D1064187

MUSIC AND THE REFORMATION
IN ENGLAND 1549-1660

STUDIES IN CHURCH MUSIC

General Editor: ERIK ROUTLEY, B.D., D.Phil.

Volumes in this series

20th CENTURY CHURCH MUSIC by Erik Routley, B.D., D.Phil.

ENGLISH CHURCH MUSIC, 1650–1750 by Christopher Dearnley, Mus.B.

CHURCH MUSIC IN THE NINETEENTH CENTURY by Arthur Hutchings, Mus.D.

THE MUSICAL WESLEYS by Erik Routley, B.D., D.Phil.

MUSIC AND
THE REFORMATION
IN ENGLAND
1549–1660

by

PETER LE HURAY

WITHDRAWN

WITHDRAWN FROM
WILLIAM F. MAAG LIBRARY
YOUNGSTOWN STATE UNIVERSITY

New York
OXFORD UNIVERSITY PRESS
1967

Copyright © 1967 Peter Le Huray
Library of Congress Catalog Card Number: 67-16680
Printed in Great Britain

ML
3131
·L44
1967b

Contents

YOUNGSTOWN STATE UNIVERSITY
LIBRARY   175344

Plates

Appearing between pages 214 and 215

Foreword

All music examples are given at original pitch, and note values are halved unless otherwise stated. Underlay variants are not shown. Editorial accidentals are given in small print as are editorial reconstructions of missing parts. The following system is used to indicate pitch: the notes from C below the bass stave to low B in the bass stave are referred to by means of capital letters, C–B; the notes in the octave above are c–b, then c′–b′ and c″–b″. Footnotes are printed collectively at the end of each chapter. Full details of the printed books listed in the footnotes may be found in the Bibliography. The following abbreviations have been used:

A or a	alto	G	Gloria
Ag	Agnus Dei	inc.	incomplete
attr.	attributed to	J	Jubilate
B or b	bass	K	Kyrie
Bar. or bar.	baritone	Ks.	key signature
Be	Benedicite	M or m	meane or medius
Bs	Benedictus	Ma	Magnificat
C	cantus	MS(S).	manuscript(s)
c.	circa, about	N	Nunc dimittis
Ca	Cantate Domino	n.d.	no date
can.	cantoris	Ps.	psalm
ch.	chorus	Q	quintus
Cr	Creed	S or s	treble or high
Ct.	contratenor		soprano
	(or countertenor)	Sa	Sanctus
d.	died	Sx	sextus
De	Deus Misereatur	T or t	tenor
dec.	decani	Te	Te Deum
f.	full	v.	verse
f5	full in five parts	V	Venite
fl.	flourished		

Acknowledgements

Many kind friends have contributed in one way or another to this book. My greatest debt is undoubtedly to Ralph Daniel, Chairman of the Musicology Department and Director of Graduate Studies in Music at Indiana University, whose researches into the English anthem have informed this study at every stage of its development. I also owe much, in innumerable ways, to Philip Brett, Alan Brown, John Buttrey, David Epps, David Keeling, John Morehen, Brian Runnett, Alan Smith, John Steele, and above all to Thurston Dart who first stimulated my interest in the music of this remarkable age. I also record with particular gratitude the help that I have received from the Librarians and Staffs of libraries both in England and in the United States, above all from the honorary librarian of St. Michael's College, Tenbury, Watkins Shaw, who first suggested that I should write this book. I remember, too, with especial pleasure the practical interest and advice of David Lumsden and Christopher Dearnley, as also of my mother and Bridget, my wife, who have both done much to speed the progress of the book. Nor can I fail to thank Marion Bavey who has spent many laborious hours translating my rough typescript into the finished product, Tom Eagle and J. M. Thomson of Messrs. Herbert Jenkins, and Paul Courtenay, whose beautifully written music examples do so much to enhance the appearance of the book. Finally I acknowledge my indebtedness to the Master and Fellows of St. Catharine's College, Cambridge, without whose support the book would never have been written.

St. Catharine's College,
Cambridge, 1966

Cathedral Music

*An Epistle to all ignorant despisers of
this Divine Part of Music*

Kind ignoramus, whosoe'er thou art,
Not having skill in this most glorious art;
Nor knowing note, and careless e'er to learn,
I prithee read this book: thou'lt then discern
Thy gross defect; and the great necessity
Of learning something in this mystery . . .
This art excelleth all without control;
The faculties it moveth of the soul:
It stifles wrath, it causeth grief to cease;
It does excite the furious mind to peace:
It stirs up love, increaseth good desires;
To heaven alone, its centre, it aspires.
It kindles heavenly raptures, and doth make
That soul that's thus enflamed for to partake
Of heavenly joys.
And canst thou think that God made this for nought?
Or that its mysteries should not be sought,
But be neglected by his chiefest creature
Man?

THOMAS MACE: *Musick's Monument* (1676)

Music and the English Reformation

Memorandum: the 13th day of March, 1549, the Parliament was prorogued which had been kept at Westminster since the 24th day of November last past, in which session divers godly acts were made . . . at this session of Parliament one uniform book was set forth of one sort of service with the ministration of the Holy Communion and other sacraments to be used in this realm of England and other the king's dominions whatsoever. To be observed after the feast of Pentecost next coming, as by an Act of Parliament against the transgressors of the same doth appear. . . .[1]

The first Edwardian Act of Uniformity, here so carefully noted by the diarist Charles Wriothesley, marked a stage in the English Reformation that was of crucial importance to church musicians.[2] Much of great moment had, of course, happened before this. During the early years of reformation—that is to say from the time of Wolsey's indictment under the Statute of Praemunire in 1529—the practical effects of reform had been to enhance the power of the Crown at the expense of the Church. There were the four anti-clerical acts passed during the four sessions of the "reformation" parliament, the Act for the Submission of the Clergy, and in particular the Act of Supremacy of November 1534, which recognised Henry as "the only supreme head in earth of the Church of England". This last measure had given Henry a power over the Church that no English monarch had ever had, and the King was quick to use it. In the following year he appointed Thomas Cromwell

Vicar-General, authorising him in consultation with the Archbishop of Canterbury, Thomas Cranmer, to draw up Injunctions "to be kept and observed" throughout the Church of England. This was seen at the time to be a radical break with the past, for in all that had gone before the King had acted with the concurrence of Convocation. One of the most striking manifestations of this new power was to be seen in the wholesale redistribution of church property, a process that began in 1536 and which continued in various guises for fifty years or more. The first and most spectacular stage was over within the space of four years. During that short time well over eight hundred monastic foundations were dissolved. Many of these were small, with annual revenues of less than £200 and communities of fewer than a dozen members, and it is unlikely that in these houses music played any important part in the daily services. Many of the greater houses, however, maintained skilled choirs—at a most conservative estimate the number cannot have been much below fifty—and, as Table 1 shows, nearly all disappeared without trace.[3]

During the course of the Henrician reformation the daily services continued to be said and sung in Latin, though steps were taken—of far-reaching consequence—to make them more intelligible to the laity.[4] Item 7 in the first set of Royal Injunctions (1536) required every parish church to purchase a copy of the newly authorised English Bible (see Plate 1). From 1543 onwards, lessons at Matins and Evensong were to be read in English. Sermons were encouraged, and—to ensure a minimum standard of competence and conformity—a system was established requiring all preachers to be licensed. And throughout the closing years of the reign a campaign was waged against idolatrous practices of all kinds: "superfluous holy-days" were discontinued, images and relics were destroyed, pilgrimages were discouraged and the "Bishop of Rome's pretended power" denounced.

From time to time, it must have seemed that further substantial reforms and perhaps even a vernacular liturgy were imminent. During the latter part of 1537 and the beginning of 1538, Henry toyed with the idea of an alliance with the Lutherans, and a Lutheran delegation actually arrived in London to begin negotiations. It was then that Cranmer and

TABLE I

Some of the Wealthier Monastic Houses, c. 1535, with Annual Revenues of £500 or more*

The Benedictines

	£		£
WESTMINSTER ABBEY	3400	ELY, the Cathedral Priory	1084
Glastonbury Abbey	3311	CHESTER ABBEY	1003
CANTERBURY, the Cathedral Priory	2349	Spalding Priory	933
St. Alban's Abbey	2102	Tavistock Abbey	902
Reading Abbey	1938	Battle Abbey	880
Abingdon Abbey	1876	NORWICH, the Cathedral Priory	874
Ramsey Abbey	1716	Winchester, Hyde Abbey	865
PETERBOROUGH ABBEY	1679	Coventry, the Cathedral Priory	808
Bury St. Edmund's Abbey	1656	Malmesbury Abbey	803
YORK, St. Mary's Abbey	1650	Winchcomb Abbey	759
Tewkesbury Abbey	1598	Chertsey Abbey	659
WINCHESTER, the Cathedral Priory	1507	Pershore Abbey	643
GLOUCESTER ABBEY	1430	Bath Abbey	617
Canterbury, St. Augustine's	1413	Selby Abbey	606
DURHAM, the Cathedral Priory	1366	St. Benet Abbey, Norfolk	583
WORCESTER, the Cathedral Priory	1290	Milton Abbey	578
Evesham Abbey	1183	Cerne Abbey	575
Crowland Abbey	1093	Shrewsbury Abbey	532
		Colchester Abbey	503

The Augustinians

	£		£
Cirencester Abbey	1051	BRISTOL ABBEY	670
Merton Priory	960	OSENEY ABBEY	654
Leicester Priory	951	Llanthony	648
Plympton Priory	912	Gainsborough Priory	628
Waltham Abbey	900	Southwark Priory	624
London, St. Bartholomew's Priory	693	Thornton Abbey	591
St. Osyth's Abbey	677	Kenilworth Priory	558

Others

Fountains, Furness, St. Mary Graces (London), Stratford, and Vale Royal (Cistercian); Sheen and Charterhouse (Carthusian) and Lewes (Cluniac).

Many less wealthy foundations also maintained choirs, including the cathedral priories at Rochester (£491) and Carlisle (£418), both of which were refounded.

* Those listed in small capital letters were refounded as cathedrals.

Cromwell began to draft proposals for a new liturgy, but the negotiations and the proposals both came to nothing.[5] There then followed a period of reaction. "Heretical" books were seized and burned in large numbers, many of them being by liberal Protestants who were later to hold office in the Somerset administration. One of the banned books was Coverdale's *Goostly psalmes*, a collection of devotional words and music in the vernacular based upon the *geistliche Lieder* that were then so popular in the Lutheran States.

That any far-reaching liturgical reforms were being considered at this time is unlikely. Wriothesley did, indeed, record in his diary that an English version of Te Deum had been sung on several occasions after meetings of a progressive London group "called by the papists the new sect".[1] But the very fact that he bothered to note this down testifies to the rarity of the event. Similarly, London gossip had it that an English form of Mass had been celebrated at least twice in small villages north of the city. Again, however, it was obviously the exceptional nature of the event that caught the popular interest.[6]

The Henrician reformation did, nevertheless, see one major liturgical change: the publication of an English Litany in 1544. During the early summer of that year England was at war, both with Scotland and France. Henry, feeling that some divine assistance would be welcome, wrote to Cranmer, as was customary in such circumstances, asking that processions be held throughout the province of Canterbury:

> We greet you well; and let you wit that, calling to our remembrance the miserable state of all Christendom, being at this present, besides all other troubles, so plagued with most cruel wars, hatreds, and dissensions, as no place of the same almost, being the whole reduced to a very narrow corner, remaineth in good peace, agreement, and concord, the help and remedy whereof, far exceeding the power of any man, must be called for of him who only is able to grant our petitions, and never forsaketh nor repelleth any that firmly believe and faithfully call on him. . . .[7]

A new English form of procession had by then been prepared, but the King insisted that the clergy should instruct the people thoroughly in it before it was actually used, and suggested a delay of a month or two in order to allow time for such instruction. His reasons for requiring an English form of words are particularly interesting. He had evidently accepted by then the basic principle that was to be the mainspring of the English liturgical reformation, namely that the laity should fully understand and take part in public worship:

> ... being resolved to have continually from henceforth general processions in all cities, towns, churches and parishes of this our realm, said and sung with such reverence and devotion as appertaineth; forasmuch as heretofore the people, partly for lack of good instruction and calling, partly for that they understood no part of such prayers or suffrages, as were used to be sung and said, have used to come very slackly to the Procession. . . . [7]

The Litany or English procession, as it was then often called, was an amalgam of several existing Latin forms of procession. In each case, the Latin procession involved a movement outwards towards a "station". For the festal and Sunday processions the station was made before the rood; during Lent the station was made at some altar within the church; whilst in times of need, and on Rogation days, the station was again made at an altar and involved the celebration of Mass. The procession then returned to the original point of departure, halting at the steps of the choir to sing a versicle, respond and collect. During the penitential processions—all but the Sunday and Holyday processions, that is—the Litany was sung. Cranmer's English procession owes something to all four Latin forms, although it was designed for a time of need.

Shortly after this, Cranmer set to work to formulate English versions of the other Latin processions—at the King's command —and to these he added some simple "plainsong" tunes of his own composing. Neither the translations nor the music have survived, unfortunately, but there remains Cranmer's interesting letter to the King on the subject of processional music. The letter deserves quotation at length, though it must be borne in

TABLE 2

The Sarum and English Processions Compared

Sundays and Holydays	In times of need	During Lent	Rogation	The 1544 English Procession
		During the outgoing procession		
Anthems with prose	Anthems, penitential psalms, Litany, Pater noster, versicles, responses and collects	Respond	as *In times of need*	Litany, Our Father, versicle, response and collect
		At the station		
(The station being made before the rood)	(The station being the altar at which Mass is to be celebrated)	(The station being made at an altar within the church)	as *In times of need*	
Antiphon, versicle, response and collect	Respond or anthem, collect, Kyrie, Pater noster, versicles, responses and collects	Kyrie, Pater noster, Preces and Miserere, collect		
Bidding of the Bedes				
	MASS			
		During the returning procession		
Anthem	Litany	Invocations of the Litany	Invocations of the Litany	Anthem (O Lord arise. O God we have heard . . . From our enemies . . .)
		Before the steps of the choir		
Versicle, response, collects	Versicle, response, collects		Versicle, response, collects	Versicle, response collects
MASS				MASS

mind that Cranmer's opinions were not necessarily those of the Church at large; nor did they refer to part-music—a fact that has often been overlooked:

... in mine opinion, the song that shall be made thereunto would not be full of notes, but, as near as may be, for every syllable a note; so that it may be sung distinctly and devoutly, as be in Matins and Evensong *Venite*, the hymns *Te Deum*, *Benedictus*, *Magnificat*, *Nunc dimittis*, and all the Psalms and Versicles; and in the mass *Gloria in excelsis*, *Gloria Patri*, the Creed, the Preface, the *Pater noster* and some of the *Sanctus* and *Agnus*. As concerning the *Salve festa dies*, the Latin note, as I think, is sober and distinct enough; wherefore I have travailed to make the verses in English, and have put the Latin note unto the same. Nevertheless, they that be cunning in singing can make a much more solemn note thereto. I made them only for a proof, to see how English would do in song. But because my English verses lack the grace and facility I would wish they had, your majesty may cause some other to make them again, that can do the same in more pleasant English and phrase. ...[7]

In the years that followed, Cranmer's more radical colleagues were to insist more and more that church music of all kinds—both monodic and polyphonic—should be in the simplest note-against-note style.

During the last two years of Henry's reign, Cranmer was at work upon a revised Latin Breviary in which he was considering the elimination of non-scriptural texts, a new yearly calendar of readings from the Old and New Testaments, a monthly rather than a weekly rota of psalms, and the compression of the eight daily office hours into two services—Matins and Evensong. For some unknown reason, however, nothing came of these projects, and it seems that the English procession was the only form of service in the vernacular to be approved during the thirty-eight years of Henry's reign.

Henry's death, on January 28th, 1547, caused Cranmer unusual distress.[8] The Archbishop undoubtedly felt a keen sense of personal loss, but he also mourned the passing of one who, he believed, was best able to carry through further reforms. Cranmer's fears for the future can well be understood, for Henry's successor was a mere nine-year-old boy. The new administration, headed by the Lord Protector Somerset, did

YOUNGSTOWN STATE UNIVERSITY LIBRARY

175344

indeed lack the firm authority to ensure the ultimate success of a liturgical reformation. It lost no time, however, in implementing a radical policy of reform.

Within six months of Edward's coronation a Royal Visitation was in progress to ensure the end of "popish" practices and ceremonies.[4] No more than two candles were to be lit at Mass; bells were to be rung before the start of service and at no other time; Latin processions were to be replaced by the 1544 English procession (a remarkable decision, this, since the original Litany had been designed for times of need and not for general use); monkish habits were to be discarded; cathedral musicians were no longer to have their hair tonsured—and so on. At the same time, new emphasis was given to the need for informed teaching and preaching.

The Royal Visitors carried out their work with great thoroughness and, as they visited each cathedral in turn, they enquired minutely into details of routine and organization. Frequently, musical matters came within the scope of their enquiry, and the decisions reached show that moves were already being made towards a simpler and more comprehensible liturgical style. At Winchester, for instance, the Visitors forbade the singing of sequences and stipulated that chapters from the Old and New Testaments should be read to the choir every day before Mass and Evensong. At Canterbury, they decreed that Mass should only be sung in the choir, and that sung Lady Mass on Holydays be discontinued in order to make way for a Sermon or a reading from the Homilies. At York, they forbade the singing of more than one Mass each day, and they recommended that the lesser hours, Dirges and "Commendations" should be discontinued. They also forbade the choir to sing responds, and ordered that all the traditional Latin "anthems" (antiphons) should be replaced by English substitutes. At Windsor, the Royal Visitors decided that the choristers should be required to say Matins and Evensong together in English before going into the choir to sing—an unusual provision, this, and one that pointed the way more than any other to future developments. The Church's representative on the Windsor commission was William May, Dean of St. Paul's, who was well known for his progressive views.

The Lincoln Cathedral Injunctions—dated April 14th, 1548—contain more specifically musical information than any of the others. In addition to many of the points already mentioned, the Visitors decreed that:

> 25. [The choir] shall from henceforth sing or say no anthems of our Lady or other Saints, but only of our Lord, and them not in Latin; but choosing out the best and most sounding to Christian religion they shall turn the same into English, setting thereunto a plain and distinct note for every syllable one: they shall sing them and none other. And after them read the collect for the preservation of the King's Majesty and the magistrates, which is contained and set forth in the English suffrage.

Injunction 28, too, would seem to imply severe restrictions in the use of music if, that is, Lady Matins and Evensong were customarily celebrated with as much music as was the Lady Mass:

> 28. To the intent the service of this Church called the Lady Matins and Evensong may be used henceforth according to the King's Majesty's proceedings, and to the abolishing of superstition in that behalf, there shall be no more Matins called the Lady Matins, Hours, nor Evensong, nor ferial dirges said in the choir among or after other Divine Service, but every man to use the same privately at their convenient leisure, according as it is purported and set forth in the King's Primer.

Under such circumstances, it is not unreasonable to suppose that in other churches, too, where the principles of liturgical reform found sympathetic support, restrictions were placed on the more extravagant forms of Latin service music, and simple settings of English texts were encouraged in their stead.

The first reports of impending change, however, came from London—and, as might be expected, from the Chapel Royal where, it seems, the prototypes of the new English services were first tried out. On April 11th, not two months after the young King had been crowned at Westminster "with great honour and solemnity" according to the Latin rite, an English form of Compline was sung by the Chapel Royal choir.[9] In November of that year, the customary service was held in Westminster Abbey to mark the opening of the new sessions of Convocation and Parliament, and Charles Wriothesley carefully noted in his diary the fact that the choir sang English versions of the Gloria, Creed, Sanctus, Benedictus qui venit and Agnus Dei. Early in the following year an English supplement to the Latin Mass was published,[10] and shortly afterwards new English versions of the daily offices were tried out by the choir at St. Paul's. In the same month, at the annual commemoration service for Henry VII in Westminster Abbey, the ordinary of the Mass was again sung in English, as in the previous November.[11]

To those who lived in London at the time, events must have seemed confusing enough. Changes were constantly being made in the established forms of service—changes that obviously had official approval. Yet, apart from the 1548 *Order of Communion*, official guidance was sadly lacking. Outside London there was even greater confusion. In an attempt to establish some kind of liturgical uniformity, until such time as an English Prayer Book could be completed, Somerset wrote to the Vice-Chancellors of Oxford and Cambridge. In his Cambridge letter he urged that the University should do its utmost to avoid "dissension and disorder", since its influence was so widespread:

September 4th, 1548: from Somerset "to our loving friend our Vice-chancellor of Cambridge, and to all masters and rulers of colleges there. . . . For so much as upon divers orders in the rites and ceremonies of the church, there might peradventure some dissension or disorder arise amongst you in the university, to the evil example of other, we have thought good to advertise you and in the king's majesty's behalf to will and command you that until such time as an order be taken and prescribed by his Highness to be universally kept throughout the whole realm . . . that you and every of you in your colleges, chapels or other churches use one uniform order, rite and ceremonies [sic] in the mass, matins and even-song and all divine service in the same to be said or sung, such as is presently used in the king's majesty's chapel, and none other". . . .[12]

While, unfortunately, the forms of service mentioned in the letter have not survived, the letter itself gives the clearest proof that the Chapel Royal was at the centre of reform during this crucial period. The Chapel Royal had always been of considerable importance in the history of English church music. One of the indirect consequences of the 1534 Supremacy Act was to make it pre-eminent.

Music was, of course, a very minor issue in the liturgical reformation, and it would be wrong to imagine otherwise. It did, nevertheless, come in for some harsh criticism on both economic and religious grounds. To the unmusical, church music of any kind must inevitably seem an irrelevance. There were many, however, who were not altogether opposed to its use but who considered that disproportionate amounts of time and money were being spent on it. Erasmus had been an early and influential critic. In the famous commentary to the New Testament, he had this to say on 1 Corinthians xiv. 19— the passage beginning "Yet in the church I had rather speak five words with my understanding, that *by my voice* I might teach others also, than ten thousand words in an *unknown* tongue":

St Paul says he would rather speak five words with a reasonable meaning in them than ten thousand in an unknown tongue. They chant nowadays in our churches in what is an unknown tongue and nothing else, while you will not hear a sermon once in six months telling people to amend their lives. Modern church music is so constructed that the congregation cannot hear one distinct word. The choristers themselves do not understand what they are singing, yet according to priests and monks it constitutes the whole of religion. Why will they not listen to St Paul? In college or monastery it is still the same: music, nothing but music. . . .[13]

Erasmus's criticisms were echoed by several writers during the early years of the Reformation, notably William Turner in a violent and wordy pamphlet called *The huntyng and fyndyng out of the Romysh foxe* (1543);[14] John Bales, Bishop of Ossory and Prebend of Canterbury, in an equally outspoken essay, *The Image of Both Churches*; and Thomas Becon, Chaplain both to Cranmer and Somerset, whose *Jewel of Joy* represents advanced Protestant opinion at about the time of the publication of the first Book of Common Prayer. In this respect, Becon's views on church music may not be without interest. They are very clearly not the views of the future Queen Elizabeth, to whom the book is dedicated!

> There have been, (would God there were not now!) which have not spared to spend much riches in nourishing many idle singing men to bleat in their chapels, thinking so to do God on high sacrifice . . . but they have not spent any part of their substance to find a learned man in their houses, to preach the word of God, to haste them to virtue, and to dissuade them from vice. . . . A Christian man's melody, after St Paul's mind, consisteth in heart, while we recite psalms, hymns, and spiritual songs, and sing to the Lord in our hearts. . . . All other outward melody is vain and transitory, and passeth away and cometh to nought. Vain and transitory it is indeed; notwithstanding, music may be used, so it be not abused. If it be soberly exercised and reputed as an handmaid unto virtue, it is tolerable; otherwise it is execrable and to be abhorred of all good men. So ye perceive that music is not so excellent a thing, that a Christian ought earnestly to rejoice in it.[15]

During the first two years of Edward's reign, the second stage in the secularisation of church property was completed under cover of the 1547 Chantries Act. Steps had already been taken in this direction during the early 1540s and several choirs of some size and importance had been disbanded, notably those belonging to the hospital of St. Leonard at York, the college of Newark in Leicester, and the collegiate churches of Holy Trinity Arundel, Higham Ferrars, St. Mary's Warwick and

Ottery St. Mary in Devon. Those that remained in 1547 were speedily dispatched, amongst them the great collegiate churches at Beverley and Ripon and the royal peculiars of Fotheringhay, and St. Stephen's, Westminster[16]—all of which had made lavish provision for music.* And amongst the humbler choral foundations was the collegiate church in the tiny Suffolk village of Stoke by Clare, with its choir of eighteen men and boys and its Dean, Matthew Parker, a future Archbishop of Canterbury.[17]

By the time that the first Book of Common Prayer came into use, in the early summer of 1549, the major programme of dissolution and reorganisation had been completed. Few changes of any substance were made after that date, though the piecemeal alienation of church property did not come to an end until the early years of the seventeenth century. Fully choral services were to be heard from then onwards in some forty or so cathedrals, churches and chapels in England, Ireland and Wales, sung by choirs ranging in size from no more than eight to as many as forty-four men and boys. There were fifteen newly founded cathedrals (Table 3), fourteen cathedrals of the old foundation (Table 4) and a number of collegiate churches and chapels (Table 5).

One or two other churches attempted choral services from time to time, especially in London. During the reign of

---

* Some of the other musical churches that were dissolved at this time were those at Hemingborough, Maidstone, Rotherham, Staindrop, Tattershall (where Taverner had for a time been Master of the Choristers), Thornton, Wallingford (where Thomas Tusser received his first schooling) and Wimborne. The account books of many other churches record payments to clerks, and in some cases to choristers as well; in many places, however, part-music can have been attempted on special occasions only, and with outside help: Astley, Auckland, Bunbury, Chester-le-Street, Bablake (Coventry), Cobham, Cotterstock, Greystoke, Irthlingborough, Lanchester, Lingfield, All Hallows (London), Guildhall Chapel (London), St. Lawrence (London), St. Martin le Grand (London), St. Michael's and Whittingtons (London), Mettingham, St. Mary in the Fields (Norwich), Noseley, Penrhyn, Pleshy, Rushford, St. Buryan, St. Cranthoe, Sibthorpe, Slapton, South Malling, Stratford-upon-Avon, Sutton, Thetford, Tong and Wingfield.

TABLE 3

Cathedral Choirs of the New Foundation

Cathedral	Statutes dated	Size of choir	Source of information and remarks
Bristol	June 4th, 1542	6 *p.* 6 *l.* 6 *c.*	[18] There were two vacant places for priest musicians in 1634 [19]
Canterbury	April 8th, 1541	12 *p.* 12 *l.* 10 *c.*	[20]
	1636	6 *p.* 18 *l.* 10 *c.*	[19] The 1636 statute confirmed a practice of at least thirty years standing
Carlisle	May 8th, 1541	8 *p.* 4 *l.* 6 *c.*	[21]
Chester	August 4th, 1541	6 *p.* 6 *l.* 8 *c.*	[22] But *Hammond* heard 16 men and 8 boys in 1635 [23]
Dublin, Christ Church	1539	8 *p.* 3 *l.* 4 *c.*	[24] In 1546 the choir was enlarged to 14 *p.* and 6 *c.*
Durham	May 12th, 1541	12 *p.* 10 *l.* 10 *c.*	[20] *Tanner* says that there were 16 laymen there, c. 1550 [25]
Ely	September 10th, 1541	8 *p.* 8 *l.* 8 *c.*	[26] Confirmed by *Hammond* in 1635 [27]
Gloucester	September 3rd, 1541	6 *p.* 6 *l.* 6 *c.*	[28] Confirmed by *Hammond* in 1634 [23]
Norwich	May 2nd, 1538		The entire foundation was taken over as it then stood, the Prior and Convent becoming the Dean and Chapter: the Elizabethan Statutes (British Museum, Stowe MS 128) confirm this, as do the Jacobean statutes of 1608. [29]
	1608	8 *p.* 8 *l.* 6 *c.*	
Oxford	September 1st, 1541	8 *p.* 8 *l.* 8 *c.*	[20] Removed to Christ Church from Oseney in 1546
Peterborough	September 4th, 1541	8 *p.* 8 *l.* 8 *c.*	[30]
Rochester	June 18th, 1541	6 *p.* 6 *l.* 8 *c.*	[20]
		5 *p.* 7 *l.* 8 *c.*	1634 [19]
Westminster Abbey	December 17th, 1540	12 *p.* 12 *l.* 10 *c.*	[31]
Winchester	March 28th, 1541	12 *p.* 12 *l.* 10 *c.*	[32]
	1638	10 *p.* 6 *l.* 6 *c.*	[33]
Worcester	January 10th, 1542	10 *p.* 10 *l.* 10 *c.*	[34]

p. = priests *l.* = lay musicians *c.* = choristers

TABLE 4

15

Cathedral Choirs of the Old Foundation

Cathedral	Date of statutes or other source	Size of choir	Source of information and remarks
Bangor	c. 1550	2 p. and an unspecified [25] number of layclerks and choristers	
Chichester	1586	4 p. 8 l. 8 c.	[35]
	1634	4 p. 8 l. 8 c.	[36] Confirmed by Hammond[23]
Dublin, St. Patrick's	1546	16 p. 4 l. 2 c.	[37]
	1554	16 p. 6 c.	
Exeter	c. 1540	20 p. plus 30 l. and c.	[25]
	c. 1563	6 p. 12 l. 14 c.	[19]
	1634	4 p. 19 l. 14 c.	[19]
	1634	4 p. 16 l. 10 c.	[23]
Hereford	c. 1534	26 p. plus at least 11 l. and c.	[38]
	c. 1583	16 p. 7 c.	[38]
	1634	16 p. 8 c.	[23] Confirmed in the charter of 1637
Lichfield	c. 1535	17 p. plus 19 l. and c.	[3]
	1634	6 p. 10 l. 8 c.	[23]
Lincoln	c. 1535	44 p. plus at least 17 l. and c.	[3]
	c. 1600	4 p. 8 l. 15 c.	
	1634	12 p. and l. 8 c.	[23] and [39]
Llandaff	c. 1535	Several p. plus 8 l. and c.	[3]
	c. 1550	5 p. and l. 4 c.	[3]
St. Asaph	c. 1535	11 p. plus 8 l. and c.	[3]
	c. 1550	4 p. 4 l. 4 c.	[25]
St. David's	c. 1535	27 p. plus 8 l. and c.	[3]
	c. 1550	8 p. plus 4 or more l. and c.	[25]
	c. 1575	Atkins states that there were places for 6 c.	[34]
St. Paul's	c. 1535	42 p. plus 70 or more l. and c.	[3]
	1634	12 p. 6 l. 10 c.	[19] These numbers were constant from 1549[40]
Salisbury	c. 1535	36 p. or more plus 12 l. and c.	[3]
	1634	6 p. 7 l. 8 c.	[19]
	1635	12 p. and l. 8 c.	[27]
Wells	c. 1535	50 p. plus 12 l. and c.	[3]
	1592	14 or more p. 6 c.	[41]
	1634	6 p. 8 l. 6 c.	[19]
York	c. 1535	36 p. 7 c.	[42]
	c. 1550	20 p. and l. 12 c.	

Since none of the old-foundation cathedrals were given new statutes at this time the figures in this table are taken in the main from Chapter Act books, Treasurers' account books and other secondary sources.

TABLE 5
Other Choral Foundations

Foundation	Date of statutes or other source	Size of choir	Source of information and remarks
1. Royal Peculiars			
Chapel Royal	1547	about 32 p. and l. 12 c: about 6 of the men were in holy orders	[43] and [44]
St. George's Chapel, Windsor	1550	4 p. 20 l. 10 c: some of the 20 l. may have been deacons	[4]
The Chapel Royal of Scotland	1501	16 men, 6 boys and an organist	[45] These numbers fluctuated considerably: see Chapter 3
2. The Universities			
King's College, Cambridge	1448	10 p. 6 l. 16 c.	[46]
Magdalen College, Oxford	1485	4 p. 8 l. 16 c.	[47]
New College, Oxford	1379	10 p. 3 l. 16 c.	[24] and [48]
Pembroke College, Cambridge	c. 1640	not known	[49]
Peterhouse, Cambridge	c. 1635	not known	[50]
St. John's College, Oxford	1558	3 p. 6 l. 6 c.	[51] The original foundation of 1555 had been 3 p. 3 l. 6 c. The choir was disbanded in 1577. In 1636 Sir W. Paddy's bequest re-established the choir as 8 l. 4 c. and an organist
Trinity College, Cambridge	1559	10 l. and c. and an organist	[52]
3. Schools			
Eton	1448	10 p. 6 l. 16 c.	[46]
	1634	2 p, 8 l. 10 c.	[19]
Winchester	1634	3 p. 3 l. 16 c.	[19] Confirming earlier statutes
4. Collegiate Churches			
Manchester (Christ Church)	c. 1555	4 l. 4 c.	[25] and [53] Dissolved in 1547 but refounded by Mary Tudor
Ripon	1604	6 l. 8 c. and an organist	[54] Dissolved in 1539 and not refounded until 1604
Southwell Minster	1582	6 p. 6 l. 6 c.	[55]

TABLE 5 (*continued*)

Foundation	Date of statutes or other source	Size of choir	Source of information and remarks
5. *Parish Churches*			
Ludlow	n.d.	6 *l*. 6 *c*.	[56] In the late 16th century the numbers of choristers fluctuated between 7 and 2
Newark	1531	at least 2 *p*. 6 *c*.	[57] and [58] The Song School was still functioning in 1640; there may have been no men after 1547, but *Hammond* heard "sweet organs, queristers, and singing-boys", in 1634[23]

Elizabeth I there are records of music at St. Botolph Aldersgate, St. Dunstan in the West, St. Mary at Hill, St. Mary Woolnoth, St. Stephen's Walbrook and, some time later, at St. Giles in the Fields. Anthems and services were sung, too, by the children of Christ's Hospital and Dulwich College. John Farrant, music master at Christ's Hospital, "pricked divers Services, very fit for the choir into eight several books together with an organ book" in 1611.[59] And a set of singing books and an organ book were purchased in 1618 for use at the newly founded Dulwich College. The inaugural service was attended by a distinguished company, including the Lord Chancellor and Inigo Jones, and the visitors were entertained to a "sermond" an anthem and a dinner.[60] A choir may have sung for much of the time at Lambeth Palace. Archbishop Parker had music of some kind in his private chapel there, for he appointed Thomas Whythorne director of music in 1571 or thereabouts. Since a later Archbishop, Abbott, is said to have discontinued the music[61] in the Lambeth Chapel (c. 1611), it could be that a choir was in residence at Lambeth for much of the time from 1560 onwards.

There are signs, too, that choral services were not entirely unheard of elsewhere, and especially in the reactionary West Country. Payments for music and for musicians are to be found in the accounts of several Devon churches, including Barnstaple, Blanchminster Charity (Stratton), Hartland, Launceston, Stratton (Bude) and Woodbury.[56]

On January 21st, 1549, the First Act of Uniformity was ratified by parliament. The act required that within the space of four months the newly published English service book, *The booke of the common prayer and administracion of the Sacramentes*, should replace all existing Latin service manuals. The anonymous compilers of the prayer book (of whom Cranmer must surely have been one) were at pains in the preface to justify its existence:

> There was never anything [they began] by the wit of man so well devised, or so surely established, which (in continuance of time) hath not been corrupted.[62]

They believed that their first duty was to restore the Word of God to its rightful and pre-eminent place in public worship "that the people (by daily hearing of holy scripture read in the church) should continually profit more and more in the knowledge of God and be the more enflamed with the love of his true religion". They believed, too, that the forms of public worship should be much simplified. The Latin services were so complex "that many times there was more business to find out what should be read, than to read it when it was found out". Moreover, services differed considerably from place to place. Some churches followed the use of Salisbury, some the Hereford use, some Bangor, some York and some Lincoln.

The new Book of Common Prayer must at first have seemed very new indeed, not least in its compactness and brevity. For all its apparent novelty, however, it was very much an amalgam of traditional elements. The services of Baptism, Confirmation, Marriage, Purification and Burial were very much direct translations of their originals, whilst the Litany was

Cranmer's English procession of 1544. Of the eight office hours, only the minor ones—Terce, Sext, and None—were abolished altogether. The other five—Matins, Lauds, Prime, Vespers and Compline—appeared in compressed form as English Matins and Evensong (Table 6).[7]

There were, indeed, many obvious similarities between the old and the new; nor must it be forgotten that translations of the daily offices had long been available in the English Primers, the latest of which was *The King's Primer* of 1545. Yet, to the musician, the Book of Common Prayer must have been a puzzling document. Within one cover were to be found Breviary, Missal, Manual, Sacramentary, Lectionary, Epistolary, Evangeliary and Directory—everything, apart from the Bible, that was necessary for the daily services; and almost everything, too, for the occasional offices. But the new Book of Common Prayer contained not a note of music, and its rubrics gave musicians little guidance as to what was expected of them. At Matins, for instance, Venite was directed to be "said or sung", but beyond this, music was not mentioned. And in the Evensong rubrics there was only a passing reference to the "Clerks":

> Then the suffrages before assigned at Matins, the Clerks kneeling likewise, with three Collects. . . .

Music was obviously to be permitted, if not encouraged, at Matins and Evensong; but there was nothing to suggest what forms this music should take. In the Sarum rites, one day in every three had been a feast of some kind—a Principal Double, a Greater Double, a Lesser Double, an Inferior Double or a simple feast of Nine or Three Lessons.[63] As Bishop Grandison's Exeter Ordinal[24] shows, the rank of the feast was reflected in the music that was used to celebrate it. At Matins, for example, on Greater Double Feasts the musicians had been permitted to sing polyphonic settings of the Hymn, the Third, Sixth and Ninth Responds and Antiphons, and the Te Deum. No polyphony at all, on the other hand, had been allowed at Matins on

TABLE 6

The English and Sarum Forms of Service Compared

Sarum Use AD MATUTINAS	The Book of Common Prayer (1549) ORDRE FOR MATTYNS
Pater noster. Ave. Credo [said privately] Domine labia . . .	The priest being in the choir, shall begin with a loud voice the Lord's Prayer called the Pater noster. Then likewise shall he say, O Lord open Thou my lips. Answer, And my mouth shall shew forth thy praise . . .
Venite with Invitatory	Then shall be said or sung without any Invitatory this psalm, *Venite exultemus.* &c. in English . . .
Hymn Psalms with *antiphons*	Then shall follow certain psalms in order as they have been appointed in a table made for that purpose
Versicle, response, Pater noster, Ave . . .	
Benedictions and Readings with responds	First Lesson
Te Deum Collect	After the first lesson shall follow *Te Deum laudamus* in English, daily throughout the year, except in Lent, all the which time in the place of *Te Deum* shall be used *Benedicite* . . . in English . . .
AD LAUDES	
Versicle, response . . . Deus in adiutorium, response Psalms with antiphons	
Chapter with *respond*	Second Lesson
Hymn, versicle, response *Benedictus with antiphon*	And after the second lesson throughout the whole year shall be used *Benedictus dominus deus Israel* in English . . .
Kyrie, Pater noster, versicles, responses, collect and Memorials . . . *Benedicamus, Deo Gratias*	
AD PRIMAM	
Pater noster . . . [privately] Deus in adiutorium, response *Hymn*, psalms and antiphon	
Quicunque vult with *antiphon* Chapter Lesser respond	In the feasts of Christmas, Epiphany, Easter, Ascension, Pentecost and upon Trinity Sunday shall be sung or said immediately after Benedictus this confession of our Christian faith, *Quicunque vult*

Table 6 (*continued*)

Sarum Use AD MATUTINAS	The Book of Common Prayer (1549) ORDRE FOR MATTYNS
Preces (Kyrie, Pater noster, Credo, prayers . . .)	Then shall be said daily through the year, the prayers following, as well at Evensong as at Matins, all devoutly kneeling . . . Lord have mercy upon us, . . . Then the minister shall say the Creed and the Lord's prayer &c. in English . . . Collects
Concluding prayers and sentences. Benedicamus	

AD VESPERAS	*ORDRE FOR EVENSONG*
Pater noster . . . [privately] Deus in adiutorium, response	The priest shall say, Our father . . .
Psalms with *antiphons*	Then Psalms in order as they be appointed in the Table for Psalms . . .
Chapter with *respond*	First Lesson
Hymn, versicle and response	
Magnificat & antiphon	After that, *Magnificat anima mea dominum* in English . . .
Kyrie, &c. as at Lauds with *Benedicamus* substitute "*ex licencia*"	

AD COMPLETORIUM	
Pater noster . . . [privately] Deus in adiutorium, response	
Psalms with *antiphons*	
Chapter with *respond*	Second Lesson
Hymn, versicle and response	
Nunc dimittis & antiphon	And after that, *Nunc dimittis servum tuum* in English . . .
Kyrie &c. Preces	Then the suffrages before assigned at Matins, the clerks kneeling likewise, with three collects

---

feast days of the lowest rank. The Rochester Cathedral injunctions, issued shortly after the refounding of the monastery in 1543, shows that similar musical distinctions were still being made between the various classes of feast.[4] In the first English Prayer Book the number of feast days had been reduced to twenty-seven, of which only six were of major importance—Christmas, Epiphany, Easter, Ascension, Pentecost and Trinity Sunday. Musicians must have wondered whether the traditional distinctions between festal polyphony and ferial plainsong were to be maintained—if, indeed, polyphony was permissible at all.

The appearance of John Merbecke's *The booke of Common praier noted* certainly did something to resolve their difficulties. The book was published by Richard Grafton, Printer to the King's Majesty, and it obviously had the full approval of Northumberland and Cranmer if it had not actually been commissioned by them. Merbecke was, of course, much in sympathy with the ideals of the liturgical reformation. He had been arrested with two of his colleagues at Windsor in 1543 and charged with heresy: he had been making a study of the writings of Calvin, and was in the process of compiling a mammoth concordance of the English Bible. He had somehow escaped punishment—unlike the other two, who were committed to the flames—and he was even reinstated at St. George's, where he remained until his death in 1585. Like Taverner before him, however, he seems to have given up composition altogether, and there is no evidence that he ever wrote any part-music for the English rites. In his *booke of Common praier noted* he supplied simple plainsong-style music for all sections of morning, communion and evening prayer, and for some of the more important occasional offices as well (see Chapter 6 for further details). His book probably represents the kind of solution that would have been acceptable to radical though not extreme churchmen at that time.

Merbecke's work had little chance to establish itself, and it did not go beyond a single edition.[64] For though the first Act of Uniformity made a return to law and order theoretically possible, the Act was far less effective than had been hoped. Even in London, where—so the Venetian ambassador said—the people were unusually compliant, the Act of Uniformity took some considerable time to make its impression. On June 20th, 1549—Corpus Christi Day—half the Londoners decided to observe the Feast as a public holiday, in spite of specific instructions to the contrary from the Council. Private masses were still going on at St. Paul's at the end of the month, though the Chantry priests had been pensioned off in May. And at Westminster Abbey, the Dean and Chapter even refused for some time to have anything to do with the new Prayer Book. This is how Bishop John Hooper, "the father of English Nonconformity", described the general situation in a letter to Henry Bullinger at Zurich, December 27th, 1549:

. . . The public celebration of the Lord's supper is very far from the order and institution of our Lord [he explained]. Although it is ministered in both kinds, yet in some places the supper is celebrated three times a day . . . They still retain their vestments and the candles before the altars; in the churches they always chant the *hours* and other hymns relating to the Lord's supper, but in our own language. And that popery may not be lost, the mass priests, although they are compelled to discontinue the use of the Latin language, yet most carefully observe the same tone and manner of chanting to which they were heretofore accustomed in the papacy. God knows to what perils and anxieties we are exposed by reason of men of this kind. . . .[65]

With time, the new Book of Common Prayer might well have won universal acceptance. But it was plain enough to those who could read the signs that the first Act of Uniformity was no more than an interim measure, and that further reforms were on the way. Certainly Martin Bucer and Paul Fagius had formed that impression on their return to England in the summer of 1549. Both men were in a good position to know, for they had been most hospitably entertained at Lambeth by Cranmer himself:

We hear [they wrote to friends in Strasbourg] that some concessions have been made [here in England] on account of the infirmity of the present times, and out of respect for ancient customs. . . . They [Cranmer and his colleagues] affirm that there is no superstition in these things, and that they are only to be kept for a short while, lest the people, not yet having learned Christ, should be deterred from embracing his religion by sudden and extensive innovations.[66]

B

As it was, many divines were impatient of delay. Holgate—
Archbishop of York, Thomas Ridley—Bishop of London, and
John Hooper—Bishop of Worcester, were especially anxious
to push the reformation farther.[67] They clearly considered
choral and instrumental music to be of little value in public
worship, and although they took no steps to ban it altogether
(this would have required an act of parliament), they whittled
it down wherever they could. This much is evident in the few
sets of Injunctions that have survived from the years 1550 to
1553. The first of these are the Royal Injunctions for St.
George's Chapel, Windsor, dated February 8th, 1550. There is
nothing particularly radical about them, and yet they do
clearly show which way the wind was blowing. The two
paragraphs that are of particular interest are numbers 27 and 30:

27. *Also*, because the great number of ceremonies in the church
are now put away by the King's Majesty's authority and act of
Parliament, so that fewer choristers be requisite, and the College
is now otherwise more charged than it hath been; we enjoin from
henceforth there shall be found in this College only ten choristers;
and their Informatour shall be yearly chosen by the Dean and
Chapter.

30. *Also*, whereas heretofore, when descant, prick-song, and
organs were too much used and had in price in the church, great
search was made for cunning men in that faculty, among whom
there were many that had joined with such cunning evil conditions, as pride, contention, railing, drunkenness, contempt of
their superiors, or such-like vice, we now intending to have
Almighty God praised with gentle and sober quiet minds and with
honest hearts, and also the Commonwealth served with convenient ministers, do enjoin that from henceforth when the room
of any of the clerks shall be void, the Dean and prebendaries of
this church shall make search for quiet and honest men, learned
in the Latin tongue, which have competent voices and can sing,
apt to study and willing to increase in learning: so that they may
be first deacons and afterward admitted priests; having always
more regard to their virtue and learning than to excellency in
music. . . .[4]

On October 26th of that year, a further set of Injunctions were issued to the Dean and Chapter at St. George's, amplifying the earlier ones and signed by Richard Cox (tutor to King Edward) and Simon Heines. Paragraph 11 took the musical reformation a stage further:

11. And whereas we understand that John Merbeck and George Thaxton hath of your grant fees appointed to them severally for playing upon organs; We take order that the said John and George shall enjoy their several fees during their lives if they continue in the College, in as large and ample manner, as if organ playing had still continued in the Church.[4]

Two years later, Archbishop Holgate issued a lengthy set of Injunctions to the Dean and Chapter at York Minster, and again we see the whittling-down process in action:

15. *Also*, we will and command that there be none other note sung or used in the said church at any service there to be had, saving square note plain, so that every syllable may be plainly and distinctly pronounced, and without any reports or repeatings which may induce any obscureness to the hearers. . . .

24. *Also*, we will and command that there be no more playings of the organs, either at the Morning Prayer, the Communion, or the Evening Prayer within this Church of York, but that the said playing do utterly cease and be left the time of Divine Service within the said Church.

This last Injunction applied not only to solo organ music but to organ accompaniments as well:

25. *Also*, forsomuch as playing of the organs ought and must be ceased and no more used within the Church of York, we think it meet that the Master of the Choristers for the time being who ought to play the same organs in times past who can no more do so, that the said Master of the Choristers do his diligence to his power to serve God in such vocation as he can conveniently and may. Therefore we will and command that the said Master of the Choristers for the time being help to sing Divine Service to the

uttermost of his power within the quire of the Church of York, specially of the Sundays and other Holy-Days.[4]

The Archbishop's language may be somewhat involved but his meaning is plain enough, and we may be sure that he gave similar instructions to the other cathedrals in his Province. And at about the same time, Cranmer, through Ridley, ordered that the organs at St. Paul's Cathedral should be silenced:

> Item; the fourth day of September [1552] was upon a Sunday, and then the choir of Paul's had a commandment from the Dean from Cambridge, at the Bishop of Canterbury's Visitation, that he [sic] should leave the playing of the organs at the divine service, and so left it.[68]

Meanwhile, in the country at large, people were slow to conform to the spirit of the first Act of Uniformity. Martin Bucer, Regius Professor of Divinity at Cambridge, gave his own analysis of the situation in an outspoken letter to the King, dated Christmas 1551:

> Your sacred Majesty has already found by experience how grave are the evils which ensued on taking away by force false worship from your people, without sufficient preliminary instruction. . . . Some have on this account made horrible sedition, others have raised perilous dissensions in the state, and to this very day wherever they can they either cause new trouble or increase what has already been excited. Some turn the prescribed forms of service into mere papistical abuse, and although these are now in the vulgar tongue, the "sacrificers" recite them of set purpose so indistinctly that they cannot be understood, whilst the people altogether refuse to understand or listen. . . .[69]

In May of that year Daniel Barbaro, a Catholic, and Venetian Ambassador in London, had reported on this very question to the Venetian Senate:

> Religion is, as it were, the heart of man, on which life depends. In Republics, and especially in Monarchies it is a wonderful power for good, leading men to acknowledge God as the giver of all kingdoms and victories. This is not so in England, however,

TABLE 7

*Holy Communion: some Rubrics from the 1549 and 1552
Prayer Books compared*

	1549	1552
Introit	Then shall the clerks sing in English for the office, or Introit (as they call it), a psalm appointed for that day	Missing
Kyrie	. . . which psalm ended, the priest shall say, or else the clerks shall sing, iii Lord, have mercy upon us . . .	Then shall the priest rehearse distinctly all the ten Commandments: and the people kneeling shall after every Commandment ask God's mercy for their transgression of the same . . .
Gloria in excelsis	Then the priest, standing at God's board shall begin, Glory be to God on high. The clerks. And in earth	Then shall be said or sung, Glory be to God on high. (This occurs after Communion)
Creed	After the Gospel ended, the priest shall begin. I believe in one God. The clerks shall sing the rest	And the Epistle and Gospel being ended, shall be said the Creed
Offertory	Then shall follow for the Offertory, one or more of these sentences of holy scripture, to be sung while the people do offer, or else one of them to be said by the minister immediately before the offering . . . Where there be clerks they shall sing one or many of the sentences above written, according to the length and shortness of the time that the people be offering.	. . . the curate shall declare unto the people whether there be any holydays or fasting days the week following, and earnestly exhort them to remember the poor, saying one or more of these sentences following, as he thinks most convenient . . .
Sanctus	After which Preface shall follow immediately . . . When the clerks have done singing then shall the priest or deacon turn him to the people and say . . .	After which Preface shall follow immediately . . .
Communion	In the Communion time the clerks sing: ii O Lamb of God . . .	Omitted
	. . . and when the Communion is ended, then shall the clerks sing the post-Communion	Omitted
	Where there are no clerks, there the priest shall say all things appointed for them to sing.	

where men change their beliefs from day to day. At this present moment everyone is dissatisfied, both Catholics and Protestants alike.... Indeed, had the Catholics a leader they would undoubtedly rebel, in spite of the severe punishment that they have suffered recently....[70]

Unsettled as conditions undoubtedly were, the Council pressed ahead with further reforms. Early in 1552, a second Act of Uniformity was pushed through parliament; and in April the Book of Common Prayer was reissued in a much modified guise. The Communion service, in particular, was radically reshaped, for Cranmer and his colleagues had by then moved very close to a Zwinglian or Calvinist interpretation of the Sacraments. Since the new emphasis was on the memorial rather than the sacrificial nature of the sacraments, the service was restated in less mystical, more immediately human terms: the altar, now described as "the table", was given a central position in church—the traditional east end position being abandoned; vestments and furnishings were drastically reduced, to avoid any possible confusion with the "popish" mass; and music, possibly the most mystical of all liturgical ornaments, was severely pruned, as the rubrics of the 1552 Communion service clearly show (Table 7).

The musical reforms that Cranmer and Holgate subsequently proposed at St. Paul's Cathedral and York Minster were fully consonant with the implicit intentions of the 1552 Prayer Book.

The second Act of Uniformity was passed in April 1552. By Christmas of the following year, the Edwardian reformation had been swept away and the English church, under Mary Tudor, was again in full communion with Rome. Had Edward lived, it is unlikely that the English church would ever have become fully committed to Geneva, for there was much in the Calvinist philosophy that was repugnant to a monarchical system of government. And yet events had been moving so swiftly in that direction during the last three years of Edward's reign that the English church may well have come to adopt many more of the external features of Calvinist worship. By the summer of 1553, the future of the English choral tradition was certainly in question. Is it too fanciful to see, in the accession of a Catholic monarch, its ultimate salvation?

NOTES TO CHAPTER I

1. Hamilton, II, p. 9.

2. See Elton for Constitutional Documents, and Dickens for a good general account of the English Reformation.

3. Authorities differ slightly in their estimates of net income, as given in Table I; cf. the figures in Hughes P., I, appendix 1; and Knowles, III. appendix IV.

4. Frere and Kennedy, XIV–XV.

5. Ridley, ch. 10.

6. Hamilton, I, p. 83.

7. Brightman, I.

8. Ridley, p. 259.

9. Bishop and Gasquet, p. 58.

10. Brightman, I, p. lxxi.

11. Hamilton, I, p. 187.

12. Bishop and Gasquet, p. 147.

13. Adapted from Froude, p. 115.

14. Banned shortly after publication; Turner later became Chaplain to Edward VI and Dean of Wells.

15. Becon, p. 429.

16. Hughes, P., II, ch. 4.

17. Brook, pp. 16–22 and p. 36; and Hope, p. 17; no trace of the collegiate church now remains.

18. Norris (and see note 20).

19. *Historical Manuscripts Commission*, fourth report and appendix (1874).

20. Falkner: the introduction to this volume, pp. xxi–lxvi, contains a good account of the new foundation cathedrals and their statutes: there is an essay on "The Cathedral Churches of the Old Foundation", by Howson.

21. Prescott.

22. Burne.

23. Hammond (i).

24. Harrison, F. Ll. (i).

25. Tanner.

26. Ely Cathedral (i) and (ii).

27. Hammond (ii).

28. Gloucester Cathedral.

29. Boston; additional information very kindly supplied by Mr. H. W. Shaw and Mr. Alan Smith.

30. Mellows.

31. Pine.

32. Kitchen and Madge.

33. Stephens and Madge.
34. Atkins.
35. Swainson.
36. Walcott.
37. Mason.
38. Bannister.
39. Cole, R. E. G.
40. Simpson.
41. Reynolds.
42. Austen.
43. Rimbault.
44. Lafontaine.
45. Rogers.
46. Heywood and Wright.
47. Wilson, H. A.
48. "Oxfordshire," III, *Victoria County History*.
49. le Huray (i).
50. Hughes, Dom A.
51. Hutton.
52. Carpenter.
53. Bridgman.
54. Information kindly supplied by Canon D. M. Bartlett.
55. Leach.
56. Information kindly supplied by Mr. Alan Smith.
57. Jackson.
58. Brown, C.
59. Pearce.
60. Warner.
61. Whythorne; and Scholes, p. 231; source not stated.
62. *The booke of common prayer*, 1549—preface.
63. Proctor and Wordsworth, pp. xl–xliii.
64. Hunt.
65. Robinson (i), p. 71.
66. Robinson (ii), p. 534.
67. See especially Ridley's Injunctions for the London diocese, in Frere and Kennedy.
68. Nichols (ii), p. 75.
69. Bishop and Gasquet, pp. 299–300.
70. Brown, R. p. 345.

2

The Elizabethan Settlement

The accession of Elizabeth to the throne in November 1558 once again threw the whole future of the English church into the balance. At first it seemed as if the Queen might be thinking of liturgical reforms on the lines of those approved by her father during the last few years of his reign. Some small changes were made almost immediately at the Chapel Royal, including the substitution of Cranmer's English Litany for the Latin forms of procession; and, within a month, similar changes had been authorised by royal proclamation for use throughout the country.[1] Beyond this, however, the Latin services remained as they had been during the Marian reaction, and the coronation service at Westminster Abbey in January 1559 followed its traditional course with only minor variations. Nor, to judge from the way in which the first session of parliament began at the end of January, did Elizabeth or her Council then intend to embark upon any major programme of reform. Certainly, events abroad made a radical home policy highly inadvisable.

With the signing of the peace of Cateau-Cambrésis, however, in mid-March, the government may have felt more at liberty to pursue the path of reformation.[2] Whether or not this was so, the opening session of parliament was unexpectedly prolonged over Easter, and during the extra time were passed *An Act restoring to the Crown the ancient jurisdiction over the state ecclesiastical and spiritual* (the Elizabethan Supremacy Act) and *An Act for the uniformity of common prayer and divine service in the*

Church (the Elizabethan Act of Uniformity). Whilst in almost every respect the Elizabethan Prayer Book was a reprint of the revised 1552 Prayer Book, certain seemingly minor modifications were made to it, one of which—the revision of the ornaments rubric—was to spark off the first major controversy of the Elizabethan Settlement: for the 1559 rubric envisaged a return not to the comparative austerity of the 1552 Prayer Book but to the earlier and unquestionably more "popish" practices of 1549. In the light of subsequent events, it can hardly be doubted that the Queen herself was directly responsible for this. That she was strongly in favour of a vernacular liturgy, however, is beyond question. Before parliament had even begun to discuss the restoration of an English prayer book, she had attended an English communion at the Chapel Royal,[3] and in May, fully six weeks before the Act of Uniformity came into force, she ordered that all the Chapel Royal services should from thenceforth follow the use of the Book of Common Prayer. As Henry Machyn, the undertaker, cryptically noted in his diary, "The xii day of May began the English in the Queen's Chapel".[4]

During the summer of 1559, some six months before Matthew Parker took up his duties at Canterbury, Elizabeth set in motion a royal visitation to administer the Oath of Supremacy and to ensure the general use of the Book of Common Prayer. The Injunctions that were issued during the course of the Visitation[5] were very similar to the Edwardian Injunctions of 1547, though some twenty or so extra clauses were added to deal specifically with current issues. One of the longest of these new clauses concerned music, and it may well have been formulated to forestall the criticisms of the Puritan exiles returning from abroad, most of whom were opposed to non-congregational music of any kind in public worship:

Item, because in divers Collegiate, and also some parish Churches, heretofore there have been livings appointed for the maintenance of men and children, to use singing in the church, by means whereof, the laudable science of music has been had in estimation,

and preserved in knowledge: the Queen's Majesty, neither meaning in any wise the decay of any thing that might conveniently
tend to the use and continuance of the said science, neither to have
the same in any part so abused in the church, that thereby the
common prayer should be the worse understood of the hearers,
willeth and commandeth, that first no alteration be made of such
assignments of living, as heretofore have been appointed to the
use of singing or music in the Church, but that the same so remain.
And that there be a modest distinct song, so used in all parts of
the common prayers in the Church, that the same may be as
plainly understood, as if it were read without singing, and yet
nevertheless, for the comforting of such that delight in music, it
may be permitted that in the beginning, or in the end of common
prayers, either at morning or evening, there may be sung an
Hymn, or such like song, to the praise of Almighty God, in the
best sort of melody and music that may be conveniently devised,
having respect that the sentence of the Hymn may be understood
and perceived. . . .

The Queen was at first prepared to allow considerable
freedom of practice and belief within the broad framework of
the 1559 Injunctions and the Acts of Supremacy and Uniformity, whilst in her own chapels she undoubtedly felt at liberty
to order the daily services as she herself wished. It soon became
clear that her tastes were very far from those of some of her
more Protestant subjects, and indeed the Spanish Ambassador,
Bishop Quadra, confidently expected another Catholic reformation, so far had he been misled by events which took
place at the Chapel Royal:

9th October 1559 [to the Bishop of Arras]
The Queen [he wrote] ordered the marriage of one of her lady
servants to take place in her own chapel and directed that a crucifix
and candles should be placed upon the altar, which caused so much
noise among her chaplains and the Council, that the intention was
abandoned for the time; but it was done at Vespers [Evensong]
on Saturday, and on Sunday the clergy wore vestments as they
do in our services, and so great was the crowd at the palace that
disturbance was feared in the city. The fact is that the crucifixes

and vestments that were burnt a month ago publicly are now set up in the royal chapel, as they soon will be all over the kingdom, unless, which God forbid, there is another change next week. . . .[6]

Even the most impartial observer must at times have wondered where Anglicanism ended and Popery began:

The xxiii day of April [1562] was St. George's Day, a[nd at White]hall the Queen's grace went from her Chapel with twelve Knights of the Garter in robes with collars of gold with garters, twenty of her Chapel in copes of cloth of gold, to the of[fering, s]inging the English procession from the Chapel round [about the] Hall and back again to the Chapel singing, and master [dean of] her Chapel bore a book and a robe, and Master Norres bore the black rod, in a robe, and master Garter, all three in crimson satin; [and] the Bishop of Winchester wore his robe of red. . . .[7]

The conduct of the services at the Chapel Royal caused the Puritans much distress. Dean Nowell of St. Paul's Cathedral was bold enough to raise the matter in a sermon at Court in the spring of 1563, but he was very quickly silenced by the Queen: "Leave that," she cried, "it has nothing to do with your subject, and the matter is now threadbare".[8] Thomas Sampson, Dean of Christ Church, could hardly have been more upset when he heard that three of the newly appointed "Genevan" bishops were to take part in "popish" ceremonies at the Chapel Royal: "What can I hope," he asked, "when three of our lately appointed bishops are to officiate at the table of the Lord, one as priest, another as deacon, and a third as subdeacon, before the image of the crucifix . . . with candles, and habited in the golden vestments of the papacy, and are thus to celebrate the Lord's Supper, without any sermon? . . . I must be silent, though I have scarcely touched upon the heads of the misery that is hanging over us. Eternal Lord, have mercy upon us. . . ."[9]

The Queen was well aware, of course, that an outwardly "Catholic" liturgy was not without its value in the game of international diplomacy. The French Ambassador and his

retinue were evidently pleased with what they saw and heard
during their visit to England in 1564, or such at least was the
opinion of Archbishop Parker, who had on that occasion been
responsible for entertaining them:

> I note this gentleman, Monsr. de Gonour, to be outwardly of a
> good gentle nature [Parker wrote to Secretary Cecil] and methink
> I espy that he hath schooled his young gentlemen attending upon
> him to note and mark not only the tract of our country, but also
> curiously to search the state of our doings [and] the order of our
> religion, as the most of them were very inquisitive therein. I
> perceive that they thought, before their coming, we had neither
> *statas preces*, nor choice of days of abstinence, as Lent &c., nor
> orders ecclesiastical, nor persons of our profession in any regard
> or estimation, or of any ability amongst us. And thereupon, part
> by word, and partly by some little superfluity of fare and provision,
> I did beat that plainly out of their heads. And so they seemed to
> be glad, that in ministration of our Common Prayer and Sacra-
> ments we use such reverent mediocrity [i.e. moderation], and
> that we did not expel music out of our quires, telling them that
> our music drowned not the principal regard of our prayer.... [10]

In the administrative circles of the English church, however,
the spirit of Geneva was very much at large. During the early
sessions of Convocation in 1562, many divines were against the
use of elaborate choral music as they were against the use of
vestments, the sign of the cross in baptism, kneeling to receive
the Sacraments and other similarly "popish" practices, many
of which stemmed directly from the revisions to the 1552
Prayer Book and from the Royal Injunctions of 1559. A group
of radicals in the Lower House of Convocation went so far,
indeed, as to propose a seven-point programme of reform, the
first stage of which was the abolition of "all curious singing and
playing of the organs". The programme was rejected by a
substantial majority; but amongst those who voted for it were
Nowell, Dean of St. Paul's, and Sampson, Dean of Christ
Church, Oxford. A much less radical programme of reform
was put to the vote on February 13th, 1562, the sixth and last

point being a proposal "that the use of organs be removed."[11]
These proposals were defeated by the margin of only one vote
—fifty-eight to fifty-nine. Even though Convocation may at
that time have contained an unusually high concentration of
Puritan opinion, church musicians must indeed have wondered
what the future had in store for them. The same puritanical
spirit permeates the second *Book of Homilies*, published in
1563, and one particular passage from the Homily on "The
time and place of prayer" is particularly outspoken in its
condemnation of non-congregational music:

> [the idolatrous] see the false religion abandoned, and the true
> restored, which seemeth an unsavoury thing to their unsavoury
> taste; as may appear by this, that a woman said to her neighbour,
> "Alas Gossip, what shall we now do at church, since all the saints
> are taken away, since all the goodly sights we were wont to have
> are gone, since we cannot hear the like piping, singing, chanting
> and playing upon the organs, that we could before? But dearly
> beloved, we ought greatly to rejoice, and give God thanks, that
> our churches are delivered out of all those things which dis-
> pleased God so sore, and filthily defiled his Holy House and his
> place of prayer. . . ."

This attack may ostensibly have been directed at the practices
of the unreformed church, but its relevance to the current
situation can hardly have gone unnoticed.

That cathedral music was then on the decline is well established. The anonymous author of an early Jacobean treatise on
the subject (British Museum, Royal MS. 18. B. XIX) attributed
this very largely to the spread of puritanism:

> The first occasion for the decay of music in cathedral churches
> [he wrote] and other places where music and singing was used
> and had in yearly allowance, began about the ninth year of Queen
> Elizabeth, and what time the pretence of reformation for church
> discipline having possessed great persons, it was thought meet by
> some of them that the foundations where such allowance was
> were needless, and more fit to be employed better, if not wholly
> suppressed, namely those stipends for singing. And that lectures

were more fit to be erected, which accordingly was done in most places, howbeit, not from any new benefice of the pretended reformers, but either from the lessening of the numbers of singing-men, some of their stipends being turned that way, or else out of some other revenues of the said colleges. . . . Then divers preachers being set a work by the humours of these aforesaid reformers, were bold to set out books, and also in their sermons did persuade the people from the reverent use of service in song, affirming it to be nothing but an unnecessary piping and minstrelsy. . . . So as few or none of the people would vouchsafe to come into the choir during the singing service, but would stand without, dancing and sporting themselves, until the sermons and lectures did begin, scorning and deriding both the service and those which were employed therein. So as hereby the practice and use of skilful music, and those which exercised the same, began to be odious, and the professors to be accounted but as rogues, drunkards and idle persons, which was the cause that all endeavour for teaching of music or the forming of voices by good teachers was altogether neglected, as well in men as children, which neglect and little better reputation continueth to this day. . . .

The author undoubtedly overstates his case. Yet, as an ornament of daily worship, music was a lively issue in the vestiarian controversy and there were many who looked forward to the eventual abolition of non-congregational music altogether. As the Bishops of London and Winchester, Edmund Grindal and Robert Horne, wrote to friends at Geneva in February 1567, "we do not assert that the chanting in churches, together with organs, is to be retained, but we do disapprove of it as we ought to do".[12] Yet without the Queen's approval little could be accomplished. Horne did, indeed, abolish the post of organist at Winchester College during his Visitation of 1571, an act which was directly against the spirit of the 1559 Injunctions. And four years later, the Visitor to St. John's College, Oxford, went so far as to order the complete dissolution of the choir there on grounds of economy.[13] These, however, were isolated incidents and there is no evidence at all that attempts were made to tamper with the larger chapel and cathedral foundations. Indeed, when Grindal made his first Visitation of York Minister in 1572 as Archbishop, he had no option but to order "that there be, and with all speed convenient, provided and placed so many vicars choral within the church of York, to be ministers there, as the lands of their house called Beddern . . . will allow".[14] There was clearly no question here (and if not here, then surely nowhere else) of appointing "lecturers" into the vacant places.

There was nothing, however, to prevent the imposition of strict controls on the music that was sung at the daily services. In 1571, for instance, Horne effectively placed a ban on contrapuntal music of any kind in Winchester Cathedral:

> Item, that in the choir no more shall be used in song that shall drown any word or syllable, or draw out in length or shorten any word or syllable, otherwise than by the nature of the word it is pronounced in common speech, whereby the sentence cannot be well perceived by the hearers. And also the often reports or repeating of notes with words or sentences, whereby the sense may be hindered in the hearer shall not be used.[15]

The Genevan spirit may also have been behind a directive to the Norwich Cathedral choir discouraging the use of harmonised music at the ferial services, though it is, of course, possible to view this simply as a continuance of pre-Reformation practice.[16] And it was certainly true, as Royal 18. B. XIX pointed out, that much outspoken criticism of Anglican church music found its way into print, especially during the 1570s and 1580s, when the vestiarian controversy had widened into an attack upon the Episcopal system itself. This extract from the first *Admonition to Parliament: a view of Popish Abuses* (1572) may serve to give the flavour of the dispute. The writers, John Field and Thomas Wilcox, were both ministers of London city churches:

> We should be too long [they wrote] to tell your honours of cathedral churches, the dens aforesaid of all loitering lubbers, where Master Dean, Master Vicedean, Master Canons or

Prebendaries the greater, Master Petty-Canons or Canons the lesser, Master Chancellor of the church, Master Treasurer—otherwise called Judas the pursebearer—the chief chantor, singingmen—special favourers of religion—squeaking choristers, organ players, Gospellers, Epistolers, Pensioners, Readers, Vergers, etc. live in great idleness and have their abiding. If you would know whence all these came we can easily answer you that they came from the Pope, as out of the Trojan horse's belly, to the destruction of God's kingdom. The church of God never knew them, neither doth any reformed church in the world know them. . . .[17]

And yet too much stress should not be laid upon the negative aspects of puritanism at that time. A proposal to abolish organs may have been defeated by only the narrowest margin in the 1563 Convocation but, ultimately, without the royal assent this could never have been put into effect. And even where the spirit of Geneva was particularly strong, the musicians were not necessarily regarded as "rogues, drunkards and idle persons". William Whittingham, Dean of Durham 1563–79, formerly a distinguished member of the community at Geneva, spent much of his private income on the Grammar and Song Schools. And as one contemporary remarked, "concerning singing in the church [he] did so far allow of that as he was very careful to provide the best songs and anthems that could be got of the Queen's Chapel, to furnish the choir withall, himself being skilful in music".[18] The charming memorials to Osbert Parsley and William Inglott in Norwich Cathedral bear witness to a surprisingly happy and fruitful relationship between the Chapter and the choir (see Plate 2), yet few cathedrals at that time can have been more subject to Puritan influences.

The decline in musical standards must also have been due, therefore, to some other and equally potent cause. The explanation is, indeed, a very simple one: inflation.[19] For although the cost of living more than doubled between 1550 and 1600, stipends for the most part remained at their pre-Reformation levels. By 1575 this had become a serious problem, as Thomas

Whythorne pointed out in his *Autobiography* (Whythorne had for a while been director of music in Archbishop Parker's private chapel at Lambeth):

> First for the church, ye do and shall see it so slenderly maintained in the cathedral churches and colleges [and private chapels], that when the old store of the musicians be worn out which were bred when the music of the church was maintained (which is like to be in short time), ye shall have few or none remaining. . . .[20]

To suggest that cathedral Chapters were entirely to blame for this, as did Royal 18. B. XIX, is to ignore hard economic facts. Revenues were drawn almost entirely from the rents on leasehold properties, and these inevitably lagged behind the rise in prices. To obtain immediate relief, many Chapters shortsightedly renewed leases for abnormally long periods—a dangerous practice which had the gravest consequences for the future and which was only stopped by a special Injunction from the Privy Council in 1575. Many of the cathedral clergy solved their financial difficulties by holding offices in plurality, a solution that was not without its drawbacks. Several of the Canons at Chester, for example, held Fellowships at Oxford and Cambridge and were thus away from the cathedral for much of the year. This, not surprisingly, had a distinctly demoralising effect on the choir and there was much slackness and incompetence.

In their humble ways, lay musicians also began to hold offices in plurality—where, indeed, this was permitted—singing in the cathedral and following some trade or profession in the city in order to make ends meet. Some left the Church altogether, as the writer of Royal MS. 18. B. XIX correctly observed, to take up more lucrative appointments in private service. Thomas Lawes, father of the Lawes brothers, resigned his place in the Salisbury Cathedral choir in 1604 since, as he told the Dean and Chapter, he was quite unable to keep a wife and family on £8 13s. 4d. a year.[21] Yet the Salisbury musicians were undoubtedly better off than most of their colleagues else-

where. Stipends at Gloucester and Carlisle,[22] for instance, were
no more than £2 19s. 2d. a year, plus a clothing and commons
allowance of just over £3 10s.; these rates had been fixed in
1540 and had been designed to meet the needs of a celibate
community. Yet the Gloucester stipends were not increased
until the 1630s, and those at Carlisle not until 1680. When
Lieutenant Hammond visited Carlisle Cathedral in 1635, he
observed acidly "that the organs and voices did well agree, the
one being like a shrill bagpipe, the other like the Scottish
tone";[23] the cause of this was clear enough! Even at Durham,
one of the richest cathedrals in the country, the musicians were
paid no more than £16 13s. 4d. a year,[24] though at that time
Gentlemen of the Chapel Royal were earning more than twice
as much.

It is hardly surprising, therefore, that standards of musicianship and conduct were often found wanting. Drunkenness was
a common complaint, brawls were all too frequent and morals
were not always above suspicion. The problems that the Dean
and Chapter of Wells had to face at the turn of the sixteenth
century were very much the problems of the times:[25]

1591: Roger Rugge, a vicar choral, was found to be keeping an
alehouse in the cathedral close and was ordered to close it.

1592: Richard Mason, a vicar choral, was convicted of revealing
the private business of the Chapter; he was excommuni-
cated.

1593: Thomas Everett, a vicar choral, was convicted of getting
his maidservant, Joan Teight, with child; he was excom-
municated.

1594: George Huishe, verger and bellringer, was also convicted
of "incontinence" with Joan Teight.

1595: In this year there began a long drawn-out dispute between
the vicars choral and the cathedral chapter, particularly
over the status and stipends of the vicars choral, vis-à-vis
the Prebendaries.

1596: The vicars choral were reminded that they were obliged
under statute to take communion at least three times a
year in the cathedral.

1597: After an unofficial absence of more than six months, Richard Mewe, one of the vicars choral was summarily dismissed.

1598: This year saw the further collapse of the pre-Reformation collegiate system when the canons decided to put an end to communal meals for the choristers (supplied in turn by each residentiary canon).

1599: Notwithstanding the warning of the Chapter, two of the vicars choral failed to make their statutory communions.

1600: William Tawswell, one of the vicars choral, was accused of "incontinence" with the wife of one of his colleagues; the case was not proved however.

In the same year the Chapter warned all the vicars choral to attend services more regularly (there had been only four men present at evensong on the Wednesday previous to the Chapter meeting), and moreover "not to frequent taverns nor walk in the streets."

1601: Tawswell was suspended for a month after an all-night gambling session with "Anthony Harrison and others".

In the same year, Richard Marwood, a vicar choral, was convicted of "incontinence". The Chapter thereupon devised a most ingenious punishment which was to their considerable financial advantage. Having knelt before the Chapter and confessed his offence, Marwood was required for a period of some months "to write and prick out services for the choir of the cathedral church of Wells, at the discretion of Mr D. Cottington, the chantor [precentor] of the said church or his deputy".

1602: The dispute between the vicars choral and the Chapter having reached an impasse, the Chapter decided that "Every canon resident shall refuse to receive his vicar choral and to admit him to his house, till he doth reform himself, and become conformable to the orders and government of this church, as he ought".

(There is a gap of three years at this point in the Chapter Act Books.)

1605: One of the vicars choral, William Moore, was found to have been secretly married to Mary Sarney, widow, by an old recusant priest "of Queen Mary's days".

In October of that year the Chapter published certain orders "for the better subordination of the vicars choral".

1607: The Chapter again admonished the vicars choral to attend the cathedral services more regularly.

1608: Richard Mason, a vicar choral, being in severe financial difficulties sought relief from the Chapter; he was given part of the offerings taken at the late Bishop's funeral.

1609: The Chapter passed a resolution ordering the vicars choral "to disclaim and withdraw all actions, suites and complaints, heretofore had and made by them ... concerning stipendia vicariorum, stall wages ... and their diet at the master's table ...".

Even at St. Paul's, where the music was reputed to be of a high standard, a great deal was amiss, as Bancroft found out when he visited the cathedral in 1598.[26] Many of the choirmen were in the habit of arriving late and leaving early. As one of the clerks told the Visitor, "we be for the most part of us very slack in coming into the choir after the bell is tolled, and when we be there divers think the service very long till they be out of it again". He pointed out, too, that while the metrical psalms were being sung quite a few members of the choir sat there talking to each other, often so loudly that they could be heard from the other side of the choir. And the noise that went on in the cathedral during service time, he complained, was often unendurable. As he put it: "there is such noise of children and others in the side chapels and church at the divine service and sermons that a man may scarce be heard for the noise of them, and such hallowing and hooting above in the steeple that it is intolerable to hear at divers times". The petty canons, in general, thought that the choristers spent far too much time and energy collecting spur money, which they were traditionally entitled to do from any gentleman who absentmindedly entered the choir with his spurs on. It appears, too, that the organ had been so badly treated "with jogging the bellows" that there was not enough wind "to give sound to the instrument". But as Thomas Harrold told the Bishop, "The nursing fault of all these disorders is because after our complaint, there followeth no amending, as though your visitation were held rather for form's sake than to reform; for these disorders have been most of them complained of at every visitation, and yet continue in their old irregularity". Although Chapter Acts and Visitation Injunctions tend to set the irregularities of the daily routine in high relief, Morley's own comments amply confirm that much was then amiss. Before joining the Chapel Royal choir in 1592, he had for a short while been organist of St. Paul's Cathedral and, before that, organist at Norwich:

... the matter is now come to that state that though a song be never so well made and never so aptly applied to the words yet shall you hardly find singers to express it as it ought to be, for most of our churchmen, so they can cry louder in the choir than their fellows, care for no more, whereas by the contrary, they ought to study how to vowel and sing clean, expressing their words with devotion and passion, whereby to draw the hearer, as it were, in chains of gold by the ears to the consideration of holy things. But this for the most part you shall find amongst them, that let them continue never so long in the church, yea though it were twenty years, they will never study to sing better than they did the first day of their preferment to that place, so that it should seem that having obtained the living which they sought for, they have little or no care at all, either of their own credit, or well discharging of that duty whereby they have their maintenance.[27]

But though slackness and incompetence may have been on the increase at the turn of the century, there can be no doubt that sterner measures were being taken to put matters to rights. John Whitgift, Elizabeth's third and last Archbishop of Canterbury, did much to confirm the central assumptions of the Elizabethan settlement.[28] By requiring the assent of all ministers to the *Articles* of 1584, he effectively silenced the Presbyterian minority within the Church. And by tackling the problem of inadequate stipends (more than half the clergy, he discovered, had salaries of less than £10 a year), he did much to improve the quality of entry into the ministry. All this work of recons-truction was continued by his able successor, Richard Bancroft.[29]

With the accession of James VI of Scotland to the English throne in 1603, the Protestants may have hoped for further reforms. The so-called "Millenary petition", presented to the King on his way to London, contained proposals that had been argued and lost some thirty or forty years earlier: that the use of the sign of the cross in baptism was "superfluous", as was the service of confirmation; that "cap and surplice" should not be insisted upon; that "the longsomeness of service" should be "abridged", and that choral services should be "moderated to better edification". James did, indeed, go so far as to convene a conference at Hampton Court in 1604, ostensibly to allow Catholics and Protestants the opportunity for discussion. But Bancroft's aphorism, which James adopted as his own during the course of the proceedings—"no bishop, no king"—can have left the non-conformists in no doubt as to the ultimate outcome of the debate.[30]

Without doubt, the general climate of opinion within the Anglican church during the early seventeenth century was far more favourably disposed to "cathedral" music than it had been since the early years of the Reformation. Richard Hooker, author of the monumental *Laws of Ecclesiastical Polity* (1593–1628), eloquently expressed the new ethos of the Anglican *media via* when he praised music as "a thing apt for all occasions", "as seasonable in grief as in joy; as decent, being added unto actions of greatest weight and solemnity, as being used when men most sequester themselves from action . . . a thing which all Christian Churches in the world have received, a thing which so many ages have held, . . . a thing which always heretofore the best men and wisest governors of God's people did think they could never commend enough . . . .". Surely, he asked, "there is more cause to fear lest the want thereof be a maim, than the use a blemish to the service of God".[31]

Visitation articles and Injunctions of the early seventeenth century reflect an increasing interest in music and a new awareness of its value as a liturgical ornament. It is probably no accident that, after an apparent lapse of some forty years or so, cathedrals once again began to spend large sums of money on the restoration and reconstruction of organs. Indeed, there seems to have been a far greater readiness to do this than to raise stipends—a situation that is not entirely without its later parallels. It cannot be entirely fortuitous, either, that many more church musicians seem to have tried their hand at composition after 1590 than before, and that a much larger proportion were from the provinces. Of the thirty-five or so Edwardian and early Elizabethan composers (c. 1540–90), almost half the number were members of the Chapel Royal. Between 1590 and 1640, on the other hand, well over a hundred and twenty composers wrote at least something for the Anglican rites; and of these, only some thirty or so were Chapel Royal musicians.

And although during the second half of James's reign the administration of the Church was greatly weakened[32]—first by the appointment of the worldly George Abbott as Bancroft's successor in 1610, and later by the delivery of church patronage into the hands of the Royal favourite, the Duke of Buckingham—there was no question of a reversion to the anti-musical puritanism of the early Elizabethan church.

The emergence of a "high-church" party within the Anglican church during the early years of the seventeenth century is not without importance in the history of English cathedral music. In part, the movement may be regarded as a reaction against the spirit of Geneva, which had been such a major force within the Elizabethan church. In part, too, it sprang from a new and positive concern to justify the existence of an independent national church. The Anglican church was seen more and more as the true continuation of all that was best in the European Catholic tradition. As the Dean of Gloucester, Richard Field, wrote, "At the Reformation we [the Anglican church] separated from a part which claimed to be the whole, that we might hold with the Church Catholic against the pretensions of the Church of Rome".[33] In no sense can the high-church movement be regarded as a popular one, nor indeed until the 1630s was it at all widespread. Wherever it flourished, however, especial attention was paid to the outward forms and observances of daily worship.

To a very large extent, the Chapel Royal provided a model for the new movement; for while the Court may have been filled with "indifferent, negligent, secular" prelates,[32] the Chapel, by design or chance, was governed by a succession of distinguished clerics—James Montague (1603–19), Launcelot Andrewes (1619–26), William Laud (1626–33), William Juxon (1633–36) and Matthew Wren (1636–41)—all of whom may justly be described as high-churchmen. As to the King's own views, there are contradictory reports; but these must surely have been to some extent reflected in the men that he chose to accompany him on his journey to Scotland in 1617—amongst whom were Dean Montague, Launcelot Andrewes, William Laud, and Richard Neile, Bishop of Durham, one of Laud's first and most influential patrons. Elaborate preparations, moreover, had been made at Holyrood Palace, prior to the visit, including the complete redecoration and refurnishing of the Chapel; and the choir, which to all intents and purposes had ceased to exist after the Scottish Reformation, was reconstituted in order to make possible the daily singing of Matins, Second Service and Evensong. Similar efforts preceded Charles' visit to Scotland in 1633, with even greater emphasis on the musical elements of the Chapel services (see Chapter 3).

Attempts at Durham during the 1620s to establish daily services on the pattern of those at the Chapel Royal achieved a certain notoriety at the time through the resulting lawsuit between the senior prebend, Peter Smart—a churchman of the old puritanical school—and a group of the younger and high-church prebendaries, led by John Cosin, a protégé of Bishop Neile's. The case is of some interest, since it illustrates in detail the influence of high-church ideals upon the musical framework of the daily services. If Smart is to be believed, the

Durham prebendaries were the first to attempt "the imitation of the king's Chapel", and it is clear that this "imitation" involved the use of much more elaborate music than had up to then been used in the cathedral. Smart's written indictment is a repetitive and excessively lengthy document, but the substance and flavour of the argument are fairly represented in the following extracts:

8. Item: We [Peter Smart and his associates] article and object that you, John Cosin, and your fellows, to the intent you might allure popish people and other schismatical sectaries, to your superstitious and idolatrous service, and ceremonies; you have not only banished the singing of psalms, in the vulgar tunes, by authority allowed and in all *Cathedral* churches, before and after sermons: but you have so changed the whole liturgy, that though it be not in Latin, yet by reason of the confusedness of voices of so many singers, with a multitude of melodious instruments (directly contrary to the Injunctions and Homilies) the greatest part of the service is no better understood, than if it were in Hebrew or in Irish. Nay the Sacrament itself is turned well near into a theatrical stage play, that when men's minds should be occupied about heavenly meditations about Christ's bitter Death and Passion, of their own sins, of faith and repentance; of the joys of heaven, and the torments of hell; at that very season, very unseasonably, their ears are possessed with pleasant tunes, and their eyes fed with pompous spectacles of glittering pictures, and histrionical gestures, representing unto us Apollo's solemnities in his temple at Delos, which the poet describeth in the 4th of his Aeneidos:—

Instauratque choros, mistique altaria circum
Cretesque Dryopesque fremunt, pictique Agathyrsi.

And this kind of administration of the Holy Communion, with so many pictures, and so strange gestures, and excessive music, at the same time, is not used in any cathedral church in England, nor in Durham, till you John Cosin became prebendary of the same, that is within these three years.

9. [moreover] . . . you would needs bestow excessive cost, in ornaments upon the choir and church. . . . You have built a new

pair of gorgeous organs, which have cost at least £700, which you command to be played upon not only at the 6 o'clock prayer in the morning (whereby you have driven away from the church all scholars and artificers, which were wont to frequent that morning prayer, when it was short and plainly said, so that they might understand it), but also you enjoin the organist to play upon the same organs, all the time that both the sacraments of Baptism and the Holy Communion are administered, to the great offence of religious people, which therefore refuse to receive the Sacrament in the said cathedral church. . . . Moreover you have set up many images about the choir, some of the angels in long scarlet gowns, green petticoats, golden wings and gilded heads: and you, John Cosin, Treasurer, and Richard Hunt, Dean, varying in opinions what colours were best, have painted, and repainted, put on, and washed off colours, still crossing one another in your conceits, trying all manner of colours upon your images: and you could find no end of your disagreement, till you had taken the counsel of your painter, a popish recusant, who told you that nothing can be too good for the church, the colour of gold was the best colour; and so you resolved to uncolour them again, and to make them all golden idols. And because you thought, in your religious wisdoms, that it were not befitting the image of poor Christ, above the Bishop's throne, should be all of shining gold and scarlet, as gay as the 50 glorious angels, by the counsel of the said popish painter, you thought good to honour him with a golden beard, a new blue cap, like a pot lid, covering his head with rays like the sunbeams. This being concluded and done, the long war, civil and intestine, ceased between Dean Hunt and John Cosin, Treasurer. And from that time forth they made a league, and joined their forces against Peter Smart, an old prebendary, and perpetual adversary of their superstitious vanities, poperies and fooleries.[34]

The changes at Durham had all been made with the approval of Bishop Neile—who had formerly been Dean of Westminster Abbey and a patron of Laud's. Interestingly enough, however, Neile's successor, Howson, found himself more in sympathy with Smart than Cosin, and Cosin was soon writing to Laud at London asking for his support. Cosin again met some opposition when he introduced choral services into the chapel at Peterhouse shortly after his election as Master of the college in 1632. One of his critics bitingly suggested that musicianship, not scholarship, was the prime prerequisite for entry to the college:

> Instead of Aristotle's *Organon*
> Anthems and organs did I study on ...
>
> I cousen'd Dr. Cosin and ere long
> A Fellowship obtained for a song ...[35]

With the elevation of Laud to Canterbury in 1633, the high-church movement came to full maturity. Laud's own archiepiscopal Visitation articles and Injunctions give evidence of an unusually keen interest in musical matters and an acute attention to detail, whether the problem concerned the rebuilding of an organ, the election of a choirman, or some more general question of discipline or administration. The following letter which Laud wrote to the Dean and Chapter at Norwich, dated December 3rd, 1634, gives a good idea of his firm grasp of a tricky situation and his determination to see justice done:

> I do very well remember the late alteration of your Statutes and the settlement of them in Bp. Harsnett and Dean Suckling's time, my predecessor and myself among others being employed in that service. At that time it troubled me very much (as it has since done upon the consideration of other churches) to see the weakness of that choir, and the small means that was left to make it better; considering that neither the choir nor anything else more about the church can flourish without some proportionable reward to service. The good old Dean, to help things on as far as he might, projected two things. The one was some proportion of corn to be allowed them, which I think was then settled, and I hope continued. The other, I do not well remember that it was settled by Statute (the more the pity), but it was generally thought fit, and approved by all of us to whom the consideration of the Statutes was then recommended, that is, that such small benefices, or cures, within the city or suburbs, as are in the church's gift, should, as they fell void, be given to the petty canons respectively

and to no other. And that the church should be very careful from time to time to choose such petty canons into vacant places, as might be fit and able to discharge both duties: both to sing in the choir, and to catechize or preach in the parish. This custom of giving these small cures to the petty canons is usual with other churches, where the choir is as mean as yours, and it being great help to them; and fit and able men will never be wanting, if this course for their preferment be held constant.

I write this unto you because I am informed that there are divers very sufficient men already in expectation of those places whensoever it shall please God to make any void; so that you need not be to seek to furnish yourselves. But I hear withall, there is a purpose amongst some of you, without any regard of the honour and good of the Church, to bestow these livings, when they fall, upon their private friends, without any respect had to the choir, which if it be, will utterly overthrow the choir service, and you will not be able to retain either voices or skill amongst you. I would be glad to hope this information were not true, but it is so constantly affirmed to me, that I cannot distrust it altogether. . . . And this I assure you, that if I shall find that you do at any time put other men into these cures, and leave the petty canons destitute to the utter prejudicing of the choir, I shall take all the ways that wisely I can to make you see your error. . . .

Your very loving friend,

W. Cant.[36]

But if the clergy were not always wholeheartedly behind Laud, the laity were by no means unanimous in their approval of his liturgical innovations. The Dean and Chapter of Canterbury, at Laud's suggestion, attempted to incorporate the popular Sunday afternoon sermons in the cathedral into the regular framework of choral evensong (the sermons had traditionally been given in the Chapter House). But many citizens strongly resented the move to enforce attendance at "the ceremonious altar service" and, not long after the change had been made, evensong one Sunday afternoon was brought to a complete standstill by an excitable and protesting congregation. After this, the Dean had no option but to move the sermons back into the Chapter House since, as he said, the times were "too much indisposed to give hopes of any speedy remedy". Troubles of a rather similar kind broke out elsewhere —notably at Chester and Worcester[37]—giving evidence of a serious lack of sympathy and understanding between the cathedral clergy and the townsfolk. Under such conditions, the cathedral musicians can hardly have been encouraged to give of their best.

It was during the 1630s, too, that anti-Episcopal (and thus anti-musical) literature became once again a serious problem. The Puritan lawyer William Prynne produced a lengthy and hotly reasoned argument against the use of elaborate church music, quoting in support of his case innumerable authors from biblical times onwards and including the Abbot of Rievaulx (c. 1160):

> Let me speak now, [saith he] of those who under the show of religion do obpalliate the business of pleasure: which usurp those things for the service of their vanity which the ancient fathers did profitably exercise. Whence then ... hath the church so many organs and musical instruments? To what purpose, I demand, is that terrible blowing of bellows, expressing rather the cracks of thunder than the sweetness of the voice? To what purpose serves that contraction and inflection of a voice? ... Sometimes, which is a shame to speak, it is enforced into a horse's neighing; sometimes, the masculine vigour being laid aside, it is sharpened into the shrillness of a woman's voice. ... And this ridiculous dissolution is called religion.

And from the pen of William Bastwick came a stream of invective, unequalled perhaps in the entire history of Elizabethan and Jacobean pamphleteering. Laud he described as "the Prior of Canterbury, William the Dragon" and Neile, "the Abbey lubber of York, that oracle of the north"; whilst of the clergy in general he wrote, "one would think that hell were let loose, and that devils in surplices, in hoods, in copes, in rochets, and with four-square cow turds upon their heads were come among

us and had beshit us all". It is hardly surprising, therefore, that
he had little time for church music of any kind:

> What holiness, I pray, is nowadays placed in churches and
> chapels? What adorning of them, to the ruining almost of the
> parishes where they are!... And now of late, what immense
> sums of money have been gathered [for the restoration of St.
> Paul's]! I have heard from Jesuits themselves, that are well
> acquainted with those businesses if not principal sticklers in them,
> who I know at least are very joyful at such preparations, that it
> amounteth to above £200,000, and that all this mighty mass of
> money must be spent in making a seat for a priest's arse to sit in;
> for it is *cathedra episcopi*—a Bishop's chair—and for the Dean, and
> sub-Dean, and for the Prebends, Canons, Petty Canons, Vergers,
> choristers and all, to keep the Pope's saddle warm, as the popelins
> themselves bragging, prate. The truth is the whole fraternity of
> that crew is but a generation of vipers. . . .[39]

Whilst the authorities managed to exert at least some control
over literature of this kind, the outbreak of civil war in England
unleashed a veritable flood of anti-Episcopal, anti-government
propaganda.

In 1637, as is well known, Charles attempted to impose a
new Prayer Book on the Scottish kirk—a move that effectively
triggered off the so-called Bishops War and the English Civil
War. In the spring of 1642, at Oxford, Charles was confronted
with an ultimatum—the Propositions for Peace—in which he
was required to agree to "the taking away of all archbishops,
bishops, and their chancellors and prebendaries, and all vicars
choral and choristers. . . .". Although Charles then rejected
the Propositions, he was powerless to stop proceedings in
parliament some two years later to abolish both the Episcopal
system and the Book of Common Prayer. Choral services came
to an end at no one particular date, however. In London they
had already been seriously interrupted by parliamentary troops
in 1642, whilst at Exeter they may well have continued until
the spring of 1647. At Ely, the Dean and Chapter received a
note from Oliver Cromwell himself (ex-Steward of the

cathedral) ordering the cessation of choral services. The note at least shows that Cromwell himself was anxious to prevent as much unnecessary destruction as he could:

> Lest [he began] the soldiers should in any tumultuous or disorderly way attempt the reformation of your cathedral church I require you to forbear altogether your choir service, so annoying and offensive, and this as you will answer it if any disorder should arise thereupon. . . . I desire your sermons where usually they have been, but more frequent.
>
> Your loving friend,
Oliver Cromwell.[40]

All too often, however, the soldiers took matters into their own hands. At Westminster Abbey "they brake down the organs, and pawned the pipes at several ale-houses for pots of ale. They put on some of the singing-men's surplices and in contempt of that canonical habit ran up and down the church— he that wore the surplice was the hare, the rest were the hounds". Similar happenings were recorded at Canterbury, Chichester, Exeter, Peterborough and Winchester, and other cathedrals doubtless suffered, too, at that time. To some, this was a matter for great exultation:

> A most rare and strange alteration in the face of things in the cathedral church at Westminster. Namely that whereas there was wont to be heard nothing almost but roaring boys, tooting and squeaking organ pipes and the cathedral catches of Morley, and I know not what trash; now the popish altar is quite taken away, the bellowing organs are demolished and pulled down, and the treble, or rather trouble and bass singers, chanters or enchanters driven out, and instead thereof, there is now set up a most blessed orthodox preaching ministry. . . .[41]

To those, however, who had devoted a life's work to the service of the Church the times must indeed have seemed bitter. And with the execution of Charles I in 1649, few men can have dared to hope for the eventual restoration of the Anglican forms of worship. Before leaving Windsor, when services at St.

George's had been stopped, Child put pen to paper for what he must have imagined would be his last anthem. The text that he chose, "in the year 1644 on the occasion of the abolishing of the Common Prayer and overthrowing the Constitution both in Church and State", came from psalm 79: "O Lord God, the heathen are come into thine inheritance: thy holy temple have they defiled, and made Jerusalem an heap of stones". This anthem forms a sad epilogue indeed to one of the greatest chapters in the history of English church music.

NOTES TO CHAPTER 2

1. Brown and Bentinck, Dec. 31st, 1558: a letter from Il Shifanoya to the Mantuan Ambassador in Brussels.
2. Dickens, p. 294.
3. Brown and Bentinck, p. 1.
4. Nichols (i), p. 197.
5. Frere and Kennedy, XVI, p. 8.
6. Hume, pp. 105–6.
7. Nichols (i), pp. 280–1.
8. Neale, p. 220.
9. Robinson (iii), pp. 63–4.
10. Bruce, pp. 212 and 214.
11. Strype, pp. 298–9.
12. Robinson (iii), p. 178.
13. Hutton, p. 52.
14. Nicholson, pp. 146–53.
15. Frere and Kennedy, XVI, p. 319.
16. British Museum, Stowe MS. 128; information kindly supplied by Mr. H. W. Shaw. At Ludlow parish church, if nowhere else, weekday services were sung to plainsong: see ch. 6 for further discussion of this question; Mr. Alan Smith has kindly supplied all the information concerning the services at Ludlow.
17. Douglas and Frere, p. 32.
18. Green (i), pp. 22–3.
19. Clapham; see also Burne for an account of the effects of inflation at Chester Cathedral.
20. Whythorne, p. 245.
21. Robertson, p. 169; six months later, the Dean and Chapter reduced the number of layclerkships from eight to six; Lawes applied for readmission.
22. The figures are taken from the Gloucester Cathedral archives, and from Prescott, p. 64.
23. Hammond (i).

C

24. Information kindly supplied by Mr. H. W. Shaw.

25. *Historical Manuscripts Commission*, "Calendar of the Manuscripts of the Dean and Chapter of Wells", II (1914).

26. Simpson, p. 272.

27. Morley, p. 293.

28. Dawley, ch. 6.

29. See Usher for an account of Bancroft's administration.

30. Barlow.

31. Hooker, sections 38–9.

32. Roper, p. 571.

33. Overton, II, p. 37.

34. Ornsby, LII, p. 144.

35. Quoted by Hughes, Dom. A.

36. Simpson, p. 420.

37. Woodruf and Danks, Burne, and Atkins.

38. Prynne (i), p. 179.

39. Bastwick, p. 19.

40. Scholes, p. 223: see ch. 15 for further account of spoliation during the Civil War.

41. Vicars.

3

The Chapel Royal

Most of our knowledge of the later history of the Chapel Royal comes from the so-called "Check Book", a large commonplace ledger into which the secretary, or Clerk of the Check as he was called, entered the business of the Chapel: appointments, resignations, decisions taken at "Vestry" meetings, special forms of service, rates of pay, and so on (see Plate 3).[1] The book was probably started by Thomas Sampson in 1592, and taken over by John Hewlett shortly after 1600. Hewlett died in 1620 and he was succeeded first by John Stevens, and then in 1630 by Thomas Day, Master of the Westminster Abbey choristers. The original Check Book remained in use until 1641, but a second book (called here for convenience Check Book B) was started in an attempt, it would seem, to correct some errors and omissions that had been discovered in the first.[2] Most of Book B is taken up with a list of appointments running from 1561 onwards, as does the similar though not identical list in Book A; but it does contain some interesting information, too, on the internal economy of the Chapel, on fees and board wages, and on travel allowances, as well as a detailed account of the preparations for Charles' visit to Scotland in 1633.

The history of the Chapel Royal before 1561 must be gleaned from the Household records (principally from those of the Lord Chamberlain[3]), and from other scattered sources, none of which—needless to say—are as complete as could be wished. Enough remains, none the less, to show that the function and organisation of the Chapel choir changed little throughout the sixteenth and seventeenth centuries. The senior official was the Dean. Under him were priests, a sub-Dean, a choirmaster, organists, lay singers, choristers and various servants—a Sergeant of the Vestry, two or more yeomen and a groom.

The Chapel foundation was a royal peculiar, under the direct control of the sovereign and exempt from episcopal jurisdiction. The business of the Chapel was discussed at meetings of the "Vestry" over which the Dean presided. No complete record of decanal appointments has survived, but the following men are known to have held office:

DEANS OF THE CHAPEL ROYAL[4]

Richard Sampson: 1516, Dean of the Chapel Royal and of St. Stephen's, Westminster; 1523, Dean of Windsor; 1536, Bishop of Chichester; 1544, President of the Council of Wales; d. 1554: widely travelled; composer of some standing; Dean of the Chapel Royal from 1516 to possibly c. 1554.

Monsignor Hutchenson: according to a letter of December 31st, 1558 (*Calendar of State Papers, Venetian*, 1558–1580, pp. 2–3), Hutchenson, Dean of the Chapel to Queen Mary, was replaced by

George Carew [or *Carey*] Doctor in Divinity, late chaplain to her Majesty when she was Lady Elizabeth: graduated from Broadgates Hall, Oxford, 1522; held many livings in plurality during the reigns of Edward VI, and Mary Tudor; 1558, Dean of the Chapel Royal[5]; 1559, Dean of Christ Church, Oxford; 1560, Dean of Windsor; 1571, Dean of Exeter; d. 1583: according to the New Year's presents lists, Carew was still Dean in 1578/9, but see below.

William Day: took his M.A. from King's College, Cambridge, in 1553, five years after election to a Fellowship; 1560, Fellow of Eton and Prebendary of York Minster; 1561, Provost of Eton; 1572, Dean of the Chapel Royal; 1575 Dean of Windsor; d. 1596. According to Stowe,[6] the deanery had been vacant for eight years when James Montague was appointed Dean in 1603 (see below).

James Montague: graduated from Christ's College, Cambridge; by 1596 he was Master of the newly founded Sidney Sussex College, Cambridge; 1603, Dean of the Chapel Royal and of Lichfield Cathedral; 1604, Dean of Worcester; 1608, Bishop of Bath and Wells; 1616, Bishop of Winchester; d. 1618.

Launcelot Andrewes: graduated from Pembroke Hall, Cambridge, and in 1576 was elected a Fellow of Pembroke; c. 1589, Master of Pembroke; 1601, Dean of Westminster Abbey; 1605, Bishop of Chichester; 1609, Bishop of Ely; 1619, Dean of the Chapel Royal; d. 1626.

William Laud: graduated from St. John's College, Oxford, becoming a Fellow of the college in 1593, and President in 1611; 1616, Dean of Gloucester; 1621, Bishop of St. David's; 1626, Dean of the Chapel Royal; 1628, Bishop of London; 1633, Archbishop of Canterbury; d. 1645.

William Juxon: Scholar of St. John's College, Oxford; Bachelor of Civil Law, 1603; 1621, President of St. John's; 1627, Dean of Westminster; 1633, Bishop of Hereford; 1633, Dean of the Chapel Royal; 1633, Bishop of London; 1636, Lord High Treasurer; d. 1663.

Matthew Wren: graduated from Pembroke Hall, Cambridge, in 1605 and was elected a Fellow of the college in the same year; 1615, Chaplain to Launcelot Andrewes; 1625, Master of Peterhouse; 1628, Dean of Windsor; 1636, Dean of the Chapel Royal; d. 1667.

Neither Sampson, Carew nor Day appear to have been unduly troubled by religious scruples. Sampson greatly shocked the Canons of Windsor by his ready support for the Supremacy Bill of 1534. And although he was imprisoned for a short while in 1540 on suspicion of reactionary activities, he had fully regained his standing at Court within the space of four years. Two motets of his[7] bear witness to a useful knowledge and skill in the art of music.

Carew, a prosperous pluralist, managed to steer himself successfully through the turbulent waters of the Edwardian reformation, the Marian reaction and the Elizabethan settlement without any very serious setbacks. At Elizabeth's coronation he was the only divine, it was said, who was prepared to celebrate the Mass in accordance with the Queen's wishes, an act of compliance that may well have won him the Deaneries of the Chapel Royal and St. George's, Windsor.

His successor, William Day, had been at odds with some of his more conservative colleagues at King's shortly after his election to a Fellowship, yet this did not prevent him from holding his Fellowship there during the reign of Mary Tudor. And, although he supported the anti-vestiarian proposals at the 1562 session of Convocation, he was evidently not so firmly opposed to the use of organs and "curious singing" as to refuse the Deanery of the Chapel in 1572 or, three years later, the Deanery of St. George's, Windsor. At Windsor, Day was not a success. He seems to have had little head for finance and no general administrative ability. Whether he took any effective part in the affairs of the Chapel, therefore, is much to be doubted: that Elizabeth left the post unfilled after his death in 1596 certainly confirms the suspicion that she can have attached little importance to it.

The seventeenth-century deans seem, on the whole, to have been more distinguished, and all were high-churchmen. James' first Dean, Montague, had already spent much of his own money, while Master of Sidney Sussex, on the provision of furnishings and ornaments for the college chapel; and as Bishop of Bath and Wells he later gave £1000 towards the restoration of Bath Abbey. His successor, Launcelot Andrewes, was the earliest friend and patron of three leading divines of the high-church movement: Laud, Cosin and Wren. William Juxon followed closely in the wake of his elder contemporary and patron Laud, first as a commoner at St. John's, Oxford, then as President of the college, and later as Dean of the Chapel Royal and Bishop of London. Wren came under the influence of Andrewes at Pembroke Hall, and was later his private chaplain and Cosin's immediate predecessor at Peterhouse.

The sub-Dean was in charge of the daily routine at the Chapel. He was normally in Holy Orders, and he was elected to the post by the Gentlemen of the Chapel. He was responsible for drawing up the yearly attendance rotas, with the help of three or more of the Gentlemen; and when the Dean was absent it was also his job to decide upon the music for each service, in consultation with the Master of the Choristers.

The Master of the Choristers was normally chosen from among the Gentlemen of the choir, a practice that made for continuity of tradition: all, except Edwardes, remained in office for a considerable time—two for periods of over thirty years:

	Year of election as a Gentleman of the Chapel Royal	Master of the Choristers
Richard Bower	before 1526	1545–(63?)
Richard Edwardes	between 1553 and 1561	1563–66
William Hunnis	between 1547 and 1553	1566–97

Richard Farrant, Master of the Choristers at Windsor, may have taken over Hunnis' duties for a while, between 1569 and 1580; see Hunnis' letter below (p. 62)

Nathaniel Giles	1597	1597–1633
Thomas Day	1615	1633 onwards

All five men led very full and active lives. Bower, Edwardes, Hunnis and Giles directed the boys in dramatic entertainments of various kinds; Giles and Day were responsible for training choristers elsewhere—Giles at St. George's, and Day at Westminster Abbey; both Edwardes and Giles were composers of some distinction, and Hunnis was the author and editor of several highly successful books of devotional verse. Of the five, Hunnis probably had the most colourful career, being imprisoned in 1555 on charges of conspiring to put Elizabeth on the throne.[8] As a reward for this, no doubt, Elizabeth appointed him surveyor of the gardens and orchards at Greenwich and collector of the tolls on London Bridge—an appointment that by rights belonged to the City Corporation!

The post of Master of the Choristers was no sinecure. The Master had not only to train the boys but also to feed, clothe and house them; he had also to act as talent scout, touring cathedrals and chapels in search of outstanding voices. Hunnis' letter to the Queen, dated November 1583, gives a clear picture of the choirmaster's various duties, and also of the difficulties that had to be faced in times of inflation:[9]

1583 November The humble petition of the Master of the Children of Her Highness' Chapel.

May it please your honours William Hunnis, Master of the Children of Her Highness' Chapel, most humbly beseecheth to consider of these few lines.

First, Her Majesty alloweth for the diet of twelve children of her said Chapel daily sixpence apiece by the day, and forty pounds by the year for their apparel and all other furniture.

Again, there is no fee allowed, neither for the Master of the said children nor for his usher, and yet nevertheless is he constrained, over and besides the usher still to keep both a manservant to attend upon them and likewise a woman servant to wash and keep them clean.

Also there is no allowance for the lodging of the said children, such time as they attend upon the Court, but the Master to his great charge, is driven to hire chambers both for himself, his usher, children and servants.

Also, there is no allowance for riding journeys when occasion serveth the Master to travel or send into sundry parts within this realm, to take up and bring such children as he thought meet to be trained for the service of Her Majesty.

Also, there is no allowance nor other consideration for those children whose voices be changed, who only do depend upon the charge of the said Master until such time as he may prefer the same with clothing and other furniture, unto his no small charge.

And although it may be objected that Her Majesty's allowance

is no whit less than Her Majesty's father of famous memory therefore allowed: yet considering the prices of things present to the
time past and what annuities the Master then had out of sundry
abbeys within this realm, besides sundry gifts from the King, and
divers particular fees besides, for the better maintenance of the
said children and office: and besides also there hath been with-
drawn from the said children since Her Majesty's coming to the
Crown a shilling by the day which was allowed for their breakfasts
as may appear by the Treasurer of the Chamber his account, for
the time being, with other allowances incident to the office as
appeareth by the ancient accounts in the said office, which I here
omit.

The burden whereof hath from time to time so hindered the
Masters of the Children, viz. Mr. Bower, Mr. Edwardes, myself
and Mr. Farrant: that notwithstanding some good helps otherwise
some of them died in so poor case, and so deeply indebted that
they have not left scarcely wherewith to bury them.

In tender consideration whereof, might it please your honours
that the said allowance of sixpence a day apiece for the children's
diet might be reserved in Her Majesty's coffers during the time of
their attendance. And in lieu thereof they to be allowed meat and
drink within this honourable household for that I am not able
upon so small allowance any longer to bear so heavy a burden.
Or otherwise to be considered as shall seem best unto your
honourable wisdoms.

When a chorister's voice broke, the choirmaster normally
informed one of the Masters of Requests, who thereupon took
steps to see that the boy was well placed, at Oxford or Cambridge, in some school, or in some congenial trade or profession.[10] On one occasion at least, Elizabeth was obliged to
intervene personally on behalf of a boy to see that justice was
done. The occasion in question arose when Dr. Dale, Master of
Requests and Dean of Wells, wrote to his colleagues at the
cathedral informing them that the Queen wished to place an
ex-chorister of the Chapel in the choir there—the boy had for
some time been a chorister at Wells before being impressed for
the Chapel Royal. For some reason, the Chapter refused to take

him back. Evidently, Dale had then discussed the problem with the Queen, for the next letter to arrive at Wells was from the Queen herself:[11]

> Trusty and well beloved, we greet you well. Whereas John Pitcher, sometime a chorister of your Church of Wells, was from thence brought hither to serve us in the room of a child of our chapel, in which place he hath remained nigh this six years, diligent in service and to our good liking, till now that his voice beginneth to change he is become not so fit for our service; and herewith understanding that there is a singingman's room void in the said church, we have thought it meet to recommend him unto you to be placed in the same, with our express commandment that according to the orders of your house ye do admit and place him, the said John Pitcher into the room of a singingman in the said church, with all manner of houses, lodgings, rooms, pays, duties and commodities whatsoever to the room of a singingman there appertaining and belonging, to be had and perceived by him during his life, in as large and ample manner as any other singingman there now hath and enjoyeth for and in respect of his room. And these our letters shall be your sufficient warrant and discharge in this behalf. Given under our signet. At our palace of Westminster, the tenth day of March in the 30th year of our reign.
>
> To our trusty and well beloved the Dean and Chapter of the cathedral church of Wells.

Dale was much upset that the Queen should have been troubled on such a small matter, and in a later letter to his colleagues he roundly upbraided them for their behaviour: no other cathedral in the country, he pointed out, would have presumed to act in such a manner:[11]

> After my hearty commendations. Her Majesty doth not take it well that a boy which have been brought up in our church and one that have served in her Chapel should not be received upon my letter which I wrote unto you. Discretion would be used in such cases, and I would be glad to make the best of all things; we must be advised in such cases. If I had written to any other church

in the realm in the like case, her Majesty should not have had made
to have written herself in so small a matter. And thus I bid you
heartily farewell. At the Court, the 18th March, 1588.

Your loving friend
Valen. Dale

To my loving friends the Prebendaries resident in the church
in Wells.

In pre-Reformation times, the duties of playing the organ
were shared out amongst the able Gentlemen of the Chapel.
With the development of the verse service and anthem, however, the duties inevitably became more arduous, and the
practice grew of electing Gentlemen especially for their skill in
organ playing. An exact succession cannot be determined, but
it probably took something like the following form:

(a) Tallis and Byrd described themselves as organists of the
Chapel on the title page of the *Cantiones, quae ab argumento sacrae
vocantur* (1575). Tallis died in 1585 and Byrd in 1623—Byrd had
relinquished these duties long before 1623, it would seem.

(b) Blitheman, an Oxford musician, is said to have become
organist of the Chapel in 1585, on the death of Tallis. Blitheman
died in 1591: the following epitaph is recorded in the later editions
of Stowe's *Survey of London*:[12]

Here Blitheman lies, a worthy wight who feared God above;
A friend to all, a foe to none whom rich and poor did love.
Of prince's chapel, Gentleman, unto his dying day,
Whom all took great delight to hear him on the organs play,
Whose passing skill in music's art a scholar left behind,
John Bull (by name) his master's vein expressing in each kind.
But nothing here continues long, nor resting place can have,
His soul departed hence to heaven, his body here in grave.

(c) John Bull joined the Chapel choir in 1586; he is later described as "organist" in a Check Book entry of May 29th, 1592.
In the Check Book minute of December 5th, 1604, he is the only
Gentleman to be so named. On December 27th, 1613, he was
replaced by a bass from St. Paul's.

(d) William Randoll, from Exeter, was elected Epistoler in 1584; he later signed himself "organist" in the Check Book (July 10th and 15th, 1592).

In 1604, Edmund Hooper (an ex-chorister of Exeter) was elected in his place; on November 2nd, 1615, he signed himself "organist".

In 1621, he was succeeded by Thomas Tomkins, who is listed as organist at the time of the coronation of Charles I. Tomkins died in 1656.

(e) Francis Wiborow was sworn Epistoler in 1599; he is no-where described as organist, but:

In 1625, John Tomkins was sworn for the next organist's place that should fall vacant. In 1626, Wiborow died at Ely and John Tomkins was elected in his stead.

At Michaelmas, 1638, Richard Portman was sworn Epistoler. Later in the year, John Tomkins died and Portman succeeded him.

(f) George Waterhouse, from Lincoln, was elected Gentleman in 1588.

In 1600, Arthur Cocke, from Exeter, was sworn Gentleman for the next organist's place that should fall vacant.

In February, 1602, Waterhouse died and Cocke replaced him.

In January, 1605, Cocke died and was replaced by Orlando Gibbons, who later signed himself "organist" (November 2nd, 1615).

On his death in 1625, Thomas Warrick succeeded him (Warrick had been Bull's assistant at Hereford). He died in 1641.

The impression emerges from this list that the best players came from a remarkably restricted circle. Tallis, the eldest of the Elizabethan organists, is said to have been Byrd's teacher, whilst Waterhouse may well have been a pupil of Byrd's at Lincoln. Bull was taught by Blitheman, and Thomas Warrick was Bull's assistant at Hereford. Hooper, Randoll and Cocke all came from Exeter (John Lugge, who became organist there in 1602, was an unusually gifted player, to judge from his extant compositions;[13] his father, Thomas Lugge, had been a vicar choral of the cathedral since at least 1586). Thomas Tomkins was a pupil of Byrd's, and John Tomkins, "Organista

sui temporis celeberrimus", was Thomas' younger brother.
He was also a student at King's College, Cambridge, while
Orlando Gibbons was there. Orlando Gibbons himself came
from a musical family. His father had lived in Oxford for some
time before 1566 and he may well have known Blitheman
while he was organist of Magdalen College. Portman was a
pupil of Orlando's and, like Orlando, he too became organist
of Westminster Abbey.

Since there were never less than two and for some of the
time three or more organists, duties were shared out according
to seniority. An entry in the Check Book dated 1615 gives a
good idea of how the system was supposed to work and of the
ruffled tempers that resulted when it did not:

> Be it remembered that in the year of our Lord 1615, there arose
> a controversy between the Organists, for the manner of their
> waiting at principal feasts. It was thereupon ordered by the
> Reverend Father in God the Lord Bishop of Bath and Wells,
> Dean of His Majesty's Chapel, that always hereafter the ancient
> custom should be observed, which was, and still must be, that the
> most ancient Organist shall serve the eve and day of every prin-
> cipal feast, as namely the eves and days of the feasts of Christmas,
> Easter, St. George, and Whitsuntide, the next Organist in place
> to serve the second day, and so likewise a third for the third day,
> if there be so many Organists, and for all other festival days in the
> year, those to be performed by the Organists as they shall fall out
> in their several weeks of waiting.

Since there were only two signatories—Hooper and Gibbons—
it would seem that neither Byrd nor Wiborow was acting as
an organist at that time.

By collating the two Check Books, and with the help of the
earlier documents in the archives of the Lord Chamberlain,
it is possible to draw up a fairly complete list of Gentlemen
from 1547 onwards. As Table 8 shows, the Edwardian reformation and the Marian reaction did not disrupt the establishment
unduly (the same would seem to have been the case elsewhere).
Column one shows the choir as it was for the funeral of Henry

TABLE 8

*The Chapel Royal Choir during the reigns of Edward VI, Mary Tudor
and Elizabeth I*

The Chapel Royal Choir at the Funeral of Henry VIII, and at the coronation of Edward VI (1547)[14]	Mary Tudor's Chapel Royal September 17th, 1553[15]	Date of retirement or death, recorded in the Check Book
John Fisher (1503)*		
Henry Stephinson (1509)		
Robert Phelipps (1524)		
Thomas Burye (1526)		
Richard Pigott (1526)		
John Allen (1526)		
Richard Stephin (1526?)		
Robert Hockland (after 1526)		
Richard Barwyck (after 1540?)		
William Poope (after 1540?)		
William Hychyns (1520)	William Hychyns	(1566)
Thomas Byrde (1526)	Thomas Byrde	(1561)
Richard Bower (1526)	Richard Bower	(1561)
Robert Perrye (1526)	Robert Perrye	
William Barber (1526)	William Barber	
Robert Richemound (1526)	Robert Richemound	(1586)
Thomas Whayt (after 1526)	Thomas Whayt	
Thomas Talys (after 1540)	Thomas Talys	(1585)
Nicholas Mellowe (after 1540?)	Nicholas Mellowe	
Thomas Wrighte (after 1540?)	Thomas Wrighte	
	Emery Tuckfield†	
	Nicholas Aurchbalde†	
	William Walker†	(1563)
	Robert Chamberlayne†	
	William Gravesend†	(1569)
	John Angel†	(1567)
	Robert Stone	(1613)
	John Benbowe	(1592)
	John Shepherd	
	William Mauperley	(1583)
	George Edwards	
	Robert Morcocke	(1581)
	William Hunnis	(1597)
	Thomas Mann	
	Richard Aylesworth	(1567)
	Thomas Pulfreyman	(1589)
	Roger Kenton	
	Lucas Caustell	
	Richard Farrant	(1564)
	Robert Adams	

TABLE 8 (continued)

The Chapel Royal Choir at the Funeral of Henry VIII, and at the coronation of Edward VI (1547)[14]	Mary Tudor's Chapel Royal September 17th 1553[15]	Date of retirement or death, recorded in the Check Book
	[Gospeller] John Singer Robert Bassocke	
	[Epistoler] Thomas Caustun	(1569)
	Richard Lever	
	John Denham	(1567)
	Walter Thirlby	
	Morris Tedder	
	Hugh Williams	
	[Richard Edwardes], c. 1555	(1566)
		plus thirteen other Gentlemen, many of whom may have joined the choir between 1553 and 1558

* In most cases the Gentlemen would have joined the Chapel choir some time before the dates given.
† Priests.

VIII and for the coronation of Edward VI (two lists have survived, but these are virtually identical). The second column is dated September 17th, 1553. Ten of the original twenty Gentlemen were still singing in the choir in 1553, and of the ten that had resigned six were probably in orders (there were only six priests in the 1553 choir and all had been appointed after 1547). Surprisingly enough, the 1553 list suggests that the choir had almost doubled in size in the course of six years; the increase may not have been as dramatic as this, however, since the junior members of the choir (the Epistolers and Gospellers) do not seem to have been included in the earlier lists.

Bearing in mind that more than half the members of the 1547 choir had then been in royal service for twenty years or more—and two for over forty—the resignations and retirements between 1547 and 1561 do not seem to have been unduly numerous.

Prospective candidates for admission to the choir were normally "heard and approved for sufficiency of voice and skill" by the sub-Dean "and the major part of the company"; recommendations were then passed on to the Dean (or in default of a Dean, the Lord Chamberlain) for his approval. Later entries in the Check Books show that the successful candidate was usually elected "Epistoler"—this was a junior post with lower rates of pay—and that he was subsequently promoted "Gospeller", and finally "Gentleman in ordinary". This practice no doubt reflected long-standing custom.

There was, however, a second method of entry whereby the candidate was first elected to an honorary post as Gentleman extraordinary on payment of a small fee; the appointment in this case was a probationary one, with the prospect of a full place at the end of one or two years if all went well. The system was, of course, open to abuse since until 1592 and even after then, candidates for honorary places were exempted from formal examination. Unsuitable and unqualified men had accordingly managed to slip in from time to time "to the no small hindrance of her Majesty's service in her said Chapel". In an attempt to put matters to rights, the Gentlemen determined in 1592 that all who sought admission to "extraordinary" places, without expressly being invited to do so by the choir, should from thenceforth be required to pay an entry fee of £5. This may well have had the desired effect, since no further measures of the kind are recorded in the Check Book. On occasion, honorary places were given to benefactors of the choir. The most unusual appointment of this kind concerned Mr. William Phelps of Tewkesbury, who was elected a Gentleman Extraordinary "at his humble suit" "for that he did show a most rare kindness to Mr. Doctor Bull in his great distress, being robbed in those parts". Elections of this kind, however, were rare.

As might be expected, the Chapel was relatively untroubled by the misdemeanours and inefficiencies that so beset cathedrals during the late sixteenth and early seventeenth centuries.

The Check Books record only three cases of expulsion: Salomon Compton, a "secondary" from Exeter had been elected Epistoler in May, 1581. He was, however, dismissed in 1588 for bigamy. Some thirty years later, one John Green was also found "to have married a second wife (the first being living)" and he too was dismissed. Some time afterwards, another Gentleman was expelled for manslaughter: he had apparently been admonished on several occasions for his "disordered and debauched" behaviour and for "distempering himself with drink". In the end, he accidentally killed his poor wife by throwing a pair of scissors at her during one of his bouts of drunkenness [March 15, 1639]. One or two Gentlemen were reprimanded for minor disciplinary offences and for neglect of duty, particularly when Laud was acting as Dean of the Chapel. Nearly all the matters are minor ones which less observant men would have missed altogether: the Sergeant of the Vestry was not to dispose of any "utensils belonging to the service of the Chapel" before the Dean or sub-Dean had passed them as unserviceable; a verger was fined a fortnight's pay for uncivil behaviour in Chapel; two layclerks, both altos, were criticised for slackness and incompetence; the Gentlemen were ordered to join in the singing of the metrical psalms "and not be silent when it is their duties to use their voices"; and poor Thomas Warwick was fined a whole month's pay for playing verses on the organ "having formerly been inhibited by the Dean from doing the same, by reason of his insufficiency for that solemn service". Measures had also to be taken in 1636 to ensure that the ferial services were adequately attended, especially when the Court lay at Hampton Court or Greenwich. On the whole, however, the Check Books are remarkably free of disciplinary decisions of the kind.

Throughout the sixteenth and seventeenth centuries, places in the Chapel Royal choir were very highly prized. That this was so is not to be wondered at, for conditions of service, rates of pay and hours of work were all outstandingly good. In the first place, the status of the Gentleman was much above that of the cathedral lay-clerk or minor canon. As we have seen, the business of the Chapel was done at meetings of the "Vestry"—all Gentlemen having the right to attend and vote. Cathedral musicians, on the other hand, had little or no say in the business of their Chapters. Chapel Royal salaries, too, were good—far better than those of any other choral foundation in the country. The daily fees amounted to 7½d. (4½d. for Gospellers and 3d. for Epistolers) to which were added expenses to cover the cost of travel and board, making a total of £30 a year (increased to £40 from 1604 onwards). The Gentlemen also received additional fees for weddings, funerals, christenings and other extraordinary services. Many of them, too, were rewarded by liberal grants of property and lucrative privileges, and they all had opportunities to earn extra money in the city. The leading members of the Chapel could, on occasion, command astonishingly high fees. John Bull, for instance, was paid no less than £20 for playing the organ at a banquet given by the Merchant Taylors Company in honour of young Prince Henry and his father.[16]

A place in the Chapel Royal carried with it the additional attraction of long holidays. No services at all were sung on ferial weekdays between St. Peter's Day (the end of June) and Michaelmas Day (the end of September), nor during the weeks after Epiphany, Candlemas, Easter, St. George's Day, or during the week before Christmas. Neither were services sung when the Court was on progress and away from a "standing house", that is to say when it was resident in some other place than Greenwich, Whitehall, Richmond, Hampton Court, or Windsor Castle. At other times, the ferial weekday services were sung by sixteen men (i.e. half the choir) and twelve boys, the Gentlemen being on duty alternate months as directed by the sub-Dean. Festal services, beginning on the eve of the Feast Day, and also the Sunday services were sung by the whole choir, as were the morning services on "Sermon days". Every Gentleman was entitled, therefore, to a hundred or more free days a year. With so much spare time, many chose to augment their stipends, as did the organists and Masters of the Choristers, by taking part-time employment in other choirs. John Hewlett, the Clerk of the Check, kept his place at Wells for nine or more years after being elected a Gentleman, and the Cathedral Chapter, though not entirely happy with the arrangement, preferred to keep him on that basis rather than lose him altogether. William Randoll kept his place at Exeter after taking up his duties at the Chapel in 1584; in this case, however, the arrangement did not work out so well, and eight or nine years later the Dean and Chapter tried to deprive him of his stipend and house in the Close. The Queen thereupon intervened in the dispute, and Randoll was reinstated.[17] During the early seventeenth century it rather looks as though more and more of the Gentlemen held appointments in plurality. The links between Westminster Abbey and the Chapel Royal certainly grew very close—so close, in fact, that by 1625 well over half the Abbey choirmen were Gentlemen:

TABLE 9

The Funeral of James I, 1625

The Chapel	Singingmen of Westminster Abbey[18]
William Heather, Doctor	[Heather was also a member of the Abbey choir, but his name does not appear]
Nathaniel Giles, Doctor and Master of the Children [also Master of the Choristers at Windsor]	
John Stephens, Gentleman, recorder of songs	
Thomas Tomkins, organist [also organist at Worcester]	
[Frost was a Gentleman, but his name does not appear here]	John Frost, chantor
Thomas Day	Thomas Day, Master of the Choristers
Walter Porter	[Porter had been a chorister at the Abbey]
John Crocker	John Croker
Thomas Peirce	Thomas Peirce
Orlando Gibbons, privy organ	Orlando Gibbons, organist
John Clark [Child of the Chapel]	John Clarke

(Table 9 continued overleaf)

TABLE 9 (*continued*)

The Chapel	Singingmen of Westminster Abbey[18]
[Nelham was a Gentleman, but is not listed]	Edward Nelham
[Greene was a Gentleman Extraordinary]	George Greene
Richard Giles	Richard Giles
[Sandie was elected Gentleman in 1627]	Richard Sandie
George Cooke	Daniel Taylor
John Woodson	Robert White
George Woodson	Henrie Northedge
Peter Hopkins	James Hooper
William West	Adrian Batten
William Crosse	Richard Patrick
John Cooke	Robert Willis
John Frost (jnr.)	Robert Williams
Crue Sharp (?)	
Humphrey Batche (?)	
George Sheffeild	
[*Gentlemen Extraordinary*]	
Nicholas Rogers and Francis Sennocke	

The system was almost bound to break down from time to time, and Laud had occasion to reprimand musicians at Salisbury, Rochester, St. Paul's and elsewhere during the 1630s for their failure to provide adequate substitutes when they were away at the Chapel Royal. At the Chapel Royal, too, Gentlemen tended to absent themselves, as we have seen, especially if the Court was away from the City. But the system did undoubtedly work whenever the musician was prepared to fulfil his obligations properly. It had its advantages, too, for it kept many provincial choirs in close touch with the highest standards of composition and performance. The presence of so much Chapel Royal music in pre-Restoration part-books must be due in no small measure to the comings and goings of "cathedral Gentlemen".

None of the chapels in which the choir had to sing were particularly large, with the exception of the Royal Free Chapel at Windsor. The chapel at Greenwich was situated at the east end of the main façade, along the waterfront (Plate 9). As Wyngaerde's drawing shows, it had three bays of windows and a shallow bay next to the gateway, projecting out towards the river, which probably housed a vestry and perhaps the royal "closet" or an organ loft. The building inside was divided into an "upper" and a "lower" chapel—these would now probably be called the chapel and antechapel. Neither can have been any higher than forty feet nor much more than forty feet long, and even if vaulted with stone (in the absence of outside buttresses this is unlikely) they would have had rather a dead acoustic—especially when hung, as they often were, with heavy curtains and gold brocade.[19] Greenwich figures prominently in the Check Book, since it was a favourite residence of both Elizabeth and James.[20]

Unfortunately, no pictures of the Whitehall Chapel have survived; nor are there any adequate descriptions—a truly remarkable state of affairs, since so much went on there.[21] Two ground plans have survived. One gives the length of the chapel as only 40 ft, a most unlikely measurement. The other —by Vertue, c. 1670—shows a building some 75 ft long and about 30 ft wide, with vestries to the north and south of the east end. The ceiling was probably stone, with moulded ribs and carved bosses; and the windows were perpendicular in style—a four-light window at the east end and four bays of three-light windows to the sides. There exists a highly stylised German engraving of a ceremony that took place there in 1623 between James I and the Spanish ambassador—the two are shown at a table before the high altar, and they are sealing an agreement connected with the projected marriage of Prince Charles to the Spanish Infanta (see Plate 10). To judge from the picture, it would seem that there must have been some sort of musicians' gallery at the north-east end of the chapel which housed the organ, instrumentalists and even some of the singers. At the west end of the chapel was the royal Closet at first-floor level; this was connected by corridors to the State apartments—the Presence Chamber and the Great Chamber—and thence to the private apartments. There were similar arrangements at Greenwich, Richmond and Hampton Court.

Distinguished visitors would wait for the King or Queen in the Presence Chamber before service, moving from there into the Closet to hear service. There was a stairway from the Closet into the Chapel, allowing access to the Altar for Communion.

The Court also spent much time at the palaces of Richmond and Hampton Court, both of which far outshone Greenwich or Whitehall in architectural splendour. Wyngaerde's sketch of Richmond conveys an exciting impression of turrets and towers, gateways and courtyards (see Plate 4). The chapel, on the east side of the middle court and opposite the hall, is clearly shown in the sketch, perpendicular in style (it dated from c. 1498) with four bays of generously proportioned windows rising well above the two-storey crenellated gateway in the foreground. In the survey made by the Parliamentary Commissioners in 1649, the chapel wing of the Court is described thus: "One fair and large structure or building, three storeys high, called the Chapel Building, covered with lead and battled; the lowest of which storeys contains one fair and spacious cellar, very well arched, called the wine cellar, and one little room in the side thereof. The middle storey contains three rooms used for the Yeoman of the wine cellar; and two rooms called the Groom Porter's Rooms. The third storey contains one fair and large room, 96 ft long and 30 ft broad, used for a chapel. This room is very well fitted with all things useful for a chapel; as fair lights [i.e. windows], handsome cathedral seats and pews, a removable pulpit, and a fair case of carved work for a pair of organs."[22]

Hampton Court remained a popular resting place for the Court throughout the sixteenth and seventeenth centuries (see Plate 5).[23] The palace had been planned and to a large extent built by Cardinal Wolsey between 1514 and 1517, and it was there that Wolsey's fine choir sang, much to the envy of Henry VIII. When Henry took the palace over in 1529, he set about rebuilding the hall and chapel. The hall was finished in a fever of activity within the space of four years, and soon afterwards work was started on the chapel. This comprised the addition of carved stalls, a new organ chamber on the south-east side of the building and, above all, the decoration of the superbly vaulted ceiling. No less than £450 was paid to work-men for "glittering and garnishing of the vault in the chapel", for "the two great bay windows of the king's and the queen's holy-day closets [at the west end on the first floor, as at White-hall], and for the decoration of the closets with the king's arms and with the queen's, with beasts gilt in fine gold and byse, set out with other fine colours . . .". The chapel, at ground-floor level, measured some 60 by 35 ft with an ante-chapel, over which the royal closets stood, measuring a further 40 ft or so in depth. Again, as at Richmond and Greenwich, there is ample evidence that the chapel was lavishly adorned with "rich cloth of gold or arras", when the sovereign was in residence.

Foreign visitors were invariably impressed with the splen-dour of the Court, and several went out of their way to mention the fine singing of the Chapel Royal choir. The simul-taneous visit of the Russian ambassador, Grigori Ivanovitch Mikulin, and Don Virginio Orsino, Duke of Bracciano, at Epiphanytide, 1601,[24] must have been one of the more brilliant occasions for feasting and jollification. Orsino, quite bewildered by so much magnificence, allowed himself to be cajoled by the Queen into attending a service in the chapel, much to the scandal of his Jesuit mentor. On Epiphany Sunday morning, Elizabeth met both the Ambassador and Orsino in the Presence chamber. As they walked along to chapel she joked with the Duke, promising to write to the Pope to ask that he should not chide him for having attended a heretical service. When the party arrived in the chapel closet, the musicians began to play on organs, cornets and sackbutts, and there was much other "wondrous music" and song. Looking down from the closet, the party beheld a dazzling spectacle: the courtiers below dressed wholly in white and richly be-jewelled; the chapel walls hung with golden tapestries; the altar covered with a rich damask cloth; the books of the Epistles and Gospels embossed with gold; the candles; the crucifix; and the golden copes of the officiating priests and the Gentlemen of the Chapel Royal. The Check Book shows that this was very far from being a unique occasion; there were solemnisations of treaties, noble marriages, births, churchings, confirmations and funerals besides the St. George's Day Garter services and the Maundy Thursday ceremonies, all of which were celebrated with great solemnity and much music. Here were ample incentives for the musician to give of his best.

Attempts to uncover the history of the choir at St. George's between 1540 and 1600 are again hampered by lack of material.[25] Unfortunately, the Chapter Act Books do not begin until 1597—the year in which Dean William Day died—and none of the other sources of information provide us with anything like a complete picture. The foundation was organised on collegiate lines, with a Dean and an executive Chapter of canons. The under officers, including the minor canons and lay-clerks, had little say in the running of the chapel and in this respect they were not as fortunately placed as their colleagues at the Chapel Royal. During the fifteenth century the choir had steadily grown in size, and in 1485 there were thirteen vicars, thirteen clerks and thirteen choristers. During the years immediately preceding the first Act of Uniformity, the Chapter were forced to admit more and more laymen into the choir for want of suitably qualified priests; and in November 1547 they decided to put the arrangement on an official footing. Provision was made at the same time for ex-choristers to be sent to grammar schools and universities, £6 13s. 4d. a year being set aside for the purpose.

A year or so later, the Visitors and the Chapter came to the conclusion that there were still too many places on the foundation for minor canons, and that the number should progressively be reduced from ten to four. To compensate for this, five more lay-clerkships were created. Laymen were to be paid £11 2s. 10d. per annum, minor canons £15 2s. 7d. This scheme was only partially carried out since the Chapter found that priest musicians were easier to come by than they had originally anticipated. By 1563, the numbers had settled to seven minor canons, thirteen lay-clerks and ten choristers. The boys were trained, housed and fed by one of the senior members of the choir. They spent four hours a day learning to read, write and say their catechism, devoting the rest of the time outside service hours to musical pursuits. Just how matters fared at Windsor in the difficult years between 1547 and 1559 we cannot say. Quite a number of the minor canons remained there during the course of at least one of the three major upheavals, and several of them held on from beginning to end. Probably the effective disruption was not particularly great.

Elizabeth gave her full support to the chapel choir and was anxious that its standards should be maintained and improved:

> Eliz. R: Whereas our Castle of Windsor hath of old been well furnished with singing-men and children. . . . We, willing that it should not be of less reputation in our days, but rather augmented and increased, declare that no singing-men or boys shall be taken out of the said Chapel, by virtue of any commission, not even for our household chapel. And we give power to the bearer of this to take any singing-men or boys from any chapel, our own household and St. Paul's only excepted. Given at Westminster, the 8th day of March, in the second year of our reign.[26]

Not, indeed, that everything went smoothly after this. During the 1570s, few of the prebendaries spent much time at Windsor, and those who did were often at odds with each other. The Chapter foolishly let a number of valuable properties on long leases, a practice that would have had very grave consequences in later years had it not been stopped by the Royal Visitors. No accurate accounts were kept and many valuables, in the form of plate and vestments, were embezzled. But these were very much the troubles of the times, and though Windsor may have been little better off than many cathedrals, it was certainly no worse. And as far as the music was concerned, standards cannot have been much below those of the Chapel Royal, since the

Court was often there, drawing to the Castle many distinguished foreigners. This extract from a report compiled by four Venetian visitors in 1575 gives a good idea of the atmosphere at Windsor when the Queen was in residence:

> After remaining three days in London we went to Windsor where the Queen was then residing, and on being conducted to the palace were introduced to what is called the Presence Chamber, at the hour when her Majesty was to pass through on her way to Chapel. The apartment was very crowded, and the nobility assembled there greeted us cordially, and with every mark of honour. After some short talk and a joke or two ... Elizabeth moved towards the Chapel, where she remained about twenty minutes until the service there ended. This service consisted first of all, of certain psalms chanted in English by a double chorus of some thirty singers. A single voice then chanted the Epistle, and after this another the Gospel, and all the voices then sang the Creed. This concluded the service, and we with the rest then returned to the Presence Chamber to see the Queen once more, and to pay due homage as she passed. ...[27]

Later, the Duke of Württemberg's secretary published an account of his master's travels in England. The Duke ("Cosen Garmombles" and "the duke de Jarmany" in the *Merry Wives of Windsor*) had a burning desire to be admitted to the Order of the Garter and was enraptured by Windsor, and not least by the music there:

> The Castle stands upon a knoll or hill. In the outer court is a very beautiful, and spacious church, with a low flat roof covered with lead, as is common with all churches in England. In this church his highness listened for more than an hour to the beautiful music, the usual ceremonies, and the English sermon. The music, and especially the organ, was exquisite. At times could be heard cornets, then flutes, then recorders and other instruments. And there was a little boy who sang so sweetly, and lent such charm to the music with his little tongue, that it was really wonderful to listen to him. Their ceremonies indeed are very similar to those of the papists, with singing and so on. After the music, which lasted

a long time, a minister or preacher ascended the pulpit for the sermon, and soon afterwards, it being noon, his highness went to dinner. . . .[28]

without it would seem, waiting for the sermon to finish!

Several famous musicians were associated with the Windsor choir: John Merbecke (c. 1531–85), Richard Farrant (c. 1564–80), John Mundy (c. 1585–1630), Nathaniel Giles (1585–1633) and William Child (1630–97). Farrant gave up his place at the Chapel Royal in order to become Master of the Choristers at St. George's—an unusual move, this, since very few left the Chapel Royal once they had established themselves there. A summary of the original indenture of his appointment has survived and is worth quoting at length, since it sets out his duties in some detail:

The 24th of [April] in the 6th of Eliz. the Dean and Canons indented Richard Farrant, one of the Queen's Chapel, to be Master of the Choristers in this church, and to have a clerk's place and to be one of the organists in this Chapel: he to have the boarding, clothing, lodging and finding of the ten choristers: to enjoy the houses and emoluments of an organist, clerk and master. On condition of the premises to have £81 6s. 8d. per annum to be paid him monthly by the treasurer besides spur money and money given by strangers for singing of ballets, and the Master of the boys is to have power of placing and displacing the boys (except the present boys before their voice is broken which are not to be displaced without order of Chapter); he is also to find a sufficient service for those he displaces: he to be absent so far as the college statutes permit. The choristers to have their chamber in the college to lie in still allowed them, but the Master of the boys to provide them not only clothes and diet but also bedding, and to leave them as well clothed as he finds them: he to have the place for his life. After the displacing of any boy he is to find another within a month or to be defaulted 18d. per week for default after the month is expired: he is not to demand anything of the augmentation granted this year to the clerks and choristers, nor be absent not above two months in the year and that by leave of the Dean. . . .[29]

The indenture makes it clear that Farrant (and presumably the other Windsor musicians too) was allowed only eight weeks official leave of absence each year. Though Farrant was still Master of the Choristers at the time of his death in 1580, he had none the less rejoined the Chapel Royal choir in 1569, the Dean and Chapter obviously having allowed him to take far more time away from Windsor than was stipulated in the original agreement. Farrant must have been very well off, for he owned two houses in London—one at Greenwich, which he used when the Court was resident there, and one at Blackfriars, close by the Chapel Royal "theatre".

Giles' indenture is very similar to Farrant's, though it is set out rather differently.[30] It shows that Giles took up the appointment there "at the request and desire" of the Dean and Canons. His duties were to teach the choristers singing, pricksong and descant, and he was also to instruct the more able choristers in instrumental playing. He was to be allowed the statutory eight weeks leave a year, though this was not to coincide with the occasions when the Queen and Court were in residence, or when the "installation or funeral of any noble person" was to be solemnised. The Dean and Chapter must again have substantially modified the attendance clauses, however, when Giles became Master of the Chapel Royal choristers twelve years later. Indeed, the Chapter agreed to Giles' request in 1605 that one of the lay-clerks, Leonard Woodson, should deputise for him since he was away from Windsor so frequently. The arrangement worked fairly smoothly, though the Chapter did have to warn Woodson some years later "to keep the whole number of choristers and to see them brought up as they ought to be in music, manners and writing".[29] During Giles' term of office at Windsor, the organist was John Mundy—Mundy and Giles both arrived at Windsor in the same year. On Mundy's death in 1630, the Chapter appointed William Child in his stead; and on Giles' death, three years later, Child became both organist and choirmaster. Much of his best and most adventurous music dates from his years at Windsor before the Civil

War. There are several fine anthems of his in the Pembroke and Peterhouse partbooks, and a Latin Te Deum and Jubilate, specially written for Dr. Cosin, Master of Peterhouse.

Two other royal foundations call for some comment in this discussion of the Chapels Royal, although neither played much part in the early history of English cathedral music. The two foundations in question are the Chapel Royal of Scotland and Queen Henrietta Maria's private chapel at Somerset House. The Scottish Chapel Royal,[31] as founded by James IV of Scotland in 1501, had consisted of sixteen canons, nine prebendaries and six boys. For ten years or so after the Scottish Reformation, some attempts were made to continue the musical traditions of the choir, largely through the encouragement of Queen Mary. On her arrival in Scotland from France in 1561, masses were sung in her chapels at Holyrood House and at Stirling, the seat of the Chapel Royal choir, but on both occasions these services aroused considerable opposition and led to "broken heads and bloody ears". For the next thirty years, little or nothing is known of the choir. Since, however, the organ at Stirling was taken down in 1571, by order of the Captain of the Castle, it is unlikely that the choir can have been singing any but the simplest kinds of music. Some half-hearted attempts were made to "search and try out the old foundation" in 1586, and in 1594 a new chapel was built at Stirling (the old one having become ruinous) in preparation for the baptism of the young Prince Henry. By English standards, the baptism service was not particularly elaborate, and yet a contemporary noted with pleasure that "the provost and prebends ... did sing the twenty-first psalm of David according to the art of music, to the great delectation of the noble auditory". James VI, father to the young prince, appeared at first to be anxious to restore the Chapel Royal to its former glory, but after he left Scotland for England in 1603 he transferred the responsibility for its upkeep to one of the grooms of his Bedchamber, James (or John) Gibb, with disastrous results. In 1615, however, a confused and very delicate situation was

clarified by Bishop Cowper, who succeeded in wresting the
patronage from Gibb's hands. In the following year preparations were begun for James' projected State visit to Scotland,
and the chapel at Holyrood Palace, which for some time had
been the principal Chapel Royal, was repaired and refurnished.
The stalls for the prebendaries and the choir were adorned with
carved and gilded angels (see the Durham controversy of 1628,
when similar refurnishing was attempted), a new altar was
provided, with sculptured candlesticks and other ornaments,
Mr. Dallam was paid £133 6s. 8d. for an organ, and Inigo
Jones was commissioned to design a case for it. James arrived in
Edinburgh on May 16th, 1617, and attended a choral service
there on the following day. On Whitsunday, James was present
at communion, which was celebrated by several of the Scottish
bishops. It would be interesting to know what part William
Laud played in the proceedings—for he was there as one of the
King's chaplains. Before James left Edinburgh, he gave full
instructions that choral services should continue. For some while
his wishes were carried out, and in the following September
Dean Cowper was able to write to him that, at the one service
he had managed to attend, "the organs and musicians, four on
every part, men and boys, agreed in pleasant harmony, to the
contentment of all, because they understood what was sung".

Cowper's successor, Lamb, was only there for two years. It
was then decided to link the Deanery with the near-by
bishopric of Dunblane to enable the Dean to attend rather
more services than his predecessor had done. Bellenden, the
new Dean, was equally anxious to improve conditions and
raise standards in the Chapel Royal, and he suggested the
appropriation of additional "prebendaries, chaplainries and
altarages" throughout the kingdom. James agreed to the
proposal. It aroused much opposition, however, and two years
later Charles, now King of England, had to reverse his father's
decision. During the course of the next seven years, Charles—
or more probably Laud—redesigned services of the Scottish
Chapel on the lines of those in England. In March 1628

Edward Kellie, a Scottish musician, servant to the High Chancellor of Scotland, George, Viscount of Diplene, was appointed a prebendary of the Chapel, director of music and receiver of the Chapel revenues. It was at about this time that members of the Scottish Council and other departments of the administration were ordered to attend communion in the Holyrood Chapel, where communion was administered at Charles' express command to the sound of trumpets! In 1630 Kellie visited London to see how services were conducted at the Chapel Royal, to order new music for the Scottish Chapel and to engage more singers. It took five months to copy out the "twelve great books, gilded, and twelve small ones with an organ book". Kellie managed to find an organist, "two men for playing on the cornets and sackbutts, and two boys for singing divisions in the verses", thus bringing the total strength of the choir up to sixteen men, an organist and six boys, "who all of them sang their psalms, services and anthems sufficiently at first sight to the organ, verses and chorus". In a report to the King, dated January 24th, 1631/2, Kellie explained that the boys practised daily in a room especially provided for the purpose, and that the men met there twice a week—no doubt for a full rehearsal. In chapel, the men wore black gowns (in marked contrast to the London surplices and copes!) and the boys wore "sad-coloured coats". As in London, the choir was seated antiphonally, cathedral fashion, with their music books placed on reading desks in front of them. Before the sermon the choir sang a full anthem, and afterwards "an anthem alone in verses with the organ".

On June 15th, 1633, Charles arrived in Edinburgh together with Dean William Laud and a section of the English Chapel Royal,[32] and on the 18th he was crowned King of Scotland in the Abbey Church at Holyrood with great ceremony and much music. The coronation and the visit passed without incident, though many Scottish prelates strongly disapproved of the way in which the services had been conducted. Two months after the court had returned to London, a letter was dispatched to

Dean Bellenden concerning the government of the chapel and requiring that services be sung twice daily "with the choir, as well in our absence as otherwise". It was not long, however, before Laud received a letter from Bellenden to say that all was not well.The chief trouble was the lack of money—the singing-men were very poorly off and paid at irregular intervals. Laud, in his reply, promised relief. Yet this did not materialise. And although nothing was proved against Kellie, the Master of the Choristers, it looks as though he had been embezzling the chapel funds. Edward Miller, who replaced him early in 1635, can have had little chance to prove himself. Two years later, the ill-fated attempt was made to impose an "Anglican" prayer book on the Scottish kirk. The book had to be with-drawn the following year, so bitter was the opposition to it, and shortly afterwards the Scottish parliament excommuni-cated Bishops Wedderburn and Bellenden. In August 1639 Charles hopefully ordered repairs to the Holyrood Chapel, which had been much damaged the year before, with a view to re-establishing services there. But on August 14th, 1641, the Episcopal system was abolished in Scotland and a prominent Presbyterian, James Henderson, was effectively made Dean of the Chapel Royal. Choral services must have ceased long before then.

Henrietta Maria's private chapel at Somerset House[33] in London was in existence for little more than ten years, yet it must have done something, at least, to influence the musical tastes of fashionable church-goers at that time. When Henrietta Maria arrived in London in the autumn of 1625 as the new Queen of England, she brought with her a large retinue of French servants, musicians and priests, expecting that a new chapel would be provided for her private use in accordance with the terms of her marriage agreement. Charles at first wished to do no more than allow her the use of a large room in Somerset House itself, and his reluctance to build a chapel was the source of much friction. But by 1627 a happy compromise had been reached: a new chapel was to be built and the Queen was to be allowed her own private retinue, if on a somewhat reduced scale. Catholic services, which had been interrupted for a year or so, began again in 1629 at the temporary Somerset House chapel. They were directed by the Bishop of Angoulême and ten Capuchin priests with the help of ten musicians, most of them French. The services drew large crowds; and although Charles at first tried to prevent the public from attending, his efforts were of little avail. By the autumn of 1632 the plans for a new chapel had been drawn up, and a service was held in the grounds of Somerset House to mark the laying of the foundation stone. The senior Capuchin, Father Gamache, tells how a temporary chapel of tapestries and fine cloth was erected on the site. The Queen's grand almoner, Mons. du Peron, granted indulgences and celebrated High Mass "while harmonious music ravished the heart". It seemed that all London had turned up to witness the ceremony. When the new chapel was finished, four years later, the Queen ordered that the first High Mass there should be celebrated with all possible pomp and splendour. The choir, organ and instruments were placed in galleries to the north and south of the high altar, but hidden from view. On December 10th, Henrietta Maria and a distinguished company took their seats in chapel for Mass. The building drew rapturous expressions of delight from all those present—as did the music, which seemed to come from paradise itself. The mass was sung to an eight-part setting (the composer, unfortunately, is not named), and the singing was so exquisite that only those with hearts of stone could have failed to be moved. In the evening Her Majesty again went to chapel, this time for Vespers, Compline and a Sermon. The musicians were so heartened by the excellent reception that had been given to their morning performance that they far excelled their earlier efforts.

So many Londoners wished to see the chapel that only on the third evening could it be cleared of visitors in order that the King might inspect it. Charles declared afterwards that he had seen nothing more ingeniously planned or more beautifully

D

executed. But within five years, all was silent again. In March 1643 the Commons appointed a commission to arrest the Capuchins and to put an end to services at Somerset House. On Thursday in Holy Week the chapel doors were broken down, the altars demolished, the furnishings destroyed and a costly Rubens thrown into the river. London was preparing itself for sterner times.

NOTES TO CHAPTER 3

1. Rimbault: Thomas Sampson was officially Clerk of the Check from 1581 to 1615; when Hewlett was elected to succeed him in 1615, however, he had been acting as Clerk of the Check "above eight years". Many of the early entries are in his hand.

2. Oxford, Bodleian Library MS. D318, pp. 25–47; see Hillebrand, p. 233.

3. Lafontaine.

4. Biographical material taken principally from the *Dictionary of National Biography*.

5. Brown and Bentinck, p. 3.

6. Stow (i).

7. British Museum, Royal MS. 11. e. xi.

8. Stopes, ch. 5–6.

9. Hillebrand (i), pp. 80–1.

10. See warrants quoted in Stopes, p. 13 and Hillebrand (i), p. 82.

11. *Historical Manuscripts Commission*, "Calendar of the Manuscripts of the Dean and Chapter of Wells", II, p. 314.

12. Stowe (ii), p. 399.

13. John Lugge, *Three Voluntaries for Double Organ*, eds. S. Jeans and J. Steele, (Novello, 1956).

14. Lafontaine.

15. Stopes, pp. 21–2.

16. Stow (i), p. 890.

17. See "William Randoll", by Lady Jeans, in the supplementary volume of *Grove V*; and Green (iii), p. 438.

18. Lafontaine.

19. Dunlop, p. 53.

20. See Klarwill and Rye for some impressions of the Court by visiting foreigners.

21. The Chapel was destroyed by fire in 1698; see the *LCC Survey of London*, XIII (1930) pp. 53–7.

22. Chancellor, p. 95.

23. Law, I, p. 183, and appendix D. There was a chapel, too, at Nonsuch but from the little information that has survived, it would seem to have been little more than a large and barely furnished room; whether the Chapel Royal ever sang there is doubtful: see John Dent, *The Quest for Nonsuch*, (1962).

24. Hotson, ch. 8.

25. See the useful series of *Windsor Historical Monographs*, and especially Fellowes (iv) and (v); see also Frere and Kennedy, XIV–XVI.

26. See the *British and Foreign Review*, XVII, 1844, p. 94.

27. Brown and Bentinck, p. 525.

28. Rye, p. 16.

29. Fellowes (iv).

30. Atkins, p. 27.

31. Much of the material for this section is taken from Rogers; see also Farmer.

32. Details of arrangements for the visit, and of the expenses involved are to be found in MS. D318, at the Bodleian Library, Oxford.

33. Taken mainly from Needham and Webster.

4

Some Performance Problems

Much attention has rightly been focused in recent years upon historical accuracy as a criterion of performance. But to what extent is it possible to reconstruct an authentic performance of a sixteenth- or early seventeenth-century service or anthem? What is known of the pre-Restoration attitude to such fundamental questions as vocal timbre, blend, pitch, speed, phrasing and dynamics? What kinds of tone-colour would have been available on the average cathedral organ, and to what extent were instruments other than the organ used in the daily services? If there are no very easy or obvious answers to these questions, much can be gleaned none the less not only from the musical sources themselves but from the archives of cathedrals, colleges and chapels, and from the comments of contemporary writers. Separately, the pieces of the jigsaw may seem of little value; together, they do afford some valuable insights into pre-Restoration performance practices.

It is important to realise, at the outset, that the musical sources are of two different kinds: the first being strictly "liturgical", the second "secular". The liturgical sources were specifically designed, as the title suggests, for the use of cathedral and chapel choirs. The secular sources, on the other hand, were printed or copied out for such "as delighted in music", and most contain very miscellaneous assortments of sacred and secular compositions.

LITURGICAL SOURCES

The liturgical sources consist both of vocal part-books and books of organ accompaniments. Most sets of choir part-books comprise no more than eight or ten volumes (excluding the separate organ books)—divided into MATB, or MAATB, decani and cantoris. The M books are not duplicated, a fact which suggests that the boys sang their parts from memory rather than from the printed or written page.

TABLE 10

The Major Liturgical Sources of pre-Restoration Services and Anthems
(tr. = triplex; m. = medius; a. = contratenor; 2a. = 2nd contratenor; t. = tenor; b. = bass; o. = organ-book; *dec.* = decani; *can.* = cantoris)

Present location	Provenance	Date
Oxford, the Bodleian Library		
MSS. Mus. sch. e. 420–2: a.a.b.	A private chapel or London parish church?	c. 1550
London, British Museum[1]		
MSS. Roy. App. 74–6: tr.a.t.	A private chapel?	c. 1550
London, British Museum		
Certaine notes set forthe in foure and three partes otherwise entitled *Mornyng and Evenyng Praier and Communion*[2] published by John Day: m.a.t.b.		1565
Tenbury, St. Michael's College[3]		
MS. 786 m.a.t.b.	Autograph of the composer Thomas Hunt ?	c. 1600
Tenbury, St. Michael's College		
MS. 1382: t.	Southwell Minster	1617
Shrewsbury: County Record Office[4]	Ludlow Parish Church	c. 1570–1640
York, the Minster Library		
MSS. M.13.S: m.; M.13/2.S: a.; M.13/3.S: b.	York Minster	1618
Durham, the Cathedral Library		
MSS. C 1: m.; C 8: a.; E 4–11: m.2a.t.*dec.* and m.a.2a.t.b.*can.*; E 11a: a. and parts of C 10: t.*can.* and C 15: t.*dec.*	The Cathedral	c. 1625
London, Royal College of Music		
MSS. 1045–51: m.a.t.*dec.* and m.a.t.b.*can.*	Compiled for John Barnard	1625
New York, the Public Library[5]		
MS. Drexel 5469: o.	King's College, Cambridge	? c. 1630
London, British Museum		
Add. MS. 29289: a.	St. Paul's Cathedral ?	c. 1625

(*Table 10 continued overleaf*)

Table 10 (continued)

Present location	Provenance	Date
Tenbury, St. Michael's College		
MS. 791: o.	Salisbury or St. Paul's?	c. 1630
Oxford, Bodleian Library[6]		
MS. Rawl. poet. 23	Chapel Royal (words only)	c. 1630
Oxford, St. John's College		
MSS. 180 and 181: b.b.	St. George's Chapel, Windsor?	c. 1635
Lambeth Palace Library		
MS. 764	The Palace Chapel?	c. 1635
Durham, the Cathedral Library		
MSS. C 4: 2a.*dec.*; C 5: 2a.*can.*; C 9: t.*dec.*; C 18: b., and parts of C 6: a.*dec.*; C 7: a.*can.* and C 10: t.*can.*; A 1–4: o. and 6: o.	The Cathedral	c. 1635
York, the Minster Library		
MS. M. 29. S: b.[7]	Durham Cathedral	c. 1635
Cambridge, Peterhouse[8]		
The "Caroline" part-books: *Set 1*: m.a.2a.b.*dec.* and m.a.b.*can.*; *Set 2*: m.a.t.b.*dec.* and m.t.b.*can.* Also an interleaved folio *Book of Common Prayer*: s.*dec.*, shelf mark G.V. and an organ-book	The College Chapel	c. 1635
Cambridge, Pembroke College[9]		
MSS. Mus. 6. 1–6: m.a.t.b.*dec.* and t.b.*can.*	The College Chapel	c. 1640
Oxford, Christ Church[10]		
MS. 6: o.	The Cathedral?	c. 1640
MS. 1001: o.	New College, Oxford?	c. 1640
MSS. 1220–4: a.t.b.*dec.* and t.b.*can.*	The Cathedral?	c. 1640
Cambridge, King's College		
The Rowe Music Library MSS. 9–17: m.a.t.b.*dec.* and *can.* and o.	Norwich Cathedral	c. 1640 (or very early Restoration)
Windsor, St. George's Chapel, the Aerary		
MSS. 48, 49, 50: a.*can.*, t.*dec.* and *can.*	The Chapel	1640
Gloucester, the Cathedral Library		
No shelf mark; kept in library safe: b.		1641
London University, the Music Library		
John Barnard's *The First Book of Selected Church Musick* in photostat—a complete copy assembled from the extant sets, all of which are incomplete m.a.a2.t.b., *dec.* and *can.*		1641

Since we have to depend to a large extent upon the liturgical sources for our knowledge of pre-Restoration church music, it is worth examining this list in some detail. Fortunately, there are books from all parts of the country and from every kind of choral foundation: from the provincial cathedrals of York, Durham and Oxford, from the collegiate church of Southwell, from several chapels at Oxford and Cambridge, from the parish church at Ludlow, from the Royal Free Chapel of St. George at Windsor, and from the Chapel Royal itself. There are, moreover, John Barnard's two important collections, reflecting, no doubt, London tastes during the 1620s and 1630s, one in manuscript at the Royal College of Music (MSS. 1045–51), the other in print and dated 1641. But although to this extent the sources are adequately representative, their chronological distribution leaves much to be desired. There are, indeed, three very early and important sources—two dating from 1550 (Oxford, Bodleian MSS. Mus. sch. e. 420–2, and British Museum, MSS. Roy. App. 74–6) and the third from 1565 (John Day's *Certaine notes*). But between 1565 and 1617 there is almost nothing, apart from the Ludlow fragments. This gap could not have been more awkwardly placed, for it completely spans the most fruitful period in the entire history of pre-Restoration English church music. To make matters worse, only three of the extant sets of part-books are complete —the two printed collections, and a set of parts containing preces and a single service by Thomas Hunt. Eight other sets lack no more than one or two books, it is true, and the missing parts can in many cases be recovered from other incomplete sources.[11] The remaining dozen sources, however, consist of no more than a single part-book or organ book. No accurate assessment can be given of the number of choir part-books that were destroyed during and after the Civil War; but if the Chichester Cathedral inventory of 1621[12] is at all typical, the total easily reaches four figures; not one of the Chichester Books has survived:

A Catalogue of all the Song-books for the performance of Divine Service; appertaining to the Cathedral Church of the Holy Trinity in Chichester: taken January 18 Annoque Domini 1621.

Ten new books in folio for Men and M[eanes]
Eight new books in folio for Men only
Eight books in a long quarto, of Mr. Weelkes his pricking
Eight books of Mr. William Cox his Service
Eight books without covers, of Anthems
Eight Scrolls in royal paper of Mr. William Cox his Anthem
Eight scrolls of the Anthem: "Thou art my king, O God"
Eight scrolls of Mr. Jurden's Anthem
Eight books in a long quarto of "Christus resurgens"
Eight scrolls of the Anthem, "The Lord hath granted"
Six books in a long quarto: "A poor desire I have to amend mine ill"
Ten books of the Gunpowder treason
Eight books of Mr. Strogers Service, called As
Ten long Anthem books, called Bs
Eight books of Mr. Tallis his Service, called Cs
Mr. Farrant's Service in books called Hs
Eight books in quarto, of Mr. Shepherd's Service
Eight books in quarto, of Mr. Bird's Service

Missing parts and, on occasion, missing works can be recovered from post-Restoration manuscripts—and no survey would be complete without at least a mention of some of the more valuable ones:

TABLE 11

Post-Restoration Manuscripts

Present location	Provenance
Berkeley, University of California MS. M2. C645. Case B: o.	Late 17th century
Cambridge, Fitzwilliam Museum[13] MS. 88	Autograph of Henry Purcell; index dated 1677—full score.
MS. 117	Once thought to be the autograph of John Blow; c. 1680—full score
Durham, the Cathedral Library The remainder of the MSS. C 1–19, and A 4 [see Table 10 above]	The Cathedral
Ely, the Cathedral Library MSS. 1: o.; 4: o.; 28: t.; and 29: b.	The Cathedral; late 17th century possibly containing fragments of pre-Restoration books
Lichfield, the Cathedral Library Barnard's *First Book of Selected Church Musick*, with additional services and anthems in MSS.—a.t.b.*dec.*, a.2a.t.b.*can.*	The Cathedral: from 1662
London, British Museum Roy. Mus. Lib. MSS. 23. m. 1–6[14] a.t.b.*dec.* and *can.*	The Chapel Royal; dating in the main from 1700, but with sections c. 1675–90.
Harley MSS. 7337–42	Autograph of Thomas Tudway, c. 1715–20; full score
London, St. Paul's Cathedral Set 1: a.t.*dec.*; Set 2: t.b.*dec.*, b.*can.*	St. Paul's Cathedral; late 17th century.
Oxford, Christ Church MS. 88: o.	The Cathedral
Wimborne, The Minster Library Unclassified: t.b.*dec.* and *can.* and a.*can.*, o.	The Minster; late 17th century
Windsor, St. George's Chapel, the Aerary MSS. 1, 1a, 2, 2a, 3, 4, 11, 23, 51: a.*dec.* and *can.*; a.a.b.*dec.*, a.t.*can*	The Chapel
York, the Minster Library m.a.t.b.*dec.* and *can.*	From c. 1675 and bearing the bookplate of William Gostling

Appropriately enough, Henry Purcell's anthology of services and anthems is the first to be arranged throughout in full score. It contains comparatively little pre-Restoration music, however, and is by no means as valuable in this respect as

Fitzwilliam 117, or the "Tudway" six-volume anthology at the British Museum.

SECULAR SOURCES

The borderlines between the sacred and the secular were by no means as sharply defined in the late sixteenth century and early seventeenth centuries as they are today. Well over two dozen printed sets of part-books contain at least some polyphonic music of a religious nature: these are listed in Appendix I. The printed books are matched by some fifty or more sets of part-books in manuscript, the most important of which are listed below: the term "anthem" is used to cover all forms and styles of sacred music to English words other than the settings of purely liturgical texts, such as canticles, preces, psalms, responses, and the like. Similarly all kinds of secular polyphony are included under the term "part-song": Joseph Kerman gives an admirable analysis of these secular styles in his account of *The Elizabethan Madrigal*.

SECULAR MANUSCRIPTS

Most of these are in part-book form and consist of five or six books, usually labelled cantus (superius or medius), altus (contratenor), tenor, bassus, quintus and sextus. It would obviously have been unpractical to copy out a score for each singer, and even to print a full score would have raised production costs appreciably.[15] A few of these secular sources do not conform to the usual part-book arrangement, however—notably the *Mulliner Book*, an anthology of arrangements and original compositions for keyboard, and one or two early seventeenth-century books of lute transcriptions. There are also full-scores of anthems and services in four interesting manuscripts: the Baldwin, Cosyn, Sambrooke and Barnard MSS.[16] Of the four, Baldwin's is the earliest (c. 1600); the original owner was evidently much interested in techniques of composition, for he scored up all manner of canons and proportional exercises, as well as sections of services by Byrd and others for study purposes. The Sambrooke MSS., unlike Baldwin's, are in score throughout and they contain an immense quantity of music: part-songs, madrigals, instrumental pieces, motets and anthems, the latter mainly by Italianate Englishmen. Cosyn's Virginal Book is primarily an anthology of keyboard music, as its title implies, but at the back of the book, oddly enough, are to be found full-scores of "the six services for the King's Royal Chapel" (the wording, rightly or wrongly, suggests that the Chapel Royal repertory of Services was not at that time very extensive). And in the Barnard MSS. there is a full-score of Ward's "First Evening Service in Verses", the actual score that Barnard's printer used when setting the type for *The First Book of Selected Church Musick*; Plate 6 shows the original score, with directions to the typesetter ("brevier" type, and so on); and Plate 7 shows the finished product, the page number conforming to the number inked in on the manuscript.

A number of anthems in these secular books are also to be found in choir part-books. The majority, however, are exclusive to the secular sources and were probably regarded as unsuitable for liturgical use on grounds of text, musical style or, more often than not, scoring. Anthems for "unusual" groupings of voices (that is to say those that failed to make use of all the four choral registers, MATB) would not have been of much use to the normal cathedral choir: Byrd's "Sing joyfully", for example, is in many pre-Restoration liturgical sources since it is scored for MMAATB; "Sing we merrily", on the other hand, is exclusive to the secular sources, being scored for SSSAT or, in the transposed version that the chiavettes seem to demand,[17] three meanes, tenor and bass. With only two minor exceptions, none of the secular sources contain music of a strictly liturgical character—Services, Preces or Festal Psalms. Distinctions, therefore, were drawn between liturgical music on the one hand and "secular" music of a devotional character on the other, whilst some of the more elaborate anthems were found to be equally well suited for use in church and in the home.

TABLE 12

The main secular sources of pre-Restoration anthems

(m. = medius, c. = cantus, a. = altus, ct. = contratenor, t. = tenor, b. = bassus, q. = quintus and sx. = sextus)

Location	Summary of contents (starred sources contain viol parts of verse anthems)	Date
London, British Museum		
Add. MS. 30513	The Mulliner Book: compositions for keyboard, and keyboard reductions of a few part-songs and anthems[18]	c. 1560
Add. MS. 15166	A treble part-book of metrical psalm tunes by Shepherd and Tallis, with anthems and two secular songs	Late 16th century
Add. MS. 22597	A small part-book for tenor containing 14 anthems, and a few motets, part-songs and instrumental pieces	Late 16th century
Add. MSS. 30480–4	Part-books (c.ct.t.b.q.) originally owned by the Hammond family of Hawkedon, Suffolk, containing anthems, part-songs, motets, instrumental pieces and settings of canticles	Late 16th century
Cambridge, King's College, the Rowe Music Library		
MS. 316	A medius part-book (labelled contratenor), containing anthems—most of which are English adaptations of Latin motets—motets, part-songs and instrumental pieces.	Late 16th century
Oxford, Christ Church Library		
MSS. 984–8*	Part-books—m.ct.t.b.q.—of almost a hundred motets, some 40 part-songs, and a small number of instrumental pieces and anthems	Late 16th century
Oxford, Bodleian Library		
MS. Mus. e. 423*	A contratenor part-book comprising many motets, a few part-songs, instrumental pieces and anthems	Late 16th century
Tenbury, St. Michael's College		
MS. 389	A treble part-book (discantus), mainly of motets, but also containing part-songs, instrumental pieces and anthems	Late 16th century

TABLE 12 (*continued*)

Location	Summary of contents (starred sources contain viol parts of verse anthems)	Date
Cambridge, Mass., Harvard University, Isham Memorial Library		
MS. Mus. 30	Part-books for a.t.b.q. of sacred and secular part-songs, mostly by Byrd[19]	Early 17th century
London, British Museum		
Add. MS. 15117	A lute book, containing arrangements of a few anthems, together with part-songs for lute and solo voice, and some solo pieces for lute	Early 17th century
Add. MSS. 29366–8*	Part-books for c.b.q. of anthems and some instrumental pieces and part-songs	Early 17th century
Add. MSS. 29372–7*	The most comprehensive source of its kind. Compiled for, or by Thomas Myriell (Precentor of Chichester Cathedral[20]); a set of books for c.a.t.b.q.sx. containing about twenty motets, over eighty part-songs, and an equal number of anthems	1616
Add. MS. 29427*	Apparently of similar date to 29372–7: an alto part-book of comparatively small size, containing instrumental pieces, part-songs and quite a few of the anthems to be found in the Myriell books	Early 17th century
New York, the Public Library		
MSS. Drexel 4180–5*	Next to Myriell's anthology, the most important "secular" source of anthems; there are six part-books—c.a.t.b.q.sx. containing some 30 motets, a few instrumental pieces, about 90 part-songs and almost 80 anthems	Early 17th century
New York, the Public Library		
MS. Drexel 4302*	An unusual collection of part-songs, motets, instrumental pieces and a few anthems, in score and in the hand of Francis Tregian, the writer of the Fitzwilliam Virginal Book, and BM Egerton MS. 3665[21]	Early 17th century

(*Table 12 continued overleaf*)

TABLE 12 *(continued)*

Location	Summary of contents (starred sources contain viol parts of verse anthems)	Date
Oxford, Bodleian Library		
MSS. Mus. sch. d. 212–16*	Five part-books—m.ct.t.b.q.—containing instrumental music, and ten anthems	Early 17th century
Tenbury, St. Michael's College		
MSS. 807–11*	A small collection of motets, anthems and one part-song: the part-books are m. ct. 1 and 2, t.b.	Early 17th century
Tenbury, St. Michael's College		
MSS. 1162–7*	Part-books for c.a.t.b.q.sx. of about 50 madrigals, over 30 anthems, a part-song and a motet	Early 17th century
London, British Museum		
Add. MSS. 17792–6*	Part-books for c.a.t.b.q. containing much instrumental music, many anthems, some motets and part-songs, and two services[22]	c. 1630
Oxford, Bodleian Library		
MSS. Mus. f. 11–15*	Part-books originally owned by the Hammond[23] family (see BM Add. MSS. 30480–4, above); c.a.t.b.q. consisting of anthems and part-songs	c. 1625–50
MSS. Mus. f. 16–19*	As above, but a.t.b.q.	
MSS. Mus. f. 20–24*	As above, but perhaps of slightly later date: most of the contents come from published collections; c.a.t.b.q.	
MSS. Mus. f. 25–8*	As above, with a few motets; c. 1 and 2, a. 1 and 2, t.b. 1 and 2 and sextus	
Oxford, Christ Church		
MSS. 56–60	An important set of part-books—c.ct.t.q.sx., consisting of a large number of anthems, part-songs, and instrumental pieces	c. 1625
MSS. 61–6*	A set of part-books similar to the above, but with comparatively few anthems: c.a.t.b.q. and sextus	c. 1625

By twentieth-century standards, all the sources are singularly uninformative, both printed and manuscript, liturgical and secular. Tempi and dynamic markings are non-existent, underlay is all too often ambiguous (especially in the manuscripts), and accidentals are inserted or omitted with bewildering inconsistency. The most reliable sources are those that were published at the end of the sixteenth and the beginning of the seventeenth centuries. Most were probably seen through the press by their composers and, as Morley himself said,[24] the standard of accuracy is consequently high. Unfortunately, the two sets of printed choir part-books (Day and Barnard) are by no means as authoritative as the madrigalian publications. Day's *Certaine notes* gives the impression of having been assembled by someone who knew very little about music: the proofs were read very carelessly indeed, for there is a slip of some kind on nearly every page—a rest or dot left out, a clef or a note misplaced, an accidental wrongly inserted or forgotten, or a passage of text mistakenly repeated. And the underlay is maddeningly erratic. In many places, the editor seems to have taken particular care to fit words and notes together, but elsewhere the singer is left to fend for himself with absolutely no guidance whatsoever. Barnard was a much more careful editor and he made far fewer mistakes, even though the music that he printed was far more complex than Day's. None of the composers who are represented in his anthology were alive at the time of printing, however, and for this reason alone it is difficult to believe that the *First Book of Selected Church Musick* is any more authoritative than the better manuscripts of the period.

Comparatively few services or anthems ever found their way into print, and it is to the manuscripts that we must turn for the bulk of our material. Proven autographs are few and far between, unfortunately, and the composers concerned are mostly minor figures such as John Amner, William Child, Michael East, Geeres, the Loosemores, John Lugge, Richard Nicholson, Palmer, Robert Ramsey and William Smith.[25] Professional copyists were undoubtedly responsible for some of the secular sets of books,[26] and possibly, too, for one or two sets of choir part-books.[27] Whether professionals were much more accurate than amateurs is to be doubted, however. Most sets of choir part-books were compiled on the spot by the cathedral and chapel musicians themselves (this is abundantly clear from the chapter acts and account books of the period), and the business of building up a repertory of service music was thus a slow and unending one. The Communars accounts of Wells Cathedral give some idea of the processes involved. In about 1550 an organist, William Parsons, came to the cathedral. He was an enterprising musician and a composer of some stature; his efforts were evidently appreciated by the Dean and Chapter, for between 1552 and 1560 he was paid several sums of money for "songs" and "masses" which he had "made" and "pricked" (i.e. copied out). Other presumably non-composing members of the foundation were encouraged to keep their ears open for new music on their travels around the country:

13½d. to Mr Lyde for a good song, viz. Te Deum in English, which he brought from Hereford.
3s. 4d. to Alexander Ward "for songs which he brought from Gloucester and Bristol".[28]

And in the same year, Mr. Lyde purchased eight quires of paper "to make books into which the same songs and others could be pricked". Much the same sort of thing must have been going on in every cathedral and chapel at that time and throughout the period.

The evils of such a system are obvious, for as copies passed from cathedral to cathedral the errors became more and more numerous. Morley knew well how easily chain reactions of mistakes could occur:

for copies passing from hand to hand, a small oversight committed by the first writer, by the second will be made much worse, which will give occasion to the third to alter much, both in the words and in the notes, according as shall seem best to his own judgement, though (God knows) it will be far enough from the meaning of the author; so that errors passing from hand to hand in written copies be easily augmented, but for such of their works

as be in print I dare be bold to affirm that in them no such thing
is to be found.[29]

The surviving sources of Hooper's full anthem "Behold it is
Christ" show very clearly how far the chain reaction could go,
particularly in matters of *musica ficta* (i.e. the use of accidentals
foreign to the key signature) and underlay; the example is
admittedly an extreme one, since Hooper had an unusual and
adventurous sense of tonality—see, for instance, his one little
"Alman" in the Fitzwilliam Virginal Book. The following extract from "Behold it is Christ" represents a collation of the
six principal sources, every accidental being included in the
transcription. All the accidentals make musical sense—with the
exception of 13 and 15, but not one of the six sources contains
every accidental, nor is there any logical pattern in the way that
the accidentals are included or omitted:

SOURCE	NO ACCIDENTAL INDICATED
New York : Drexel MSS 4180-5	4,13,15,17,19,20
BM : Add.MSS 29372-7	2,4,13,15,20
BM : Add.MSS 17792-6	1,5,8
Cambridge : Pembroke College	5,8,15,20
Cambridge : Peterhouse Set I	12,13,15,17,20
Cambridge : Peterhouse Set II	1,2,3,4,8,15,17,20

This rather suggests, therefore, that the errors in this case
were of omission rather than commission.

A somewhat different approach to the problem of *musica
ficta* also leads to the conclusion that accidentals tended to be
left out rather than added. During the closing years of the
sixteenth century, English words were adapted to a number of
Latin motets by Tallis and Byrd—the motets had all appeared

in print, Tallis' in 1575 and Byrd's in 1575, 1589 and 1591. All three collections were undoubtedly seen through the press by their composers and they may be regarded with some confidence as primary sources. On comparing the printed motets with their later English adaptations, it is immediately apparent that almost nothing in the way of *musica ficta* has been added to the adaptations but that a great deal, on the other hand, has been left out. It is particularly noticeable, too, that Tallis' music lacks many more of the original accidentals than does Byrd's. As the table below shows, most of the manuscripts are of early seventeenth-century origin. Most of them, indeed, were compiled some fifty years after Tallis' death.

TABLE 13

Musica ficta: a Comparison of some Primary and Secondary Sources of Music by Tallis and Byrd

Motet and primary source	English adaptation	Comparison of numbers of accidentals in original and adapted versions
		Tallis
ABSTERGE DOMINE 1575	Wipe away my sins	43: 1575, Ks. B♭ E♭
		6: 30480–4, superius Ks. B♭ only, giving 4 extra E♮
		17: 17792–6, bassus Ks., and opening lines of superius B♭ only, giving 8 extra E♮
		13: 4180–4, superius Ks. B♭ only, giving 4 extra E♮
MIHI AUTEM NIMIS 1575	Blessed be thy name	19: 1575, Ks. B♭, but opening of tenor, and closing section of bassus B♭ E♭
		7: 1641, the bassus Ks. remains B♭ only, giving 5 extra E♮
		7: 4180–4, Ks. B♭, except tenor which is B♭ E♭ throughout (the accidentals omitted in this source differ from those of 1641). There is one extra F♯.
		11: 17792–6, Ks. B♭ only, giving 3 extra E♮
O SACRUM CONVIVIUM 1575	I call and cry	30: 1575, Ks. B♭ E♭
		18: 1641, Ks. B♭ E♭; an extra E♮ and F♯
		20: 29372–7, Ks. superius B♭, the others B♭ E♭, one extra E♮ and F♯
	O sacred and holy banquet	30: 29372–7; in all respects as 1575; this is a unique source, and may well have been directly adapted by Myriell from the original

TABLE 13 (continued)

Motet and primary source	English adaptation	Comparison of numbers of accidentals in original and adapted versions
SALVATOR MUNDI I 1575	Arise, O Lord	22: 1575, superius Ks. B♭, the others B♭ E♭, tenor changes to B♭ midway
		6: Durham MSS. C1, 2, 3, 11 and 16; superius and bassus Ks. B♭, the others B♭ E♭ giving 6 extra E♭; there are also an extra F♯ and a B♮
	With all our hearts and mouths	15: 1641, Ks. as 1575; there are 4 extra E♮ in superius, and one B♮
		6: 30480–4, discantus and tenor Ks. B♭ E♭, others B♭, giving 2 extra E♮
		7: 17792–6, superius and bassus Ks. B♭, others B♭ E♭, bassus changes to B♭, giving an extra E♮
SALVATOR MUNDI II 1575	When Jesus went	This adaptation is incomplete in the one extant source; comparative figures are 1575:17, 30480–4:1

Byrd

ATTOLITE PORTAS 1575	Lift up your heads	91: 1575, open Ks.
		82: Durham MSS. E4–11, with 5 extra B♭
CIVITAS SANCTI TUI 1589	Bow thine ear	29: 1589, Ks. B♭
		27: 1641
		20: 17792–6, with 1 extra B♭
		28: 29372–7, the controversial E♯ is missing
		18: 4180–4, one line of one part lacks Ks. and the E♯ is missing
NE IRASCARIS 1589	O Lord, turn thy wrath	17: 1589
		15: 1641

Summary

	Percentage
Total number of printed accidentals missing in manuscripts	49
Extra accidentals arising through the omission of an original E♮ in the key signature	10
Other additional accidentals in manuscripts	10

Key

1575	Byrd, William and Tallis, Thomas, *Cantiones, quae ab argumento sacrae vocantur*
1589	Byrd, William, *Liber Primus Sacrarum Cantionum*
1591	Byrd, William, *Liber Secundus Sacrarum Cantionum*
1641	Barnard, John, *The First Book of Selected Church Musick*
30480–4	British Museum Add. MSS. Late 16th century
29372–7	British Museum Add. MSS. 1616
17792–6	British Museum Add. MSS. c. 1630
4180–4	New York, Public Library, Drexel MSS. Early 17th century

Few primary sources of English liturgical music have survived from this period, unfortunately, and no extensive checks of this kind are therefore possible. Such evidence as we have, none the less, tends to the conclusion that accidentals should be added, in cases of difficulty, rather than subtracted. But in the last resort it must be admitted that such problems were very much a matter of taste and subject to no hard and fast rules. Even Morley refused to dogmatise on the subject of *musica ficta*, beyond the bare statement that the leading notes of final cadences ought to be sharpened.[30]

Underlay is undoubtedly the most troublesome problem of all. In Hooper's anthem—a typical example in this respect there are considerable differences not only between the separate sources but also between decani and cantoris books of a single source:

(a) British Museum Add. MS. 29374 (1616)
(b) Tenbury, St. Michael's College, MS. 1382 (1617)
(c) British Museum Add. MS. 17794 (c. 1630)
(d) New York Public Library, Drexel MS. 4182 (c. 1620)
(e) Durham Cathedral MS. C 12 (c. 1635)
(f) Cambridge, Peterhouse, decani and cantoris books (c. 1635)
(g) Windsor, St. George's Chapel, decani and cantoris books (c. 1640)
(h) Cambridge, Pembroke College, decani and cantoris books (c. 1640)

Nor were such problems confined to the compositions of the minor masters. Orlando Gibbons' "Short Service" simply bristles with difficulties of the kind. For while there are few ambiguities or awkwardnesses of underlay in the outer parts, many of the problems involved in setting words to the alto and tenor parts defy satisfactory solution. A case in point is the opening of Nunc dimittis; there are no underlay variants for the upper part, but for the alto there are almost as many variants as there are sources. The inference is inescapable that Gibbons himself cannot have been unduly concerned over the question of "just accentuation" (in the inner parts, at least).

A further point, in connection with underlay, and about which it is only possible to speculate, is the extent to which melismatic underlay was filled in during the process of copying and recopying. The lack of authenticated primary sources makes this question impossible to answer at all fully. It is none the less interesting to note that passages of melismatic underlay in Byrd's "Have mercy upon me O God" (published by the composer in his *Psalmes, songs and sonnets* of 1611) are much altered in the Durham manuscripts of the 1630s. Below are two extracts for comparison:

Undoubtedly, choirmen were themselves often confused by underlay difficulties—and, if Morley is to be believed, words were often left out altogether in performance!

> ... I see not what passions or motions [a motet or anthem] can stir up being sung as most men do commonly sing it, that is leaving out the ditty and singing only the bare note, as it were a music only for instruments, which indeed will show the nature of the music but never carry the spirit and, as it were, that lively soul which the ditty giveth. ... [31]

Underlay problems were by no means peculiar to England, of course. The eminent composer and theorist, Gioseffo Zarlino, complained bitterly of the careless manner in which notes and words were usually put together:

> the notes are often so badly adapted to the words that the singer cannot possibly see how to perform them. In one place he may find two syllables beneath a whole series of notes, in another a whole series of syllables under two notes. During performance he may hear the singer of another part eliding the vowels of a particular word; but when he attempts to do likewise in his own part he finds that he has placed a long syllable under a short note, or vice versa, with unfortunate and inelegant results. ... Thus hearing such diversity he becomes more and more confused and bewildered. [32]

Zarlino went on to offer some simple rules which he hoped would be useful to both singer and composer:

1. Short notes require short syllables, and long notes long ones.
2. Not more than one syllable should be set to a single note.
3. Syllables should not be set to notes shorter in value than the quaver [reducing Zarlino's note-values by a half].
4. Whenever repetition of text is unavoidable, care should be taken that a whole phrase is repeated, and that it makes sense in itself.
5. Repetition should be avoided as much as possible.
6. Melismatic passages should be treated in the following manner: as far as possible, every note should be given a syllable,

the melisma being taken on the penultimate stressed syllable of the last word, the last syllable being reserved for the last note.

Problems of underlay are further complicated by the fact that English pronunciation was by no means standardised at any time between 1540 and 1640. Even the "upper-class" accent, cultivated by well-to-do Londoners, admitted many variations. The word "spirit", for instance, could equally well be given two syllables, to rhyme with "inherit", or one (sprite), to rhyme with "quite". Many polysyllabic words, too, were open to more than one accentuation. In each of the following words, the accent could well occur on the first syllable if the word in question was immediately followed by a stressed syllable: condemn, confess, contrite, create, despise, distress, divine, entire, express, extreme, maintain, proclaim, remiss, renew, reveal, resolve, revenge, secure—and so on. There were, moreover, the regional dialects, all of which had their own peculiar accentuations and pronunciations. There may well have been fashions in pronunciation, too, which changed with the years. According to the underlay in Merbecke's *book of Common praier noted*, for instance, polysyllabic words such as "patience", "temptation", "precious" and "gracious" were being pronounced "pa-ti-ence", "temp-ta-ti-on", and so on. Kökeritz suggests that by 1580 fashionable people were tending to pronounce these words much as we do today: "pa-tience", "temp-ta-tion" . . . , but that the older pronunciation was still alive in 1620.[33]

Bearing in mind these many difficulties—the ambiguities of the manuscripts, the errors of the copyists, regional differences in pronunciation, changes in fashionable pronunciation, and a basic indifference to the principles of "just note and accent"—modern editors and performers need have no fear of altering the underlay if a more natural solution can be worked out in conformity with Zarlino's principles.

On the question of speed there has perhaps been a tendency in the past to be over-dogmatic. There is, indeed, a very clear direction in the *pars organica* of Tomkins' *Musica Deo Sacra* (the

Tenbury copy only) that the semibreve equals two beats of the human heart, or the swing of a pendulum 2 ft long:

○: Sit mensura duorum humani corporis pulsum, vel globuli penduli, longitudine duorum pedum a centro motus

Whereas such a speed would be quite reasonable, however, for Tomkins' most elaborate music (in which there are many semi-quavers—as for example in "Arise, O Lord"), it would certainly be too slow for Edwardian and early Elizabethan music, in which the crotchet (in reduced note-values) formed the basic pulse. Yet it is probably true to say, nevertheless, that modern performances tend to err on the fast side. In his *Brief Discourse*, Thomas Ravenscroft (formerly a chorister at St. Paul's under Edward Pierce) criticised composers for their failure to distinguish between the two time signatures of C and ¢.

> ... But herein now the ignorance of our times is such, not knowing the differences of this imperfect prolation (C) and the diminutions thereof (¢), that [composers] commonly character the church songs and motets with the greater diminution thus: ¢; according whereunto if those songs should be sung, it would not only alter the nature of those harmonies, but also make them seem rather some dancing or revelling measure, than a religious note to be used in God's service. 'Tis then the less prolation (thus C) wherewith all such divine compositions (especially all those which are with fugues) ought to be charactered, and that is the slowest and gravest measure now in use. ...

But Ravenscroft admitted that when all was said and done, speed was ultimately a matter "for the discretion of the singer". Acoustics, too, must to some extent have been a controlling factor; the more resonant the building the slower, in general, must have been the performance. It is interesting in this connection to compare the two extant versions of Weelkes' "Alleluia, I heard a voice". In the secular sources the dramatic solo at the beginning of the anthem appears as in the first example; in the second, taken from the choir books at Durham Cathedral, the semiquaver interjection by the trebles, altos and tenors has been slowed down to half speed:

While on the question of tempo, the modern editorial practice of using a variable bar-line deserves some comment. It seems that the custom of beating time was not uncommon, and that the speed of beating was governed by the basic time signature. The symbol C indicated that the semibreve was to be regarded as the time unit or "tactus", and that it was measured by one down-up movement of the hand: beat one (a minim duration) downwards, beat two (also a minim) upwards. Similarly, the time signature C3, or O normally showed that the time unit was the dotted semibreve and that it was to be measured again by a downward movement of the hand (first two minims) and a shorter upward movement (last minim). It was rare for triple metres to be used in church music, and never were rapid, single-bar changes made between duple and triple time. The following extract from a modern edition of Byrd's *Venite*, thus gives a wholly false impression that the time signatures change in the original at Figures A, B, C and D.

This is not so, however, and the hand that beat out the measure would have continued to move in duple time (crotchet one down, crotchet two up—the note-values here having been halved). It follows, therefore, that the singer would have experienced a feeling of syncopation wherever the musical accents conflicted with the literary accents. To iron out this syncopation is to destroy a vital feature of the style. The existence of regular barring in all sixteenth- and early seventeenth-century scores underlines this essential point.[34]

The problem of pitch is very involved and is closely bound up with organ design. The main questions to be asked are these: whether there was in fact any such thing as a standard "church" pitch in pre-Restoration England; and, if so, what the standard was in terms of cycles per second. According to a printed note, again in the *pars organica* of *Musica Deo Sacra* (the Tenbury copy only) an organ pipe 2½ ft long produced a note that was called f—tenor F that is, on the bass stave: 𝄢 Using the modern standard (a′ = 440 c.p.s.), the pitch of such a pipe would lie somewhere between g and a♭. It is important to realise, however, that church musicians were using two different pitch standards at that time: "organ" pitch and "choir" pitch. As Nathaniel Tomkins explained to a friend at the Chapel Royal:

> ... The great organ which was built at Worcester, 1614, consisted of two open diapasons of pure and massy metal, double F fa ut of the choir pitch 𝄢 or as some term it, double C fa ut according to the keys [of the organ].[35] 𝄢

The "choir pitch" to which Nathaniel referred was the pitch at which the music was invariably written out for the singers. "Organ pitch", on the other hand, referred to the names of the notes on the keyboard. On Dallam's instruments (including the one which he built at Worcester in 1614) the lowest note on the *keyboard* was called C fa ut 𝄢 and this actuated pipes 10 ft, 5 ft, 2½ ft and 1¼ ft in length.³⁶ Now, as the *Musica Deo Sacra* directive indicated, these pipes produced notes that in terms of "choir pitch" were called and written F. If the bottom C of the Worcester Cathedral great organ was depressed, therefore, all the stops being out, the following notes would have sounded, according to "choir pitch" standard:

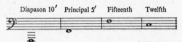

Since basses were rarely asked to sing below written F, it follows that the 10 ft diapason stop could double the lowest voice part at the octave below to produce what would now be termed 16 ft tone, whilst the "principal" rank was, in effect, *the* principal rank in the organ, since it did most nearly cover the full choral tessitura, from the lowest (sung) bass note upwards.

When compared with the organs that were being built in the Netherlands and north Germany at the time, the English organ was sober and unimaginative. It lacked pedals, and it had none of the exciting reeds, mixtures and mutations that the larger continental instruments had. Dallam's Worcester instrument was probably typical of its kind:³⁷

Great Organ

1–2	Two open diapasons of metal	10 ft
3–4	Two principals of metal	[5 ft]
5–6	Two small principals or fifteenths	[2½ ft]
7	A twelfth	[3¾ ft]
8	Recorder of metal, stopped	[Sounding 5 ft ?]

Chaire Organ

1	Principal of metal	[5 ft]
2	Diapason of wood	[10 ft]
3	Flute of wood	[5 ft]
4	Small principal or fifteenth of metal	[2½ ft]
5	A twenty-second of metal	[1¼ ft]

Limited as such an instrument may have been for solo work, it was surprisingly flexible for accompanying purposes since, by playing either a fourth below written choir pitch or a fifth above, a very considerable range of tone colours could be produced. Here are a few of the effects that could be obtained:

	Effect in 20th-century *terms*
1. ff., to accompany full choir Full Great—played a fifth above choir pitch	8 ft, 4 ft, 2⅔ ft, 2 ft
2. f., to accompany full choir in solemn, slow-moving music Full Great, less the Twelfth—played a fourth below choir pitch	16 ft, 8 ft, 4 ft
3. For full-choir music of a bright but rather quieter kind Full Chaire organ, less flute—a fifth above choir pitch	8 ft, 4 ft, 2 ft, 1 ft
4. For solo accompaniments when a bright quality of sound is required Chaire Organ: Flute and Twenty- second, a fourth below choir pitch	8 ft, 2 ft
5. For soft solo accompaniments either the Great Recorder or the Chaire Flute —played a fourth below choir pitch	8 ft

The double pitch standard gave organists a good deal of work, for it meant that every accompaniment had to be transposed, either beforehand or at sight. The organ-books do indeed contain a great many transposed accompaniments, some a fourth below choir pitch, some a fifth above, whilst others alternate between one interval of transposition and the other. In general, the left-hand clef was used to indicate whether or not the accompaniment had been transposed and, if so, whether up or down: an "F" clef on the first or second lines was used more often than not to show that the music was a fourth below choir pitch, and "C" clefs on the second or third lines that it was a fifth above, the "F3" and "C1" clefs being reserved for music copied out at choir pitch. Plate 12 shows the opening of the organ accompaniment to Morley's "Te Deum" for "verses" as it occurs in Christ Church MS. 1001 (c. 1640). The first left-hand clef that the copyist has used is "F2", to show that the music is a fourth below choir pitch; hence the pencilled reminder which someone scribbled into the copy: "play it not four notes lower, but as it standeth". For the chorus sections "C3" clefs are used, the music being copied out a fifth above choir pitch. Plate 11 shows the "Te Deum" as it is in the "Batten" organbook; here the music is written out at "choir pitch", hence the use of the "F3" clef. As Morley pointed out, organists were often called upon to transpose at sight, and since in this case transposition would have involved nothing more than a substitution of clefs, the task would have been a relatively easy one.

It can hardly be doubted that stops and even manuals would have been changed wherever the clefs changed, and on the lines suggested in the discussion of the Worcester specification above.

The organ-books contain keyboard scores of every kind of Anglican service music, from preces and festal psalms to anthems and canticles.

Whether, indeed, all this music was actually played on the organ is open to question. Organ accompaniments were obligatory when the music was in verse style, of course, but keyboard reductions of "full" services and anthems may have been copied into the organ-books as much for rehearsal purposes as for performance. At Chichester it very much looks as though the organ remained silent when full services and anthems were sung; such, at least, is the sense of a resolution which was passed at a Chapter meeting in 1616:[38]

> the organist [Thomas Weelkes] shall remain in the choir until the last psalm be sung and then go up to the organs and there, having done his duty, return in to the Choir again to bear his part all along.

His "duty" presumably was to play the customary voluntary before the first lesson. And from the way in which the end of the resolution is phrased, it would seem that this procedure was followed in many other cathedrals at that time:

This is thought a meet matter in all double choirs, much more is it necessary in all half choirs, such as ours is.

A similar minute is to be found in the Act Books of Hereford Cathedral.[39]

Most of the extant organ accompaniments leave much to the imagination of the player, and no two separate accompaniments of any one work are identical. This much can be seen from the two versions of Morley's "Te Deum" for verses— though the variants in this particular case are comparatively few. Figured basses do not appear in organ-books until the late seventeenth century, but there are one or two unfigured basses in the Tenbury organ-book (c. 1630) and many organ accompaniments consist of no more than a top and a bottom line.

To what extent skilled organists embellished their accompaniments with runs and ornaments is an open question. Here and there are to be found such signs as $\sharp$ and $\sharp$, the meaning of which is unclear. There are indications, however, that runs and turns of various sorts were occasionally indulged in. The published organ accompaniment to "O Lord, let me know mine end" in *Musica Deo Sacra* (1668) is comparatively straightforward, but the "Batten" organ book version of c. 1630 is in places quite difficult to play:

Musica Deo Sacra (1668)

Tenbury MS 791 (c.1630)

The existence of ornamentation in organ scores prompts one to ask whether there is any evidence of improvised vocal ornamentation in England during the late sixteenth and early seventeenth centuries. In her discussion of "Improvised Embellishment in the performance of Renaissance Polyphonic Music",[40] Imogene Horsley concludes that the practice originated in Italy and the Netherlands, that it was firmly established in both countries by 1540, and that it was known of in Spain, Germany and France. One of the earliest theorists to discuss the art of vocal ornamentation was Adrian Coclico, a pupil of Josquin des Prèz.[41] In his *Compendium musices* of 1552 the author stressed that skill in ornamentation was one of the hallmarks of the good singer, and he gave a number of interesting examples of the kinds of melodic formuli that would commonly have been used, as Coperario was later to do in his *Rules how to Compose* (c. 1610).[42]

There are rather more extended examples in Hermann Fink's *Practica musica* (1556), and dalla Casa's *Il vero modo di diminuir* (1584). It is clear, however, that by no means everyone approved of the practice and least of all Zarlino, possibly the most eminent authority of his day. It is clear, too, that ornamentation of the kind described by Coclico, Fink and dalla Casa could only be practised by solo voices, and successively rather than simultaneously. For this reason, therefore, it is extremely unlikely that ornamentation was ever practised in English churches in the performance of full services and anthems. It does seem, however, that with the development of the verse forms of service and anthem, soloists—in one or two places at least—were trained to sing "divisions" on their solo lines. When the Duke of Württemberg visited St. George's Chapel, Windsor, one Sunday morning in 1592, he was much impressed with the little boy who sang so sweetly to the accompaniment of all manner of wind instruments: "Es sang auch ein kleines Knäblein so lieblich darein, und *colorirt* dermassen mit seinem Zünglein, dass es wundersam zuhören" (my italics).[43] At that time the verb "coloriren" was well known in its musical sense of "to embellish". Ammerbach's second book of tablatures of 1575, for instance, is described on its title page as "auffs beste colorirt"—embellished in the best possible manner.[44] It does, therefore, seem highly probable that the boy at Windsor was ornamenting his part. Some thirty years later, when Edward Kellie visited London to find out how services were sung at the Chapel Royal and to engage singers for the newly reformed choir at Holyrood Palace, he took back to Scotland "two boys for singing divisions in the verses".[45] Walter Porter's one extant anthem, "Praise the Lord", gives a good idea of the kind of ornamentation that might then have been attempted by the highly skilled singer. There can be little doubt, therefore, that some kind of improvisatory tradition was alive in England, at least from the late sixteenth century onwards. Whether it was at all widespread is not certain although, in view of the fact that much of a musician's early training consisted of improvising "descants" upon a plainsong,[46] the extemporisation of embellishments on a given line would have caused the intelligent singer no difficulty at all.

Surprisingly little attention was paid—at least in the published singing tutors of the times—to methods of voice production. Humphrey Bathe's *Introduction to the skill of song* (1597) is quite typical in this respect: the only instructions that bear upon the problems of voice production appear in a brief paragraph at the beginning of the book, under the heading "ante-rules of song" (the heading in itself is revealing). The remainder of the book is devoted to theoretical matters: clefs, time-signatures, scales and the like. Bathe's "ante-rules" are:

1. Practise to sunder the vowels and consonants, distinctly pronouncing them according to the manner of the place.
2. Practise to have the breath long to continue, and the tongue at liberty to run.
3. Practise in striking [i.e. time keeping] to keep a just proportion of one stroke to another.
4. Practise to have your voice clear.

Vague as instruction 4 is, the implication is that the singer must aim at a natural, unforced tone, and the maximum clarity of diction. Subtlety certainly seems to have been preferred to power, and sweetness to brilliance. As Richard Mulcaster wrote,[47] music "stands not much upon straining or fullness of the voice", but is "delicate and fine in concent [harmony]." Again, in the words of William Barley[48] [*The Pathway to Musicke*, 1596] "Music is a science which teacheth how to sing skilfully: that is to deliver a song sweetly, tunably and cunningly". John Dowland emphasised the same point in his translation of Ornithoparcus' *Micrologus* (1606): "Let every singer [he wrote] take heed, lest he begin too loud, braying like an ass; ... for God is not pleased with loud cries, but with lovely sounds. ... The uncomely gaping of the mouth, and ungraceful motion of the body, is a sign of a mad singer." Charles Butler, too, urged cathedral musicians to avoid "all harsh straining of their voices beyond their natural pitch", as also "too much shaking and quavering of the notes".[49]

In most cathedrals today, boys outnumber the men by more than two to one, whereas in the late sixteenth and early seventeenth centuries exactly the reverse was true. The full Chapel Royal choir, to take an extreme case, numbered thirty-two men and only a dozen boys. Although the boys may well have been trained to use the more penetrating chest voice,

E

the men must obviously have sung with constraint, for had they not done so the effect would have been excruciatingly coarse. As it was, musicians and writers were all agreed upon the sweetness of the best English choral singing. When Lieutenant Hammond and his friends made their tour of the English cathedrals in 1634 and 1635, this indeed seems to have been their main criterion of judgement.[50] They found that the voices and organs at Lichfield were "deep and sweet", and they were much impressed by the solo voices—two trebles, two counter-tenors and two basses—who "most melodiously acted and performed their parts". At Winchester they heard the cathedral choir and were charmed by "the sweet and heavenly anthems" which were sung. But they reserved their highest praise for the music at Exeter, for the "rich and lofty organ", for "the viols and other sweet instruments" and for the "tunable voices" all of which in consort made "a melodious and heavenly harmony, able to ravish the hearers' ears". "Sweetness" was certainly con-sidered to be a prime ingredient of any satisfying performance. When—as at Carlisle—it was lacking, the Lieutenant and his friends were unmerciful in their criticism: "The organs and voices did well agree", they noted sarcastically, "the one being like a shrill bagpipe, the other like the Scottish tone".

Before leaving the question of vocal timbre, two small points should perhaps be noted. The first concerns the tenor voice, which then had a written range corresponding closely to that encompassed by the tenor clef: c to f^1. It is quite clear, from the comments of both Archbishop Laud and the theorist Charles Butler, that the tenor was then the commonest of the three ranges of men's voices. Laud asked the Dean and Chapter of Salisbury, during the course of his Episcopal visita-tion in 1634, whether they took care to elect men of "skill and good voices" into the choir, "so that there be not more of tenors therein, which is an ordinary voice, than there be of basses and counter-tenors, which do best furnish the choir".[51] Two years later he wrote to the Dean and Chapter of Wells Cathedral about the vacancy in the choir, urging them to elect either a bass or a counter-tenor; the election of the tenor, he said, would be a great mistake in such a small choir as theirs.[52] Butler, too, gives the impression that the tenor voice was the commonest and least useful of the three.[53] Tenor parts, he said, avoided the extremes of compass, "neither ascending to any high or strained notes, nor descending very low . . ."; they were therefore well within the range of an "indifferent voice . . .". This comment could well be applied to the present-day baritone—who, incidentally, would have no difficulty in singing tenor parts of sixteenth- and early seventeenth-century anthems at the original written pitch. This may help to explain why tenors were so rarely given solos in the verse services and anthems of the period. The alto or counter-tenor, on the other hand, was perhaps the most popular voice—and it was often required to cover a range from low tenor D to high alto A (untransposed "choir pitch"). This suggests that the chest voice must have been used for the lower notes.

The second point concerns the boy's voice. There were two kinds of voice, apparently—the normal "meane" with a compass from a to e":

and the treble, with a compass from d' to g":

As the anonymous author of MS. Royal 18. B. XIX put it:

Nature has disposed all voices, both of men and children, into five kinds, viz: Basses (being the lowest or greatest voices), Tenors being neither so low or so great, Countertenors (being less low and more high than tenors) of which three kinds all men's voices consist. Then of children's voices there are two kinds, viz. Meane voices (which are higher than men's voices) and Treble voices, which are the highest kind of Children's voices.[54]

And, again, in the words of Charles Butler;

Of the parts of a song:

Setting, is the framing of a song in parts: which, for the most part (especially in counterpoint) are four, of which in some songs is wanting one or two: and in some, for a voice of high pitch is added a treble. . . . The treble is so called, because his notes are placed (for the most part) in the third Septenari [i.e. g′-g″], or the treble clefs: and is to be sung with a high, clear, sweet voice. . . . The Meane is so called, because it is a middling or mean high part, between the countertenor, (the highest part of a man) and the treble (the highest part of a boy or woman) and therefore may be sung by a meane voice.

The treble voice was evidently something of a rarity. Nearly all Services and anthems are scored for meanes—and for a total choral range of no more than two octaves and a fifth (low bass F to top meane d″). The few works that do call for the treble as well as the meane are nearly all of a rather special kind and half of them come from one manuscript—the Tenbury organ-book, MS. 791. In this particular manuscript the Services and anthems for trebles are grouped together between ff. 398–407 and 437–48, and in the index they are carefully listed under four headings: "Morning service with trebles", "Evening Magnificat with trebles", "Psalms with trebles" and "Anthems with verses for trebles". No more than twenty works "for trebles" are still extant. In each case, the choral range is three octaves or more, from low F to high treble f″ and frequently g″ (starred items in the following list are unique to the Tenbury organ-book: works that are only to be found in secular sources are not included):

Byrd[55]	Laetentur coeli
	Fac cum servo tuo
	Have mercy[56]
Gibbons	This is the record of John[57]
	*Praise the Lord, O my soul
	*Unto Thee, O Lord
Giles	*I will magnify Thee
Holmes, J.	Preces and psalms
	*Magnificat "in medio chori"
Juxon	Christ rising (the Easter anthem)
Lugg, J.	Let my complaint
Mundy, W.	Evening Service "in medio chori"

Parsons, J.	*All people clap your hands
Parsons	*Jubilate
Shepherd	*Magnificat "in medio chori"
	*Cantate Domino "in medio chori"
Tallis	*O give thanks
Tomkins	Know ye not[58]
Weelkes	Te Deum
	Magnificat "for trebles"
	and Nunc dimittis
White, R.	Praise the Lord
Wilkinson	Behold, O Lord

The tessitura of the treble parts is high; and if the normal interval of transposition is applied, top B♭s frequently occur—as in the William Mundy "in medio chori"[59] Service of nine parts, from which the following example is taken; few cathedral choristers, surely, can have had the range to sing music of this kind:

The outer voices of William Mundy's "in medio chori" Magnificat.

With two exceptions, nothing is known about the balance of voices in the various choirs. The Jacobean statutes for Norwich Cathedral (confirming earlier Edwardian statutes, now lost) do, however, clearly state that the choir was to consist of eight choristers, five altos, five tenors and five basses, subject to the choice and nomination of the Dean.[60] It is also known that there were eight boys, six counter-tenors, four tenors and six basses in the reduced Chapel Royal choir that accompanied Charles to Scotland in 1633—a balance that does something to confirm Laud's disparaging remarks about the usefulness of the tenor voice.[61] To judge from Charles Butler's comments in *The Principles of Musik* (1636), the aim was to achieve a smooth blend, with no one part predominant except, that is, in imitative music, where the entries were to be slightly emphasised: "[singers are] in their great variety of tones to keep an equal sound (except in a point), that one voice drown not another".[62]

Pre-Restoration sources contain no dynamics and, to all intents and purposes, no speed markings either.[63] Yet even from pre-Reformation days singers were trained to think of music in expressive terms. This much is clear from the analogy that Roger Ascham chose to draw between the arts of oratory and singing:

> ... truly, two degrees of men which have the highest offices under the king in all this realm shall greatly lack the use of singing —preachers and lawyers—because they shall not without this be able to rule their breasts for every purpose. For where there is no distinction in telling glad things and fearful things, gentleness and cruelty, softness and vehemence and such-like matters, there can be no great persuasion.[64]

Some years later, Archbishop Parker urged all those who used his Psalter (c. 1567) "to conjoin a sad tune or song with a sad psalm, and a joyful tune and song with a joyful psalm, and an indifferent tune and song with a psalm which goeth indifferently." Thomas Morley criticised church musicians in no uncertain terms for their failure to sing expressively. It was a matter on which he evidently felt very deeply:

> ... though the song be never so well made [he wrote] and never so aptly applied to the words, yet shall you hardly find singers to express it as it ought to be, for most of our churchmen, so they can cry louder in the choir than their fellows, care for no more, whereas by the contrary they ought to study how to vowel and

sing clean, expressing their words with devotion and passion, whereby to draw the hearer, as it were, in chains of gold by the ears to the consideration of holy things.[65]

The anonymous author of Royal MS. 18. B. XIX also stressed the need for an expressive approach, both to the composition and performance of church music:

> ... it were good that those who do compose the songs and music for the church would both in the composing and the acting [i.e. performing] thereof (whether the words of the song do tend to prayer or thanksgiving, as do all that part of the church service which is sung) that I say themselves would religiously put on the affection and devotion of those that are well prepared, either to prayer or thanksgiving. ...
> (c. 1610)

And again, in John Dowland's translation of Ornithoparcus' *Micrologus*, singers are asked to keep in mind both the sense of the text and also the liturgical occasion:

> Let every singer conform his voice to the words, that as much as he can he make the concent sad when the words are sad, and merry when they are merry. ... Let every singer discern the difference of one holyday from another, lest on a slight holyday he either make too solemn service, or too slight on a great. ...[66]

Certainly, therefore, a good choir would then have sung "with devotion and passion", but with a devotion and passion suitably tempered by the solemnity of the liturgical occasion.

Opinions have differed as to the extent which musical instruments—other than the organ—were used in the daily services. Cornetts and sackbutts may possibly have been used at Canterbury as early as 1532, and places for players of cornetts and sackbutts may have been established at Carlisle Cathedral when the new statutes were drawn up in 1541.[67] One of the earliest references that can be substantiated concerns Queen Elizabeth's visit to Oxford, where she heard in the cathedral, "an anthem called the Te Deum sung to cornetts".[68] Otherwise there is no reason to suppose that cornetts, sackbutts or any other kinds of wind or stringed instruments were used in church before about 1575. From then onwards, references to wind instruments, and particularly to cornetts and sackbutts, become increasingly numerous, rising to a peak in the decade before the Civil War. It was in 1634 that the Dean and Chapter of Canterbury Cathedral took the (probably) unprecedented step of putting the cathedral sackbutts and cornetts—four players in all—on the foundation, a step which had the full approval of Archbishop Laud. Elsewhere, however, the instrumentalists were super-numerary. At first they seem to have been engaged only for very special occasions, but during the early years of the seven-teenth century they could be heard in many cathedrals on Sundays and Feast Days. Two of the earliest references date from 1575. In the summer of that year the Queen visited Worcester, and to mark the occasion the Sunday services in the cathedral were sung to the sound of cornetts and sackbutts. In the same year the Christmas services at Norwich Cathedral were enlivened by the presence of the city waits.

At the beginning of the sixteenth century the town or city wait had been, above all, a municipal watchman with sub-sidiary civic duties as a musician. His principal instrument had been the shawm (or wait-pipe, as it was often called)—a loud, reedy instrument eminently suited to outdoor occasions. During the course of the century, however, the nature of the office changed considerably and the wait became, above all, a municipal musician. From the middle of the century, most of the larger companies of town and city waits numbered four or five players, plus apprentices: the city of London maintained an unusually large company, consisting of six and later seven qualified waits, plus twelve and later eighteen apprentices. As their musical duties increased, the waits learned to play new kinds of instruments: viols, cornetts, recorders and lutes. The London waits, for instance, seem to have purchased their first set of viols in 1561, and seven years later their first sets of cornetts and recorders—instruments that were all much more suited to indoor use than the shawms of earlier times. Other companies of waits elsewhere were doing likewise.[69]

The cornett and sackbutt were the two instruments most frequently used in church. The cornett was thought to be similar in timbre to the human voice. It was not a very loud instrument but it had a useful dynamic range, with a *piano* as soft as a recorder's. In tonal quality it was bright and round, rather like the tone of a modern cornet when played softly but without that instrument's rather fat and brassy quality. According to Mersenne, a good player could manage a melody of anything up to eighty measures (i.e. 20 bars of 4/4 in *mm* = 60) without pausing for breath. Opinions differed as to its usefulness. The Italians considered that it was best suited to accompany voices, being too unsteady and uncertain in tone for solo work. The French and Germans, on the other hand, greatly liked its sound both as a solo and accompanying instrument. Mersenne became quite lyrical in its praise:

> Quant à la proprieté du son qu'il rend, il est semblable a l'esclat d'un rayon de soleil qui parait dans l'ombre ou dans les ténèbres, lors qu'on l'entend parmi les voix dans les Eglises Cathédrales, ou dans les Chapelles.[70]

In English cathedrals, cornetts were used to support the upper voices, sackbutts the lower. The sackbutt greatly resembled the modern trombone in appearance. It had thinner walls, however, and it was capable of a very soft, clear sound, ideal for consort work with viols, organs, recorders and voices.

Other instruments beside the cornett and sackbutt were undoubtedly played in church, although they are rarely referred to in contemporary writings. Usually they were included under some such blanket description as "and other excellent instruments of music". The Solicitor General in Ireland and Master of Requests, Sir Roger Wilbraham, recorded in his journal that at the St. George's Day celebrations at Whitehall in 1598 "two psalms and two anthems [were] sung with great melody [with] organs, voices, sackbutts and other instruments

... ".[71] And when Queen Anne attended the service of churching at Greenwich Chapel, in May 1605, the Chapel Royal choir sang sundry anthems to the sound of "organs, cornetts, sackbutt and other excellent instruments of music". Just two years beforehand, the choir of St. Paul's Cathedral had welcomed James and Anne into the city with an anthem sung to the music of "loud instruments", a description that hardly fits sackbutts and cornetts. And then there were organs, cornetts, and other instruments of music at Durham in the 1620s and 1630s.

In most cases we can only guess at the nature of these "other instruments". Viols seem rarely to have been used, for they are mentioned only twice in contemporary accounts—once by Lieutenant Hammond in his diary:

> At Exeter there is a delicate, rich and lofty organ which has more additions than any other, as fair pipes of an extraordinary length, and of the bigness of a man's thigh, which with their viols and other sweet instruments and tunable voices, and the rare organist, together makes a melodious and heavenly harmony, able to ravish the hearer's ears.[73]

and once by Bishop Bedell's son-in-law—the Rev. Alexander Clogy. The Bishop was apparently unable to stand the music at Christ Church Cathedral, Dublin, which

> ... was attended and celebrated with all manner of instrumental music, as organs, sackbutts, cornetts, viols, etc., as if it had been at the dedication of Nebuchadnezzar's golden image in the plain of Dura. ...[72]

Viols may well have been played by cathedral musicians, but rather for their private recreation than for the daily services: certainly there are no instrumental parts in any of the extant pre-Restoration "liturgical" sources. The Dean and Chapter of Ely, for instance, provided viol lessons for the choristers during the later years of the sixteenth century. There is nothing to show that viols were ever used in the cathedral, however; but in 1615 the cathedral organist, John Amner, published a set of

Sacred Hymnes for voices and viols designed for the amateur. The organist of Lichfield Cathedral, Michael East, also published quite a few verse anthems for voices and viols: he had been for a short time under Amner at Ely. But again there is no evidence that viols were actually used in the cathedral. Hammond certainly heard only voices and organ when he visited Lichfield in 1634. Many London musicians, too, wrote anthems for voices and viols—notably Hooper, Bull, Gibbons and Ravenscroft—many of which have alternative accompaniments for organ. Viols would probably have been used during the course of an evening's music at Court, or at the concerts which took place from time to time in the Jerusalem Chamber of Westminster Abbey, or in the private houses of gifted amateurs, whilst the organ would have been used in church. From the purely practical point of view, viols would have been much less convenient to use in the daily services than wind instruments; the players would have required spaced seats and music stands, and not even the most expert violist would have been able to accompany the choir in procession! To what extent viols would have doubled the solo voices is an open question. Plate 13, showing the beginning of the quintus part of Amner's splendid Christmas anthem "O ye little flock", gives a clear idea of the problem: the first two lines are not underlaid, and are therefore instrumental; a solo passage for counter-tenor begins with the words "The shepherds" and continues to the end of the first verse. At no point in the verse, or in the succeeding choruses and verses, is there any direction to the viol player to stop. Yet experience has shown that the effect of doubling a solo voice with viol is not entirely satisfactory and that the words, in particular, tend to be obscured.

There can be no doubt that wind instruments other than sackbutts and cornetts were used from time to time in church, although the available evidence is again extremely nebulous. The most detailed description is to be found in the account of the Duke of Württemberg's visit to St. George's Chapel, Windsor, 1592, mentioned on page 80. The Duke, we are told, listened for more than an hour to the beautiful music, the usual ceremonies and the English sermon. He was specially impressed with the music, with the solo boy, and with the organ, cornetts, flutes, recorders and other instruments that accompanied him.

Wind instruments seem to have been introduced into the services at the Chapel Royal shortly after James came to the throne in 1603. At first, instrumentalists were only brought in for special occasions: a noble wedding or a state funeral. By 1633, however, the King's musicians "for the windy instruments" were present at both festal and ferial services.[74] A rota, dated December 1633, gives "the order to be observed throughout the year by His Majesty's musicians for the wind instruments for waiting in the Chapel and at His Majesty's table". Fifteen musicians in all are named in the list. The three senior members were required to attend only on "principal feasts and collar days"; the other twelve were required to attend on alternate weeks—six on one, six on the other. Most, if not all, of the musicians could play at least two different instruments, and some could play even more. Cornetts and sackbutts would probably have been considered most appropriate for general use in the Chapel, but there is no reason to suppose that recorders, flutes and "hoboys" were not also used from time to time, as the occasion demanded. The fifteen musicians in the 1633 list played between them a wide variety of instruments (H = hoboy; S = sackbutt; F = flute; R = recorder; C = cornett; V = viol):

> Senior players: Jerom Lanier, HSC; Clement Lanier, SRC; Anthony Bassano, FR.
> Other players, group one: Andrea Lanier, FRCV; Henry Bassano, HSF; Alfonso Ferrabosco, FCV; Henry Ferrabosco, FC; Robert Parker, HS (a low tenor); Thomas Mell, FRC.
> Other players, group two: Richard Blagrave, HS; Robert Baker (junior), HSC; John Mason, HS; Christopher Bell, HS; William Gregory, FV; John Adson, FC.

A similar rota of December 1637, has also survived. The players and groups are essentially the same, although by then an extra player had been added to each of the weekly groups. As before, the whole company was required to attend on the "solemn feast and collar days of the year". In general, the wind musicians are unlikely to have done more than double the full choir during performances of services and anthems. During the christening of James' daughter Mary at Greenwich in 1605, for example, the Chapel Royal choir sang a verse anthem and the choruses "were filled with the help of wind instruments". And at the end of the service there was a grand procession from the Chapel to the Nursery, during which "the Chapel and the Musicians joined together, making excellent harmony with full anthems". There is, however, one anthem in the Chapel Royal anthem book of c. 1630 which had a separate and independent accompaniment for cornetts and sackbutts. Unfortunately, the music of this piece—Henry Lawes' "When the mountains were brought forth"—has not survived. The very fact that it was labelled "with verses for cornetts and sackbutts" suggests very strongly that it was at that time unique, and it dates from the time when the wind musicians became a permanent part of the Chapel establishment.

NOTES TO CHAPTER 4

1. Hughes-Hughes.
2. Schnapper; also in the Bodleian Library and the library of Westminster Abbey.
3. Fellowes (vi).
4. Information kindly supplied by Mr. Alan Smith.
5. Dart (i).
6. Arkwright (i), p. 108.
7. Ford.
8. Hughes, Dom. A.
9. le Huray (i), pp. 181–5.
10. Arkwright (ii).
11. The contents of all the known liturgical and secular sources are listed in Daniel and le Huray.
12. Welch, p. 10.
13. Fuller-Maitland and Mann.
14. Shaw (i), p. 38.
15. A collected edition of Cipriano da Rore's four-part madrigals was published at Antwerp in 1577. It was aimed specifically at the student of da

Rore's music, and seems to have been the first scorebook to have been published: printed scores were rare before 1650.

16. The manuscripts are, British Museum, Royal Mus. Lib. MS. 24 d. 3 and 23 l. 4; New York, Public Library, Drexel MS. 4302; and London, Royal College of Music, MS. 1051.

17. For a discussion of the function of chiavettes, see Mendel; see also Andrews (ii) for an account of Byrd's use of chiavettes.

18. Stevens, D. (iii).

19. Brett and Dart.

20. Dart (ii), p. 221.

21. See Botstiber, p. 738, for list of contents. For biographical information see Cole, E., and Dart and Schofield.

22. Willetts, p. 71.

23. Crum.

24. Morley, p. 255.

25. Information very kindly supplied by Mr. John Morehen.

26. Brett and Dart.

27. The handwriting of Durham Cathedral MSS. E 4–11, Christ Church MSS. 1220–4, and Pembroke College MSS. Mus. 6. 1–6 all bear a close resemblance to the very unusual type of Barnard's *First Book*, which they may well antedate.

28. *Historical Manuscripts Commission*, "Fourth Report".

29. Morley, p. 255.

30. Morley, p. 243.

31. Morley, pp. 292–3.

32. Strunk, pp. 259–60.

33. Kökeritz, p. 293 *et passim*.

34. Lowinsky (iii) and (iv); see also Morley, p. 256, and *Journal of the American Musicological Society*, XIII (1960), p. 161.

35. Steele, J.

36. Only one sixteenth-century specification of an English organ has yet been found giving pipe measurements—the organ at All Hallows, Barking, of 1519. This, too, had a manual range upwards from double C fa ut, and its longest pipe measured 10 ft; see Freeman, A. (i). The few early seventeenth-century specifications that have so far come to light show that the 10 ft standard was still the norm.

37. Steele, J. Concerning the arguments for and against pedals on English organs see B. J. Maslen, "The Earliest English Organ Pedals" *Musical Times*, September 1960, p. 578, and the subsequent correspondence in the *Musical Times*, February 1961, p. 107, and April 1961, p. 248.

38. Walcott, p. 90.

39. Referring to Hugh Davies, organist of the cathedral from 1630–44.

40. Horsley.

41. Coclico. For further references to improvisation practices abroad, see R. Haas, "Aufführungspraxis der Musik", *Handbuch der Musikwissenschaft* (New York, 1931), and especially pp. 112 and 115 for coloured motets by Finck and Palestrina; "Improvisation in Nine Centuries of Western Music":

an *Anthology of Music*, ed. K. G. Fellerer (Köln, 1961); and *Acta Musicologia*, XXII (1950), pp. 148–52.

42. Coperario.

43. Rye, p. 16.

44. Reese, p. 665.

45. Rogers.

46. Morley, p. 140.

47. Mulcaster, ch. 11.

48. Barley.

49. Butler, p. 116.

50. Hammond (i and ii). The quality of sweetness was also admired by the Italians; see Fortune (ii), pp. 211–19.

51. *Historical Manuscripts Commission*, "Fourth Report."

52. *Historical Manuscripts Commission* (i).

53. Butler, p. 40–2.

54. The division of boys' voices into meanes and trebles goes back to pre-Reformation times: the Earl of Northumberland's choir included two "tribills" and three "meanys": see Hawkins, p. 385, and Wulstan (ii).

55. Many of Byrd's other motets, of course, contain treble parts: these two are, however, to be found in a liturgical source—the Caroline books at Peterhouse; the Peterhouse books are unique in that they contain motets (though few), as well as music to English words.

56. The anthem has a full three octave range, and is printed with a G clef in the 1611 edition. In the Durham MSS., however, the G clef is replaced by C 5.

57. The Peterhouse version is for solo treble, instead of the usual alto.

58. Although the upper part is scored in the G clef it does not go above f″.

59. The meaning of "in medio chori" is obscure. In 1569 an organ was installed in the chapel of Winchester College, "in medio chori", see the Wykehamist, vol. 523 (December 1913), p. 216, for details. In the cathedral at Winchester was "one great branch candlestick, hanging in the midst of the choir"—see Ford, p. 158. Perhaps a group of solo singers stood in the middle of the choir, somewhat apart from the decani and cantoris sections of the full choir, to produce a kind of polychoral effect.

60. Information very kindly supplied by Canon Noel Boston.

61. Lafontaine, p. 84.

62. Butler, p. 98.

63. The direction "long tyme" at the beginning of the second verse of Henry Palmer's "Lord, what is man" (Durham MS. A1) may well be unique. See Kirby.

64. Ascham (i), p. 42.

65. Morley, pp. 292–3.

66. Ornithoparcus, p. 88.

67. Grove, V., "Cornett"; and Woodfill, p. 149: neither give the source of this information.

68. Mr. Alan Smith, who has kindly supplied this information, believes that instruments were at first associated with royal events and festal services.

69. Woodfill, ch. 2.
70. Mersenne, V, Proposition 22.
71. Scott, p. 16.
72. Hammond (ii).
73. Clogy, p. 140.
74. And probably by 1630, or even earlier: see Lafontaine, p. 72, "1630, May 6".

5

Trends and Influences

The history of church music in England during the sixteenth and early seventeenth centuries is very largely concerned with the development of an increasingly personal and dramatic musical language. The extent to which the English Reformation influenced this development is an open question. It has been argued that the immediate effect of the Reformation was to focus attention on the need for a simple and comprehensible musical style, a style suitable for the "presentation" of the Word in the clearest possible terms. It has been suggested, moreover, that this initial concern for "presentation" quickly led to an increased interest in the musical "representation" of the Word and to the use of more immediately expressive techniques of composition.[1]

Whilst the liturgical reformation was undoubtedly a major event in the history of English church music, there is perhaps a danger that too much importance may be attached to it— that it may be seen as the primary cause of change rather than as the catalyst in a process that had been steadily at work since the middle of the fifteenth century. A fundamental factor in this process had been the gradual shift from "successive" to "simultaneous" techniques of composition—from a primarily horizontal method of working, in which the separate parts were composed one after the other, to a vertical method in which all parts were developed simultaneously. To what extent the change was due to the search for a more expressive musical language, and to what extent "expressive" composition followed as a product of change, is a matter for speculation.[2] There can be no doubt, however, that the simultaneous method opened up new and exciting musical possibilities— possibilities which were speedily realised by Flemish, French and Italian musicians, and above all by Josquin des Préz. "Absalom fili mi" and "Planxit autem David"—two of Josquin's greatest compositions—demonstrate beyond question the immense superiority of the simultaneous system in the expression of dramatic emotion. In "Planxit autem", the composer skilfully controls the speed of harmonic change— as his younger contemporary and admirer Glarean pointed out—to portray the mourner in his despair, "wont at first to cry out frequently, subsiding gradually with ever longer intervals between his passionate outbursts of grief".[3] In "Absalom fili mi", the composer exploits even more movingly the declamatory and pictorial potential of melody, harmony, tonality and texture. The rise and fall of the opening imitative point reflects the rise and fall of the speaking voice, whilst the extended modulation to the remote "key" of B♭ aptly symbolises the descent into hell:

Neither the opening imitation nor the sequential modulation would, of course, have been possible had the separate voice-parts been composed one after the other.

Although Josquin may very largely have abandoned the medieval techniques of successive composition, and although in his most advanced work he may have anticipated the mature style of the High Renaissance, he was to some extent a conservative in his approach to the problems of liturgical composition—and especially to the composition of music for the ordinary of the Mass—as were the majority of his contemporaries and immediate successors. The words of the Kyrie, Gloria, Creed, Sanctus and Agnus Dei may offer less scope for word-painting than do those of the Absalom and Jonathan laments, yet even the most obvious opportunities are often ignored and the elements of harmony and tonality are rarely used with expressive intent.[4] The inference must be that, in such essentially liturgical works as these, the aim was not primarily the production of "expressive" music—in the sense, that is, that Josquin's devotional laments are "expressive". This conclusion is perhaps confirmed by the somewhat curious practice of "parody" composition, which remained in vogue throughout the sixteenth century. This technique was used almost exclusively in the composition of Masses, and it involved the assimilation into the Mass of sections of a pre-existent composition—or, in some cases, the pre-existent composition as a whole. Taverner based his *Mater Christi* Mass, for instance, on his own antiphon "Mater Christi sanctissima". The way in which he incorporated parts of the motet into the Gloria may serve to illustrate the technique in practice[5]:

A Parody Mass and its original

elements common to the *Mater Christi* antiphon and the Gloria of the *Mater Christi* Mass by Taverner

Antiphon	Mater Christi sanctissima	
Gloria	Et in terra pax hominibus bonae voluntatis (11–32 new material)	$\left\{\begin{matrix} 1\text{–}10 \\ 1\text{–}10 \end{matrix}\right\}$

| Ant. | filium | $\left\{\begin{array}{l}31\text{--}33 \\ 33\text{--}35\end{array}\right\}$ |
| Glor. | omnipotens | |

| Ant. | Ergo fili, decus patris, Jesu | $\left\{\begin{array}{l}34\text{--}43 \\ 36\text{--}45\end{array}\right\}$ |
| Glor. | Domine fili unigenite, Jesu | |

| Ant. | vitalis cibus | $\left\{\begin{array}{l}56\text{--}58 \\ 46\text{--}48\end{array}\right\}$ |
| Glor. | Christe | |

| Ant. | vescamur in palacio. Amen | $\left\{\begin{array}{l}131\text{--}141\ (\text{end}) \\ 154\text{--}164\ (\text{end})\end{array}\right\}$ |
| Glor. | in gloria Dei patris. Amen | |

A single musical idea is often to be found, moreover, in many different contexts, further emphasising the absence of links between words and notes:

from the Motet and Mass, Mater Christi   Taverner

Viewed in its historical context, the phenomenon is by no means as puzzling as it might at first appear. If, indeed, few obvious connections can be traced between musical techniques and literary ideas in medieval music, it either follows that the medieval composer had little interest in developing an expressive musical language or that he lacked the necessary techniques to do so. But part-music was of itself an unusual and impressive phenomenon, and by its very presence it could lend dignity and weight to an important occasion. No doubt Bishop Grandisson had this in mind when he drew up regulations for the performance of polyphony at Exeter Cathedral. The higher the class of festival the more chance he allowed for the performance of polyphonic settings:[6]

Rank of Festival	Greater and Lesser Doubles	Semi-Doubles	Ordinary Sundays and Feasts with the ruling of the choir	Ferias and Feasts of Three Lessons
		Vespers		
	Antiphon Respond	Antiphon		
				No polyphony (plainsong only)
	Hymn Magnificat and its	Hymn	Hymn	
	Antiphon	Antiphon to Magnificat	Antiphon to Magnificat	
	Benedicamus substitute Deo gratias			
		Compline		
	Hymn Nunc dimittis and Antiphon	Hymn	No polyphony (plainsong only)	No polyphony (plainsong only)

Taverner's eight extant Masses suggest how such musical distinctions might have been achieved shortly before the Reformation, the simple *Playn Song* Mass being suitable for the more modest festal and Sunday services, the three Flemish-style Masses and the *Western Wynde* Mass for perhaps Semi-doubles, and the great cantus firmus Masses (*Gloria tibi Trinitas, Corona spinea* and *O Michael*) for major festivals. While some very obvious instances of word-painting are to be found in each of the eight Masses, there is little consistency in this matter, a fact suggesting that word representation can still only have been a very secondary consideration at that time. It is significant, too, that cantus firmus methods of composition lost none of their appeal for English musicians during the early years of the sixteenth century, hampering as these were to the development of an expressive musical idiom. That there had none the less been considerable progress in this direction is clear enough to see in the music of the younger Tudor composers. Christopher Tye's *Euge bone* Mass, in the highly compressed and imitative French style, is the equal of anything that was then being written abroad; the short declamatory points of imitation contrast markedly with the long, melismatic lines of the festal cantus firmus Mass:

Agnus Dei of the 'Euge bone' Mass — Tye

*this part is missing in the original

During the early years of the Reformation in England, great emphasis was placed upon the need for full congregational comprehension of what was said and sung in daily worship. It is hardly surprising, therefore, that much of the earliest English church music is simpler in style and considerably more concise in structure than the music which it replaced. Yet many precedents for change are to be found in the music of the pre-Reformation rites: Taverner's *Playn Song* Mass is to all intents and purposes a Short Service setting. The *In nomine, Small Devotion* and *Meane* Masses are clear and straightforward to listen to; whilst John Shepherd's somewhat later

French Mass illustrates the tendency to brevity and clarity within an imitative idiom, and it shows, as does the remarkable *Euge bone* Mass by Tye quoted above, the native indebtedness to French and Italian models.[7] Nor, indeed, at the time of the Reformation did composers lack experience in setting English devotional texts to music. Pygott's "Quid petis O fili/The mother, full mannerly" is strikingly imitative and unmelismatic, and yet it must have been written some twenty or thirty years before Cranmer raised the question of syllabic word setting in his much quoted letter to Henry VIII.

It would be wrong, therefore, to think of the Reformation as the sole or even the principal cause of change. Yet in one respect at least it was of immense importance, for it encouraged the composer to exercise a more direct control in that necessary but preliminary stage of composition, the selection of a text. This was especially true in the strictly liturgical fields of composition, for the first Book of Common Prayer gave little guidance to the composer, and later Prayer Books gave even less. Very many of the earliest English anthems already reveal a preference for "subjective" texts of clearly defined mood, and it is certainly wrong to think of the dramatic, subjective anthem text as a late-Elizabethan phenomenon. Similar changes are to be observed in the Latin music of the period.[8] As Dr. Harrison has shown, church music in England immediately before the Reformation was still centred very largely upon the liturgy and its chant. The early-Renaissance motet, based upon texts of non-liturgical origin and lacking a specifically liturgical function, did not begin to appear in England until the very eve of the Reformation. It may well have found its way there from France and the Low Countries by way of Scotland, through the work of such Anglo-Scottish composers as Robert Johnson and William More, probably no more than "ten or xii yeiris before reformation". Whether, in fact, English composers were already writing free motets before the Edwardian Reformation or whether these are of later date is not known. There are, however, a number of such works by

Tye and Tallis and by their younger Edwardian and early-Elizabethan contemporaries, Mundy, Shepherd, Robert Parsons and Robert White.

Many of the earliest English motets are settings of complete psalms or sections of psalms, and it seems that composers were slow to attempt the compilation of texts from multiple sources (this would also seem to be true of the anthem). It is probably no accident that one of the first "English" composers to do so was the elder Alphonso Ferrabosco, most of whose extant motets are based on "composite" texts. Ferrabosco was born in Bologna in 1543—his father had himself been a composer of some note—but by 1562 he was already living in London as one of Elizabeth's most privileged musicians. Both Morley and Peacham speak of the high regard which Englishmen then had for Alphonso's work, and there are several authenticated stories of friendly rivalries between Alphonso and his English contemporaries, notably William Byrd.[9]

A comparison between Byrd's early and later non-liturgical motets shows clearly that the composer became increasingly selective in his choice of words. Of the sixteen items in the 1575 collection, no fewer than eight are based on texts of liturgical origin. In the later *Cantiones Sacrae* of 1589 and 1591, liturgical texts and cantus firmus compositions are very few indeed. This is not to suggest, of course, that a liturgical motet is necessarily inexpressive or a free motet expressive. In his psalm-motets, for instance, William Mundy shows only a very superficial concern with the relationship between word and note. On the other hand, Byrd was certainly aiming at an expressive interpretation of several of the 1575 liturgical texts. Yet the change from the liturgical to the composite text suggests a new concern for the expression of the personal situation, a concern that is also increasingly manifest in the music itself.

During the second half of the sixteenth century, progress towards a more personal musical language seems, if anything, to have been accelerated. It is only necessary to compare early

and late Elizabethan settings of identical Latin texts to appreciate
the extent of change. Tallis' "Laudate Dominum", a lively
work by Elizabethan standards, moves for the most part in
minims and crotchets, the polyphony is well developed in the
best Flemish-Italian style, and the motet as a whole is reminiscent of the work of the elder Alphonso Ferrabosco. Byrd's
setting of the same text is, by comparison, highly dramatic—
opening with a brilliant "duet" for two basses and building up
section by section to a fine conclusion.

Similar comparisons may be made between Edwardian and
early-Jacobean settings of English texts. Tallis chose to set the
words of the Easter-morning anthem "Christ rising" to five-
part imitative polyphony of great solemnity: the rubric of
the 1549 Prayer Book, from which he took his text, reads
"In the morning before Matins, the people being assembled in
the church, these anthems shall be first *solemnly* sung or said"
(author's italics). The mood of solemnity is not altogether
absent from Byrd's setting of the same text, but the more
immediately human reaction of joy is also there. The use of
solo voices as well as a full chorus at once adds a more personal

note to the setting; the bright solo timbres contrast well with the sombre viols, and the entry of the chorus for the first time at the words "death from henceforth hath no power upon him" is highly dramatic (see extracts from this anthem on page 244). Moreover, the second part of the anthem, beginning "Christ is risen", is in triple time almost throughout, a metre that was considered as suitable then, as it is now, for joyful occasions:

> The use of this Perfect Prolation [i.e. triple metre] is, in Service Divine for Jubilees and Thanksgivings, and otherwise for Galliards and Revellings....[10]

Even in the simplest anthems a new, personal note is much in evidence. The upper, and dominant, voice in Richard Farrant's lovely little anthem, "Hide not Thou thy face", rises and falls with the speaking voice; two important phrases of text are emphatically repeated, whilst shape is given to the anthem as a whole by the skilful disposition of cadences.

Yet it would be wrong to imagine that the unreserved expression of mood was ever aimed at, either in the composition of devotional or liturgical music. This may have been the composer's legitimate goal in the fields of secular composition, and Morley, who in this respect was heavily indebted to Zarlino, had much advice to offer on the subject:

> You must therefore, if you have a grave matter, apply a grave kind of music to it; if a merry subject you must make your music also merry, for it will be a great absurdity to use a sad harmony to a merry matter, or a merry harmony to a sad, lamentable, or tragical ditty.... So that if you would have your music signify hardness, cruelty, or other such effects you must cause the parts proceed in their motions without the half note, that is you must cause them proceed by whole notes, sharp thirds, sharp sixths, and such like (when I speak of sharp or flat thirds and sixths you must understand that they ought to be so to the bass); you may also use cadences bound with the fourth or seventh which, being in long notes, will exasperate the harmony. But when you

would express a lamentable passion then must you use motions proceeding by half notes, flat thirds and flat sixths, which of their nature are sweet. . . .

But those chords . . . are not the sole and only cause of expressing those passions, but also the motions which the parts make in singing do greatly help; which motions are either natural or accidental. The natural motions are those which are naturally made betwixt the keys without the mixture of any accidental sign or chord, be it either flat or sharp, and these motions be more masculine . . . than those accidental chords which are marked with these signs, ♯♭, which be indeed accidental and make the song, as it were, more effeminate and languishing than the other motions. . . .

Also if the subject be light you must cause your music to go in motions which carry with them a celerity or quickness of time, as minims, crotchets, and quavers; if it be lamentable the notes must go in slow and heavy motions as semibreves, breves and suchlike. . . .[11]

As the Elizabethan divine, Richard Hooker, put it, music had indeed an "admirable faculty" to express and represent to the mind "the very standing, rising and falling, the very steps and inflexions every way, the turns and variations of all passions whereunto the mind is subject".[12] But if, as Hooker suggested, church music's function was to allay "all kind of base and earthly cogitations" and to drive away the "secret suggestions" of the "invisible enemy", it followed that a special, unsecular kind of music was required. Upon this point there was general agreement. The anonymous author of Royal MS. 18. B. XIX recommended that church music should be composed in "passionate notes" and "tunes of long measure", and that "wild, sudden, quick and skittish notes" should at all costs be avoided. Morley had much the same advice to offer, with the additional recommendation that passing dissonances and suspensions would add greatly to the solemnity of the music. He wrote:

. . . you must cause your harmony to carry a majesty, taking discords and bindings as often as you can, but let it be in long notes, for the nature of it will not bear short notes and quick motions, which denote a kind of wantonness.[13]

Notwithstanding such excellent advice, the natural tendency was to exploit ever more dramatic modes of expression, a tendency that was accelerated by the arrival of the Italian madrigal in England in the 1580s, and one which led simultaneously to the collapse of the polyphonic style and to the cultivation of a deliberately archaic and, by contemporary standards, "inexpressive" liturgical style. The extremes are best seen in Italian music of the early seventeenth century, the "prima prattica" being essentially polyphonic in the Palestrinian tradition, the "seconda prattica" being homophonic and monodic. Many composers, and among them Monteverdi, happily made use of both old and new. Monteverdi's *Sacrae Cantiunculae* and the Missa "In illo tempore" are firmly in the "prima prattica" idiom; the Mass is, in fact, a parody composition based upon an early sixteenth-century motet by the French composer Gombert. The Vespers music, on the other hand, is in a comparatively modern style; there are elements of Florentine monody in it, and much polychoral writing in the best Venetian tradition. In Italy, the dividing line between the sacred and the secular was in many cases a very fine one indeed.

English music of the same period covers by no means the same wide range of forms and styles. Yet the leading English composers tended to adopt an increasingly fragmented and dramatic style, whilst their less adventurous contemporaries clung firmly to the past. In his *Gradualia* of 1605 and 1607, Byrd used within the course of a single piece a far wider range of rhythms and textures than he had done in his early 1575 *Cantiones*, whilst at the same time compressing his ideas into a much smaller framework. Byrd's younger Anglo-Catholic contemporaries, Philips and Dering, went even further in this direction. Dering's intensely dramatic setting of "Factum est silentium", for instance, makes an interesting

comparison with the earlier and rather austere setting by
Clemens non Papa:

English devotional and liturgical compositions, and especially
those in verse form, show a similar process of fragmentation.
The verse form is, of course, by its very nature somewhat
sectional, with clear divisions between the "verses" and

"choruses". But the collapse of the mid sixteenth-century polyphonic style involved not only the differentiation of textures and an increasing sectionalisation of structures but also the further expansion of melodic and harmonic rhythms and the break-up of the classical modal system. Much of the simpler and more chordal Elizabethan music is already very tonal in feeling. Farrant's "Hide not Thou thy face" does in fact "modulate" into the related keys of G minor and B♭ major. This new feeling for tonality is particularly apparent in the work of William Byrd. "Sing joyfully", perhaps the composer's greatest anthem, has a particularly clear tonal scheme:

1.	Sing joyfully unto God our strength	C major
2.	Sing loud unto the God of Jacob	G major
3.	Take the song and bring forth the timbrel	G major to its dominant
4.	The pleasant harp with the viol	D minor to A minor
5.	Blow the trumpet in the new moon	beginning with an interrupted cadence in F, and moving upwards by fifths to the dominant of G major
6.	Even in the time appointed and at our feast day	D minor to G major
7.	For this is a statute for Israel, and a law of the God of Jacob	C major to F major followed by a long section in A minor, and final cadence on C

Although the mention of major and minor keys may in this context seem somewhat anachronistic, Morley's comments, quoted on page 144 show that musicians were already then thinking in such terms even though the word "key" is not yet used in its modern sense. The anonymous author of Royal MS. 18. B. XIX went a step further than either Zarlino or Morley had done when he suggested that there were effectively no more than three "keys": one beginning on C—the Ionian, another on D—the Dorian, and a third on E—the Phrygian. To these keys the author attributed distinctive moods: the

Phrygian mode was best suited, he considered, for the expression of harshness and aggression (interestingly enough, Archbishop Parker described Tallis' Phrygian psalm-tune in much the same terms), the Dorian for "tragedies", "melancholy actions" and "petitionary ditties" (i.e., prayers), and the Ionian for songs and anthems of "rejoicing" and "thanksgiving".

In general, English composers were fairly conservative in their use of harmony and tonality. A factor here may well have been the church organ, which was probably tuned to a meantone system of temperament. Madrigalian chromaticisms of the kind to be found in Weelkes' "Cease sorrows now" or Farnaby's "Construe my meaning" are extremely rare, though there are one or two isolated passages of the kind in the verse anthems of Nathaniel Giles inserted by the composer, it would seem, as much for their novelty as for any clearly expressive purpose:

Thomas Tomkins used this kind of chromaticism only once in his liturgical music, and for an occasion of particular poignancy—the death of young Prince Henry:

Shock-modulations in the Italian vein, of the kind to be found in some of the more exotic motets of Gesualdo and even here and there in English madrigals, are non-existent in the liturgical and devotional music of the period:

Early seventeenth-century composers learned to manipulate the important element of harmonic rhythm with great subtlety and effect. Gibbons' superb verse anthem "See, see the Word is incarnate" illustrates this particularly well (see below, page 315); and in a cruder form it appears in every extant setting of Psalm 81 ("Sing joyfully", or "Sing we merrily"). Nobody seems to have been able to resist the obvious invitation:

Elements of the *stile nuovo* first appeared, however, in the Latin music of the Anglo-Catholic composers Philips and Dering, both of whom spent much of their time abroad.

F

The continuo motets of these two composers develop an idiom that had first been worked by Viadana, in his *Cento Concerti Ecclesiastici*, of 1602, an idiom that owed something to the old and the new:

Dering's "Latin songs" were especially popular in England, and they may well have first been heard in Queen Henrietta Maria's private chapel at Somerset House in the 1630s (see Chapter 3, page 86). The genre found several English admirers and imitators—notably the Lawes brothers and William Child, whose continuo psalms date from the 1630s, and George Jeffries, a musical eccentric of the first water. The especial fondness for jigging Alleluias suggests, none the less, a stylistic ancestry going back to Sweelinck himself:[14]

In the fields of liturgical music, composers tended on the whole to be less adventurous. Walter Porter, a Monteverdi pupil and from 1616 until the Civil War a member of the Chapel Royal choir, was probably the first to make use of *seconda prattica* techniques in compositions for the Church. The words of ten of his anthems are in the 1630 Chapel Royal anthem book. Unfortunately not a note of music has survived in manuscript—a sure indication of its limited appeal; and only one of the ten was ever published—"Praise the Lord", a verse anthem with continuo organ accompaniment. The verses for solo treble and tenor call for virtuosity of a high order.[15] The church anthems of William and Henry Lawes are in many ways more traditionally English than are their psalm settings. The same stylistic contrasts are to be found in the music of William Child, the devotional psalms being distinctly more advanced in harmonic idiom than most of the Services and anthems. Yet some of Child's more interesting pre-Restoration anthems do certainly owe something to the *seconda prattica*. "O God, wherefore art Thou absent" is perhaps reminiscent of the Monteverdian *stile concitato*, both in its declamatory choral textures and its restless tonal scheme:

And Child was probably the first church musician to adopt an openly "major" and "minor" system of tonality, and to use sharps as well as flats in his key signatures. The very popular Service in D sol re ♯ is indeed in D major, with a key signature of two sharps and with modulations to nearly related "keys"; the service is to be found in quite a few pre-Restoration manuscripts. In this respect, at least, Child was well ahead of his time.

These few introductory observations on the changing function and style of church music during the sixteenth and early seventeenth centuries may, it is hoped, serve to set the following musical chapters in some general context. An attempt has been made to show that a new and more subjective musical language was made possible by the change during the early sixteenth century from successive to simultaneous techniques of composition. It has been suggested that the late-medieval concept of music as a ceremonial adjunct of the liturgy gave way slowly to one in which both the objective and the subjective had expression. The part that the English Reformation played in this process of change is open to argument. That it focused attention both on problems of "presentation" and of "representation" seems undeniable.

It is clear, none the less, that the more volatile, surface emotions of the kind expressed in the secular music of the period were considered unsuitable for the Church. Church music's function, as Thomas Morley put it, was "to draw the hearer, as it were, in chains of gold by the ears to the consideration of holy things".[16] This called for a musical style lacking pronounced secular associations, a style that was "grave" and "sober" as well in thanksgiving as in sorrow. Since, however, the tendency in secular composition was to seek for ever more dramatic and personal modes of expression, it is not surprising that the language of church music developed along similar if comparatively conservative lines. By 1640 the continuo-motet genre established by Viadana had become very popular in England through the work of such composers as Dering, Child and the Lawes brothers. There were signs, too, that English composers were learning to incorporate elements of the *seconda prattica* into their liturgical works. Although this progressive movement would seem to have been centred almost exclusively on the Court, it might well have gone much further had not "the Divell Incarnate" (as Roger North put it) "confounded the public with his civil wars".[17] Or might perhaps the forces of conservatism have succeeded in containing the English baroque within the Chapels Royal? The very conservative repertory of pieces in John Barnard's *First Book of Selected Church Musick* suggests that "old" music may already have had a bigger appeal for church musicians than the new.

NOTES TO CHAPTER 5

1. Stevens, J., ch. 5.
2. Lowinsky (i), p. 57.
3. Strunk, p. 226.
4. Harrison, F. Ll. (i), p. 322 for further discussion of this point.
5. In *Tudor Church Music*, I & III, "Taverner" (1923–24).
6. Harrison, F. Ll. (i), p. 110. See also K. Jeppesen, *The Style of Palestrina and the Dissonance*, 2nd. Edn., 1946, pp. 276–294.
7. By 1539 five Bassanos had taken up residence at Court, and in the same year six other Venetians joined the King's Music; see Izon, p. 329. Foreign musicians continued to play an important part in the musical life of the Court throughout the late sixteenth and early seventeenth centuries; see Westrup (ii), p. 70.
8. Kerman (ii), p. 279.

9. Cockshoot; the motets of the elder Alphonso Ferrabosco are shortly to be published in the *Early English Church Music* series. See also Arkwright (ed.), *Old English Edition*, "Alphonso Ferrabosco", XI–XII—the madrigals of Alphonso Ferrabosco.

10. Ravenscroft.

11. Morley, p. 290.

12. Hooker, section 39.

13. Morley, p. 293.

14. Arnold, F.T., pp. 21–33 for further examples of Viadana motets. For an interesting seventeenth-century account of the emergence of the new style see Giustiniani. See also Platt, p. 135 *et passim*, and Lefkowitz, p. 242.

15. "Nine out of ten monodies were written for a high voice—soprano, mezzo-soprano or tenor"; Fortune (ii), p. 206. See le Huray (ii) for the music.

16. Morley, p. 293.

17. Wilson, J., p. 294.

" . . . the order of Common Prayer as it is to be sung in Churches"

1549-1600

Enough part-music has survived from the earliest years of the Reformation to show that choral services were quickly established on lines that are familiar to us today. Paired "Service" settings of the canticles and music for the "ordinary" and "proper" of the Mass are already to be found in Edwardian manuscripts, together with anthem-like compositions based on texts from the Bible, the Prayer Book and elsewhere.

Surprisingly little is known of the ways in which the daily psalms and the Responses were sung in cathedrals during the late sixteenth and early seventeenth centuries. The Elizabethan divine, William Harrison, said that services in cathedrals and collegiate churches were "so ordered" that the psalms only were sung "by note, the rest being read (as in common parish churches) by the minister with a loud voice".[1] Since choirs did not process to and from the chancel before and after service, and since in many places fines for lateness were only imposed when offenders had arrived after the first psalm had started (at Matins this was of course Venite, exultemus), it may be that the Preces and Responses were either said or else sung to simple Sarum intonations of the kind that Merbecke printed in his *booke of Common praier noted.*

It would seem, too, that the psalms were sung to adaptations of the eight Sarum tones, similar in style to those that Merbecke published in his prayer book. Some light is shed on this question by an interesting and unusual document in the Shrewsbury County Record Office (Ludlow deposit) concerning conduct of the services in the parish church at Ludlow.[2] It is dated 1581 and it records, amongst other matters, an agreement "That all the prayers (excepting psalms) shall be said in such places as they have been used to be said since the being here of the Right Honourable the Lord President, which is at the choir door, and the psalms as well before the chapters [i.e. the lessons] as after shall be sung in plainsong in the choir". In other words, all prayers were to be said where they could best be heard by the congregation (which was at the door leading from the nave to the choir), whilst the psalms and canticles (rather loosely described as the psalms before and after the lessons or "chapters") were to be sung in the body of the choir and to plainsong. It was agreed, furthermore, that the organ was to be played "between the psalms or with the psalms and with the anthem or hymn", whilst the anthem was to be, in "pricksong", and chosen by "Mr. Parson", if he were present. These arrangements were to be observed when the Lord President was present at divine service, and perhaps, too, on Sundays throughout the year, though this is not entirely clear.

Altogether, no more than five groups of psalm-chants have so far come to light, but all are closely related to the pre-Reformation psalm-tone system.[3] The earliest of the five is Merbecke's. The second is to be found in Morley's *Plaine and Easie Introduction to Practicall Musicke* (1597). Here the eight Sarum tones are set out in order, in very simple four-part harmonisations, the tone in each case being in the tenor. Morley made no attempt, however, to provide variant endings for the tones, nor did he set out the structure of each chant at all clearly. The third group consists of five harmonised chants in one of the "Caroline" part-books (c. 1635) at Peterhouse, Cambridge. Though the chants are in two parts as they now stand, it may well be that the originals were arranged for four voices. All five are set out rather carelessly as for the first

verse of the Venite, and like the Merbecke chants they have
pronounced Sarum characteristics.

The fourth and fifth chant groups date from the early years
of the Restoration.[4] The fourth was published by Edward
Lowe at Oxford in 1661 in an attempt, as the preface clearly
shows, to revive the lost traditions of earlier times. Lowe
prints only two monodic chants—Sarum I, ending 4, and
Sarum 8—and a four-part harmonisation of Sarum I, called
the "Canterbury tune". The fifth and much more comprehensive collection of chants was published by the Rev. James
Clifford in the second edition of *The Divine Services and Anthems*
in 1664. It consists in all of thirteen "Sarum" monodies,[5]
with varied endings, together with four harmonised chants,
including Lowe's "Canterbury tune", a setting of the eighth
tone—called "Imperial"—and two settings of the first tone:
one entitled "Christ Church tune", the other "Adrian Batten's

Sarum : [first mode, fourth ending]

Lae - ta - tus sum in his quae dic - ta sunt mi - hi In do - mum Do - mi - ni i - bi - mus

Merbecke: *booke of Common praier noted (1550)* [first mode, second ending]

My soul doth mag - ni - fy the Lord ; and my spi - rit hath re - joic - ed in God my Sav - iour.

For he hath re - gard - ed the low - li - ness of his hand - maid, for be - hold from-hence-forth all

gen - e - ra - ti - ons shall call me bless - ed . . . .

Morley: *A Plaine and Easie Introduction (1597)* " The First Tune " [fifth ending]

Peterhouse, Cambridge, MS 34 (c.1635) [Chant measured out for the first line of the Venite]

Lowe : *A Short Direction for the Performance of Cathedral Service* (1661) [first mode, fourth ending]

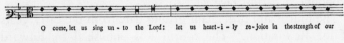

O come, let us sing un - to the Lord : let us heart - i - ly re - joice in the strength of our

sal - va - ti - on

Clifford : *Divine Services and Anthems* (1664) "Adrain Batten's tune in four parts" [first mode, fourth ending]

O come, let us sing un - to the Lord : let us... re - joice in... our sal - va - ti - on.

tune of four parts". Evidently, therefore, the psalms had been sung to harmonised Anglican-style chants for some time before the outbreak of civil war, since Batten himself had died in 1637 (see above, pages 159–60).

Both Lowe and Clifford were at pains to point out that although they had printed the chants in notes of specific duration, the time values were intended as an indication of natural word stress rather than of precise length. As Clifford put it:

> The reader is to observe that although the ordinary tunes are done in notes yet are they not intended to signify any exact time, but to take notice that the minim and semibreve are commonly put where the syllables are to be sung slower and more emphatically than the rest.

It may well be that Merbecke's system of notation should be interpreted with equal freedom, the natural word rhythm being the prime consideration. How the psalms were set to these chants is an open question. *The psalter or Psalms of David, corrected and pointed as they shall be sung in churches after the translation of the Great Bible* was first published in 1549, but in practice this must have been quite inadequate for its purpose, there being no "pointing" other than the colon dividing each verse into two. No doubt each choir arrived at a workable solution by a process of trial and error; and, as nowadays, both pointing and chants must have varied in detail from cathedral to cathedral.[6]

On festal occasions the practice grew, during the late sixteenth century, of singing specially harmonised settings of the Preces, Responses and proper psalms, and many festal psalms are directly associated with sets of Preces and Responses:

TABLE 14

Some Sixteenth- and Early Seventeenth-century Preces, Psalms, Responses and Litanies

Amner	First Preces and Psalm 89 (verses 1–30 and 50)	Christmas Day Evensong
Barnard	Preces à 5 Preces à 6 "for trebles" Responses for March 27th and November 5th	
Batten	Preces for trebles Preces and Psalms: (i) Psalms 20 and 124	
	(ii) Psalm 114	"for Easter Day"
	(iii) Psalm 21	"for March 27th"
	(iv) Psalms 67 and 113	
	(v) Psalm 145	
	(vi) Psalm 45	"for Whitsunday"
	Litany Litany (from Short Service for Men)	
Butler	Litany	
Byrd	First Preces and Psalms 47	9th Evening and Whitsun Evensong
	54	10th Evening
	Second Preces and Psalms 114: 1–6	Easter Evensong
	55: 1–8	10th Evening and
	119: 33–40	Epiphany Evensong
	Psalm 24: 7–10 (adapted from, Attollite portas)	Ascension Evensong
	Third Preces and Responses Litany	
Child	Preces and Psalm 67	
Davies	Preces and Psalms 136 and 24	
Farrant (?)	Psalms 21, 146 and 147	"for obiit Sunday"
Frith (Freeth)	Preces and Responses	
Gibbons, O.	First Preces and Psalms 145: 15–20	Whitsunday Evensong
	57: 9–12 and	
	118: 19–24	Easter Evensong
	Second Preces and Psalm 145: 1–14	

(*Table 14 continued overleaf*)

TABLE 14 (*continued*)

Giles	Preces	
Holmes, J.	Preces and Psalm 89 "for trebles"	Christmas Evensong
Hooper	Preces and Psalm 24	
	Preces to the "Flat Service"	
Hunt, T.	Preces	
Juxon	Preces	
Lugg, R.	Litany	
Merbecke	Preces, Psalms, Responses and Litany	
Marson, G.	Preces and Psalm 16	
Molle	Litany (Latin)	
	Litany "made for Dr Cozens"	
Morley	Preces, Responses and Psalm 119: 145–76	
Palmer	Preces and Psalm 118: 24–end	Easter Evensong
Parsons (?)	Preces and Psalms 6–8	
Ramsey	Litany (Latin)	
	Litany I	
	Litany II (from Service in F)	
Smith, Edward	Preces and Psalm 8	Ascension Matins
	Preces and Psalm 119: 1–8, 169–76	All Saints
Smith, W.	Preces and Responses	
	Preces and Psalms 85	Christmas Matins
	110	Christmas Evensong
	111	Easter Matins
	57: 9–12 and	
	118: 19–24	Easter Evensong
	67	Whitsunday Matins
Tallis	First Preces and Responses	
	Second Preces and Responses	
	Psalm 119: 19–32	24th Evensong
	Psalms 110 and 132	Christmas Evensong
	Psalm 119: 145–end	26th Evensong
	Litany I	
	Litany II	
Tomkins, T.	Preces and Psalms 15	Ascension Matins
	47	Ascension Evensong
	Litany I	
	Litany II	
Wanless	Litany	
Wilson, T.	Psalm 85	Christmas Matins
	Litany (Latin)	

Tallis would seem to have been the first to write festal-psalm settings. His extant psalms consist of the three proper to Christmas Evensong and the ordinary psalms for the 24th and the 26th evenings of the month — evidently a Christmas cycle. The psalms for the 24th and 26th evenings are, unfortunately, too incomplete to be restored. The Christmas evensong chants, which are complete, are chordal harmonisations of the first and seventh Sarum tones. Tallis' simple system was adopted by several later composers, notably Amner and Farrant (Psalm 21, the first of the three for "obiit Sunday"), but the majority of the settings are of a more complex kind. The psalms by Byrd (excepting Psalm 114 and the "Attolite portas" adaptation), Gibbons (Psalm 145: 1–14), Marson, Morley (Psalm 119: 145–68), Edward Smith, Tomkins and Wilson are less obviously chant-like in structure but they none the less include elements of repetition, though none are based on the Sarum tones. Several psalms are in a simple verse style, including Byrd's Psalm 119: 33, Child's Psalm 67, and Farrant's third "obiit" psalm, and there are others in a surprisingly elaborate verse idiom, notably those of Gibbons (Psalms 145: 15–20, 57 and 118), Palmer and William Smith. There are even two festal psalms—the "Attolite portas" adaptation, and Edward Smith's "O Lord our governor" (also attributed to William Mundy)—which were also used independently as anthems.

The earliest Litany dates from 1544, when Cranmer's English version first appeared in print. Its notation is remarkably similar to that of Merbecke's *booke of Common praier noted* and the style of the music owes much to Sarum originals, as does Merbecke's. The first harmonised versions of the Litany are to be found in the Wanley books and, like all the later settings, they are in a straightforward chordal style. No fewer than six different harmonisations by Cambridge composers were copied into the Peterhouse part-books during the 1630s.

Before embarking upon a discussion of the main liturgical forms—the Service and anthem—a word should perhaps be said of that much despised appendage, the organ voluntary (see Appendix II). At St. Paul's, after the Restoration, there were usually organ voluntaries before the reading of the first lesson at Matins and Evensong.[7] How far this reflected earlier practice it is hard to tell. Certainly in early Elizabethan times many divines were opposed to the use of the organ in church, and evidence is not hard to find of the neglect and destruction of instruments. As Dr. Steele has remarked, "the Elizabethan period, while not exactly poor in organ music, was nevertheless restricted. All the major organists were connected in some way or other with the Chapel Royal, and royal patronage may well have kept organ music alive in England during critical times ...."[8] The "renaissance" in organ building that occurred during the early 1600s[9] closely followed the new fashion for verse Services and verse anthems, and there are signs that there was a parallel revival of interest in the art of solo organ playing.

Several musicians won praise from their contemporaries for their prowess at the keyboard: William Blitheman, organist of the Chapel Royal from 1585 until his death in 1591; John Bull, his most distinguished pupil and even today still something of a legend; Orlando Gibbons, "the best finger of the age", organist of the Chapel Royal and Westminster Abbey, and privy organist to James I; John Tomkins, who became organist of the Chapel Royal the year after Gibbons died and who, in his turn, was described as "organista sui temporis celeberrimus"; Thomas Holmes, organist of Winchester Cathedral and for a short while Gentleman of the Chapel Royal, whom Hammond described as "one of the rarest organists" of his day; and John Parsons, organist of Westminster Abbey, whose unusual epitaph found its way into the 1657 edition of Camden's *Remaines Concerning Britain*:

> Death passing by and hearing Parsons play,
> Stood much amazed at his depth of skill,
> And said, this artist must with me away,
> (For death bereaves us of the better, still)
> But let the choir, while he keeps time, sing on
> For Parson[s] rests, his service being done.

In all probability customs differed from cathedral to cathedral as to the use of organ music. At Exeter, for instance, where Edward Gibbons was choirmaster, there may often have been a short voluntary before the anthem.[10]

Prelude . . before the Anthem.   Edward Gibbons

The Chapel Royal Check Book furnishes more evidence than any other single source on the liturgical use of the organ.[11] "Offertories" were commonly played during the course of the communion and ante-communion services as, for example, at the christening of Princess Mary in May 1605. And on the same occasion, organ music heralded the arrival of the "noble babe" at the Chapel door and covered up the clatterings and scufflings of the outgoing procession.

One of the more unusual occasions which the Chapel Royal organists witnessed was the signing of the oath between Spain and England "for the maintenance and continuance of the league between them" in August 1604. A table had been placed some 3 ft or so in front of the altar "whereupon there lay writings and a stand with pen and ink". As the king and the Spanish ambassadors arrived, "the organs played". The ceremony then began with an anthem, after which came the signing of the treaty, a further anthem and an outgoing voluntary. A similar event took place six years later—the ambassadors on that occasion being French. At every musical service described in the Check Book, indeed, organ music was used to cover those unavoidable and uncomfortable pauses that inevitably attend any extraordinary ceremony.

One of the most charming accounts of the use of organ music—other than at the Chapel Royal—is to be found in a description of the entertainment offered to the French ambassadors by John Williams, Dean of Westminster Abbey, in 1624;[12] the Frenchmen were in London to negotiate the marriage of Henrietta Maria to Prince Charles. Prior to a banquet in the Jerusalem Chamber at Westminster Abbey, the visitors were taken into the Abbey itself "that they might cast their eyes on the stateliness of the church."

> At their entrance, the organ was touched by the best finger of that age, Mr. Orlando Gibbons . . . and while a verse was played, The Lord Keeper presented the ambassadors and the rest of the noblest quality of their nation with [the] liturgy as it spake to them in their own language. The Lords ambassadors and their great train took up all the stalls, where they continued half an hour while the choirmen, vested in their rich copes, with their choristers, sang three several anthems, with most exquisite voices before them. . . .

When we come to examine the repertory of Elizabethan and early seventeenth-century keyboard music we are faced with the considerable difficulty of differentiating organ music from virginals music. No instrumentation is specified in the extant sources, the two printed collections only excepted— *Parthenia or the Maydenhead of the first musicke that ever was printed for the Virginalls* (1612–13), and *Parthenia In-Violata or Mayden-Musicke for the Virginalls and Bass-Viol* (1625?). The only categories that can be excluded with certainty from this survey of liturgical organ music are the dance forms, and the sets of variations on secular tunes. The fugal forms— the Voluntary, Verse and Point—are in general well suited for the organ and entirely appropriate for use in church. Plainsong fantasias, on the other hand, which form the bulk of the repertory, are less easy to categorise. Plainsong had no place in the reformed services, of course, though it has been suggested that the psalms and responses continued to be sung to Sarum intonations, in forms adapted to suit the English words. The plainsong fantasias, however, make use of far more highly developed Sarum chants; and in the large virtuoso fantasias, at least, the plainsongs are clearly audible from start to finish. This alone would seem to disqualify them from use in the reformed services. They are, moreover, so difficult to play that they must surely have been beyond the reach of all but the very greatest organists. Tallis' two long settings of the Offertory, "Felix namque", are of this kind; and although it is just possible to imagine them in performance at the Chapel Royal, it is surely more probable that they were originally written to provide an evening's entertainment at Court.

Some of the principal ideas used by Tallis in the first setting of "Felix namque"

It is worth recalling, in this context, the visit of Dionisius Memo, one of the organists at St. Mark's, Venice, to London in 1516, during which he played to a distinguished company, including the king himself, for some four hours on a small chamber organ.[13] No doubt Elizabeth was equally appreciative of good organ music, for she too was a more than competent performer on the virginals. The smaller plainsong fantasias to be found in Elizabethan sources, on the other hand, are for the most part so short that they must surely have been designed for use in conjunction with the liturgical plainsongs. Tallis' "Ecce tempus idoneum" is typical of this genre, the plainsong being used as a basis for an imitative texture rather than as a set cantus firmus:

Apart from a single psalm-prelude in the Mulliner Book, two substantial Voluntaries and a handful of smallish Verses and Points, the "organ" repertory in Elizabethan sources consists entirely of imitative and cantus firmus plainsongs.

The forms and figurations explored by the composers of Tallis' generation were exploited to the full by the younger Elizabethans and above all by John Bull, possibly the only English organist of the age with a truly international reputation. It must be admitted, again, that much of this music is of ephemeral interest. Carleton's extraordinary expedition into the remote keys may herald the development of the classical tonal system but it would be idle to pretend that it or Bull's chromatic "Ut, re, mi, fa, sol, la", which attempts the same thing, are at all coherent.

Nor can Bull's curious essay in 11/4 time be now regarded as of more than historical interest. Of all the major organist-composers, Orlando Gibbons managed to produce the most consistently satisfying work, possibly because he altogether avoided (as far is as known) the plainsong fantasia forms. His fantasias are freely imitative and, in this sense, forward-looking. His "Fantasia for Double Organ" is the first of its kind, involving the fugal and sequential interchange of melodic fragments between "Great" and "Chaire".

There are four other double-organ fantasias by pre-Restoration composers: one by Richard Portman, the Westminster Abbey organist (1633–Civil War), and three by the virtuoso organist of Exeter Cathedral, John Lugge. Portman's composition, though rambling, clearly foreshadows the Restoration organ style of Blow and Locke:

A Verse for Double Organ   Richard Portman

Lugge's compositions, and the Voluntaries in particular, are strikingly idiomatic, the ideas being developed with commendable economy. Hammond described the organ at Exeter as "delicate, rich and lofty . . . having more additions than any other, as fair pipes of an extraordinary length and of the bigness of a man's thigh". Lugge would seem to have been fully worthy of such an instrument.

Most of Tomkins' extant organ music dates from the late 1640s and early 1650s, when the composer was nearing his seventieth birthday.[14] It is, from the formal point of view, a retrospective collection, most of the compositions being based on plainsongs and soggettos. If indeed such pieces as the Offertory and the eight Misereres are properly organ music

(Dr. Steele rejects the four undated Misereres and the Offertory on stylistic grounds), they show the transference to the organ of techniques that would normally be considered more appropriate to the virginals (see foot of page 169).

Yet again the cantus firmus settings tend to ramble, the ideas being bewilderingly profuse and all too often unmemorable. For Tomkins was far more successful, as were his distinguished contemporaries, in the more disciplined secular forms of the dance and the variation.

NOTES TO CHAPTER 6

1. Harrison, W., ch. 1: "saving that in the administration of the Communion the choir singeth the answers, the Creed, and sundry other things appointed but in so plain, I say and distinct manner, that each one present may understand what they sing, every word having but one note, though the whole harmony consist of many parts, and those very cunningly set by those skilful in that science . . ."; presumably "canticles" come under the general heading of "psalms": Harrison clearly knew very little about church music.

2. Information very kindly supplied by Mr. Alan Smith.

3. Palmer; the chapter entitled "Psalmody", and its appendix. No evidence has yet been found to show that the tones may have been simply harmonised in faux bourdon style, though the simpler type of Anglican festal psalm is very obviously in the faux bourdon tradition. Morley's "first tune" (see below) was adapted by Burgess and Shaw as a *Magnificat and Nunc Dimittis . . . with verses in faux bourdon* (Novello, 1913).

4. Excluding, that is, John Playford's "Order of Performing the Divine Service in Cathedrals and Collegiate Chapels", which did not appear in the *Introduction to the Skill of Musick* (first edition 1654) until the seventh edition 1674).

5. The third and sixth tones are lacking.

6. In 1562 a motion was debated in the Lower House of Convocation, "that the psalms appointed at common prayer be sung distinctly by the whole congregation, or said with the other prayers by the minister alone, in such convenient place in the church as all may well hear and be edified . . ." (Strype, p. 298); the wording of this motion confirms that the proper psalms must often have been sung chorally, and that the words of the psalms can rarely have been intelligible.

7. Clifford (1664).

8. Steele, J., p. 144; the greater part of this brief survey is based upon this study.

9. Clutton; Steele, J.; Sumner.

10. British Museum, Harley MS. 7340.
11. Rimbault.
12. Hacket, p. 210.
13. Wooldridge, p. 459.
14. Stevens, D. (i), "Music for Keyboard Instruments", p. 120.

7

Edwardian and Early Elizabethan Church Music

At least a dozen composers were writing for the new English services during the early years of the Reformation, including Tye and Tallis (already in their late forties or early fifties when the first Prayer Book was published), John Shepherd (then about thirty), William Mundy (Shepherd's junior by some ten years), and a number of comparatively minor figures, most of them London and Chapel Royal musicians: Robert Adams, John Brimley, Thomas Caustun, Richard Farrant, John Heath, Robert Johnson, Robert Morecocke, Robert Okeland, Osbert Parsley, Robert Stone and [Thomas] Whytbroke. Little of their music can be dated with any certainty and, as most of them were still very much alive during the early years of Elizabeth's reign, it will be at once convenient and practical to consider the Edwardian and early Elizabethan periods as one.

THE EDWARDIAN AND EARLY ELIZABETHAN SOURCES

1. *The Wanley Books* are easily the most valuable of the extant Edwardian sources. Originally there were four part-books in the set—two altos, a tenor and a bass—but the tenor book was already missing when the set passed into the hands of Humphrey Wanley early in the eighteenth century. Most

of the Wanley music is in four parts and scored for men's voices, though there are one or two four- and five-part settings for men and boys. The Wanley books would seem to have been copied out for a small parish church or private chapel, where services were normally sung by "clerks"—as was the case in many London churches at that time—and where, on festal occasions, boys were borrowed from a neighbouring choir school.[1] To judge from appearances, the books were

TABLE 15
The Wanley Part-Books

Number	Title		Text source (where known)
[Part I]			
1	A Kyrie	K	1549
2	The Communion	K.G.Cr.Sa.Ag. [Heath]	?; Apostles' Creed 1545
3	Magnificat	Ma	1539
4	Nunc dimittis	N	1545
5	Domine, secundum actum	In judgement, Lord	
6	Magnificat	Ma	1539
7	Nunc dimittis	N [Tye]	1535
8	Antem	I give you a new commandment [Shepherd]	
9	Antem	O praise the Lord (Psalm 147)	
10	Postcommunion	Happy are those servants	1549
11	Antem	In no kind of creature	
12	The Communion	K.G.Sa.Ag.	1549
13	Offertory	Charge them that are rich	1549
14	Postcommunion	The night is passed	1549
15	At Burial	Funeral sentences: I am the resurrection I know that my redeemer liveth We brought nothing Man that is born In the midst of life I heard a voice	1549
16	Antem	Make ye melody unto the Lord	
17	Antem	I am the true vine	
18	Antem	Submit yourselves [Shepherd]	
19	Antem	Happy is the people	
20	Christus resurgens	Christ rising again: Christ is risen	1549
21	Antem	O most merciful Jesu Christ	
22	Antem	Lord Jesu Christ, Son of the living God	1545

(*Table 15 continued overleaf*)

TABLE 15 *(continued)*

Number	Title		Text source (where known)
23		Bs	1549
24	Antem	This is my commandment [Tallis or W. Mundy]	
25	Weddings	Blessed art thou that fearest God	Sternhold, 1549
26	Usque quo Domine	How long wilt Thou forget me	
27	Antem: Deus in adiutorium	Haste Thee, O God	
28	Antem	Hear the voice and prayer [Tallis]	
29	Antem	Praise we the father [Okeland]	1535
30	Te Deum	Te	
31	Postcommunion	I am the voice of a crier	
[Part II]			
1		Ma	1549
2		N	1549
3		Ma	1545?
[there are no further		Bs	1549?
numbers or titles in this		Ma	1549
volume]		N	1549
		Te	1549
		Bs	1549 (or 1545?)
		V	1549
		Let all the congregation [Caustun]	? : metrical
		All people hearken	Sternhold, 1549
		Praise be to God; come Holy Ghost	
		The spirit of the Lord	
		Be	1545
		O clap your hands together	
		O eternal God almighty [Johnson]	
		Remember not, Lord, our old iniquities	1545
		If ye love me [Tallis]	
		Praise the Lord, O our souls [Okeland]	
		Verily, verily . . . except ye eat	
		Christ rising again: Christ is risen	1549
		O Lord, the maker of all things	1545
		O God, the father of heaven (the Litany)	1549
		Our father	1535 and 39
		Our father [Stone]	1545
		K.G.Cr.Sa.Ag.	1549
		Christ our paschall lamb	
		K.G.Cr.Sa.Ag.	?; Apostles' Creed 1545
		K.G.Cr.Sa.Ag.	?; Apostles' Creed 1545
		Christ our paschall lamb [Shepherd]	
5 parts		God be merciful unto us [Taverner,	

TABLE 15 (continued)

Number	Title		Text source (where known)
		adapted from "Mater Christi"]	
		An untexted hymn (?) tune	
		Let your light so shine	
[Part III]			
[1]	The Communion	K.G.Cr.Sa.Ag.	1549
2	Antem	O Lord of hosts [Shepherd]	
3	After the Communion received	O almighty God, the father	
4	Antem	Praise the Lord, O ye servants	
[5]		O God, in whose hands are the hearts	
6	Venite	Come let us rejoice unto the Lord	1545
[7]	Te Deum	Te	1549
8	Benedictus	Bs	1549
9	The Procession	O God the father of heaven	1549
10	Pater noster	Our father	1545
11		I have not my hope	
12	The Communion	K.G.Cr.Sa.Ag. and including	?; Apostles' Creed 1545
	Offertory	Lay not up for yourselves	1549
	Postcommunion	If any man will follow me	1549
13	Magnificat	Ma [Whytbroke]	1549
14	Christus resurgens	Christ rising again; Christ is risen	1549
15	For Ash Wednesday	Turn Thou us, good Lord	
16		Ma	1535?
17		N	1549
18	Antem	Walk while ye have light	
19	Offertory	Do ye not know	1549
20	Postcommunion	If any man will follow me	1549
21	Antem	If a man say I love God	
22	5. parts for men	K.G.Cr.Sa.Ag.	1549
23	5. parts	G.Cr.Sa.Ag. [adapted from Taverner's "Meane" Mass]	1549
[24]	5. parts	G.Cr.Sa.Ag. [adapted from Taverner's "Small Devotion" Mass]	1549
		Come let us sing unto the Lord	1549
		K	1552

Key to reference numbers:

1535	A Goodly Primer [Marshall's Primer]
1539	The Manual of Prayers [Hilsey's Primer]
1545	The Primer set forth by the King's Majesty [The King's Primer]
1549	The booke of the common prayer
Sternhold, 1549	Certayne Psalmes, Thomas Sternhold, 1549
1552	The Boke of common prayer

completed within a comparatively short space of time—in all probability between 1549 and 1552—since at the very beginning of the books are settings of texts from the 1549 Prayer Book and at the very end is a single 1552 Prayer Book text: "Lord have mercy upon us".

The Wanley repertory is a large one, covering a wide range of forms and styles. The music throughout is anonymous, though concordances with later sources have in one or two cases revealed the name of a composer.

Most of the Wanley music is likely to date from the experimental years of 1547 and 1548 and afterwards. The possibility cannot altogether be ruled out, none the less, that one or two pieces were written for private devotional use some little time before the Edwardian reformation. Two of the earliest texts come from the so-called "Marshall" Primer of c. 1535;[2] one is an anthem by Okeland—"Praise we the Father" the other a setting of "Nunc dimittis" by Tye. Text and music do not necessarily date from the same year, of course, but the strangely melismatic underlay and the lengthy imitative points of Tye's "Nunc dimittis" suggest that this, at least, is an early work.

At least three English Primers were published during the 1530s and 1540s. The earliest—"Marshall's" of c. 1535—was officially banned in 1542, though copies of it remained in circulation for many years afterwards. The others were Hilsey's Primer of 1539 and the so-called King's Primer of 1545 which replaced it. All three contain English translations of the daily offices of Matins, Lauds, Prime, Terce, Sext, None, Vespers and Compline, together with English versions of the Apostles' Creed and the Lord's Prayer and private prayers for all occasions. During the years immediately before the publication of the first English Prayer Book, the Primers furnished the most readily available and most acceptable translations of the daily offices, and it is hardly surprising therefore to find that many of the Wanley texts come from these books.

Music for the communion service occupies by far the most important place in the Wanley repertory. Six of the ten complete settings follow the wording of the 1549 Prayer Book, with only very minor variants. Numbers one, four, five and seven, however, use an earlier version, possibly the first draft translation drawn up for use in Westminster Abbey in November 1547 at the state opening of Parliament and Convocation (see page 10). This early version seems to have been made in something of a hurry, since the King's Primer translation of the Apostles' Creed was used in place of the correct Nicene Creed, of which no published translation was then available. All but the last two Masses are for men's voices. They cover, none the less, a remarkably wide range of styles. The first and fifth are simple chant-like settings suitable for daily parish-church use:

Mass No. 1   Heath

Tenor or   And peace on the earth, and un-to men a good-will
Bass missing

The third, fourth, sixth and seventh are contrapuntal, with frequent exchanges between the upper and lower voices, in the Flemish manner, and mainly syllabic underlay:

The eighth is a rather more elaborate and highly imitative five-part setting for men's voices:

The second, ninth and tenth are adaptations of Latin originals; the second does not readily lend itself to such treatment but the ninth and tenth—Taverner's Flemish "Sine nomine" and "Small Devotion" Masses—are admirably suited to the purpose:

The settings of the "proper" of the Mass—in this case the Offertory and Postcommunion—are by comparison disappointing, being for the most part in a syllabic, chant-like idiom.

The Wanley books also contain much music for other liturgical occasions: for weddings, for funerals, for the Litany and for the daily offices of Matins and Evensong. There are three paired settings of the canticles for Matins and five for Evensong, besides half a dozen or so separate settings. Four of these are in a fairly elaborate polyphonic idiom: the "Nunc dimittis" by Tye discussed above, and three English adaptations of Latin originals. The others are again predominantly chant-like in structure.

In neither of the two Edwardian Prayer Books is there any mention of the "anthem". Nevertheless, there are seventeen "antems", so-named, in the Wanley books and another dozen or so anthem-like compositions besides. At what points in the service these would have been sung is an open question, but some may well have been fitted in after Matins and Evensong as votive antiphons had been after Lauds, Compline and Vespers.

The texts of the Wanley anthems are mainly biblical, though there are three metrical psalms (two by Sternhold) and a number of prayers.[3] Quite a few of these works are in binary form, the second half being repeated. Shepherd's "I give you a new commandment", Tallis' "Hear the voice and prayer" and the two Okeland anthems are all in this category. It is curious that this one particular repeat form should have been so popular at that time. Repetition forms were much used abroad for both sacred and secular compositions, but the A|: B:|| structure seems to have been one of the rarer ones.

Few of the Wanley anthems are of any great musical interest, though here and there a composer attempted and achieved something out of the ordinary. The opening of "How long wilt Thou forget me", for example, sets the mood of the text in a way that Zarlino would have applauded; the word accentuation is acceptable, and there are some telling minor intervals, chords, suspensions and passing dissonances:

2. *The Lumley Books.* Of the other Edwardian sources, British Museum MSS. Royal App. 74–6 is the most important. Like Wanley, there were originally four part-books—Triplex, Contratenor, Tenor and Bass—though one (the bass) is now missing. These were apparently the property of the Fitzalans during the 1560s—if not earlier—and later of the Lumleys. A galliard, added in a later hand, is dedicated to one of the Fitzalans—"Mi Lord Mark's galiarde, My Lord of Arundell". —and the name Lumley is scribbled into one of the books. The earliest sections of the Lumley books date from 1549 or thereabouts and contain anthems, metrical psalms, and a few canticles. But there is no music at all for the communion service, apart from one short setting of the 1552 Kyrie. This suggests that the books may well have been designed for private use—perhaps even for the family chapel at Arundel Castle. The music is predominantly homophonic in texture and there are none of the highly melismatic adaptations from Latin

originals that are to be found in the Wanley books. One or
two pieces, however, are of considerable length, notably a
Magnificat based on the Marshall Primer translation which is
over 150 measures long (four minims to a measure).

3. *Certaine notes* (1565). Of the few extant Elizabethan
sources, John Day's *Certaine notes set forth in fowre and three
parts* is at once the earliest and the most important. Recent
research has established that this work passed through no more
than one edition and that its publication, originally planned
for 1560, was delayed for five years.[4] The cause of this delay
can only be guessed at, but Day may well have felt for a time
that the future of church music was too uncertain to justify
such an undertaking (see chapter 2, page 31). Most of the
music that Day included in *Certaine notes* must have been composed during the Edwardian period: the first half of the bass
book (to folio M ii) had already been set up and printed by
1560 when work stopped, and no fewer than six of the anthems
to be found in the subsequent pages are in the Edwardian
Wanley books. Heath's Communion Service—the first in
Wanley (cf. p. 177)—reappears, too, in *Certaine notes*, greatly
modified to fit the wording and form of service in the 1552
Prayer Book. That so simple a setting should have been thought
worthy of preservation in this way suggests that music of the
kind can then have been none too plentiful:

Like Wanley, *Certaine notes* seems to have been intended as
much for the parish church as the cathedral since more than
half the settings are for men's voices and all are in a fairly
simple four-part idiom (Day may have intended to include
some three-part pieces in the collection as the title page suggests,
but for some reason these did not materialise). There are

altogether three complete Morning, Communion and Evening Services, two for men and one for full MATB choir. Each Service includes the Venite, Te Deum, Benedictus, Kyrie, Creed, Sanctus, Gloria, Magnificat and Nunc dimittis. There are also two alternative Evening Services—both for men—sixteen anthems, and some incidental items—Offertories, a setting of the Lord's Prayer and a Litany. Day's choice of music is an odd one, since he included none at all by Tye and Mundy—two of the foremost composers of the time—but a very great deal by Caustun, a composer who hardly figures at all in any other sources. The work, as a whole, gives the impression of having been thrown together without a great deal of knowledge or care.

Had no music survived from this early period other than the Wanley, Lumley, and Day compositions, enough material would still exist to show that a wide variety of forms and styles were being tried out during the early years of the Reformation. Much additional music is also to be found in late Elizabethan and early seventeenth-century sources to supplement this picture:[5]

TABLE 16

Edwardian and Early Elizabethan Services and Anthems
(All are for full four-part choir unless stated)

Robert Adams (fl. 1550)	Venite* Nunc dimittis
John Brimley (c. 1500–76)	Creed to Shepherd's Second Service Te Deum, Benedictus and Kyrie*
Thomas Caustun (?–1569)	A Morning, Communion and two Evening Services for men (Ve. Te. Bs. [K.] Cr. Sa. G. Ma. N.) A Morning, Communion and Evening Service for full choir (as above) In trouble and adversity (adapted from Taverner) Let all the congregation* Most blessed Lord O most high and eternal King Rejoice in the Lord Show us thy light Turn Thou us

(*Table 16 continued overleaf*)

G

TABLE 16 (*continued*)

Richard Farrant (?–1581)	A Morning, Communion, and Evening Service (Te. Bs. K. Cr. Ma. N.), called the Third, High or Short Call to remembrance Hide not Thou thy face Lord, for thy tender mercy's sake (or Hilton snr.) When as we sat in Babylon
Farrant	A Benedicite for men*
Ferying	O merciful Father, we beseech Thee
William Fox (?–1579)	Teach me thy way
John Franclynge	O God, for thy name sake
Heath (fl. 1550)	A Morning and Communion Service* (V. Te. Bs. K. Cr. Sa. Ag. G.) for men
Robert Johnson (c. 1490–c. 1560)	A Morning, Communion and Evening Service (Te. Bs. Cr. Ma. N.)* (f5?) A Te Deum and Jubilate Benedicam Domino/O Lord with all my heart I give you a new commandment O eternal God almighty* O happy man, if thou repent Relieve us, O Lord
John Merbecke (c. 1510–85)	A virgin and mother* (f3) *The booke of Common praier noted** (monodic)
[Robert] Merricocke, or Morecocke (?–1581)	A Te Deum, Magnificat and Nunc dimittis*
William Mundy (c. 1525–)	(see below, p. 209)
Robert Okeland (fl. c. 1550)	Praise the Lord, O our souls* Praise we the Father*
Osbert Parsley (?–1585)	Two Morning Services (Te Deum and Benedictus)*
Robert Parsons (?–1570)	The First Morning, Communion and Evening Service (V. Te. Bs. K. Cr. Ma. N)* (f4–8) The Second Morning Service for meanes, in five parts (V. Te. Bs.) The Service for two counter-tenors of five parts (Te. Bs. K. Cr.) Deliver me from mine enemies (f6) Holy, Lord God almighty I (f5) Holy, Lord God almighty II (f5)
William Parsons (fl. c. 1550)	Almighty God, whose kingdom Out from the deep (or Tallis) Remember not, O Lord Wherewithal shall a young man

TABLE 16 (continued)

John Shepherd (?–c. 1560)	(See below p. 205)
Robert Stone (1516–1613)	The Lord's Prayer*
Thomas Tallis (c. 1500–85)	(See below, p. 193)
[John] Thorne (?–1573)	A Te Deum*
Christopher Tye (c. 1500–71)	(See below, p. 199)
Robert White (?–1574)	Lord, who shall dwell (f5) O Lord, deliver me (adapted from, Manus tuae) O Lord, how glorious (or Hooper) (f5) Praise the Lord (adapted from, Domine, non est exaltatum) The Lord bless us and keep us (f5)
[Thomas] Whytbroke (c. 1495–1568)	A Magnificat and Nunc dimittis* Let your light so shine
Thomas Whythorne (1528–96)	A Venite and Jubilate Almighty God, thy loving care Behold, now praise the Lord . . . ye that by night Is there no choice for me I will yield thanks to Thee My soul and all that in me is O good Lord, have mercy upon me O Lord above, send us thy grace O our father Out of the deep have I called Since I embrace the heavenly grace The divers chance that God doth send The great offence of my most sinful ghost Though fortune frown on me Unto Thee lift I up mine eyes When I remember of this world (There are also a dozen or so two-part devotional songs)
Philip van Wilder (?–1552)	Blessed art thou that fearest God (possibly by Peter Philips) (f5)

* Items marked thus are based on texts not later in date than 1552.

Most of the musicians named above came from London and were at some time or other members of the Chapel Royal choir. Nothing is yet known of three—Ferying, Franclynge and Robert Johnson. Of the rest, only six lived and worked for much of the time in the provinces—Brimley at Durham,

Fox at Ely, Merbecke at Windsor, William Parsons at Wells, Parsley at Norwich and Thorne at York; Robert White moved from Ely to Westminster Abbey (probably via Chester) in about 1570, [Thomas] Whytbroke spent some time at St. Paul's Cathedral; Heath may be identified with the Conduct, Lawrence Heath, whose name appears in the records of several London city churches between 1549 and 1590; whilst Thomas Whythorne, though not primarily a church musician, did none the less direct the music in Archbishop Parker's private chapel for two or three years. Most of the other dozen or so musicians listed above had graduated to the Chapel Royal through one or other of the London parish-church choirs.

The quantity of "provincial" music surviving from this earliest period is very small indeed. The compositions that have so far come to light do, nevertheless, show a wide variation of styles. Thorne's Te Deum is by far the simplest—to judge, that is, from the single part that has survived—and it may well have been written to meet Archbishop Holgate's stringent requirements (see Chapter 1, page 25). Certainly it has none of the "reportings" and "repeatings" that the Archbishop was so keen to avoid.

Te Deum   Thorne

All the earth   doth worship Thee,   the Fa - ther e - ver - last - ing.   To Thee Che -

- ru - bin and Se - ra - phin   con - tin - u - al - ly do   cry.

The Brimley Te Deum and Benedictus, based on the 1549 Prayer Book translation, is in a more sophisticated Short Service style with occasional points of imitation and some repetitions of phrase. The same composer's Kyrie to Shepherd's Second and most elaborate Service is itself an extraordinarily complex work. With all repeats, it is almost a hundred bars long. Whether or not so grand a setting as Shepherd's Second Service was in the Durham repertory during Brimley's time is perhaps unlikely. Brimley was seriously involved in the

Catholic rising in 1569, and there can be little doubt that he was at heart a Catholic. His Creed may not be entirely typical, therefore, of the music that was in the cathedral repertory at the time (but see page 39):

Robert Johnson's Services and anthems are in the simpler, more compressed idiom of the day. The Morning, Communion and Evening Service is not without interest, since in places the composer seems to be working towards a freely unmetrical *musique mesurée* style, of the kind that Claude le Jeune was using at about the same time for his settings of metrical psalm verses.[6]

(the barring is original)

Thomas Whythorne spent most of his career in secular musical activities of one kind or another.[7] Unfortunately, none of the music that he wrote for Archbishop Parker's private chapel has survived, but the canticles and anthems in the *Songs for three, fouer and five Voyces* published in 1571, very shortly before the composer took up his duties at Lambeth, probably give a fair idea of his "liturgical" style. Although the composer was widely travelled—he had spent at least two years abroad in the Low Countries, Germany, Italy and France—his music shows little evidence of this and the technical quality of his work leaves much to be desired. This Venite, for instance, is in a "Short" Service style, but it lacks both the structural ingenuity of Tallis' Short Service and its melodic charm (the use of chiavettes in the original edition suggests a downward transposition of the music to bring it into the normal MATB compass):

Apart from the plainsongs in *The booke of Common praier noted* and a devotional three-part anthem, none of Merbecke's English music has survived—if indeed it ever existed. Nor has any music yet come to light by several of Merbecke's distinguished contemporaries, including Richard Edwardes and William Hunnis (Masters of the Chapel Royal choristers) and the organists John Redford, Philip ap Rhys and William Blitheman.

Of the non-Chapel Royal composers of this period Robert White is unquestionably pre-eminent, though for his Latin rather than for his English work. White was probably born some time between 1530 and 1535—the University grace recording the award of his Mus.B. mentions that he had been a student of music for ten years. In 1561 he went to Ely Cathedral as Tye's successor, probably moving from there to Chester in about 1567 and from thence to London towards the end of 1568 or soon afterwards. At the time of his death in 1574—he died of the plague—he was Master of the Choristers at Westminster Abbey. A substantial amount of his Latin music is for the Sarum rite and must therefore date from the Marian reaction: there are four *alternatim* settings of the Compline hymn "Christe qui lux es", an *alternatim* Magnificat, a "Libera me" from the Burial Service, two fine sets of Lamentations, and two cantus firmus antiphons, "Tota pulchra es" and "Regina celi", this later setting being remarkably "expressive" in spite of its traditionally English structure.

The other Latin compositions are based on texts from the psalms, and as they lack any specific liturgical function they may well be of somewhat later date. White shows here a predilection for the penitential moods and a fondness for richly expressive melodies and textures.

In view of the outstanding quality of his Latin work, it is particularly unfortunate that so little of his English music has survived. There are no festal psalms, Responses or Services, and only five anthems. Of these five, two are adaptations of psalm motets ("O Lord deliver me" is from "Manus tuae fecerunt me", and "Praise the Lord" from "Domine, non est exaltatum"), whilst a third, "O Lord how glorious", is also attributed to Edmund Hooper. The other two—"Lord who shall dwell" and "The Lord bless us"—are both in a learnedly imitative motet style and of unusually large proportions. "Lord, who shall dwell" is some eighty-five measures long, "The Lord bless us" well over sixty, and both are for five-part choir. The possibility cannot be ruled out, of course, that these, too, are adaptations, for the underlay is, in places, far from satisfactory.

Of the minor Chapel Royal composers, neither Adams, Morecocke, Okeland nor Stone are of any great consequence, though Stone's charming setting of the Lord's Prayer rightly has a place in the modern repertory. Three other minor figures do, however, deserve some notice—Richard Farrant, Master of the Windsor and Chapel Royal choristers, Robert Parsons and Thomas Caustun, both Gentlemen of the Chapel. Not a note of Caustun's music is to be found in the pre-Restoration liturgical sources, nor is the composer's name mentioned in either the Chapel Royal anthem book (c. 1630) or in Clifford's *Divine Services and Anthems* of 1663 and 1664. Most of the composer's extant work is likely to date from the Edwardian period, since it was already being set up by Day in 1560 (and perhaps in 1559) for the *Certaine notes*. The two Services for men's voices—a complete Morning, Communion and Evening Service, and an alternative Magnificat and Nunc dimittis—are in chant form and of little musical interest. The Service "for children"—that is to say for MATB—is, on the other hand, well written and in its way quite as "expressive" as Tallis' Short Service. Two of Caustun's anthems are adapted works, one originally being an instrumental "In nomine":

by Taverner: the second being an adapted viol song (see p. 223). Two of the other four anthems are for men—"Rejoice in the Lord" and "Shew us, O Lord". Both are in binary form and in a workmanlike part-imitative, part-chordal style. "O most high" is in Day's ... *the whole psalmes* of 1563, a simple, homophonic anthem for MATB with a strange semi-imitative opening. "Most blessed Lord Jesu", also for MATB, is by far the largest of Caustun's anthems, being well over seventy bars long. It is also one of his most attractive, especially in the conflict of modalities between the four voices, two of which have an open key signature, two a key signature of one flat.

Richard Farrant is mainly of interest for his pioneering work in connection with the early verse anthem, of which more will be said below (see page 217). The two well-known four-part anthems and the Short Service are the only compositions of his in the full style that have yet come to light. The Service was widely sung during the late sixteenth and early seventeenth centuries, being in a simple, singable idiom and well within the capabilities of the smallest cathedral choir. In at least one pre-Restoration source it is numbered the Third, implying that there were two or more others, now lost, perhaps of "Great" Service dimensions and thus of limited use. "Hide not Thou thy face", the simplest of the two anthems, has been discussed above (page 144) as showing, in a modest way, the late sixteenth-century trend towards a new and subjective liturgical style. Similar qualities characterise the Service and the other anthem, "Call to remembrance", though the composer's rhythmic limitations tend to stand out rather more obviously.

Robert Parsons had only been a member of the Chapel Royal choir for seven years when he came to an untimely end in the River Trent at Newark. Nothing is known of him before 1563—the year in which he joined the Chapel Royal choir—but it does seem as though he must have written his massive First Service by 1553, since it is based on texts from the 1549 Prayer Book. This Service is one of the most elaborate of all the extant Edwardian and Elizabethan settings, and it would be interesting to know where it was first performed.

Though the composer used neither harmony nor melody with any very obviously "expressive" intent, he does seem at times to have used texture with this end in view. The Nunc dimittis of this Service, for instance, is scored in the following manner: "Lord, now lettest Thou thy servant depart in peace, according to thy word" (5 parts). "For mine eyes have seen thy salvation" (4 parts dec.), "which thou hast prepared before the face of all people" (4 parts can.); "to be a light to lighten the Gentiles" (5 parts full), "and to be the glory of thy people Israel" (increasing from 4 to 8 parts). The Gloria is in seven parts throughout. Parsons' two other incomplete Services are also on the grand scale; and the anthems, too, are amongst the largest of their kind. "Deliver us" is a highly contrapuntal work with a great deal of passing and suspended dissonance. Impressive as the sound of such music may be, it tends to pall quickly since the rate of harmonic change varies little from a basic crotchet pulse, and there are few modulations to "related" cadences. The same criticism can be applied to the two versions of "Holy, holy" and, indeed, to a great deal of music in the grand manner by Parsons' contemporaries. So far, no setting of the Mass by Robert Parsons has been found, and no more than a handful of Latin compositions.

THOMAS TALLIS

Of all the composers of the Edwardian and early Elizabethan period, Tallis, Tye, Shepherd and William Mundy are undoubtedly pre-eminent. Nothing at all is known of Tallis' early career. By the year 1531 he was "joculator organorum" of Dover Priory. Six years later he was singing in the choir of the London city church of St. Mary-at-Hill. In the summer of 1538 he left St. Mary's, presumably for Waltham Abbey, where he remained until the dissolution of the foundation on March 23rd, 1540. Waltham was the last abbey to make its surrender. From there Tallis went to Canterbury Cathedral, and within two or three years he had been elected a Gentleman of the Chapel Royal, a post which he kept until his death in 1585. Since he described himself as "very aged" in a petition to the Queen dated June 27th, 1577, he was probably little short of eighty when he died. His Latin music, which forms the major part of his work, covers the entire range of forms and styles that were then currently in use. The gigantic setting of "Gaude gloriosa" looks back to the English votive antiphon of the early sixteenth century. It is well over four hundred measures long, and it is sectionally scored in Eton Choirbook fashion for various groupings of voices of from two to seven parts. The "Sine nomine" Mass, on the other hand, is in an up-to-date "Short Service" style, with brief, highly compressed points of imitation and a good deal of animated homophony.

In his old age, Tallis entered into a music-publishing partnership with a young colleague of his at the Chapel Royal, William Byrd. Under licence from the Queen, the two were given the exclusive right to print music and ruled music paper for a period of twenty-one years. The scheme unfortunately went wrong but not, luckily, before the two composers had jointly published a comprehensive collection of their own Latin hymns, antiphons, responds and psalm-motets, the *Cantiones quae ab argumento sacrae vocantur* (1575). Tallis' contribution is hardly less enterprising than that of his young partner. In such works as the canonic and highly complex

"Miserere nostri", the boldly harmonic "In jejunio et fletu" with its remarkable "modulations", and in the beautifully simple "O nata lux", Tallis shows himself to be one of the most imaginative and accomplished composers of his day.

No fewer than six of Tallis' motets were adapted to English words—five of which came from the 1575 *Cantiones*. "Absterge Domine" was especially popular, and four different English versions of it are to be found in pre-Restoration manuscripts:

Absterge Domine	1. Discomfit them, O Lord; 2. Forgive me, Lord, my sin; 3. O God, be merciful; 4. Wipe away my sins
Mihi autem nimis	Blessed be thy name
O sacrum convivium	1. I call and cry; 2. O sacred and holy banquet
Salvator mundi [I]	1. Arise, O Lord; 2. With all our hearts and mouths
Salvator mundi [II]	When Jesus went forth
O salutaris hostia (unpublished)	O praise the Lord

The existence of so many adaptations suggests that there must have been a need for large-scale anthems in motet style, a need that could not be satisfied from the current repertory of English anthems. The adaptations are on the whole close in spirit to the Latin originals, with one very glaring exception:

Salvator mundi, salva nos
With all our hearts and mouths we confess, praise and bless thee,
qui per crucem et sanguinem redemisti nos
God the Father unbegotten and Thee the Son only begotten, with the Holy Ghost the comforter
auxiliare nobis, te deprecamur, Deus, noster.
Holy and inseparable Trinity, to Thee be glory for evermore.

The five-part "anthem", "Blessed are those", would also seem to be an adaptation. It is very similar in outline to the "Salve intemerata" antiphon and Mass, with duos, trios and antiphonal contrasts between the upper and lower voices—features that suggest an undiscovered Latin original. The

Ludlow copy of this work, moreover, is given the Latin title "Beati immaculati in via", which further underlines the possibility. The adaptation, if such it is, may even have been the work of Tallis himself, for the translation used comes from Coverdale's bible of 1535:

Tallis' English church music is of considerable importance, though the table of his compositions is a modest one:

TABLE 17

Tallis' English Compositions

Service music

A set of Preces and Responses, and an alternative set of Preces

A set of Festal Psalms for the 24th, 25th and 26th evenings of the month

A Litany* (the alternative version in four parts may not be original)

Benedictus: in five parts, for men's voices

A five part Te Deum*

A Full Service in five parts, consisting of Venite, Te Deum, Benedictus, Kyrie, Creed, Sanctus, Gloria, Magnificat and Nunc dimittis*

A Short Service, called "The First", as above*

An isolated Sanctus and Gloria (probably a seventeenth-century adaptation)

Anthems for men, in four parts

A new commandment give I unto you

Hear the voice and prayer*

If ye love me*

This is my commandment* (possibly by Robert Johnson I, or William Mundy)

(*Table 17 continued overleaf*)

TABLE 17 (*continued*)

Anthems for MATB
O Lord, give thy holy spirit
O Lord, in Thee is all my trust
Out from the deep (possibly by William Mundy, or Robert Parsons)
Purge me, O Lord
Remember not, O Lord
Verily, verily I say unto you

Anthems in five and six parts
Blessed are those (see above) MAATB
Christ rising again* MAATB
O sing unto the Lord (possibly by Shepherd)

Fragmentary anthems
Lord, for thy tender mercies sake (music lost)
O give thanks unto the Lord (listed as a psalm in Tenbury MS. 791)
O Lord God of hosts
O praise the Lord, all ye heathen
Teach me thy way
The simple sheep (music lost)

---

* Items marked thus were probably written before 1553; others too may date from the Edwardian period.

There are also two chant-like "anthems" of no more than a dozen bars each: "Holy, holy holy, Lord God of hosts", and "Not everyone that saith".

None of the four-part anthems seem to have been at all popular. "O Lord in Thee" is in fact a harmonisation of a melody that first appeared in the 1562 Sternhold and Hopkins psalter. It is an attractive work with a good melodic shape and a clearly defined tonal scheme (see page 197).

The other four-part anthems are imitative, in the rather clipped, short-winded idiom of the time, and all are in binary form with optional second-half repeats. One of the more attractive of these is "O Lord, give thy holy spirit", the textures being more varied than those of the other anthems (the repeat, not shown in the published edition, begins at the words "that we may know").

Of the fragmentary anthems, "O give thanks", a setting of Ps. 136, is particularly interesting in that it foreshadows to some extent the late Elizabethan verse idiom (see page 217).

O Lord, in Thee is all my trust, Give ear un-to my woe-ful cries;

Re-fuse me not that am un-just, But bow-ing down thy hea-venly eyes Behold, how

I do still la-ment My sins, where-in I do of-fend. O Lord for them I

shall be shent, Sith Thee to please I do in-tend.

The psalm refrain "for his mercy endureth for ever" is sung by full choir, whilst the first half of each verse is scored for a group of high voices—probably altos, meanes and trebles (the psalm is headed "for trebles" in the organ-book). The refrain music remains the same throughout, but it modulates from the tonic of D "minor" to the related keys of F "major", G "minor" and A "minor" thus:

> Verses 1–2, D minor / 3–4, F major /5–7, D minor /8–9, G minor /
> 10–12, D minor / 13–14, A minor / 15–17, D minor / 18–19,
> F major / 20–21, D minor / 22–23, G minor / 24–27, D
> minor / and Gloria, D minor.

Time has not dealt kindly with Tallis' Service music, but enough has survived to show that some of it was on a much larger scale than any of the extant anthems—the Easter anthem "Christ rising" not excepted. Tallis' Service in five parts uses the text of the 1549 Prayer Book. Only a single bass part has survived, but the title of the Service "of five parts, two in one" suggests that it must have been something of a canonic *tour-de-force*. The evening canticles are the most elaborate—the Magnificat, in particular, is highly contrapuntal and it is not far short of the large Morley verse Service in length. The five-part Te Deum, also using the 1549 text, is rather more complete, and a convincing reconstruction by Dr. Fellowes is available. This, too, is on a large scale, being scored for independent decani and cantoris choirs and divisi meanes. The Short Service (c. 1550) still deservedly has an important place in the cathedral repertory. The formal principle which Tallis used is simple and most effective. Brevity being the first essential, the composer dispensed with imitation altogether —apart, that is, from one very short point at the end of the Nunc dimittis. In its place he used a sequence-like structure $AA^2BB^2CC^2 \ldots$, the repeated music being either stretched or squeezed by the phrase-lengths and rhythms of the accompanying text in this manner:

In such a simple idiom as this, the scope for expressive word setting is necessarily limited. Yet even here Tallis manages to achieve a sensitive and dignified liturgical style that is entirely appropriate to its purpose.

CHRISTOPHER TYE

Scant justice has yet been done to Christopher Tye, a close contemporary of Tallis and little inferior to him in stature. No more than a handful of his compositions are now available, and the few that have been published in recent years are by no means representative of his best work. The known facts of his life are few.[8] In 1536 he took his Mus.B. at Cambridge, and nine years later his Mus.D. By 1543 he was Master of the Choristers at Ely Cathedral, having for some years previously sung in the choir of King's College. We learn from the title page of his *Actes of the Apostles* (1553) that he was by then a Gentleman of the Chapel Royal, and it has been suggested that he may have been one of the king's tutors. Notwithstanding his Chapel duties, Tye continued to direct the choir at Ely until 1561, when he resigned to take up the living of Doddington-cum-March, having the previous year entered Holy Orders. His name is not to be found in the Chapel Royal Check Book, which begins, albeit spasmodically, in 1561; and the chances are, therefore, that he had resigned before then. His successor at Doddington was appointed in March 1573, "per mortem venerabilis viri Christopheri Tye musices doctoris ultimi incumbentis . . ."

Tye's reputation lived on long after his death, and even long after most of his music had been forgotten. A striking tribute to him is to be found in Samuel Rowley's historical drama *When you see me you know me*, published in 1613. The play contains a long dialogue between Tye and the young Prince Edward,[9] the kernel of which occurs just after one of Tye's songs has been sung:

Prince: Doctor, I thank you and commend your cunning,
   I oft have heard my father merrily speak

In your high praise; and thus his highness saith,
England one God, one Truth, one Doctor hath
For music's art, and that is Doctor Tye,
Admired for skill in music's harmony.

Much of Tye's Latin music is now sadly incomplete, but it is evident from what has remained that the composer delighted in rich sonorities and that he was a master of the French techniques of imitation. The three cantus firmus settings are short and semi-imitative; the other liturgical settings, of which "Ad te clamamus" (i.e. Salve regina) is a fair example, are freely imitative. Some—especially the seven-part "Peccavimus cum patribus" and the two five-part psalm motets, "Miserere mei Deus" and "Omnes gentes plaudite"—are on an exceptionally elaborate scale. "Peccavimus" is no less than 250 measures long. Of the three Masses, the "Western Wind" Mass is the simplest, being constructed, much like Taverner's Mass, on the variation principle. The Peterhouse Mass is imitative but of "Short-Service" proportions, whilst the *Euge Bone* Mass represents Tye's most ambitious style—splendidly sonorous in the best English tradition but fully up to date in its "expressive" use of texture and imitative counterpoint. It is one of the very finest settings of its kind (see the Ex. on p. 140).

Although Tye's work for the English rites is not extensive, it is of considerable importance, for it covers a particularly wide range of styles and techniques. The musical sources are of little help in dating either the canticles or the anthems, although "O God be merciful" was certainly written before 1552 since it occurs anonymously in the Wanley books. The texts of no fewer than six compositions come from the 1545 *King's Primer*. Another text comes from the first edition of Sternhold's metrical psalms (1549), and two others from the 1549 Prayer Book. The others are as yet untraced and may well be the work of Tye himself.

The separate Nunc dimittis in Wanley has already been discussed (page 176) and it has been suggested that this may be one of Tye's earliest English works. The paired Magnificat and

Nunc dimittis is somewhat later. Doubt remains as to the identity of the composer, for the Service is described variously as "Mr Parsley's Evening Service" (one source only) and as "Dr. Tye's Magnificat and Nunc dimittis to Mr Parsley's [Morning] Service". On stylistic grounds it would certainly be more convenient to attribute the work to the Norwich musician Parsley, who was much the less accomplished composer of the two. It contains some very awkward and mechanical points of imitation—and some crude progressions which are not characteristic of Tye.

TABLE 18

Tye's English Compositions

Service Music
Magnificat and Nunc dimittis "to Mr Parsley's Service"
Nunc dimittis
Deus misereatur

Anthems à 4 (MATB unless stated)
Blessed are all they
Deliver us, good Lord
From the depth I called (MMAB)
Give alms of thy goods
I have loved
I will exalt
O God, be merciful unto us
Praise ye the Lord
Save me, O God, for thy name's sake

Anthems à 5
My trust, O Lord
O Lord, deliver me/I lift my heart
To Father, Son and Holy Ghost (inc.)
Christ rising again

The thirteen anthems are all for full choir of men and boys (there are fourteen anthems in the EECM catalogue, but the music of two—"I lift my heart to Thee", and "O Lord, deliver me"—is the same). In most of the four-part pieces, Tye clearly had the problem of word audibility uppermost in his mind. "Blessed are all they" represents the simplest solution to the problem. The texture is practically note-against-note

from start to finish, with only the briefest point of imitation. In Tallis' hands this technique could produce interesting
results, for he took good care to vary the cadences and to
secure both variety and continuity in phrasing. Tye's anthem,
however, sticks closely to cadences on F and C for much of the
time and, although at the beginning of the second (triple-
time) section there is a clear "modulation" to G minor, the
music starts and stops in the most disconcerting way. Much the
same is true of "Save me, O God". In most of the other four-
part anthems Tye turned to a different scheme, using imitation
as the basis of the structure. To ensure that word audibility
would not be impaired by the polyphony, he used very sparse
textures, repeating not only single words and phrases of text
but entire points of imitation, note for note and word for
word, in this manner:

"From depth I called", "Give alms", "O God be merciful"
and "Praise ye the Lord" are all built on similar lines. The
solution is not ideal, particularly if used at all frequently, and
it seems that none of Tye's contemporaries adopted it.

Tye's best anthems are undoubtedly the most complicated
ones. These include two fine four-part anthems, "Deliver us
good Lord" (AB, optional repeat of B, C structure) and "I
have loved", together with the three five-part anthems and
the six-part "Christ rising". Tye manages, more successfully
than any other composer of his generation perhaps, to escape

from routine imitative formulae to produce an arresting and expressive idea. "My trust, O Lord" begins with a square, rock-like point of *Ein feste Burg*-like character and it ends with a kind of sequential, perpetual-motion figure to the words "world without ending". (Weelkes used a similar idea in "Alleluia" and in the Service "for trebles". See page 302.)

In "I have loved" Tye uses a downward quaver melisma to express the running of tears and the sliding of feet:

in "Christ rising" a colourful range of sonorities to emphasise the Easter message "death from henceforth hath no power upon him":

in "I lift my heart to Thee" a poignant figure of imitation which is strangely similar to one that Weelkes used in his verse anthem, "Give ear, O Lord" (c.f. p. 305):

and in an otherwise routine setting of Ps. 67 this very insistent point of imitation, with its jubilant melismatic countersubject:

In this expressive approach to the problems of liturgical composition Tye was more forward-looking than any of his contemporaries. For this reason, if for no other, his music deserves wider recognition.

JOHN SHEPHERD

John Shepherd was appointed Master of the Choristers at Magdalen College, Oxford, in 1542. The Fellows were then at odds with each other on political and religious issues and it may well have been on that account that Shepherd resigned in the following year. Two years later, however, he had resumed his former post at the college. Sometime between 1547 and 1553 he secured for himself a place in the Chapel Royal choir, and in 1556 or 1557 he left Magdalen for a second time, perhaps to devote himself fully to his Chapel Royal duties. His name does not appear in the Chapel Check Book—a fact suggesting that he may have retired or died before 1561, the year in which the Check Book List of appointments and resignations begins.

In terms of sheer quantity Shepherd has no mid sixteenth-century rival. There are five complete Masses: the well-known "French Mass", possibly the most up to date of all the extant compositions—a tightly knit, highly imitative four-part setting in the manner of Gombert (c. 1505–c. 1556); a Mass on the "Western Wind" tune—a rather obvious and unadventurous work in which the tune appears almost continuously in the highest voice; a four-part imitative Mass, "Be not afraid" for men; a four-part "plainsong" Mass; and a festal Mass, in the Taverner "Small Devotion" idiom, for six voices. There are also some fifty or more Latin compositions, most of which are liturgical and of cantus firmus structure, the plainsong being presented in even and unvarying note-values. The six-part "Gaude Maria virgo" is a particularly colourful example of this genre, with a long five-part central section scored for divisi trebles, meanes and a bass. Shepherd does not seem to have written any non-liturgical psalm-motets, a form of Latin composition that came into fashion after 1558 and which was developed by Tallis, Tye, William Mundy and the younger Elizabethan composers.[10]

Shepherd's English music, though by no means as extensive, is of considerable interest:

TABLE 19

Shepherd's English Compositions

Service music

Isolated settings of Te Deum, Benedictus, a "short" Kyrie, Creed and Offertory (Lay not up for yourselves), two additional settings of the Creed, a Deus misereatur, and a setting of the Lord's Prayer

The First Service, consisting of Venite, Te Deum, Benedictus, Creed, Magnificat and Nunc dimittis*

The Second Service, as above

Two settings of Te Deum, Magnificat and Nunc dimittis

A Magnificat and Nunc dimittis "for trebles"

Anthems for men

Christ rising again*

I give you a new commandment*

Rejoice in the Lord (also attr. Strogers)

Submit yourselves*

Anthems for MATB

Haste Thee, O God (Pt. II, But let all those)

O Lord of hosts (also attr. Tye)*

Incomplete anthems

Christ our paschall Lamb (for men)*

Lay not up for yourselves

Let my complaint (Pt. II, Let thine hand)

Lord, how are they increased (à 6)

Of all strange news

O God, be merciful

---

* On grounds of text or source the items marked * would seem to date from 1553 at the latest: other items in the list may be of equally early date.

There are also thirty-three simple settings of metrical psalms (see British Museum, Add. MS. 15166) and two three-part compositions, "Steven first after Christ" and "What comfort at thy death".

Of the anthems, "Haste Thee O God" is one of the longest (over seventy measures) and most attractive. Although largely imitative, it contains rather more homophony than is to be found in many of the other English compositions, and there are clearly defined "modulations" to related keys. The only six-part anthem—a setting of the eight verses of Psalm 3—is unfortunately too incomplete to permit reconstruction; but it, again, is of considerable length—in all, over a hundred measures. Of the three complete anthems for men, "Christ rising" is the most distinguished. Like Tallis' setting, it is based on the 1549 Prayer Book text. It, too, is in a "solemn" liturgical style, with a harmonic richness that characterises the best of the composer's work and with little obvious attempt at "expressive" word setting:

Shepherd's Service music, like that of his contemporaries—Tallis, William Mundy and Parsons—is on a much larger scale. The First Service, which dates from the Edwardian period, can conveniently be sung by men, as the modern edition suggests. It is probable, none the less, that Shepherd intended the work for men and boys since it covers the usual two-octave and a sixth range. For some unknown reason, low clefs are used in all the extant manuscript sources—implying, it would seem, some kind of upward transposition (see page 208). The Service is basically in four parts, but there are divisi decani and cantoris sections in five or more parts.

The Second Service is probably late Edwardian or Elizabethan. It is considerably more elaborate than the first, with divisi passages in as many as seven parts, much in the style

of the Mundy and Parsons "Great" Services. In it there are a surprisingly large number of melismas, much antiphony and imitation (see page 209).

Shepherd evidently assumed that the listener would be familiar with the words of the ordinary of the Communion Service, as also with the Morning and Evening canticles, for there are places (as in "and of all things visible and invisible") where the meaning is hard to follow without some prior knowledge of the text.

Little of Shepherd's other Service music is complete enough to make reconstruction practicable. The two settings of Te Deum, Magnificat and Nunc dimittis are both contrapuntal, as is the second Creed, whilst the Third Creed is a Short Service setting. The loss of Shepherd's Evening Service "for trebles" is particularly to be deplored, for—to judge from the one extant source, the "Batten" organ-book—this was a setting on the

grandest scale. The Magnificat is over 130 measures in length, the Nunc dimittis well over sixty, with parts for trebles as well as meanes in the best pre-Reformation manner.

WILLIAM MUNDY

William Mundy spent much if not all of his life in London— first as a chorister of Westminster Abbey (he became head boy there in 1543), then as a member of the choirs at St. Mary-at-Hill and St. Paul's Cathedral, and finally, from 1563 until 1591, as a Gentleman of the Chapel Royal. He was a prolific composer of vocal music, both English and Latin, and his work is of considerable interest and importance. It falls roughly into four main categories: Latin music in the old, florid votive antiphon style; music in the imitative French style (English

TABLE 20

*Mundy's English Compositions**

Services for men
A "Whole" Service, including Venite, Te Deum, Benedictus, Kyrie, Creed, Magnificat and Nunc dimittis*
A Service in three parts, lacking Venite, Kyrie and Creed*
A Service in four parts, lacking Venite*
A Te Deum

Services for full choir
The First Service, including Venite, Te Deum, Benedictus, Kyrie, Creed, Magnificat and Nunc dimittis*
The Second Service, lacking Kyrie and Creed*
The Short Service
A Magnificat and Nunc dimittis to Mr. Parson's [Morning] Service in five parts
A Magnificat and Nunc dimittis in C fa ut
A Magnificat and Nunc dimittis "in medio chori", in nine parts
The First and Fourth Evening Services, including Magnificat and Nunc dimittis

Anthems for men's voices by "Mundy"
A new commandment give I unto you
Behold, it is Christ
He that hath my commandments
Let us now laud
Praise the Lord, O ye servants
Rejoice in the Lord alway

Other anthems (including incomplete anthems) by "Mundy"
Blessed is God in all his gifts
God be merciful unto us   (inc.)
Lay not up for yourselves   (inc.)
Let the sea make a noise
Teach me, O Lord   (inc.)
(the above anthems are *full*)

Anthems by "William Mundy"
Ah, helpless wretch   vs
Bow down thine ear   f6 (inc.)
Increase my joy   text only
My song shall be of mercy   (inc.)
O Lord, I bow the knees   f5
O Lord, the maker of all things   f4
O Lord, the world's saviour   f4
Prepare you, time weareth away   f4
Save me, O God, for thy name's sake   (text only)
The secret sins   vs (text only)
This is my commandment (also attr. Tallis and Johnson)*   f4 for men's voices

---

* On grounds of text or source the starred items would seem to date from 1553, at the latest.

and Latin); English music in a basically chordal, non-imitative idiom; and English music in the new "verse" style.

The least accomplished works are, without question, the anthems for men's voices. Many of the imitative entries are forced, and there are some crude dissonances and ugly holes in the harmony.

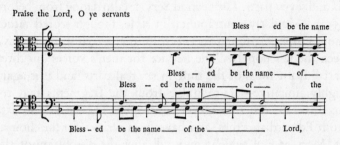

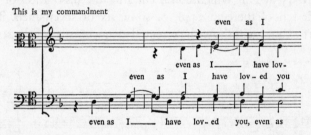

These anthems for men's voices present a curious problem since they are all on a strikingly lower technical level than the first two Services, which are known to be comparatively early works. It may be no accident, therefore, that with only one exception these anthems are ascribed equivocally to "Mundy", no Christian name being given. It is very unlikely indeed that any could be the work of William Mundy's son John. They might well have been written, on the other hand, by his father, Thomas, who was sexton and musician at St. Mary-at-Hill from 1527 until 1558. The only one of these anthems that is actually ascribed to *William* Mundy (and the ascription is in a seventeenth-century source) is also attributed elsewhere to Tallis and to Johnson.

By the time that he came to write the First Service (some time before 1552) Mundy had acquired a fluent if limited contrapuntal technique. The layout of the First Service is quite elaborate, being scored in the main for five-part choir (MAATB), with frequent exchanges between decani and cantoris (mostly in four parts), and some divisi full sections in six and seven parts. The Second Service (also dating from before 1552) is similarly contrapuntal in style, though scored rather more simply for four-part choir. Of the two, it seems to have been the less popular. The Service for men's voices "in three parts" is for most of the time in six real parts, and it is again highly imitative—as, to judge from the fragments that remain, are the other two services for men. These may also date from Edwardian times, and have been written for the choir at St. Mary-at-Hill which consisted, after the dissolution of the choir school there in 1548, of some six or seven men. This short extract will show the essential characteristics of the style:

Service for Mens' Voices, in three parts

Although Mundy managed to solve the basic problems of writing imitative counterpoint in a strictly non-melismatic idiom, it cannot be denied that he was somewhat cramped by this severe discipline, as indeed were his contemporaries. No doubt he was stimulated by its challenge, but he does all too often seem to have been reduced to ringing the changes on a rather limited number of cadential and harmonic formuli without attempting any close relationship between note and word.

During the Marian reaction, Mundy tried his hand at the florid votive-antiphon style, in which no problems of underlay or imitation arose to fetter the imagination. The contrast between this music and the imitative music (whether to Latin or English words) could hardly be more marked:[11]

Maria virgo sanctissima

The nine-part Magnificat and Nunc dimittis is easily Mundy's most ambitious English work. Indeed, it is one of the most elaborate liturgical compositions of the entire century —the Eton Choir Book antiphons not excepted. In the sole surviving source (the Peterhouse Caroline books), it is headed "in medio chori", a direction that has so far eluded satis-- factory definition. In all probability a group of soloists from the choir stood, literally, "in the middle of the choir" between the decani and cantoris stalls to produce an additional antiphonal effect. This Service is one of the few calling for high treble voices, and there are long divisi passages scored for high trebles, meanes and altos—a most exciting sound. The odds are that Mundy wrote this work for the Chapel Royal choir after he became a Gentleman in 1563, and for some special occasion (see top of page 214).

Mundy's setting of the evening canticles to Parson's Morning Service is somewhat similar to the First Service in scale. There is, however, considerably more homophony, and a clearer differentiation between chordal and imitative textures. Above all, however, there is a noticeably closer relationship between words and music (see "He hath put down the mighty from their seat", page 214).

The two other completable Services (there are two very fragmentary settings, besides) are both predominantly chordal, and for this reason, perhaps, more tonal in character than the imitative settings. "Modulations" are indeed to be found in

the early works. But in none is the feeling for tonality so pronounced as in the C fa ut Service, which is in every way the direct predecessor of Byrd's two full Services, particularly in its sequential development and phrase repetition (see page 215).

The absence of large-scale anthems to match the Services is

Plate 1

The title page of the "Great Bible" of 1539, symbolizing the
royal supremacy. Henry VIII (top centre) is dispensing the Word
of God to the unmitred Cranmer (left) and to Thomas Cromwell
(right), intermediaries between the "Supreme head of the Church
of England" and his people.

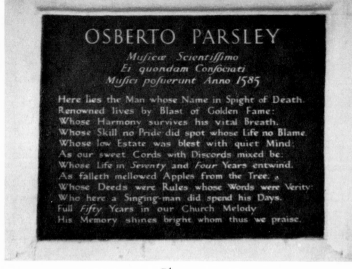

Plate 2

Osbert Parsley's memorial tablet in Norwich Cathedral.

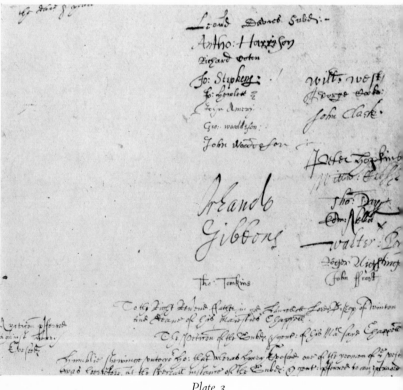

Plate 3

Signatures of Gentlemen of the Chapel Royal in the Check Book, attached to a minute of a meeting held on June 6th, 1620, and the first few lines of a "petition offered against Henry Eveseed," one of the yeoman of the Vestry, "by the Subdean and Gentlemen of His Majesty's said Chapel".

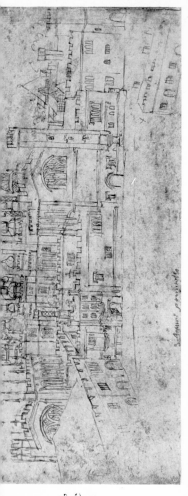

Plate 4 Right
Wyngaerde's sketch of Richmond Palace, showing the Chapel on the left of the picture. *By courtesy of the Ashmolean Museum*

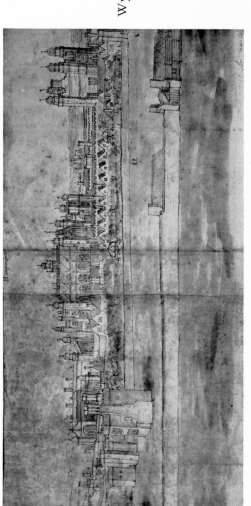

Plate 5 Left
Wyngaerde's impression of Hampton Court. *By courtesy of the Ashmolean Museum*

Plate 6 Left and Right

Part of Ward's first Verse Service, scored up in preparation for the printer. Directions to the typesetter are to be found at the top left and right of the page, e.g. "brevier[type] begin here for 2 Con:Can: fo:67". See also Plate 7.

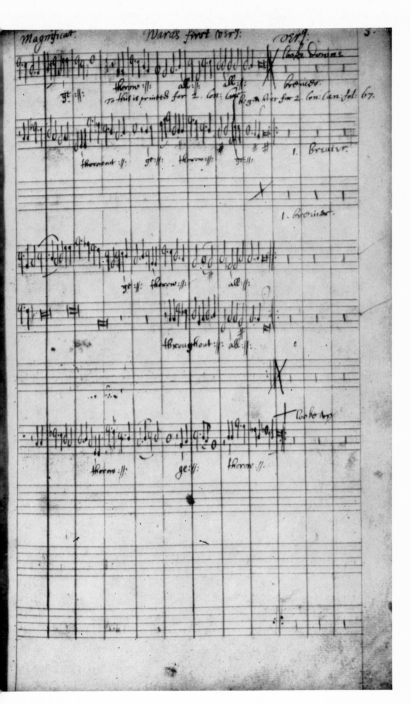

Plate 7

Folio 67, of the second contratenor cantoris part of John Barnard's *First Book of Selected Church Musick* (1641), as printed from the manuscript score (see Plate 6).

THE FIRST SET OF PSALMES OF. III. VOYCES

Fitt for private Chappells or other private meetings with a continuall Bafe either for the Organ or Theorbo newly compofed after the Italian way

By

William Childe Bacheler in Muficke and Organift of his Maties free Chappell of Windfor.

London printed by Iames Reaue. 1 6 3 9

Plate 8

The title page of William Child's *Psalmes* of 1639. The flowing italic script accords well with Child's Italianate music.

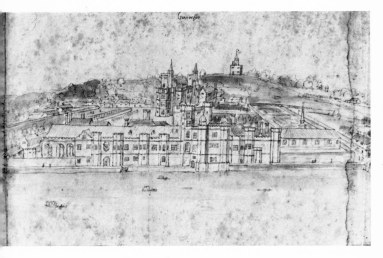

Plate 9

Greenwich Palace; a sketch of the waterfront by Antonius van den Wyngaerde (1559) showing the Chapel at the extreme left of the façade.

By courtesy of the Ashmolean Museum

Plate 10

The ratification of the Spanish marriage treaty in the Chapel

Plates 11 and 12

The opening of Morley's Te Deum as it appears in the
"Batten" organ-book, Tenbury MS 791 (above) and in
an organ-book at Christ Church, Oxford, MS. 1001; both
sources are dated c. 1635. The setting opens with a verse
for solo counter-tenor—"We praise Thee, O God"; this
is followed by a verse for solo trebles and altos in four parts
—"We knowledge Thee to be the Lord"—and an extended
section for full choir beginning with the words "All the
earth".

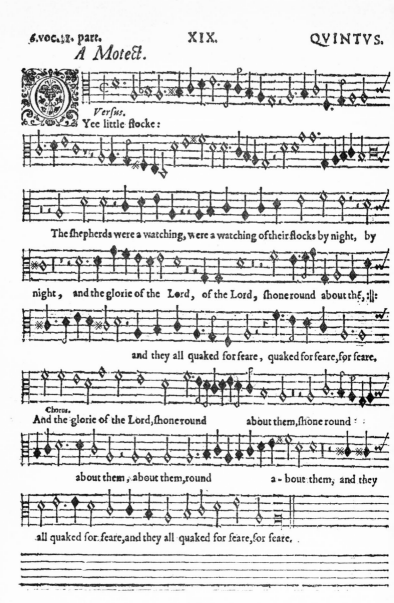

A Motect.

Verſus.
Yee little flocke:

The ſhepherds were a watching, were a watching of their flocks by night, by night, and the glorie of the Lord, of the Lord, ſhone round about the,

and they all quaked for feare, quaked for feare, for feare.

Chorus.
And the glorie of the Lord, ſhone round   about them, ſhone round

about them, about them, round   a-bout them, and they

all quaked for feare, and they all quaked for feare, for feare.

Plate 13

A page from the Quintus part of John Amner's *Sacred Hymnes* (1615), showing the beginning of the composer's Christmas verse anthem, "O ye little flock".

Here beginneth the fifth Booke
of Pſalmes.

§ *The Argument. Pſalme. CVII.*

This hath fiue partes diſtinct: where diuers men be bid:
The Lord to prayſe: to preach bys power: who them from perils rid.

§ *The Quiere. The rearefreyt of the Pſalme.*

Od graunt that we would: prayſe euer agayne,
⸭ The Lord for hys grace : ſo to fing in our quiere
⸭ The wonders he doth : for the children of men,
Whoſe mercy ſo nere : to all doth appeare.
To all doth appeare.

[margin: Confitemi ni domino]

§ *The Meane.*

1 Prayſe the Lord allye,
Due thankes to hym extende :
For good he is : whoſe gentilenes,
Shall laſt full woeld both ende.

2 Let them ſay thus in thankes: who were by God made free:
Whom he redemd: from cruell hand: of troublous enmitie.

3 And whom he gathered wye: from countries ſtrange and wyde:
From Eaſt and Weſt: from ſtoth and South: in citie ſafe to hyd.

4 Who wandred out of way : in deſertes wildernes:
And found no way: to dwelling towne: to ſtay in reſtfulnes.

5 When hunger felt and thirſt: wee pynde by farniſhment:
whoſe hartes within: dyd melt away: for needefull nouriſhment.

The

6 Who thus afflict: when they did cry,
To God in meeke complaintes :
He then dyd faue: moſt louingly,
From all they; hard conſtrayntes.

7 For he led them : the way full kynde,
Both ryght and proſperous :
Wherby they dyd: a citie fynde,
To dwell commodious.

§ *The Quiere.*

God graunt that they would: prayſe hartely then:
⸭ The Lord for hys grace : ſo to fing in they quiere :
The wonders he doth : for the children of men,
Whoſe mercy ſo neare : to them dyd appeare,

9 For that he refreſht : their bodely neede,
⸭ Where thirſty they frayd : as wyth anguithe oppreſt:
⸭ Theyr foule dyd heaſe : of theyr hunger in ſpeede,
To ſet them in reſt: wyth foode of the beſt.

§ *The Meane.*

10 And they that ſate in darke: in deadly ſhadowes blacke:
Afflict in bondes: and iron chaynes : and felt all comfortes ſlacke.

11 They thus deferud for: why: gods wordes they did deteſt,
The counſaples eke: they did defpife: of all the woorthieſt.

12 He then brought downe their hartes: wyth griefes moſt tedious:
They fell full faynt : none helping them : ſo far rebellious.
CC.iiij. *The*

Plate 14

The opening of Ps. 107, as it appears in Archbishop Parker's *Psalter* (c. 1567). The directions, "The Quiere", "The Meane" and "The Rectors" would seem to foreshadow the "verse" and "chorus" directions to be found in verse Services and anthems.

Plate 15

From the preface to Sir William Leighton's *The Teares or Lamentacions of a Sorrowfull Soule* (1614). The addition of Thomas Weelkes' name was evidently an afterthought!

somewhat puzzling and yet quite characteristic of the period. There are now no more than three major MATB anthems of his. Two of these use texts that first appeared in the 1545 King's Primer: "O Lord the world's saviour", for Evensong, and "O Lord the maker of all things" for Compline. Both hymns were reprinted, unchanged, in the Edwardian and Elizabethan Primers. The most popular of these, then as now, was "O Lord the maker", which has the benefit both of a superior text and a more colourful tonality. Like so many

anthems of the period, it is in AB form with an optional repeat of B. Its style is deceptively simple. To achieve so effective a contrast of textures while at the same time avoiding over-much text repetition or melisma is no easy task, as any student of composition will know. There are, admittedly, one or two loose ends—the unexpected continuation of a line beyond its logical conclusion or the premature demise of some prominent phrase—but as a whole the various parts tie in remarkably well with each other, and there is a fine sequential middle section.

The other English anthem is the five-part setting of "O Lord I bow the knees of my heart", the words of which are

H

to be found in the Henrician, Edwardian and Elizabethan Primers (from "the Prayer of Manasses, King of Juda"). It is easily the largest of the English anthems (87 bars in length, as against 48 and 58) and, like Mundy's Latin psalms, it is consistently imitative throughout. If indeed this is an original work—and the possibility cannot be ruled out that it was adapted from one of Mundy's Latin motets, now lost—it does show that attempts were being made at that time to write anthems akin in scale and design to the larger motets of Lassus and the elder Ferrabosco. The almost complete lack of anthems in this vein, however, lends weight to the theory that in the Chapel Royal, at least, motets may have been sung as anthems for some little time after the accession of Queen Elizabeth. If this were so, Mundy's Latin psalms would certainly have been entirely suitable for liturgical use.

Perhaps the most interesting of Mundy's compositions, Latin or English, are the two verse anthems, "The secret sins" and "Ah helpless wretch". The music of "The secret sins" has apparently been lost, but it is more than likely that the setting printed in the complete works of Orlando Gibbons is by him (see page 313). Certainly it is remarkably like "Ah helpless wretch", a setting of words from *The poore Widowes mite*, published by William Hunnis in 1583. That Mundy, at the age of fifty or more, could adapt himself so successfully to this new idiom is quite remarkable.

Mundy's music, both for the English and Latin rites, is undeniably limited in its appeal, for the composer seems to be preoccupied so frequently with problems of a purely technical nature that he has little time to think of establishing any close relationship between word and note. Yet Mundy, one of the most prolific composers of his time, did much to build a sure foundation for the future, not only in the "full" style but also in the new "verse" idiom that was to be the vehicle of much of the finest Elizabethan and early seventeenth-century church music. The Oxford scholar Robert Dow likened Mundy as the moon to Byrd's sun:[12]

Dies lunae
Ut lucem solis sequitur lux proxima lunae
Sic tu post Birdum Munde secunde venis

a donnish yet just observation!

THE EARLY VERSE ANTHEM

Only passing reference has yet been made to the new "verse" style of composition which made its appearance in England during the second half of the sixteenth century. The use of solo voices in choral music was in itself no novelty, of course: the late medieval antiphon is based upon the opposition of solo and choral groupings as, in a different and very much simpler way, is the vernacular carol. The Elizabethan verse anthem and Service differ from these, and from all earlier solo-chorus forms, however, in the use of obbligato instrumental accompaniments. Pre-Reformation verse music can well be performed without instrumental support; late sixteenth-century verse music would be hopelessly incomplete without it.

The direct antecedents of the verse anthem and Service would seem to have been the metrical psalm or prayer and the consort song. The prefaces to Sternhold's *Certayne Psalmes* (1549) and Tye's *Actes of the Apostles* (1553) show that devotional songs and metrical psalms were already very popular in Court circles. The verses were apparently set to simple tunes and sung as solos, to the accompaniment of a lute or other suitable instrument. It needed only an *alternatim* performance of a song or psalm to create a simple type of verse anthem. Indeed, there is a strophic setting of a metrical prayer in the Wanley books which takes this very form, each stanza of the prayer being sung twice—on the first occasion by a solo voice and on the second by a four-part chorus. No instrumental accompaniment is supplied for the solo verses, it is true, but one might well have been improvised upon the lute or organ from the "chorus" bass (see page 218).

Tallis' setting of the Benedicite (Psalm 136) represents a

further step in the direction of the verse anthem. The psalm refrain "for his mercy endureth for ever", which forms the second part of each verse, is scored for full choir, whilst the non-repetitive verse sections are arranged for trebles accompanied either by organ or by meanes and altos (the exact scoring is not known, since only an organ bass is now extant). Archbishop Parker suggested a similar plan for his metrical version of this psalm, men singing the verses and a "Quire" the refrain. Parker went one stage further in his

Anon

Now let___ the congre - ga - ti - on   that is within this place   · Cry un-to God,   that

[Lute or keyboard harmonisation, bars 1 - 11 ?]

ho -ly Lord,   to send him of his grace.   `Now let___ the con-gre - ga - ti - on

arrangement of Psalm 107: the psalm has two refrains, both recurring four times: "O that men would therefore praise the Lord . . ." and "So they cried unto the Lord in their trouble . . .". The first, Parker suggested, should be sung by the "Quire", the second by men's voices ("The Rectors"), and the intermediate verses by a "meane" as in Psalm 136 (see Plate 14). As we shall later see, most of the early verse anthems are settings of metrical texts and many have refrain or repeat structures of various kinds.

The song for solo voice and viols was especially popular during the second half of the sixteenth century. Some forty or so early Elizabethan consort songs have so far come to light and nearly all of them are for boys to sing. Some are sacred or moral in tone, and others are unequivocally secular. Quite a few of them can be directly associated with the choir-boy plays that were so much the rage at the time.

That so many of the songs are for boys' voices is no accident, for the boys of the leading London choirs took a surprisingly active part in London's musical life. They played and sang at the dinners of the city merchants and they staged dramatic entertainments of various kinds for the pleasure of both Court and City. Concerts at banquets were already much in vogue during the 1560s. Henry Machyn recorded two such occasions in his diary.[13] The first took place in 1561, when the Grocers engaged the boys of St. Paul's to supply the music for their annual feast. "All the dinner time" Machyn wrote, "the singing children of St. Paul's played upon their viols and sung very pleasant songs to the great delectation of the whole company." Evidently, the music was a huge success! Shortly afterwards Machyn went to a dinner given by the London Guild of Parish clerks, where he heard with much pleasure "a goodly concert of the children of Westminster with viols and regals."

The boy-play tradition, though of considerable antiquity, reached the peak of its popularity during the second half of the sixteenth century. Indeed the Elizabethan stage was teeming with boys—those "little eyases" as Shakespeare called them, who cried out "on the top of question" and were so "tyrannically clapped for it".[14] The fashion for boy plays seems to have originated at Court, where during the first twenty or so years of Elizabeth's reign well over half the plays were acted by boys, principally the boys of St. Paul's and the Chapel Royal. Richard Farrant, the composer, was particularly involved in Court theatricals, and it was during his time as joint Master of the Windsor and Chapel Royal choristers (c. 1567 to 1581) that "rehearsal" rooms were procured at Blackfriars for the Windsor and Chapel Royal boys. The "rehearsals" were open to all who were prepared to pay generously for the privilege of admission and it is clear that London Society took full advantage of the offer, greatly to the inconvenience of the aristocratic Blackfriars tenants nearby; much to the annoyance, too, of at least one pamphleteering puritan, who considered play-acting a pursuit quite unworthy of those whose duty it was to sing God's praises:

> Plays will never be suppressed, while her Majesty's unfledged minions flaunt it in silks and satins. They had as well be at their popish service, in the Devil's garments. Even in her Majesty's Chapel do these pretty, upstart youths profane the Lord's Day by the lascivious writhing of their tender limbs, and gorgeous decking of their apparel, in feigning bawdy fables gathered from the idolatrous heathen poets. . . .[15]

If the choirboy play which the Duke of Stettin-Pomerania saw in 1602 was at all typical, music must have been one of the major attractions of this kind of entertainment:

> The Queen keeps a number of young boys, who are taught to sing and to play on all sorts of musical instruments—they are also expected to continue their school studies at the same time. These boys have special instructors in the various arts, and especially in music. As part of their education in courtly manners they are required to put on a play once a week, and for this purpose the Queen has provided them with a theatre and with a great deal of rich apparel. Those who wish to see one of the performances must pay as much as eight shillings of our Pomeranian money [that is in English terms, the equivalent of a shilling—about four times the price of a normal theatre seat]. Yet there are always a good many people present, including ladies of the highest repute, since the plots are always well developed, and of a suitably elevated character. All the performances are by candlelight and the effect is indeed spectacular. For a whole hour before the play begins there is a concert of music for organs, lutes, pandoras, citterns, viols and recorders. When we were there a boy "cum voce tremula" [does this, perhaps, imply some kind of vibrato?] sang so charmingly to the accompaniment of a bass viol that with the possible exception of the Nuns at Milan, we heard nothing to equal him anywhere . . .[16]

Richard Farrant, William Mundy and Byrd, three of the most distinguished members of the Chapel Royal, would seem to have been among the first composers to develop the verse forms of anthem and Service.[17] The anthems of Farrant and Mundy particularly suggest the influence of the metrical psalm; those of Byrd, the consort song. Farrant's one extant verse anthem is scored for organ and voices and, like the embryo Wanley anthem discussed above, it is a strophic setting of a metrical psalm, though on a considerably larger and more elaborate scale. Only the last phrase of each solo is in fact, repeated by the chorus; and completely new music is supplied for the last verse. No voice-parts of the anthem have survived, but the two extant organ parts are complete enough to show what the original must have been like. The first verse and chorus are given below as they appear in the Christ Church version; small notes and words in brackets are editorial:

William Mundy's one extant verse anthem (but see Orlando Gibbons, page 313) is also strophic in form, with new triple-time music for the last verse. In both settings the solos have the simple dignity of the metrical psalm tune and the choruses are plainly harmonised, with little attempt at polyphony of any kind.

There are quite a few consort songs by Byrd's elder colleagues at the Chapel Royal, notably Robert Parsons, Richard Farrant and Richard Edwardes (Hunnis' predecessor as Master of the Chapel Royal choristers). The songs, mostly in five parts, fall between two stylistic extremes—the simpler and probably the earlier being essentially chordal, the upper voice dominating the texture as in some of the shorter anthems and Services of the period:

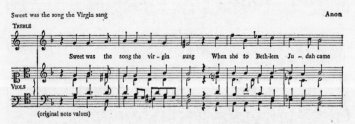

the other being freely contrapuntal, with the solo line moving independently of the accompaniment in sustained and fairly concise phrases:

Caustun's "Turn Thou us" (which Day published as a full anthem in 1565) must surely in its original state have been a song for solo meane and three viols:

Byrd was especially attracted to the form, it would seem, for well over sixty of his consort songs have survived, nearly all for meane or treble and a trio or quartet of viols.[18] Byrd adapted no fewer than twenty-six of these songs as full anthems for publication in the 1588 *Psalmes, Sonets and songs*. One or two of the consort songs also appear as simple verse anthems in contemporary sources. "Lord to Thee I make my moan" is one such dual-purpose song/verse anthem. It has a short closing phrase of some three bars, which is repeated once. In one source, however, words appear beneath the instrumental parts of the repeated phrase, suggesting "chorus" treatment of the closing bars. "O Lord within thy tabernacle" also appears both as a solo song and a simple one-chorus verse anthem, and there are one or two other refrain-structure songs that could very well have been treated in a similar way, notably "O Lord, who in thy sacred tent", "The Lord only is my support" and "The man is blest", all of which, incidentally, are settings of metrical psalm texts.

TABLE 21

Early Verse Anthems and Full Anthems

	Verse anthems	Full anthems
Richard Farrant (d. 1581)	1	2
William Mundy (c. 1525–91)	2	c. 20
William Byrd (1543–1623)	17	c. 60 but see below, p. 239
Edmund Hooper (1553–1621)	11	9
Thomas Morley (1557–1603)	3	3
Nathaniel Giles (c. 1558–1633)	20	4
John Bull (c. 1562–1628)	9	5
Thomas Tomkins (1572–1656)	50	41 but see below p. 288
Thomas Weelkes (c. 1575–1623)	23	18
Orlando Gibbons (1583–1625)	24	10
John Holmes (before 1580, and after 1610)	18	0
Edward Smith (d. 1611)	4	0

Farrant and Mundy may have anticipated Byrd in the use of an instrumental verse style, but there can be little doubt that Byrd was the first to make any extensive use of it. And it is not altogether impossible that Byrd had already composed some verse music before leaving Lincoln, as a rather ambiguous Chapter Minute of September 29th, 1570, required him to "set the tune" before the beginning of Te Deum, Benedictus, Magnificat and Nunc dimittis, and to accompany the anthem. Nor were Byrd's younger contemporaries slow to appreciate the advantages of the new idiom. The figures in Table 21 above show clearly that Gibbons was by no means the "pioneer" in this field that he was once thought to be!

There were many good reasons for the sudden popularity of the new style. From the purely practical point of view, the verse anthem and Service had obvious advantages since the burden of performance could be placed upon the ablest singers—a particularly important factor in the provinces, where good musicians were so hard to come by. Moreover as the author of Royal MS. 18. B. XIX pointed out, the solo voices tended to stand out against the instrumental accompaniment, thus making a more immediate impact upon the listener. And as Charles Butler observed, the new idiom was infinitely more colourful than the old: for him there was no better music than a solemn anthem "wherein a sweet melodious treble or countertenor singeth single and a full choir answereth, much more when two such single voices and two full choirs interchangeably reply to one another and at the last, close all together..."[19]

NOTES TO CHAPTER 7

1. Baillie.

2. Burton, pp. xlii–xliii.

3. None of these texts are "composite" compilations from multiple sources. The second "antem" is, however, based on a selection of verses from a psalm, unlike the others of the kind, which are settings of complete psalms or complete sections of psalms: this reflects a similar pattern of development already observed (p. 142) in the motet.

4. Information very kindly supplied by Mr. H. M. Nixon of the British Museum.

5. For a discussion of the minor Edwardian and Elizabethan sources see Frere.

6. See Pattison, p. 62, for a discussion of the use of quantitative verse by English writers.

7. Whythorne.

8. The preface to Arkwright's edition of Tye's "Euge bone" Mass contains a good account.

9. Hawkins, p. 453.

10. See Harrison, F. Ll. (i), for a discussion of the Latin music.

11. The Latin works are being published in the *Early English Church Music* series.

12. Brett and Dart.

13. Nichols (i), June 16th, 1561, and May 11th, 1562.

14. *Hamlet*, Act 2: sc. 2; Rosencrantz. See Hillebrand (ii), for an extended account of Elizabethan choirboy plays.

15. Warton, p. 217; the original broadside entitled "The Children of the Chapel Stript and Whipt " (1569) cannot now be traced.

16. Bulow.

17. Shepherd's "Of all strange news", a six-part anthem for Christmas, is divided into sections for chorus and sections for solo voices; the work is unfortunately incomplete but it would seem to be more akin to the medieval carol than to the Elizabethan verse anthem; it is unlikely, in other words, that the solo sections required obbligato instrumental support.

18. Brett (i).

19. Butler, p. 41.

The Late sixteenth and Early seventeenth Centuries: William Byrd and his Contemporaries

The quantity of Edwardian and early Elizabethan church music is such as to permit at least passing reference to every composer. From 1580 onwards, however, omissions are inevitable; for during the late sixteenth century well over a hundred musicians tried their hand at the composition of Services, anthems and devotional songs. The number of extant works cannot fall much short of two thousand. The difficulties of summarising this enormous repertory are much complicated by the fact that few Services and anthems can be dated at all accurately. Primary sources are few and far between, and most pre-Restoration sets of cathedral part books were compiled in the 1630s.

WILLIAM BYRD

William Byrd was the most distinguished musician of his generation and, indeed, of the entire period from Reformation to Restoration. Of his early career nothing at all is known. He was born in 1542 or 1543[1] and he may have been the son of Thomas Byrd, composer and Gentleman of the Chapel Royal. Antony à Wood, that gossipy and unreliable Oxford

historian, states that he was "bred up under Tallis", implying
that he was either a chorister of the Chapel or that he was a
private pupil of the composer. In this instance, Wood may
not have been very far from the mark since his statement
seems to be corroborated in one of the poems prefacing the
1575 *Cantiones quae ab argumento sacrae vocantur*. On February
27th, 1563, Byrd became organist of Lincoln Cathedral; and

TABLE 22

The Younger Contemporaries of Byrd (1543–1623)

	Hooper*	*1553–1621*
	Morley	*1557–1603*
	Giles	*1558–1633*
also		
	Bevin	*1555–1640*
	Bull	*1562–1628*
	Hilton (snr.)	*1565–1612*
	John Holmes	fl. 1600
	Matthew Jeffreys	fl. 1600
	Leighton	fl. 1600
	Milton	*1563–1647*
	John Mundy	*1555–1630*

Other composers
  Alison, Barcroft, Bathe, Bennett, Boyce, Carlton, Cobbold, Crosse, J. Farrant
(there were at least two composers of this name), Edward Gibbons, *Heardson*, Inglott,
Juxon, John Mudd, John Parsons, Randoll, Edward Smith, Elias Smith, John Smith,
Wanless, West, Matthew White, Wigthorpe, Yarrow.

* Italicised dates are only approximate. Italicised names indicate that no liturgical
anthems or Services are known by the composers in question.

seven years later, almost to the day, he was sworn a Gentleman
of the Chapel Royal in succession to the composer Robert
Parsons, who had been drowned a month previously in the
River Trent at Newark, not twenty miles from Lincoln.
For the next three years he travelled between London and
Lincoln, but in December 1572 he left Lincoln for good to
devote himself to his Chapel Royal duties. His final departure
from Lincoln may mark the date of his appointment as co-
organist of the Chapel with Tallis, although the first mention
of this is to be found on the title page of the 1575 *Cantiones*.

A good deal is known of Byrd's subsequent career, and the composer is seen in a double rôle—on the one hand a convinced and practising Catholic, on the other a distinguished member of her Majesty's reformed Chapel. Byrd made no secret of his Catholic sympathies, and his name and the names of the members of his family figure prominently in the recusant lists of Harlington, where they lived until 1592, and subsequently in the registers of the Essex parish church of Stondon Massey. That Byrd felt able and that he was allowed to lead this dual existence is perhaps not so surprising as it might seem. For Byrd can hardly have been the only recusant member of the Chapel Royal choir. No fewer than sixteen of the Gentlemen had been in the choir during the Marian reaction, and one or two of the older members could look back to the time of Henry VII. Moreover, the reformed services in the Chapel Royal were by no means as "reformed" as some of the Queen's subjects could have wished, nor was the Queen herself especially interested in the doctrinal niceties of the Reformation, especially when artistic matters were at stake. She had, after all, intervened to prevent the dismissal of Sebastian Westcott from St. Paul's Cathedral, in 1559, and again through Lord Robert Dudley in 1563, though Westcott was known to be a Catholic.[2] It is possible to see, therefore, how Byrd may have felt able to compromise to the extent of singing, playing and even writing music for the reformed services.[3]

There is certainly nothing to show that Byrd ever chose, or that he was ever asked, to sacrifice the interests of his musical career to his faith, in spite of assertions to the contrary by Father William Weston.[4] And as the years went on, he revealed ever more openly his Catholic sympathies. Shortly after 1590, three Latin Masses appeared from an anonymous press with Byrd's name attached to them, whilst in 1605—the very year of the Gunpowder Plot—the composer published his first book of liturgical motets, following these with a second book only two years later. Yet at the time of his death in 1623 he was still a Gentleman of the Chapel and, as the unique entry in the Check Book shows, greatly respected and beloved of his colleagues. No other composer of the time, indeed, inspired quite the same universal admiration and affection. As early as 1597 Thomas Morley, possibly his most distinguished pupil, had described him as a "great master", "never without reverence to be named of the musicians"— an opinion that was echoed again and again by his contemporaries.

Byrd was a prolific composer, though like his colleagues Bull, Tomkins and Gibbons he preferred the more serious forms of vocal and instrumental music. Altogether well over fifty keyboard dances have survived, together with Preludes, Fancies, Voluntaries, Variations and Plainsongs of various kinds for both keyboard and viols, a hundred or more English part-songs of sundry natures, more than fifty songs for solo voice and viols, three settings of the ordinary of the Mass, nearly two hundred motets and much English church music besides.

Most of the extant motets are contained in the five published collections of 1575, 1589, 1591, 1605 and 1607, and amongst them are numbered many of his finest compositions. Recent studies by Joseph Kerman[5] have enabled us to see more clearly the process of growth from the early to the late motets. By the time that Byrd came to write "Aspice Domine", one of the earliest motets in the 1575 collection, he had already acquired a fluent contrapuntal technique and an ear for impressive sonorities. In this he had even then outpaced his elder contemporary William Mundy, especially in the expressive handling of melodies and textures. Note, for instance, the setting of "desolata civitas", the full six-part polyphony to the words "plena divitiis", and the curiously restless rhythms of "non est qui consoletur eam" in "Aspice Domine." Similarly expressive qualities characterise some of the other large-scale imitative settings in this collection, and notably the very popular "Attollite portas".

The contents of the 1575 *Cantiones* show that Byrd was then experimenting with a very wide range of forms and styles. There are the "virtuoso" compositions (this was after all Byrd's first appearance in print), including a fine canonic "Miserere mihi Domine", a rather dull crab-canon "Diliges Dominum" in which the second half reverses the first (on the face of it a remarkably difficult feat, but in practice comparatively straightforward), and the doxology to "O lux beata Trinitas"—a canon three in one. In addition to these, there are several chordal hymns, a long cantus firmus setting of "Libera me Domine de morte aeternam", and the large imitative motets.

The motets that Byrd published in his next anthology, the *Cantiones Sacrae* of 1589, show that the composer was working towards a more concise and expressive musical style. The earlier motets in the collection include "Domine praestolamur", "In resurrectione tua", "Laetentur coeli", the very popular "Ne irascaris Domine" (adapted to several English texts during the late sixteenth and early seventeenth centuries), "O Domine, adiuva me", "Peccavi super numerum" and "Tribulationes civitatum", all of which are to be found in manuscripts predating the year of publication. Of these, "In resurrectione tua" is remarkable for its brevity, its rhythmic vitality, and its economy of construction (see page 232). The polyphonic padding that clogs the texture of the earlier imitative works is here drastically pruned. Similar qualities are to be found in many of the other 1589 motets, and especially "Laetentur coeli", "Deficit in dolore" and "Vigilate", the last two being, as Kerman suggests, comparatively late works.

In the 1591 *Cantiones* are again to be found both "old" and "new" motets. "Cunctis diebus", "Infelix ego" and "Recordare Domine" were all circulating in manuscript some time before the date of publication, and all three are in the diffuse, extended style of "Aspice Domine". On the other hand, eight of the most vividly drawn motets do not occur in any pre-1591 manuscripts: "Laudibus in sanctis", "Miserere mei Deus",

"Quis est homo", "Salve regina", "Cantate Domino", "Domine non sum dignus", "Domine salva nos" and "Haec dies".

None of the 1575, 1589 or 1591 motets have a specifically liturgical function, though some are based on Sarum texts and plainsongs. Byrd designed his last two collections of motets, however—the *Gradualia* of 1605 and 1607—with a clear liturgical purpose in mind. For this reason if no other, these later works must be approached from a rather different standpoint. As James Jackman has recently shown in an admirable study of the "Liturgical aspects of Byrd's *Gradualia*",[6] the two books must be viewed as collections of sectionally constructed motets, the sections of which may be rearranged in many different ways. The two sets of *Gradualia*, as he puts it, are assemblies of "Mass-motet elements, rather than of discrete pieces each inviolably whole in its own right". An example may serve to make this point clearer. As it stands in the 1605 print, the Introit of the Lady Mass "Post Nativitatem Domini" (Vultum tuum) lacks both its psalm verse (Eructavit cor meum) and a doxology. Byrd intended, however, that the missing sections should be supplied from "Salve, sancta Parens". Using this principle of sectional transference, music for every liturgical occasion mentioned in the 1605 preface can be assembled—and, indeed, for other occasions besides. And, as Jackman has observed, the interchangeable elements interlock perfectly with each other in every instance, both as to key and the number of voices required. Forty-eight of the sixty-three numbered motets in the first book, and forty-four of the forty-six in book two are relevant to Byrd's main liturgical plan.

The qualities of brevity and economy already observed in the 1589 and 1591 collections are here even more pronounced as can be seen in this comparison of the opening bars of "Attollite portas" (1575) and "Tollite portas" (1605):

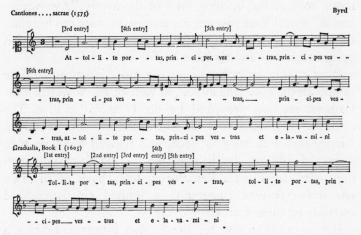

There is, too, something of a reaction against the almost madrigalian brilliance of the great 1589 and 1591 motets. There are certainly well over a dozen motets in the two sets of *Gradualia* of remarkable power and invention: there are the six-part settings from the 1607 print, "Alleluia, ascendit Deus", "Ascendit Deus", "Psallite Domino", and "Venite exultemus"; there are the three-part motets from the first book: "Alleluia. Quae lucescit", "Haec dies", and "Regina

coeli"; there are the four-part settings of "Alleluia, Cog-
noverunt discipuli", "Ave Regina", and "Puer natus" and
several superb five-part motets, including the two beginning
"Gaudeamus omnes", and "Assumpta est Maria", a third version
of "Haec dies" and "Tollite portas". Yet, for the reasons
already touched upon, these motets do not have either the
breadth or unity of the earlier works. Many of the liturgical
texts, moreover, offer little obvious scope for musical invention,
and the penitential vein that Byrd worked so fruitfully in
the earlier motets is almost completely absent. Nor, indeed,
did Byrd always fully exploit the available opportunities.
"Stabat mater", from the 1605 print, is strangely flat and
colourless, though the hymn is one of the most poignant in
the Latin repertory. The composer might well have made
more, too, of the opening lines of the lovely "Ave verum
corpus" text: "Vere passum, immolatum in cruce pro homine:
Cuius latus perforatum unde fluxit sanguine: Esto nobis
praegustatum in mortis examine."

Byrd could hardly have chosen a more inopportune time
to publish the *Gradualia* motets, in view of the powerful anti-
Catholic reaction provoked by the Gunpowder Plot. The
evidence suggests, indeed, that he withdrew both sets from
sale, probably in 1607 or 1608, and reissued them in 1610
as second editions, simply replacing the old title pages with
new ones dated 1610. Remarkably few copies of the two
sets have survived, suggesting a limited circulation and
certainly no more than a single edition.

Byrd's extant music for the English liturgy comprises a
set of Preces and Responses, two other sets of Preces (the second
of which has survived in two different versions), two sets of
original festal psalms, a Litany, two complete Services (one
in Short Service style, the other the elaborate Great Service),
two sets of canticles for Evensong and fragments of an early
Te Deum and Benedictus. The "First" or "Short" Service was
undoubtedly the most popular of them all, though less so
perhaps than the Gibbons Short Service in F fa ut. It defies all

attempts at dating, for its earliest source cannot have been copied out much before 1620 and the music is, in style, quite unlike any of the anthems, motets or devotional songs. Its structure is very similar to that of Tallis' Short Service, the musical plan being essentially A, B1, B2, C1, C2....

In places the repeat pattern coincides with the binary structure of the verse but as often as not Byrd evolves a binary scheme of his own, just as Tallis had done. The melodic style of the Short Service (and of the Third Service, too, which corresponds closely to it) falls half way between the simpler kind of festal psalm and the chordal full anthem. Apart from the repetitive B1, B2 design, each movement of the Short Service is through-composed. There are no recapitulations or imitative developments and, with one short exception, no canons. Here and there, however, the upper line does seem to spring from some short melodic figure, as if Byrd were writing free variations on a theme. In this passage from the Third Service, for instance, the intervals of the third and fourth predominate:

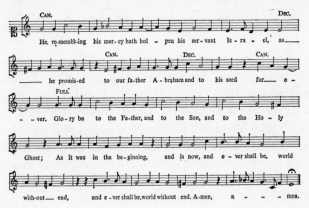

The passage also illustrates Byrd's fondness for syncopation (his keyboard dances are remarkable for their rhythmic vitality). Much of the original intention is lost if a flexible duple/triple barring system is used, for the original duple time signature holds throughout this passage, and the singers would undoubtedly have felt the syncopations as off-beat stresses against the main "tactus" or pulse.

Byrd wrote only one verse Service—a Magnificat and Nunc dimittis, which Barnard called the Second Service. It is an enigmatic work with features that are both ancient and modern. The limited use of solo voices suggests that it may be an early work (probably c. 1580), for it is in effect a Full Service with short interludes for solo voices and independent organ accompaniment. It is in the choruses, however, that Byrd is particularly adventurous, and especially in his use of sequence, as indeed was William Mundy in his C fa ut Evening Service.

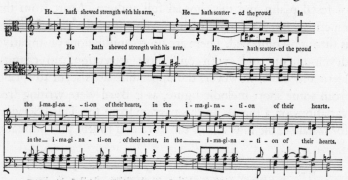

Byrd's most substantial work for the English rites is, of course, the "Great" Service, comprising Venite, Te Deum, Benedictus, Kyrie, Creed, Magnificat and Nunc dimittis. It is in the early Elizabethan Great Service tradition established by John Shepherd, Robert Parsons and William Mundy, being neither "full" nor "verse" in the early seventeenth-century sense, but calling none the less for soloists as well as full choir. It was not widely known, being doubtless too complex for the average cathedral choir (see page 237).

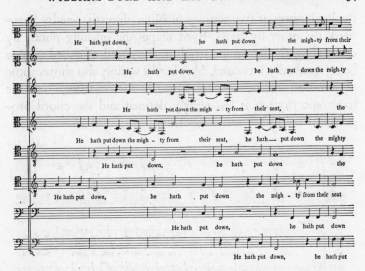

The extant sources are at York Minster (1618), Pembroke College Cambridge (1640), Peterhouse Cambridge (1635) and Durham Cathedral (1625), and fragments of the morning canticles are to be found in score in John Baldwin's commonplace book (c. 1590–1615). Though the setting was generally entitled the "Great Service", it is described in the York Minster books (c. 1618) as "Mr Byrd's new sute of service for meanes", a title that suggests a comparatively late date. Several missing parts have come to light since the original *Tudor Church Music* score was published in 1922, and the editorial reconstructions may now be dispensed with. Though the version in the Stainer and Bell edition is, in this sense, more complete, it omits all original scoring indications and is thus by no means as satisfactory as the 1922 edition. The textural subtleties of the original are indeed remarkable, the alternations between decani and cantoris and between soloists and full choir being an essential part of this impressive work. Although Byrd took the idea of the "Great" service from his elder contemporaries at the Chapel Royal, he differed from them in his use of a far wider range of melodic and harmonic rhythms. Here for comparison are

the beginnings of two settings of Nunc dimittis, one by Shepherd, the other by Byrd. Byrd shapes the opening phrase by
controlling the harmonic rhythm, the speed of chord change
being gradually increased. Shepherd's setting also shows some
acceleration of movement towards the cadence, but the
harmonic rhythm is less clearly defined and the chord progressions are rather more repetitive:

Byrd would also seem to have had some sort of broad tonal
scheme in his mind for each movement. In outline the
Magnificat, for instance, runs as follows:

Verse	"Modulations" during the course of the verse
1	C to D and G
2	C to G
3	a to C
4	a to d and C
5	C to a, d, G and F
6	C to G and d, ending in a
7	a to d and F and ending in G
8	F to a, d and F, ending in C
9	C to G and F
	Doxology in C, touching G, d and a.

It seems probable, on the evidence of the manuscript sources,
that Byrd wrote no more than a handful of anthems for
liturgical use, though well over sixty anthem-like compositions
are extant:

TABLE 23
The Anthems of William Byrd[7]
(i) Full anthems

	Separate voice-parts
All ye people clap your hands	5
*Arise, Lord, into thy rest	5
Arise, O Lord, why sleepest Thou [I] (Pt. II: Help us, O God)	5
Arise, O Lord, why sleepest Thou [II] (adaptation of Exsurge Domine)	5
*Attend mine humble prayer	3
Behold, how good a thing (Pt. II: And as the pleasant morning dew)	6
Behold, I bring you (Pt. II: And there was with the angel) (Adaptation of, Ne irascaris)	5
Behold, now praise the Lord (adaptation of, Laudate pueri, or of an instrumental canzona)	6
Be not wroth very sore (adaptation of, Civitas sancti tui)	5
*Be unto me a tower	4
Blessed art Thou, O Lord	(inc.)
Blessed is he that fears the Lord†	5
Come help, O God	5
*Come, let us rejoice	4
Even from the depth†	5
From depth of sin	3
Have mercy on us, Lord	5 (consort song)
Help Lord, for wasted†	5
How long shall mine enemies	5
How shall a young man†	5
How vain the toil	5 (consort song)
If that a sinner's sighs†	5
I have been young	3
I laid me down	5
I will give laud	(inc.)
Let not our prayers (adaptation of, Nos enim)	5
Let not thy wrath (adaptation of, Ne irascaris)	5
Let us arise (adaptation of, Attollite portas)	6
*Look down, O Lord	4
*Lord, hear my prayer	3
Lord, in thy rage	3
Lord, in thy wrath correct me not	3
Lord, in thy wrath reprove me not†	5
Lord, to Thee I make my moan	5 (consort song)
Lullaby, my sweet little baby†	5
*Make ye joy to God	5
Mine eyes with fervency†	5
My faults, O Christ	5 (consort song)
My soul oppressed†	5
O God, but God, how dare I	5 (consort song)

(*Table 23 continued overleaf*)

TABLE 23 (continued)

	Separate voice-parts
O God, give ear	5
O God, the proud are risen against me	6
*O God, which art most merciful	3
O God, whom our offences	5
O heavenly God	5 (consort song)
O Lord, bow down thy heavenly eyes	5 (consort song)
O Lord, give ear to the prayers	6
O Lord, how long wilt thou forget†	5
O Lord, how vain	5 (consort song)
O Lord, make thy servant	6
*O Lord, my God, let flesh and blood	4
O Lord, turn thy wrath (Pt. II: Bow thine ear) (Adaptation of, Ne irascaris)	5
O Lord, who in thy sacred tent†	5
O Lord, within thy tabernacle	5 (consort song)
O praise our Lord (Pt. II Extol the greatness, Pt. III Praise him on tube Pt. IV The gladsome sound)	5
O that we woeful wretches	5 (consort song)
Out of the deep [I]	5
Out of the deep [II] (or Orlando Gibbons)	6
*Praise our Lord, all ye gentiles	6
Prevent us, O Lord	5
Prostrate, O Lord, I lie†	5
Rejoice unto the Lord	5 (consort song)
Remember, Lord	5 (consort song)
*Retire, my soul	5
*Right blest are they	3
Save me, O God, for thy name's sake [I]	5
Sing joyfully unto God our strength (Pt. II: Blow the trumpet)	6
*Sing we merrily (Pt. II: Blow up the trumpet)	5
*Sing ye to our God	3
The Lord only is my support	5 (consort song)
The man is blest	5 (consort song)
*This day Christ was born	6
*Turn our captivity	6
*Unto the hills†	6
What unacquainted cheerful voice	5 (consort song)

Anthems in roman type are only to be found in non-liturgical sources; starred anthems do not appear in any manuscript source, but in the 1588, 1589 and 1611 publications only: anthems marked † are adapted consort songs.

(ii) Verse Anthems

	Total length	Scoring and length of full sections	Scoring of verses
Alack, when I look back	120 with repeats	40 (MAATB)	7 verses for solo alto
An earthly tree		(MMAT)	MM

TABLE 23 (continued)

	Total length	Scoring and length of full sections	Scoring of verses
Behold, O God, the sad and heavy case	185 with repeats	45 (MAATB)	4 verses for AA
Behold, O God, with thy all prospering eye			(text only)
Christ rising again	65	25 (MATTB)	4 verses for MM
Pt. II: Christ is risen	55	30 ([M]MATTB)	4 verses for MM
Exalt thyself, O God			(inc.)
From Virgin's womb	60	25 (SSMM)	M
Glory to God on high			(text only)
Have mercy upon me	75	40 ([S]MATTB)	4 verses for S
Hear my prayer, O Lord, and consider	65	35 (MAATB)	5 verses for M
Let us be glad			(text only)
Now Israel may say			(inc.)
O be joyful			(text only)
*O God that guides	120	30 (SMATBB)	1 verse for M
O Lord, rebuke me not	115	50 (MATTB)	4 verses for M
Thou God, that guid'st	80	30 (MAATB)	M/M/M/MM/M/MM

Italicised anthems are to be found in liturgical sources: starred anthems do not appear in any manuscript source, but in the 1588, 1589 and 1611 publications only. Full sections are represented in the fourth column by diagonal lines.

Of the nine motet adaptations, four are versions of "Ne Irascaris"—one of Byrd's most popular motets. Three of these are similar in mood to the original; but the fourth— "Behold, I bring you glad tidings"—serves as a salutary reminder that a great deal of Byrd's early work, whether English or Latin, has no very pronounced emotive character of its own. Absurd as it may seem to replace so stern a text as 'Ne Irascaris" with a joyful Christmas narrative, the adaptation does not in practice seem particularly incongruous. With the possible exception of "Exsurge, Domine", all the adapted motets are early works, and it may well be that the adaptations were made fairly soon after the originals had first appeared. Certainly there would have been less need for "Englished" motets after 1600, for by then a substantial repertory of anthems would have been available both for liturgical and devotional use.

Altogether, nine "original" full anthems are to be found in liturgical sources. Three of these are to be found in late sixteenth-century manuscripts: "How long shall mine enemies", "O Lord, make thy servant Elizabeth" and "Prevent us, O Lord". On stylistic grounds, the earliest of these would seem to be "O Lord, make thy servant", and "Prevent us, O Lord", together with a third anthem, "Out of the deep"— if, indeed, this is by Byrd. All three might excusably be mistaken for the work of William Mundy. The imitative ideas are developed in a regular and very compressed French style, the melodic lines move predominantly by step, the underlay is insistently syllabic, and the overall texture is dominated by the crotchet pulse. The scoring, too, is typical of early Elizabethan practice, with thick chords occasionally occurring in the lower registers.

The second group of English anthems would seem to follow closely upon the first, and there are both structural and stylistic parallels with the large imitative motets in the 1575 *Cantiones*. The works in question are "Arise, O Lord", "How long shall mine enemies", "O God whom our offences", and "Save me O God". None are quite on the scale of "Aspice, Domine" or "Attollite portas", and the underlay is at once more syllabic and less repetitious. The two latest liturgical anthems would seem to be "O God, the proud are risen against me" and "Sing joyfully". Of the two, "O God the proud" is perhaps the less successful work, partly because the tonality hangs rather too firmly around the centre of C. None the less, the scoring is imaginative and the melodic ideas highly dramatic, if at times a little naïve—as was often the case when Byrd was working in a pictorial vein. The text of "Sing joyfully" offers some unusually vivid opportunities for word painting—opportunities which Byrd seized with gusto, using every available technique to heighten the impact: abrupt oppositions of tonality, exciting harmonic and melodic rhythms and some highly colourful textures.

Of the seventeen extant verse anthems, five were published by the composer in the 1589 and 1611 collections. Of these five, three consist of no more than a single verse and a concluding chorus—"An earthly tree", "O God that guides" and "From Virgin pure". The two published verse anthems proper —"Christ rising" and "Hear my prayer"—were quite popular at the time and are to be reckoned amongst the composer's finest works. "Christ rising" was circulating in manuscript

some ten or so years before it was published, complete with
accompaniment for viols. The scoring is comparatively simple
—as indeed it is in the other verse compositions: the solos
throughout are sung by two meanes, and the full sections by
a five-part chorus which divides near the end into six parts.
The anthem opens with a brief "In nomine"-like introduction
for four viols, based on the Sarum plainsong "Alleluia, Christus
resurgens". This idea is then developed in the ensuing solo
verse, with dramatic effect:

Drama is, in fact, the most striking quality of the anthem: see
especially the bold first entry of the chorus at the words "Death
from henceforth hath no power upon him"; the joyful
rhythms of "he liveth unto God"

and the arresting contrast between the slowly moving "For
as in Adam all die" and the jubilant "So by Christ shall all

men be restored to life"—the musical climax of the whole
work.

"Have mercy", the other published verse anthem, is penitential in mood, lacking the brilliant contrasts of "Christ
rising" but, in a very much more subdued and expansive
way, no less fine.

The unpublished verse anthems are exclusive to the liturgical
sources and all are for organ and voices. Both "Behold, O
God" and "Thou God that guidest" are settings of indifferent
prayers for the royal health.

> O Lord Thou knowest that if the head but ache
> The body must partaker be of pain
> And every limb will tremble, shake and quake,
> Till health possess her wonted course again.

Words of this kind have little to offer, and Byrd is hardly to
be blamed for the results.

Of the other two complete anthems (the others are too
fragmentary to make restoration practicable), "Alack, when
I look back" is perhaps the most striking. It is based on verses
from Richard Edwardes' *Paradice of Dainty Devises*, published
posthumously in 1578, and like the early Mundy and Farrant

anthems it is strophic in form, with long solo verses and short choral interjections. "O Lord, rebuke me not" is a rather more complex piece, with comparatively long choruses in which substantial sections of the previous verse are repeated, some in reharmonised versions, as in "Hear my prayer".

THOMAS MORLEY

We now know that Morley came from a Norwich family and that he spent some years there as organist of the cathedral.[8] His father, who was a brewer, may also have been head verger of the cathedral for a while—a conjugation of activities that would not then have seemed at all unusual. No record of Thomas Morley's birth has yet been discovered but a note in the Sadler part-books at the Bodleian Library, Oxford (MSS.Mus. e. 1–5), suggests that the composer must have been born in 1557. If so, he would have been just seventeen years old when the Dean and Chapter of Norwich Cathedral granted him the reversion of the office of Organist and Master of the Choristers, proof enough that they were anxious not to lose him. Exactly when it was that Morley took up the reversion is not known; but by the year ending Michaelmas 1583 he was sharing the salary—and presumably the duties—of Master of the Choristers with Edmund Inglott, who had been in the service of the cathedral long before Morley was born.[9] By 1586–87 Morley seems to have been doing most of the work. But a year later his name disappears from the cathedral records and that of William Inglott—a son of Edmund—replaces it. It was in that year that Morley took his Mus.B. at Oxford. Shortly afterwards he settled in London, and his career there is nothing short of remarkable. Within the space of four years he had established himself as organist of St. Paul's Cathedral and a Gentleman of the Chapel Royal. In 1593 he published his first set of madrigals, the *Canzonets to Three Voices*, following these during the next seven years with no fewer than nine collections of vocal and instrumental music, comprising two sets of Italian madrigals "Englished", a collected edition of madrigals by English composers (*The Triumphs of Oriana*), and six sets of his own compositions. And, as if this were not enough, he managed to find time to bring out his monumental treatise on the theory and practice of music, the *Plaine and Easie Introduction to Practicall Musicke*.[10] How he combined all these activities with his duties as a professional church musician (not to mention his family responsibilities) will remain a mystery. When he died, in 1603, overwork must surely have been one of the contributory causes. Certainly he must have been a man of immense energy and ambition. As a musician, he possessed a remarkable breadth of vision and a truly cosmopolitan approach to the techniques of composition. Among his early works is the motet "Domine non est exaltatum", written, if the date in the Sadler part-books is correct, only a year after Tallis and Byrd had published their *Cantiones quae ab argumento sacrae vocantur*. It owes much to the motet style of the elder Alphonso Ferrabosco—it is expressive in harmony, melody and rhythm, and it is of prodigious length.

Later, in London, Morley was one of the first to exploit the new demand for Italianate ballets and madrigals. As Kerman has demonstrated:

No other musicians of Morley's generation distinguished themselves in Italianate composition, and the younger men looked instinctively to him as their model. But Morley looked instinctively to Italy; his historical position is that of a pioneer who digested the continental style, naturalised it, and presented it to his countrymen in a form that they could immediately appreciate and utilize further.... The popularity and cultivation of the English madrigal was in large measure due to him alone.[11]

It is against this background that we must review his achievements as a composer of church music. His extant compositions include settings of sentences from the Funeral Service, three full anthems—one of which is a composite Latin/English work, another being an English adaptation of "De profundis"

I

—three verse anthems, a set of festal psalms, a short four-part service, a full five-part Evening Service, and a highly elaborate verse Service.

The funeral anthems are in the simplest four-part chordal style—but even so they show a sensitive feeling for word accent and melodic line. There are a few short early Elizabethan settings of isolated sentences from the Burial Service, but Morley's "Service" is the earliest work of its kind to survive. Oddly enough, no pre-Restoration sources of the work have yet come to light, and indeed, until recently, the earliest authority was Tudway (c. 1720)—not the most reliable of copyists. Within the last three years, however, an early Restoration organ-score has materialised, confirming Tudway's ascription.

The habit of using both Latin and English consecutively in the same work goes back to pre-Reformation times. "Nolo mortem," rather more than Weelkes' Latin/English "Gloria in excelsis", looks back to these earlier works. It is in a simple imitative-cum-chordal style that would seem to place it amongst Morley's earliest works. The melodic outlines of no fewer than three imitative points boldly cover the span of a seventh in characteristic early Elizabethan style:

The two full Evening Services are both fairly straightforward. The "Short" Evening Service in four parts is probably the earlier of the two. Its melodic lines show affinities with those of the festal chant, as do all "Short" Services of the period, though they have an unquestionably expressive function; the proud are scattered in a rush of quavers, and the meek are exalted to heights that are reached nowhere else in the Service:

Although Morley attempts none of Byrd's formal experiments, he manages to give the four-part Service a sense of direction and movement forward by the skilful manipulation of cadence. In this respect, he was rather in advance of his time:

Magnificat of the Short Service

	First half	Second half
Vs. 1	d–A	d–D
Vs. 2	d–A	d–A (through E)
Vs. 3	F–F	F–D (through B♭)
Vs. 4	d–A	F–F
Vs. 5	F–A	A–d (with plagal IV–I cadence)
Vs. 6	d–D	d–D
Vs. 7	d–A	d–D
Vs. 8	d–F	F–G (through g)
Vs. 9	C–C	C–C (through B♭)
Gloria	G–G	C–D
	d–A	a–D

The parallels between the five-part Evening Service (called Mr. Morley's "Three Minnoms" in many sources) and Byrd's five-part Evening Service (also called "Three Minnoms") are too numerous to be coincidental. Perhaps Morley wrote his Service as a tribute to his master, or even while studying with him (see page 250).

Fine as the full Services and anthems are, it is the verse music that is of especial interest and importance. Although none of it can be dated with any certainty, there is more than a hint from manuscript evidence that Morley had written at least two of the verse anthems before he left Norwich for London. The only complete set of parts of "O Jesu meek" are in the Norwich Cathedral books—the earliest sections of which may date from 1640, and which, in turn, may have been copied from earlier books. The anthem seems to have been very little known in pre-Restoration times for it is to be found in only two other sources—the "Batten" organ-book, and the bass part-book from Barnard's manuscript collection (Royal College of Music MS. 1051). "How long wilt thou forget me" was admittedly more popular than "O Jesu meek", and its appearance in the Norwich books is perhaps less significant. It is none the less possible that both pieces were being sung whilst Gibbons, the "pioneer" of the verse anthem, was still in the cradle!

As Table 26 shows, Morley was little concerned with the structural integration of verse and chorus, although he did frequently repeat the words of a verse—or some of them, at least—in the succeeding chorus. His deservedly popular "Out of the deep" is to some extent uncharacteristic of his work in that it is by far the simplest, being scored for a single soloist and five-part MAATB choir. Yet in the solo verses Morley achieved a new and astonishingly vivid power of expression. The bold melodic lines, the superbly balanced phrases and the imaginative "key" scheme combine to create an impression that is not easily forgotten:

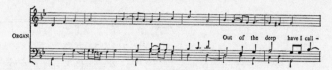

It has to be admitted that neither of the other verse anthems quite achieves this level, remarkable though they are. "O Jesu meek" bears some resemblance to Weelkes' "Give ear, O Lord". The texts of both come from the very popular collections of devotional verse, published by Mr. Hunnis, Master of the Chapel Children (1566–1597). Both are penitential in mood, and both have short refrains: Morley's ends "... have mercy now on me", and Weelkes' (see Ex. on page 305), "Mercy, good Lord, mercy".

Weelkes develops one musical idea with great economy at each reappearance of the refrain—and to superb effect. Morley's anthem is more loosely constructed. The ideas are less memorable, and their development less intense. "How long wilt thou forget me", on the other hand, falls very little below "Out of the deep" (see page 252).

The most ambitious of Morley's verse compositions is the verse Service. This is a curious work, for it covers in its seven movements—Venite, Te Deum, Benedictus, Kyrie, Creed, Magnificat and Nunc dimittis—almost the complete gamut of pre-Restoration Service styles. Venite, Kyrie and Creed

are full throughout, rather in the manner of Byrd's full four-part Venite but lacking the repetitive verse structure. The Te Deum opens with an intonation for solo alto, to which there is an independent organ accompaniment. The intonation follows the Sarum use. The canticle then continues in full style, with solo verses at the beginning of part two ("Thou art the everlasting Son of the Father") and at verse twenty-seven ("O Lord, have mercy upon us"). There is rather more solo music in the Benedictus. It begins with a solo intonation, and there are further solos at verse six and in the Gloria. The Magnificat and Nunc dimittis, on the other hand, are in a highly elaborate and colourful verse idiom, very little less ornate than that which Gibbons used in his most ambitious works. It would be fascinating to know which came first—Morley's Evening Verse Service or Hooper's. Both composers were born at about the same time (Hooper was just four or so years older). Hooper arrived in London six years before Morley—he had been at Exeter before then—and he became

Organist and Master of the Westminster Abbey choristers in 1588, a year or two before Morley went to St. Paul's. Yet by the time that Hooper joined the Chapel Royal Morley was dead, and it is for the Chapel Royal that these two verse Services must surely have been written.

The scheme of Morley's Magnificat is set out in Table 24 (see pages 254–55). The scoring is to some extent expressive. Verses one, eight and nine are set for high voices, as might be expected. On the other hand, the use of only three solo voices for verse six ("He hath shewed strength") after a full section to the words "And his mercy is on them" is certainly unexpected. For most of the time, the lowest line of the organ part doubles the lowest vocal line—always in the full sections; and indeed, in only forty bars out of the two hundred or more does the organ play an independent bass of its own. In this, it is closely akin to the early Elizabethan "Great" Service, with its oppositions of full, dec., and can., and its varieties of textures, arranged versewise.

OTHER YOUNGER CONTEMPORARIES OF BYRD

Of Morley's many immediate contemporaries, Edmund Hooper and Nathaniel Giles deserve especial mention. Both were prolific composers and both were distinguished members of the Chapel Royal.

Hooper was born at Halberton in Devon in about 1553, and he is said to have been a chorister at Exeter Cathedral.[12] By 1582 he was in London as a member of the Westminster Abbey choir. In December 1588 he became Master of the Abbey choristers, and in March 1604 a Gentleman of the Chapel Royal in succession to William Randoll, an Exeter musician. Some time before 1615 he was appointed an organist of the Chapel Royal, Orlando Gibbons being then his junior colleague. He died in 1621 and was buried in the cloisters of the Abbey on July 16th.

As far as is known, Hooper's interests lay almost entirely in church music. The little "Alman" in the Fitzwilliam Virginal

TABLE 24

Morley's Anthems and Service in Verse Style

Italicised MATB markings indicate repetition of text from the previous section. Broken lines dividing sections indicate that musical ideas in the first section are developed in the second

	V₁	Ch₁	V₂	Ch₂	V₃	Ch₃	V₄	Ch₄	V₅	Ch₅
How long wilt Thou forget me	A	MAAATB	M	*MAAATB*	MMAA + MAT	*MAAATB*	MAT	*MAATB*	MMAT	MAATB
[length in bars]	15	13	11	2	7	2	4	5	9	12
O Jesu meek	*AA*	*MATTB*	M	*MATTB*	A + MM	*MATTB*	A	*MATTB*		
	24	14	10	18	32	3 triple metre	20 triple metre			
Out of the deep	A	MAAATB	A	*MAAATB*	A	MAAATB	A	MAAATB		
	13	8	9	11	7	8	10	12		
Let my complaint	A	MATB	A	MATB	A	MATB	A	MATB	*Gloria* A	MATB
	10	7	6	6	5	7	8	9	6	16

(TABLE 24 *continued*)

Magnificat	*Verse* 1a:	1b*	4a:	4b	6a:	6b	8a:	8b	9a:	9b
	M^c	M^d	M^dM^c	M^dM^c	M^d	M^d	M^dM^c	M^dM^c	M^c	
		Ar^dAr^c	Ar^c	Ar^c	Ar^c	Ar^c	Ar^c	A_1^c	A_1^d	
								A_2^c	A_2^d	
		T^c	T^d	T^d					T^c	T^d
					B^c	B^c			B^c	B^d

* The Gloria, and verses not listed here are scored for full MAATB choir.

(^{d} = decani; ^{c} = cantoris)

Book shows him to have been an adventurous and very individual composer for keyboard—the dance is to all intents and purposes in the unusual key of A major. His other compositions include psalm settings for Este's psalter, two part-songs for Leighton's *Teares or Lamentacions*, two sets of Preces (one belonging to the "Flat" Service), a festal psalm, five Services, eight full anthems and ten verse anthems. The five Services do not seem to have been very widely known. The "Flat" Service—consisting of Venite, Te Deum, Jubilate, Magnificat and Nunc dimittis—has survived in only one source, the "Batten" organ-book, where it is at the very end and described as "the last that he ever made". There is also a Te Deum and Benedictus in the "Batten" organ-book which is unique to that source. The other three Services—all more or less complete—cover the full range of Service styles then current: "Short", "Verse" and "Great". The "Short" Service—Venite, Te Deum, Benedictus, Kyrie, Creed, Magnificat and Nunc dimittis—is one of the more substantial of its kind, being scored for full choir of MAATB. It is not imitative, though its textures are very far from chordal. The following extract from the Nunc dimittis may serve to give some idea of the composer's unusually advanced tonal idiom. The basic "key" of the setting is C "major":

The very elaborate Verse Service is very similar to Morley's Evening Service "for Verses", the scoring for the solo voices being especially colourful:

Hooper's unusual feeling for tonality is again much in evidence, and there are frequent "modulations" from tonic "major" to tonic "minor" keys, resulting from the use of the sharp accidentals of F and C. The underlay may not, on the whole, be as satisfactory as Byrd's—although one hesitates to comment on this point, since many of the faults may be due to careless copying—but in other respects Hooper's work is very little inferior to the best of the period.

The "Long" or "Full" Service is, as might be expected, the most elaborate of the three, being in effect a "Great" Service in the Robert Parsons, Mundy tradition. Its Magnificat is some 150 bars long, as against 75 for the "Short" Magnificat, 150 for the Tomkins "Third" or "Great" Magnificat, and 220 for the Byrd setting—easily the longest of its kind. Hooper's Service, like the others, is highly contrapuntal, with divisi writing in up to ten parts (see page 258).

Of the eight full anthems, "O how glorious", "Submit yourselves" and "Teach me thy way" may well be the work of

other composers. On stylistic grounds, the four-part "Teach me thy way" would certainly seem to be either a very early anthem or else the work of William Mundy, to whom it is attributed in the Durham MSS. Of the eight full anthems, "Behold it is Christ" is undoubtedly the most unusual—and the most successful. It is to be found in no fewer than eighteen separate pre-Restoration sources and, thus it would seem to have been one of the most popular anthems of its day. Its unusually rich and dissonant counterpoint evidently appealed to Hooper's contemporaries, and indeed it is an unusual and most effective setting (see page 103 for an extract).

TABLE 25

Anthems by Edmund Hooper

Full anthems
Almighty God, which hast given us (for Christmas Day)
Behold, it is Christ
I will always give thanks
I will magnify Thee, O God my king
O how glorious (attr. uncertain)
O, thou God Almighty
Submit yourselves (attr. uncertain)
Teach me thy way, O Lord (attr. uncertain)

Verse anthems
A fruitful branch of Jesse
Almighty God, which madest thy blessed Son (for the Circumcision)
Hearken, ye nations (for November 5th)
O God of Gods (for the King's Day)
O Lord, in Thee is all my trust
O Lord, turn not away thy face
Remember not, O Lord God
Sing, O sing unto the Lord
The blessed Lamb (for Easter Day)
Unto the hills

Sacred songs
Alas, that I offended ever
Wellspring of bounty

Splendid as Hooper's verse music is, it is unlikely ever to come into general use again since nearly all of it is set to very inadequate Elizabethan and Jacobean verse. The two occasional pieces, "Hearken ye nations", and "O God of Gods", are veritable cantatas, each lasting for between four and five minutes and richly scored for voices and viols.[13] The Easter anthem is on a similar scale, and there are string parts, too, for this work. Hooper's younger colleague at the Chapel Royal, Orlando Gibbons, must surely have learned much from him, for the two composers have much in common:

O Lord, turn not away

The Blessed Lamb

Nathaniel Giles came from a musical family. His father, Thomas, had been senior chorister at Westminster Abbey in 1543, and later organist and Master of the Choristers at St. Paul's Cathedral. Nathaniel was born in 1558, a year or so after Thomas Morley. He was for a while Organist and Master of the Choristers at Worcester Cathedral, moving in 1585 to a similar post at St. George's Chapel, Windsor, by special request—so his indenture says—of the Dean and Chapter there. He must have been an outstandingly gifted choir trainer, for on the death of William Hunnis in 1597 he was invited to take charge of the Chapel Royal choristers. He then held both appointments concurrently until a year or two before his death in 1633.

During the early days at Windsor and the Chapel Royal he was deeply involved in theatrical activities (see page 219). The fashion for choirboy plays was still at its height, and the choristers of both St. George's and the Chapel were busily engaged in the production of plays at the Blackfriars Theatre and at Court. As has already been mentioned, music formed an important part of these entertainments. There would have been up to an hour's music beforehand, as well as songs and dances during the course of the play. Although Giles does not appear to have written any "theatrical" music himself, secular influences are very apparent in his church music. Nearly all of it is in the new "verse" style, and elements of the "consort song" are apparent in the solo and instrumental lines of the verses. In all, there are some twenty verse anthems and two verse Services, both consisting of Te Deum, Jubilate, Kyrie, Creed, Magnificat and Nunc dimittis, a Morning Service (of which only fragments remain), three full anthems and three sacred songs.[14] With so much to do at St. George's and the Chapel Royal, it is a wonder that Giles found any time at all to compose. Much of his music is, indeed, competent if unmemorable. The full anthem "O give thanks", for instance, is rather an exercise in counterpoint than an attempt at expressive word setting, and there is nothing especially joyous or festive about it:

Much of the verse music, too is equally characterless. The harmonies tend to gravitate firmly around a central chord and the melodies to spring from a few cadential clichés. One or two of the anthems do, however, deserve an occasional hearing. Giles' setting of "Out of the deep" was one of his more popular anthems, and it compares interestingly with Morley's superb setting of the same text. Though Giles' music is rather more drawn out—it lasts for 114 bars as against Morley's 78—his solo lines also have a declamatory quality about them and there are, here and there, curious parallels between the two:

No voice parts of "Have mercy" have yet come to light, but to judge from the extant organ part, this anthem would have been equally interesting, its tonality being unusually adventurous. The chromatic verse after the first chorus is especially striking. "God which as at this time" also contains a chromatic verse and chorus. Its text, the Collect for Whitsunday, is not a particularly easy one to set to music, being for the most part "indifferent" in mood—to use Archbishop Parker's apt definition. Giles has none the less managed to produce a colourful, festive Whitsunday anthem of a rather distinctive kind (see page 149 for an extract from the last verse and chorus).

Perhaps the most unusual feature of Giles' music is the variety of its forms. In some anthems there are no links at all between the various verses and choruses; in some, large sections of verses, both text and music, are redeveloped in the succeeding choruses, and in others there are exact rondo-like repetitions. "What child is he", for example, takes the following musical form: aBcBaB (the small letters being verse, the large being chorus), whilst "O Lord my God" is in the form aBcBdBeB. As a melodist and contrapuntist, Giles is undoubtedly inferior to his more famous contemporaries. The best of his music none the less deserves a place in the cathedral repertory (see Table 26, page 264).

Of the other Chapel Royal composers, John Bull is undoubtedly the most important. Before he finally left England in 1613 he had written more than a dozen devotional songs and anthems to English texts. Five of his anthems, all in verse form, are listed in the Chapel Royal anthem book (c. 1630), and a further four verse anthems are in pre-Restoration music manuscripts. Two were especially popular at the time. One is the well-known setting of the Epiphany Sunday collect "Almighty God, who by the leading of a star", and the other is based on verses from Psalm 38, "In Thee, O Lord, put I my trust". There are string parts for both anthems. The history of the "Star" anthem, as the Epiphany one was commonly called, is difficult to determine; but there is evidence to suggest that the work was originally a motet "Deus omnipotens", or possibly a string fantasia with that title.[15] John Baldwin, the Windsor musician, copied it into his commonplace book in score format, leaving the separate parts untexted but with the Latin incipit. Baldwin's score dates from about 1600 and is the earliest of the extant sources. In the Thomas Myriell books, dated 1616, it appears as a verse anthem for voices and viols, and in two separate versions —one arranged for six singers and instrumentalists, the other

TABLE 26

The Anthems of Giles

Full Anthems
He that hath my commandments
O give thanks unto the Lord
O Lord almighty

Sacred songs
Almighty Lord and God of love
Out of the deep (f3)
Out of the deep (f5)

Verse anthems	Total length*	Scoring and length of full sections	Scoring of verses
Blessed are all they	—	—	text only
Blessed art thou that fearest God	120	40	(inc.)
Everlasting God, which hast ordained	95	40 (MAATB)	AT/MAAT/MAT
Except the Lord	120	35 (MATB)	A/A/M/A/MM
God, which as at this time	130	60 (MAATB)	MM/MAT+B/MMA/ MMA+ATB/A/ MAATB
Have mercy on us Lord	110	40	(inc.)
Have mercy upon me	150	57	(inc.)
I will magnify Thee	135	40 (SMAATB)	S+M+B+SMAT/A/ A+S (i.e., this anthem is scored for trebles and meanes, plus altos, tenors and basses)
Lord, in thy wrath	120	45 (MAATB)	M/MA/MA/M+M (inc.)
O hear my prayer, Lord	90	35 (MAATB)	M/M/M/M/M
O how happy a thing it is (I)	100	25 (MAATB)	M/M/A+T/M (inc.)
O how happy a thing it is (II)	125	40	—
O Lord, in Thee is all my trust	—	—	text only
O Lord, my God, in all distress	160	50 (MAATB)	M/AA/MA/MM. (A thanksgiving for a victory: the Armada?)
O Lord of hosts	140	60	(inc.)
O Lord, of whom I do depend	100	25	(inc.)
O Lord, turn not away thy face	180	40 (MAATB)	M/A/T/M/A/MM
O sing unto the Lord . . . let the congregation	120	65	(inc.)
Out of the deep	115	30 (MAATB)	B+A/AB/MM/B+A
What child was he	160	65 (MAATB)	A+M/M+A+M/A+A

+ = the entry of a voice during the course of a verse.
/ = chorus (scoring as indicated in column 3).
* = to the nearest five bars: four crotchets to the bar, note-values reduced by half.

for five (the music is identical in the two, however). If indeed the original was a motet, the work of adaptation was skilfully done, perhaps by the composer himself.

Dr. Fellowes' criticisms of "In Thee, O Lord" must have done much to prevent its inclusion in the modern repertory. This is a pity, for it is a fine anthem constructed on even broader lines than "Almighty God". It was generally known as the "roaring" anthem, since the words "I have roared for the very disquietness of my heart" (Psalm 38, verse 8) are developed at length by solo voices and full choir. While this may look somewhat incongruous in black and white, the anthem has proved to be remarkably effective in performance. The verses are scored principally for two solo meanes and four consort instruments—presumably viols, though the instrumentation is not, of course, specified—and there are subsidiary solo parts for alto, tenor and bass. The full sections throughout are for the normal five-part cathedral choir. Bull's use of passing and suspended dissonance is especially daring and superbly effective:

Time has dealt very harshly with the work of Elway

Bevin. The composer was for a while a member of the
Wells Cathedral choir before moving to Bristol as Master
of the Cathedral choristers in 1585. In 1605 he was made a
Gentleman Extraordinary of the Chapel Royal, and Anthony
à Wood asserts that he subsequently became a Gentleman
in Ordinary, though there is no evidence to support this
claim. In documents dealing with an archiepiscopal visitation
of Bristol Cathedral in 1635, Bevin is described as a "very
old man". Wood suggests that he was expelled two years
later as a recusant, but there is again nothing to corroborate
this. Bevin died in 1638. Of his six anthems, four are incomplete, the fifth is a setting of a composite text beginning
"Praise the Lord, and call upon his name"—a simple and
undistinguished work for MATB—and the sixth is a devotional
song for three voices. His two Services are of rather greater
interest. The so-called "Dorian" or "Short" Service has been
in the repertory almost without a break since Boyce printed
it in the first volume of his *Cathedral Music*. The Service
includes all the usual movements—Venite, Te Deum, Benedictus, Commandments, Creed, Magnificat and Nunc dimittis
—Venite, Kyrie and Creed being in four parts throughout,
the remaining canticles being alternately scored for full
MAATB choir and decani and cantoris subdivisions of MATB.
The texture is essentially homophonic, but there are one or
two small points of imitation in the evening canticles. The
other Service—so far unnoticed—is the Evening Service called
"Mr. Bevin's Gimill", a title implying the extensive use of
paired voices (gemellus = a twin) and especially of paired
meanes or trebles. Unfortunately, the boys' parts and an alto
part are lost, but enough remains to show that the setting was
of "Great" Service proportions, with exciting contrasts of
texture and divisi sections in perhaps as many as eight real
parts. This extract from the Gloria of the Magnificat will
serve to give some idea of Bevin's style, which looks back to
the early Elizabethan work of William Mundy and Robert
Parsons (at least two parts are missing here):

Four other minor Chapel Royal composers deserve at least a mention: William West, the Canterbury musician who "did attend by the space of eight days at the great solemnity of the league of Spain to his great charge" and who was duly rewarded in 1605 with a full place in the choir; William Randoll, the Exeter musician who sang in the Chapel choir from 1584 to 1603 (see page 66); William Crosse, "servant" to the Dean of the Chapel, the Bishop of Bath and Wells, and Matthew White, "Minister and bass from Wells".

Not a note of Crosse's music has survived, though the texts of six of his anthems are in the Chapel Anthem Book of c. 1630, whilst Matthew White's one undisputed anthem lacks at least two of its voice parts. West's two anthems and his "Short" Service suffer from shortwindedness, and even Randoll's six-part setting of Psalm 43—"Give sentence with me"—proves on closer acquaintance to be a very dull affair, barely escaping the chords of the tonic, dominant and sub-dominant.

The more important minor provincial composers include John Mundy, Organist of St. George's Chapel, Windsor, John Holmes, Organist of Winchester Cathedral, Matthew Jeffreys, a vicar choral at Wells and John Hilton the elder, of Trinity College, Cambridge. Of the four, John Mundy is perhaps the best known, both for his *Songs and Psalmes* of 1594 and for his vigorous and attractive consort anthem "Sing joyfully". The composer's blunt, forceful style is well suited to the mood of "Sing joyfully" and, although the trumpet blowings in the third and fifth choruses may lack the subtlety of Byrd's, the anthem has much to recommend it. Mundy's other anthems do not, unfortunately, measure up to this standard, having much of the dry exactness that characterises the work of the elder Mundy, John's father.

Of Holmes' sixteen anthems and two Services, not one is complete enough to justify an attempt at restoration. This is particularly unfortunate since his music is of unusual historical interest, nearly all of it being in verse form. Several of the anthems bear dates between 1602 and 1610, and are thus very early examples of verse music by a provincial composer: three of them, "All laud and praise", "O God, Thou art the wellspring" and "O heavenly Father" are described as anthems "for the King", suggesting some as yet undiscovered link between Holmes and the Chapel Royal. Certainly the composer was known to Morley as one of the contributors to *The Triumphs of Oriana*. The loss of the evening Service "in medio chori" is particularly to be deplored, as also the Preces and Psalms "for trebles" which precede it.

Much of Matthew Jeffreys' music is, by contrast, in the established full style. There are some seven full anthems and fragments of two full Services (one called the Service "for meanes"—implying divisi boys' voices—and the other the "Second" or "Full" Service), together with five verse anthems (two of which have parts for stringed instruments) and a verse Service (called the "First"). Jeffreys preferred rich sonorities and imitative textures. His full anthems are all in five and six parts, and they display surprising technical assurance and even, here and there, real imagination. Although the composer is not the equal of his more illustrious contemporaries in either melodic or rhythmic invention, his work certainly deserves an occasional hearing:

Rejoice in the Lord

John Hilton is now known for his "Lord, for thy tender mercy's sake" (if indeed this is by him and not by one of the Farrants) and for his seven-part "Call to remembrance". There are, in all, some sixteen extant anthems by "John Hilton", as well as two settings of the morning and evening canticles (both incomplete), a Te Deum for men, and a Magnificat and Nunc dimittis "for verses". Rather shortsightedly, John the elder christened his musical son John, thus sowing the seeds of much confusion and uncertainty. There is, for instance, a world of difference between the sober polyphony of "Call to remembrance" and the madrigalian texture of the verse anthem "Teach me, O Lord":

Teach me, O Lord

None of the elder John Milton's anthems are to be found in liturgical sources, and we may safely assume that the composer must have written them for performance at the weekly music meetings which took place at his house in Bread Street just off Cheapside, between about 1600 and 1632.[16] All are a-capella works for four and five voices, and all are available in modern reprint. Milton's music provides a pleasant evening's entertainment, and there are indeed some memorable moments, especially in the setting of "When David heard", which captures much of the spirit of the great settings by Weelkes and Tomkins:

One other composer, a mysterious "Wilkinson", would seem to deserve mention here. In all there are thirteen of his verse anthems (most of which are consort anthems for voices and viols), three full anthems, and settings of Te Deum, Benedictus, Commandments, Magnificat and Nunc dimittis.[17] Contrapuntal as this music is, the dominant influences are the consort song and the lute song. The solo lines of the verses move in shortish phrases, punctuated by brief instrumental interludes. Wilkinson was a careful craftsman, and his respect for the principles of underlay is exemplary if a little unimaginative. He evidently preferred to work to a set pattern, for each of his completable verse anthems consists of three verses and three choruses. The texts are mostly composite ones assembled from the psalter but with modifications—either with the idea, it would seem, of producing a more immediately intelligible text or of increasing the personal impact. The scoring of the verse anthems is on the dull side, something like half of the total number of solo verses being for one or two meanes.

As Alison remarked, music for trebles and meanes was then much in demand for use "in private families".

All the verse anthems are of considerable length. At crotchet = 72 (reducing the original note values by half), the three longest would take five minutes or more to perform and the shortest would take little less than four. Wilkinson, like Dowland, was more attracted to the darker moods,

TABLE 27

Anthems by Wilkinson

Full anthems
I am the resurrection
O Jerusalem, thou that killest the prophets
O Lord God of my salvation
Why art thou so full of heaviness

Verse anthems with strings
(there are alternative organ parts for most of these)

Deliver me, O Lord, from lying lips
Hear my prayer, O Lord, and with thine ears
Help Lord, for there is not one
Lord, how are they increased
O Lord, consider my distress
O Lord, my God, in Thee have I put
Praise the Lord, O ye his servants
Preserve me, O Lord
Put me not to rebuke

Other verse anthems
Behold, O Lord
In Thee, O Lord, do I trust
Unto Thee, O Lord, will I lift up

nearly all his anthem texts being penitential or prayerful in character. Several of the anthems would have been appropriate for use in time of plague, and one—"Behold, O Lord" —suggests that the composer must himself have experienced its horrors:

Behold, O Lord and deliver thy people, O ponder the voice of our humble desire. Thy hand is heavy upon us; Lord, how long wilt Thou hide thy face from us? Be not angry with us for ever. We consume in thy displeasure and are afraid of thy wrathful indignation. O remember not our old sins, but according to thy goodness think upon thine inheritance, whom Thou hast purchased of old. Comfort us again, after the time that Thou hast plagued us, and for the time wherein we have suffered great affliction. Turn Thee again, O Lord, thou God of hosts; shew us the light of thy countenance and we shall be whole.

Within the limits of a very conservative style, Wilkinson's church music is certainly "expressive". The anthems are enlivened by many subdued madrigalian touches:

But in general, his music is probably too self-effacing to appeal to twentieth-century ears.

NOTES TO CHAPTER 8

1. Fellowes (ii), ch. 1.
2. Flood, p. 149.

3. Though Byrd may not have taken a very active part in the administration of the Chapel choir, for he signed not a single minute in the *Check Book*.

4. Weston, ch. 9.

5. Kerman (iii).

6. Jackman.

7. It is hard to draw a distinction between the sacred and the secular, especially in the case of Byrd: his "Care for thy soul", for example, could conceivably be considered as a devotional part-song.

8. Harrison, F. Ll. (ii), p. 98.

9. Boston, and Shaw (ii).

10. Morley.

11. Kerman (i), p. 131.

12. Grove V.

13. Possibly some of this music may have been commissioned by John Williams, for a time Dean of Westminster Abbey and a noted patron of the Arts; see Hacket; and Phillips.

14. Mr. Brian Runnett and Mr. David Keeling very kindly placed their transcriptions of Giles' music at the author's disposal.

15. Information very kindly supplied by Professor Dart.

16. Brennecke, ch. 3.

17. Mr. Alan Brown very kindly placed his transcriptions of Wilkinson's music at the author's disposal.

9

Thomas Tomkins and his Contemporaries

Tomkins was well over eighty when he died, early in the summer of 1656.[1] With the exception of William Child, he was the longest lived of all the major sixteenth- and early seventeenth-century composers, and one of the most prolific, too. He wrote an immense amount of music for stringed

TABLE 28

*The Younger Contemporaries of Thomas Tomkins
(1572–1656)*

	Orlando Gibbons*	1583–1625
	Weelkes	1575–1623
also		
	Amner	1585–1641
	Batten	1590–1637
	East	1580–1648
	Peerson	1572–1650
	Ravenscroft	1590–1635
	William Smith	fl. 1630
	Ward	1600–1641

Other composers
   Bateson, Coperario, Benjamin Cosyn, Cranford, Dering, Fido, *Ford*, John Gibbs, Richard Gibbs, Heath, Hinde, Thomas Holmes, John Hutchinson, Richard Hutchinson, Jewett, *Robert Johnson II*, *Kirby*, John Lugge, Robert Lugge, Thomas Lupo I (d. 1628) or/and Thomas Lupo II (d. 1637), Marson, Molle, Nicholson, Palmer, Robert Parsons II, Pilkington, Portman, Stonard, Daniel Taylor, Giles Tomkins, John Tomkins, Tucker, Warwick, *Wilbye*, Wilson, Woodeson

---

* Italicised dates are only approximate. Italicised names indicate that no liturgical anthems or Services are known by the composers in question.

and keyboard instruments,[2] thirty or more secular and sacred madrigals,[3] at least seven Services, one hundred and thirteen anthems, a set of Preces, two festal psalms and several metrical psalm tunes.[4] Tomkins came from a very musical family and he was for a while a chorister at St. David's Cathedral, where his father was organist. He later moved to London to study with Byrd, before taking up an appointment at Worcester Cathedral early in 1596. Although he was Organist and Master of the Choristers there until the Civil War, he none the less kept in close touch with London. He contributed one of the madrigals to Morley's *Triumphs of Oriana* (1603), and it looks as though he supplied a setting of the *Confortare* for James' coronation in 1603.[5]

By 1620 he was a Gentleman of the Chapel Royal. His name first appears in the Check Book as witness to the appointment of another Gentleman, Thomas Piers, in June of that year. It is more than likely, however, that he had been a Gentleman Extraordinary for some considerable time before that—perhaps even from 1603 or thereabouts. In August, 1621, he succeeded Edmund Hooper as Organist of the Chapel and for the next few years he must have spent much time in London. It may well have been this appointment that encouraged him to publish his one book of madrigals, *Songs of 3. 4. 5. and 6. parts*, in 1622. The book is of considerable interest, not least for the dedications that head each piece. These reveal the composer in many different lights: as a loving son ("Our hasty life away doth post", "to my dear father Mr. Thomas Tomkins", the first work in the collection) —a humble pupil ("Too much I once lamented", "to my ancient and much reverenced Master, William Byrd")— and as a lively and quizzical friend ("O let me live", dedicated to "Doctor Dowland", and parodying Dowland's well-known *Lachrymae antiquae* pavan).

The dedications reveal a wide range of friendships. Chapel Royal musicians naturally predominate (Byrd, Gibbons, Giles, Heather and the Clerk of the Check, John Stevens), but

Tomkins was on good terms with some of the leading secular musicians at Court, including Dowland and Coperario. And among the other dedicatees are Dr. Aylmer, the Bishop of Worcester, the poet Phineas Fletcher, and Humphrey Withy—one of Tomkins' Worcestershire friends. Upon the death of Byrd in 1623, Tomkins became the senior organist and composer of the Chapel. Much of the music for Charles I's coronation in 1625 is by him, and it was possibly in belated recognition of his services on that occasion that Charles made him "composer in ordinary" some three years later. There is no record of him at Court after 1628, and it is reasonable to assume that with advancing age he found the long journey from Worcester to London increasingly arduous. Yet the 1630 Anthem Book of the Chapel Royal contains more anthems by him than by any other single composer, proof enough of the esteem in which he was then held.

The years at Worcester before the outbreak of civil war were troubled ones. The Dean and Chapter became involved in a series of petty and nagging disputes with the townsfolk. Indeed, if the Dean is to be believed, the Bishop was largely to blame since he had on many occasions criticised the cathedral services, and in terms which could only plant "faction and contempt of the church in the citizens". Choral services finally came to an end on July 23rd, 1646—just three days after the city had surrendered to parliamentary troops:

> July 23. This day at 6 of the clock prayers, many gentlemen went to take their last farewell and meeting at the collegiate common prayers of the church and to receive the Bishop's blessing, saying "The grace of our Lord", etc. . .

Tomkins none the less stayed on at his house in College Green, quietly composing, revising and copying. But in 1654 he joined his son and daughter-in-law at their house in the village of Martin Hussingtree, not far from the city, and within two years he was dead. The parish registers there contain this simple record of his death:

Mr Thomas Tomkins, organist of the King's Chapel and of the Cathedral Church of Worcester was buried the 9th day of June, 1656.

Happily, however, the story does not end there; for twelve years later a comprehensive collection of his church music was published (probably edited by his son Nathaniel) under the title *Musica Deo Sacra*. The editor may not have been particularly expert, yet had it not been for him all the three-part compositions would have been entirely lost and well over half the liturgical anthems and Services would have been hopelessly incomplete. All but seventeen of the extant anthems are to be found in *Musica Deo Sacra*. Of the seventeen, three are sacred madrigals that had already been published in 1622, and three others are sacred madrigals that were not especially suited to liturgical use. Even the superb sacred madrigal "When David heard" was only included in *Musica Deo Sacra* as an afterthought at the time the errata sheets were being printed.

In all probability, Tomkins wrote the three-part anthems for the private recreation of his family. All but three are based on texts from the psalms. Two of the odd three use Prayer Book texts, and the third is a composite text possibly phrased by the composer himself: "O Lord do away as the night so do away my sins. Scatter my transgressions as the morning cloud." Of the nineteen three-part compositions, the settings of the seven penitential psalms are consistently the best. The opening of Psalm 130 is typical of its kind.

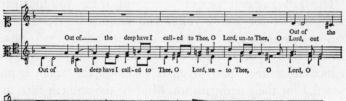

These three-part pieces, and indeed the Services and anthems as a whole, have many madrigalian qualities.

And yet, words apart, they could not conceivably be mistaken for madrigals. Tomkins' church style is, for want of a better term, more "learned" than the secular. There is a greater continuity of mood, the imitative points are developed at greater lengths, and extremes of mood are never contrasted as sharply as they are in the livelier madrigals.

The full anthems proper consist of some six four-part compositions for men's voices and another thirty-five for various combinations of meanes, altos, tenors and basses (see Table 29, pp. 288–95). All are provided with keyboard reductions in the "pars organica", though the organ is not essential for their performance. Most of the anthem texts are taken from the psalter and Book of Common Prayer, though there are one or two settings of contemporary verse. Three of the full anthems were written for special occasions, two— "Be strong" and "Zadok"—for coronations, and one—

"Almighty and everlasting God which hatest nothing"—
for Ash Wednesday (three other full anthems may perhaps
have been written for the Maundy Thursday service: "Arise,
O Lord God", "Blessed is he that considereth" and "He that
hath pity"). Most of the "occasional" anthems are, however,
in verse form—for All Saints, Christmas, Holy Innocents,
Whitsunday, St. John the Evangelist, St. Stephen, St. George,
and for Prince Henry's funeral—an indication, perhaps, of
Tomkins' own preference for the verse style.

The general level of achievement is again remarkably high,
although Tomkins is undoubtedly at his best when setting
texts of clearly defined mood. The formality of the Ash
Wednesday anthem is, indeed, quite in keeping with its
"indifferent" text:

but a work of this kind cannot possibly have the immediate
appeal of the more dramatic anthems and sacred madrigals—
and especially of "Arise, O Lord, into thy resting place",
"Great and marvellous are thy works", the seven-part "O
sing unto the Lord a new song", and the settings of the laments
"When David heard that Absalom was slain" and "Then
David mourned".

Tomkins rarely attempted feats of unusual technical skill
in his church music, nor was he especially successful when he
did. There is a strange and awkward canon, 4 in 1, to the
words of the Commination Service prayer, "Turn thou us,
O good Lord". Its melodic lines begin and end abruptly, and
the harmonic scheme seems forced and crude:

K

It may be, of course, that the original was an abstract exercise and that words were added to it when it was included in *Musica Deo Sacra*. Certainly there is much in the opening bars to suggest adaptation. There is, for instance, the irregular entry of the alto in the first bar and the ugly subdivision of the word "favourable".

The twelve-part "O praise the Lord" is something of a technical exercise, too, though of a rather different order. The chief problem that is likely to arise when writing imitative counterpoint for so many voices is the maintenance of an interesting harmonic rhythm. Tomkins does not pass the test especially well; for though the tonality of "O praise the Lord" is not altogether static, it lacks subtlety and flexibility. The real bass line of the first seventeen bars runs as follows, for example (simple "continuo" figures have been added to indicate the harmonies):

And if the harmonic scheme is not especially imaginative, nor are the textures. Oddly enough, the composer made no attempt to subdivide the large choir into three MATB groups

—though this would have been quite practicable—and all twelve voices are kept going fairly continuously throughout the anthem.

There is little or nothing to suggest that Tomkins changed or developed his style as the years went on. He attempted no radical experiments with the established forms and techniques of composition, and he remained unmoved by *seconda prattica* developments in Italy. If indeed he composed the five *Musica Deo Sacra* Services in the order in which they are numbered, he would seem increasingly to have preferred the verse style.

The first two *Musica Deo Sacra* Services are "short", being scored in the main for full four-part choir. The third is called the "Great" Service and is scored for two antiphonal choirs (decani and cantoris MAATB) and a small solo group (MMAT). An organ part for these first three Services is supplied in the "pars organica" but it does no more than double the voices. The other two Services in *Musica Deo Sacra* are in the verse style proper, with independent obbligato accompaniments for organ.

There are two incomplete Services, both "for verses", in the Durham Cathedral part books.[6] The most popular Service by far was the first, in "C fa ut", for MATB with decani and cantoris subdivisions. The second Service, though of similar proportions, and of equal merit, has survived in no more than a single pre-Restoration manuscript. Both follow closely the pattern used (and probably evolved) by Tallis in his "Short" Service, the treble line dominating an essentially homophonic texture. Tomkins uses a semi-sequential method of melodic extension—a device perhaps borrowed from Byrd—and this serves to give a feeling of unity to an otherwise through-composed structure (see "For mine eyes have seen", page 282).

In the fifth Service the sequential extension is even carried through from one canticle to another. The third, fourth and fifth Services seem to have been no more popular than the second. The third and the fourth call for large choirs and are of festal proportions (see "O be joyful in the Lord all ye lands", page 282).

The Te Deum of the third lasts for close on eight minutes—
or twice as long as the average "short" setting. *Musica Deo Sacra*
is the sole source of the fifth Service, though it must surely have
been within the range of the average cathedral choir of the
time.

Rather more than half of the liturgical anthems are in
verse form. Like his contemporaries, Tomkins kept closely
to the basic formula of instrumental introduction, solo verse,
chorus—the sequence being repeated as often as required.
Only one of the fifty or so verse anthems departs from
this scheme—"Rejoice, rejoice", a consort anthem for the
Annunciation, which opens with a full chorus and which
then continues with the usual instrumental—solo—chorus

alternations. This work, however, is rather different from the other anthems in general style. It was not included in *Musica Deo Sacra*, and it may well be by some other composer.

The verse anthems have much in common, both in broad outline and in structural detail. There is much semi-sequential development of the kind discussed above. The opening verse of "Give sentence with me, O God" well illustrates the advantages and disadvantages of the technique:

A norm is established in this verse of threefold repeats and one- and two-bar phrase lengths during the course of the first sixteen bars. The norm is then broken by an irregular entry on the accented beat at bar sixteen. The repetitions of the fourth phrase—bar eighteen onwards—are unevenly spaced, and the last phrase is extended slightly on its third appearance to produce a feeling of conclusion. Yet Tomkins was perhaps mistaken to repeat each of the five phrases three times, for despite the interesting organ accompaniment the listener is only too well prepared to expect a threefold scheme of repetition by the time that the twenty-third bar has been reached.

Only four of the verse anthems have accompaniments for consort instruments (presumably viols, though the instrumentation is never specified). These are "Above the stars",[7] "Know ye not", "Rejoice, rejoice" and "Thou art my king, O God". The organ accompaniments of many other verse anthems none the less give the impression of having been condensed from viol parts. Like the Services and the full anthems, the verse anthems are built upon a fairly conservative tonal system. Here and there are to be found unexpected touches—the use of a tonic major tonality in a basically "minor" mode, or the use of some unconventional modulation:

My beloved spake

Almighty God whose praise this day

Hear my prayer

But though Tomkins rarely went to the available extremes of chromatic modulation (the superb "When David heard" and the verse anthem "Know ye not" are exceptions to prove the rule), his music gains much of its shape from well-defined "modulations" or cadences in related tonalities. The opening verse of "Give sentence", quoted above, shows this clearly. And in the use of the sharp keys Tomkins was, if anything, ahead of his immediate contemporaries.

Tomkins has often been taken to task on the matter of text repetition, and it is indeed true that there are occasional instances of very inept and obvious word spinning. Word repetition is none the less at the very heart of the composer's style. Morley, being a superb melodist, preferred to set texts of considerable length with practically no word repetition. Tomkins, on the other hand, required time in which to develop his ideas. He was less interested in melody than in the imitative and sequential development of melodic fragments. A comparison between the settings of Psalm 130 by the two composers serves to underline this point:

	Morley	Tomkins
Verse 1		
Out of the deep have I called unto thee, O Lord: Lord, hear my voice	bars 1–13 (verse)	bars 1–17 (verse) and 17–23 (chorus)
Verse 2		
Let thine ears consider well: the voice of my complaint	13–21 (chorus)	23–30 (verse) 30–35 (chorus)
Verse 3		
If Thou, Lord, wilt be extreme to mark what is done amiss: O Lord, who may abide it?	22–31 (verse) 31–36 (chorus)	35–48 (verse) 48–55 (chorus)
Verse 4		
For there is mercy with Thee: therefore shalt thou be feared	36–41 (chorus)	55–70 (verse) 70–76 (chorus)
Verse 5		
I look for the Lord; my soul doth wait for him: in his word is my trust	42–48 (verse)	——
Verse 6		
My soul fleeth unto the Lord: before the morning watch, I say, before the morning watch	49–56 (chorus)	——

Verse 7

O Israel, trust in the Lord, for with   57–66   ——
the Lord there is mercy: and with   (verse)
him is plenteous redemption

Verse 8

And he shall redeem Israel: from all   67–74   ——
his sins   (chorus)

Amen   74–78   76–79
                                        (chorus)   (chorus)

As Table 29 (pages 288–95) will show, no two verse anthems are at all alike. In many, the verses are linked to the following choruses (though never the other way about) by the use of words and musical phrases common to both. In one or two there are no links at all between verses and choruses; but these through-composed anthems, lacking sectional links, are on the whole the least successful. Formal musical repeats, of the kind to be found particularly in the anthems of Giles and Weelkes, are entirely lacking. The quotations from "Hear my prayer", and especially from "When David heard" and "Know ye not", will have shown that the composer possessed an unusually imaginative ear. It is equally clear, however, that he considered

TABLE 29

Anthems of Thomas Tomkins

Title	Vs. 1	Ch. 1	Vs. 2	Ch. 2	Verse anthems in Musica Deo Sacra Vs. 3	Ch. 3	Vs. 4	Ch. 4	Vs. 5	Ch. 5	Vs. 6	Ch. 6	Total length (to nearest 5 bars)
Above the stars	A 7	*MATB* 3	A 6	*MATB* 2	A 8	*MATB* 5	A 15	*MATB* 6	MMAATB 13	MMATBB 10			75
Almighty and everlasting God (for the Feast of the Purification)	MA 8	MATB 3	MA 6	*MATB* 6	A 18	MAATB and	MMA	(alternating in short sections for 28 bars)					65
Almighty God, which has instructed (for St. Mark's Day)	B 15	*MATB* 7	B 9	*MATB* 4	MATB 19	*MATB* 11							65
Almighty God, which hast knit together (for All Saints)	MMAATTBB 38	MMAATBB 9	MMAA • 3	*MMAATTBB* 8	MMAATTBB 23	MMAATTBB 18							100
Almighty God, which hast given us (for Christmas)	MM 19	*MAATBB* 3	MMATB 11	*MMAATTBB* 16	MMABB 4	*MAATB* 2	MMAABB 30	*MMAATBB* 19	MMAATB 15	*MAATBB* 15			135
Almighty God, whose praise (for Holy Innocents' Day)	MMAB & T 43	MAATB 20	MMATB 9	MMAATB 14									85
Behold, I bring you glad tidings	M 35	MMAAA ATTBB 40											75
Behold, it is Christ	MMB 26	MMAATTBB 19	MMBB 32	*MMAAT B (B)* 18									95
Behold the hour cometh	A 26	*MATB* 10	MMA 15	*MATB* 21									70

TABLE 29 (*continued*)

Verse anthems in Musica Deo Sacra

Title	Vs. 1	Ch. 1	Vs. 2	Ch. 2	Vs. 3	Ch. 3	Vs. 4	Ch. 4	Vs. 5	Ch. 5	Vs. 6	Ch. 6	Total length (to nearest 5 bars)
Blessed be the Lord God of Israel	MA 21	MMAAT BB 28											50
Christ rising again	B 14	MATB 5	ATB 12	MATB 2	ATB 9	MATB 10	MATB 9	MATB 11					70
Pt. 2. Christ is risen	ATB 18	MAATB 15	ATB 15	MATB 5	ATB 15	MATB 16							85
Come let us go up	MAATB 25	MMAATT BB 15	MMAA TB 7		AB 11 and 10	MATB 6	MATB 7	MATB 3	MMA 4	MATB 3	MMA 6	MMATB 10	105
Deliver me from mine enemies	MMBB 23	MATB 16	MMBB 16	MATB 7	MATB 21	MAATB 18							100
Give sentence with me	BB 28	MAATB 6	BB 26	inc. 3	BB8	inc. 10	BB 11 and 17	MAATB 9	BB 36	MAAT BB 16			170
Glory be to God on high	MA 12	MAATB 28	MMAA TTB 11	MAATB 3	M 7	MAATB 4	M+AA TB 13	MMAA TBB 30					110
God, who as at this time	MA 18	MATB 3	MMAT 3	MATB 3	B 3	MATB 3	B 4	MMA TTB 4	MAATB 18	MMAA TTBB 18			80
Hear me when I call	MMA 19	ATB 17	MMA 16	ATB 18	MMA 35	MAATB 4	MMA 5	MAATB 20					135
Hear my prayer, O good Lord	A 8	MAATB 4	AA 5	MAATB 4	AA 3	MAATB 3	AA 4	MAATB 4	AA 9	MAATB 12	AA 28	MAATB 17	95
Hear my prayer, O Lord (Ps. 39)	B 8	MATB 4	B 7	MATB 3	B 10	MATB 11	MB 24	MATB 30					95
I will lift up mine eyes	AA 13	MAATB 7	AA 14	MATB 8	AA 11		B 11		MATB 12	MAATB 18			95

TABLE 29 (continued)

Verse anthems in Musica Deo Sacra

Title	Vs. 1	Ch. 1	Vs. 2	Ch. 2	Vs. 3	Ch. 3	Vs. 4	Ch. 4	Vs. 5	Ch. 5	Vs. 6	Ch. 6	Total length (to nearest 5 bars)
Leave, O my soul	B 20	MAATB 12	M 12	MAATB 6	M 12	MAATB 12	B 24	MAATB 10	A 14	MAATB 8	MMB 36	MAATB 24	190
Merciful Lord (for St. John's Day)	MAATB 17	MAATB 15	MAATB 21	MAATB 16									70
My beloved spake	MMAB 9	MATB 3	MMAB 11	MATB 6	MMAB 21	MATB 4	MMAB 22	MATB 15					90
My shepherd is the living Lord	A 20	MAATB 11	AA 23	MATB 13									65
Not in the merits	A 16	MATB 3	A 24	MATB 9	M 13		MAB 17	MATB 5	MAB 15	MATB 11			115
O Lord God of hosts (for St. George's Feast)	MMAABB 32	MAATBB 22	MMAATTBB 21	MAATBB 11									85
O Lord, grant the King a long life (the Coronation anthem)	B 26	MAATB 22	MAB 23	MAATB 20									90
O Lord, let me know mine end	A 21	MAATB 10	A 35	MAATB 14	A 25 +18	MAATB 16							130
O Lord, thou hast dealt graciously	B 18		AB 19		MMAT 14	MAATB 17	MMAATB 16	MMAA TTBB 16					100
O pray for the peace	MAB 9	MAATT B 4	MAB 13	MAATT B 4	MMAB 13	MAATB 14	AB+MT 16	MAATB 12					85
O that the salvation	M 11	MMAA TTBB 7	MM 16	MMMAATT BB 13	MMBB 17+9	MMMAATT BB 4+11							90
Out of the deep	M 17	MATB 6	M 7	MATB 5	M 13	MATB 8	MAB 16	MATB 10					80

TABLE 29 (continued)

Verse anthems in Musica Deo Sacra

Title	Vs. 1	Ch. 1	Vs. 2	Ch. 2	Vs. 3	Ch. 3	Vs. 4	Ch. 4	Vs. 5	Ch. 5	Vs. 6	Ch. 6	Total length (to nearest 5 bars)
Praise the Lord, O my soul	M 9	MATB 4	M 5	MATB* 3	M 5	MATB 3	MATB 37	MATB 13					80
Praise the Lord, O ye servants	T 20	MATB 12	T 19	MATB 5	T30+ 12	MATB 12	T 11	MATB 13					135
Sing unto God	B 24	MATTB 11	B 31	MATTB MATB 18	MB 45	MATB 13							140
Stephen being full of the Holy Ghost (for St. Stephen's Day)	MMAAATB 38	MATB 5	MMAA BB 20	MAAATB 13									75
The Lord, even the most mighty	B 35	MAAATB 10	MAB 33	MAAATB 16	MAB 47	MAAATB 19							160
Thou art my king	B 17	MAAATB 10	B 23	MAAATB 7	B 28	MAAATB and B (alternating in short sections for 22 bars)							110
Turn thou us	A 8	MAAATB 6	T 6	MAAATB 6	M 10	MAAATB 6	MA+ T 11	MAAATB 14	MB 15	MAAATB 11	MMAATB 11	MAATB* 9	155
Who can tell how oft	A 19	MATB 10	A 29	MATB 11	AA 25	MATB 11							105
Who is this that cometh (for St. John's Day)	A+MA TB 27	MAAATB 20	AB 7	MAAATB 3	MATT BB 21	MAAATB 11							90

Turn thou us (continued): * Vs. 7 — MMAATBB 24; Ch. 7 — MAATB 19; Total 155

(Italics indicate text repeated from previous verse. A division between Vs. and Ch. indicates that there is no thematic connection between the two.)

Verse anthems not in Musica Deo Sacra: Death is swallowed up; Jesus came when the doors were shut; Know ye not (Prince Henry's Funeral anthem); My dwelling is above; O think upon thy servant; Rejoice, rejoice (probably not by Tomkins); Sweet Saviour; The Lord bless us; Ye people all.

TABLE 29: *Anthems of Thomas Tomkins (continued)*

Full anthems

Title	Voices	Bars	
Blessed is he whose unrighteousness is forgiven	MAT	38	The Penitential Psalms: No. 2 (Ps. 32)
Have mercy upon me, O Lord	MAT	32	The Penitential Psalms: No. 4 (Ps. 51)
Hear my prayer, O Lord, and consider	MA Bar	47	The Penitential Psalms: No. 7 (Ps. 143)
Hear my prayer, O Lord, and let my crying	MAT	40	The Penitential Psalms: No. 5 (Ps. 102)
Out of the deep have I called	MAT	37	The Penitential Psalms: No. 6 (Ps. 130)
Put me not to rebuke	MAT	64	The Penitential Psalms: No. 3 (Ps. 38)
Whom have I in heaven	MAT	40	
Arise, O Lord, and have mercy	M(T)A Bar	41	
Awake, up my glory	MAT	9	
Deal with me, O Lord	MAT	51	
Glory be to the Father	MTB	38	"Gloria patri", with Alleluia
I have gone astray	MAT	37	
O Lord, do away as the night	MAT	49	
O Lord God of hosts who is like unto thee	M(A)T Bar	41	
O Lord, how glorious	MAT	13	
O Lord, open thou our lips	MA(T) Bar	42	
O Lord, rebuke me not	MAT	41	The Penitential Psalms: No. 1 (Ps. 6)

TABLE 29 (continued)

Full anthems

Title	Voices	Bars	
The hills stand about Jerusalem	MAT	23	
Thou healest the broken in heart	M(A)T Bar	38	
Give ear unto my words	AATB	60	
Pt. II. My voice shalt thou hear	AATB	40	
O give thanks unto the Lord	ATTB	48	
O how amiable are thy dwellings	ATTB	52	
O Lord, how manifold are thy works	AATB	38	
Remember me, O Lord	ATTB	45	
The heavens declare the glory	AATB	52	
Almighty and everlasting God which hatest nothing	MATB	55	Collect for Ash Wednesday
I am the resurrection	MATB	19	⎫
Pt. II. I know that my redeemer	MATB	27	⎬ Funeral anthems
Pt. III. We brought nothing	MATB	33	⎪
I heard a voice	MATB	29	⎭
O be favourable unto Zion	MMTB	37	
O pray for the peace	MMTB	30	
Praise the Lord, O my soul	MMTB	38	
Turn Thou us	MATB	55	[Commination service] Canon 4 in 1
Almighty God, the fountain	MAATB	90	A collect after the Offertory [when communion is not celebrated]

TABLE 29 (continued)

Full anthems

Title	Voices	Bars	
Arise, O Lord, into thy resting place	MAATB	65	
Arise, O Lord God, lift up	MATTB	86	A prayer
Great and marvellous	MAATB	49	
Have mercy upon me, O God	MAATB	50	
He that hath pity	MATTB	80	
Holy, holy, holy, Lord God of Sabaoth	MMATTB	24	
Lord enter not into judgement	MAATB	57	
O God wonderful art thou	MAATB	49	
O Lord, I have loved	MAATB	45	
O praise the Lord, all ye heathen	MMATTB	30	
Then David mourned	MMATB	45	
When David heard	MMATB	69	(Also 1622)
Why art thou so full of heaviness	MMATB	61	
Withdraw not Thou thy mercy	MAATB	77	
Blessed is he that considereth	MMAATB	85	Alternative text, O Lord graciously accept. A prayer
Dear Lord of life	MMAAATB	86	Not in MDS
From deepest horror of sad penitence	SSMAT Bar		Not in MDS

TABLE 29 (*continued*)

Full anthems

Title	Voices	Bars	
It is my well beloved's voice	MMAATTB	46	(1622) Not in *MDS*
O Israel, if thou return	MMAATTB	33	
Turn unto the Lord	MMAATTB	42	(1622) Not in *MDS*
Who shall ascend the hill of God	MMAAATB	43	
Woe is me	MMAATBB	48	(1622) Not in *MDS*
Be strong and of a good courage	MMAATBB	**51	[Coronation anthem]
O sing unto the Lord a new song	MMAAATBB	81	(ps. 149: 1–2)
O God, the proud are risen up	MMAAATTBB	71	
Glory be to God on high	MMAAAATTBB	39	[the chorus of, Behold I bring you]
O praise the Lord, all ye heathen	MMMAAAATTTBBB	89	

Full anthems incomplete

Title	Voices	Bars	
Grant us, gracious Lord			"For the Communion"
Holy, holy, holy, Lord God of hosts			
O Lord, wipe away my sins	à 5		
Zadok the priest			[Coronation anthem]

** The organ part in *Musica Deo Sacra* continues for a further 20 bars.

harmonic and rhythmic extremes to be inappropriate for normal liturgical use, that they were too striking, too theatrical, tending to draw attention to the musical technique rather than to the words which the music aimed to serve. Of all the elements, he used rhythm with the greatest freedom; words with a joyful connotation invariably produced exciting effects. If there are occasional lapses, this is only to be expected in the work of so prolific a composer. The wonder is that Tomkins maintained a standard that was so consistently high, and one that was so marvellously varied.

THOMAS WEELKES

Nothing is known of Thomas Weelkes before 1597, the year in which he published his first set of *Madrigals to 3. 4. 5. and 6. voyces.* The composer dedicated this work to a Master George Phillpot, and in terms which suggest that Phillpot must have been one of his earliest patrons—the Phillpot family kept a house in London and also an estate on the outskirts of Winchester, besides a country house at Thruxton, near Andover.[8] Perhaps the Phillpots were responsible for introducing him to London musical circles, for he subsequently spent a short while in the service of Edward Darcye, groom of her Majesty's privy chamber; and if we are to believe the title page of his last madrigal publication—the *Ayeres or Phantasticke Spirites* (1608)—he was by then a Gentleman of the Chapel Royal.

His first professional appointment of which we have any certain knowledge, however, was at Winchester, as Organist of the College.[9] He went there, it would seem, in the summer or early autumn of 1598. For the previous twenty years or more there had been no college organist, the post having been abolished by the Visitor, the Bishop of Winchester, in 1576. Clearly, musical standards could not have been particularly good when Weelkes took up his duties there. The college treated him well, placing him on an equal footing with the chaplains and paying him a stipend which, if small by Chapel

Royal standards, was well above the stipend that his successor received. The job had serious drawbacks, however. The composition of the choir was unusual in that there were only six men to balance the sixteen choristers (there were no less than twenty-four men in the cathedral choir at that time) and the situation was aggravated by the fact that the men frequently absented themselves from service. Moreover, the choristers were in some respects treated as menials—it being part of their duties, for instance, to wait upon the scholars of the college at mealtimes.[10]

Weelkes remained at Winchester no more than four years. On July 13th, 1602, he took his B.Mus. from New College, Oxford, and by the autumn of that year he was Organist and Master of the Choristers at Chichester Cathedral—at the invitation, perhaps, of the new Dean, William Thorne, a Wykehamist and Fellow of New College, who had himself taken a degree from New College in July 1602.

From this point, the story of Weelkes' life becomes clearer.[11] It is a puzzling and unhappy one. In February 1603 the composer married Elizabeth Sandham at All Saints, Chichester, and on June 9th their first child was born. From 1609 onwards his behaviour gave the Dean and Chapter mounting cause for concern. At first he was charged with nothing more than unauthorised absence—a charge that was also levelled at one or two members of the Chapter. But in 1613 he was accused of "a public fame". By 1616 the cathedral music had reached such a low ebb that the Dean and Chapter were obliged to reprimand him for his neglect and issue him with detailed instructions as to his future duties. In January of the following year, Bishop Harsnett ordered the Dean and Chapter to dismiss him. But despite this, Weelkes was allowed to remain as a lay-clerk. In 1619, his colleagues in the choir had this to say to the visiting Bishop of his behaviour:

... most of the choir and the other officers of the same demean themselves religiously all the time of prayer, save one, Thomas Weelkes, who divers times and very often come[s] so disguised

either from the tavern or alehouse into the choir as is much to be
lamented, for in these humours he will both curse and swear most
dreadfully, and so profane the service of God (and especially on
the Sabbath days) as is most fearful to hear, and [to] the great
amazement of all the people present. And though he have often-
times been admonished by the late Lord Bishop [and] the Dean
and Chapter to refrain these humours and reform himself, yet he
daily continue[s] the same, and is rather worse than better
therein.[12]

But in 1623, at the time of his death, Weelkes was still in the
service of the cathedral.

Although Weelkes was one of England's very greatest

TABLE 30

Anthems of Thomas Weelkes

Full anthems	Verse anthems
Alleluia, I heard a voice (for trebles)	All laud and praise
All people clap your hands	*An earthly tree*
Behold, how good and joyful (f?)	*Behold, O Israel*
Deliver us O Lord (attr. uncertain)	*Blessed be the man*
Gloria in excelsis Deo	*Blessed is he*
Hosanna to the Son of David	*Christ rising*
Lord, to Thee I make my moan	*Deal bountifully*
Most mighty and all knowing Lord	Give ear, O Lord
O Absalom (attr. uncertain)	Give the king thy judgements
O happy he whom Thou protec'st	If King Manasses
O how amiable are thy dwellings	*If ye be risen again*
O Jonathan	*I lift my heart to Thee*
O Lord, arise into thy resting place	*I love the Lord*
O Lord God almighty	In Thee, O Lord (Ps. 31)
O Lord, grant the king	In Thee, O Lord (Ps. 71)
O Lord, preserve thee (f?)	*Let us lift up*
O mortal man	O Lord, how joyful is the king
Rejoice in the Lord	*O Lord, turn not away*
Sing unto the Lord, O ye princes	Plead Thou my cause
Teach me O Lord	*Successive course*
Thy mercies great	*The Lord is my shepherd*
When David heard	What joy so true
With all our hearts and mouths (f?)	*Why art thou so sad*
and one motet, possibly written as his B.Mus.	*Ye people all*
exercise: Laboravi in gemitu meo	

(The italicised anthems are incomplete.)

madrigalists and a prolific composer of church music, few of his Services and anthems are to be found in contemporary choir part-books. The "Batten" organ-book, with its markedly southern repertory, is by far the most important source, whilst the post-Restoration part-books at Wimborne Minster (sadly incomplete, alas) contain a good deal of his music, too. Of the forty-eight anthems, only twenty-seven are complete enough to be restorable (see Table 30, page 298).[13]

Weelkes is most consistently at his best in the full style of composition and in the dynamic and dramatic moods. His most impressive anthems include "Alleluia", "Gloria", "Hosanna to the Son of David", "O Lord, arise" and the two laments: "When David heard that Absalom was slain" and "O Jonathan". Of these, "O Lord arise" is the most conservative in style. Its text is a composite one made of verses from the Te Deum and Psalm 132, with a clear-cut shape mounting to a final climax (Weelkes shows an unusual concern for words in many of his best anthems, and a particular fondness for working up to a dramatic conclusion):

Ps. 132:8 O Lord, arise into thy resting place; Thou and the ark of thy strength.

Te Deum Save thy people good Lord, and bless thine inheritance.

Ps. 132:9 Let thy priests be clothed with righteousness, and let thy saints sing with joyfulness.
Alleluia.

Tomkins, by comparison, was content to set verses 8 to 10 of the psalm without alteration (see "Arise, O Lord"). The anthem is scored for seven voices (MMAATBB) and is consistently contrapuntal throughout. This section from the Alleluia will serve to give some idea of its immense melodic and rhythmic vitality (see "Alleluia, alleluia," top of page 300).

"Gloria", "Hosanna" and "Alleluia" all have well-defined musical structures. "Gloria" is in a straightforward ABA form with a final jubilant "Amen" as a coda; "Alleluia" is also in ternary form, with an extra twelve bars added to section A

on its repeat to form a most exhilarating conclusion; and "Hosanna" is in a kind of rondo form, ABACA, but lacking the precise formality of the classical scheme. These three anthems are all intensely dramatic. The cries of "Hosanna", from the crowd, which open "Hosanna to the son of David":

become, on the first repetition at bar 18:

On the third and last appearance, at the very end of the anthem, the cries are still further intensified by the use of the rest in bar 34 (during which all voices are silent), the subsequent thickening of the texture, and the ostinato-like figure in the last four bars which finally comes to rest on the chord of G:

And in "Gloria" there is a daring change of key at the words "crave thy God to tune thy heart":

Of the three anthems, however, "Alleluia" is in many ways the most remarkable, not only for the extraordinary bass solo that occurs at the beginning:

but also for the "sequential" pattern of imitation which forms the structural basis of the anthem. Immediately following the bass solo, all five voices take up this imitative phrase:

which "modulates" through the keys of d minor, D major, G major, C major, and back to d minor through its dominant A major. A large part of section B follows a similar plan:

In both sections, the music could continue indefinitely, as the words indeed demand: "Alleluia. Salvation, and honour, and glory and power be unto the Lord our God, and to the Lamb *for evermore*." Interestingly enough, section A of "Alleluia" appears note for note in the Gloria of the Nunc dimittis "for trebles", and to words of similar meaning: "and ever shall be, world without end. Amen".

The two superb sacred madrigals "When David heard" and "O Jonathan" are to be found in none of the liturgical sources (nor indeed are any of the other settings of these very popular texts). The occasions on which the laments could have been sung at matins and evensong were few, and nearly all the settings were perhaps too chromatic for such a purpose.

Weelkes' magnificent six-part setting of "When David heard" surpasses all the others in this respect. The composer has managed to portray with remarkable vividness the rhythm of David's lament, with its sudden outbursts of grief and its heavy periods of silence:

Of the other full anthems, "All people clap your hands", "O happy he", "O how amiable", "O Lord, grant the king a long life" and "O mortal man" are predominantly polyphonic. The words of "O happy he" and "O Lord, grant the king" offer little scope for musical invention. Of the others, "O mortal man" is of particular interest as its text would seem to be Scottish in origin and its music to be based on a late sixteenth-century setting by an anonymous—and presumably Scottish—composer. Both have a common musical structure—AABCC—and there are curious melodic and harmonic parallels between the two. Neither the poem nor the anonymous setting are to be found in English sources of the period.[14]

"O Lord God almighty" and "Lord, to Thee I make my

moan" are slight works, written in a simple note-against-note style. Weelkes is here in a workaday mood, for neither text offers any scope for dramatic representation, the one being a fulsome prayer for King James and "the royal progeny", the other a Sternhold and Hopkins metrical psalm.

"Most mighty and all-knowing Lord", the last of the complete anthems listed above, is in fact a simple consort song. The words are by Sir William Leighton, and the music appears in the *Teares or Lamentacions* of 1614. Weelkes' setting was a late addition, so late, in fact, that the title page of the anthology had already been engraved without the composer's name. Plate 15 shows the page in question, Weelkes' name having very obviously been added at the bottom, thus throwing the symmetrical design askew.

The nine restorable verse anthems are scored for modest forces, though all are of surprising length:

	Total length	Length of full sections	Scoring of verses
All laud and praise	131	29	MA/MMA/MA/ MMA
Give ear, O Lord	108	20	AA/MM/MAATB
Give the king thy judgements	106	38	MA/MM/MMA/
If King Manasses	145	43	M/A/B/MAB/MAB/ [MMAATB]
In Thee, O Lord (Ps. 31)	74	21	B throughout
In Thee, O Lord (Ps. 71)	144	48	[uncertain: editorial reconstruction]
O Lord, how joyful is the king	180	73	M/A/T/[M]AT/ [M]/[A]/[MAT]
Plead Thou my cause	93	30	A/[B]/MAT/T/ MAA
What joy so true	107	34	M/A/MM/MMA

"Give ear, O Lord" can rightly be considered as one of the very greatest verse anthems of the period. The text is by William Hunnis, Master of the Chapel Royal choristers.

There are three stanzas in all, each ending with the refrain "Mercy, good Lord, mercy". Each complete stanza forms a solo verse of the anthem—the first being sung by two altos, the second by two meanes, the third by a meane, two altos and tenor. After each verse, the refrain is developed as a chorus to form a kind of rondo structure:

The sections of the anthem are integrated not only by the recurrence of a refrain but by the extension of each verse into the succeeding chorus, whilst the refrain itself is developed to produce the crescendo shape that is so marked a feature of many of the full anthems.

One or two of the other verse anthems deserve mention, notably the penitential anthems "In Thee, O Lord", "Plead thou my cause" and "Give the king thy judgements"—a vigorous festal anthem for "the King's Day".

"Plead thou my cause" is attractively scored for a variety of solo voices (for details see page 304), and the full sections are arranged for MAATB chorus. It lacks the continuity of "Give ear", however. There are no linking devices of any kind between verses and choruses; the choruses are, on balance, too short; and there are too many pauses between the sections.

The solo bass anthem "In Thee, O Lord" is open to similar criticisms, though the effective solo part does much to compensate for the other deficiencies.

Of the three, "Give the king" is possibly of the greatest interest. The full sections are well sustained and they have much of the brilliance of "Alleluia"

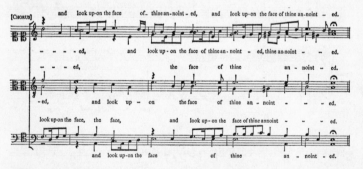

whilst a sense of formal unity is achieved by the partial repetition of the first chorus before the final "Amen".

Nine of Weelkes' Services have survived, though five of them are too fragmentary to permit reconstruction.[15] They range from the four-part setting in "Short" Service style—

a through-composed and mainly chordal work—to the Magnificat and Nunc dimittis of seven parts, a full setting in the "Great" Service tradition.

1. First Service to the organs in Gam ut, the Service in verse for a meane (Te, Ma, N) (verse)
2. Second Service to the organs in D sol re (verse) (Te, J, K, Cr, Ma, N: also Offertory)
3. Magnificat and Nunc dimittis to the organs in F fa ut (verse)
4. Magnificat and Nunc dimittis "for trebles" (verse)
5. Magnificat and Nunc dimittis "in medio chori" (verse)
6. Magnificat and Nunc dimittis "in verse for two counter-tenors", the "flat" Evening Service (verse)
7. Service in "four parts" (full) (Te, J, Ma, N)
8. Service in "five parts" (full) (Te, J, Ma, N)
9. Magnificat and Nunc dimittis in "seven parts"

Two of the Services, the "in medio chori" and the "seven-part" Services, are on an unusually large scale. To judge from the organ part of the "in medio chori" setting (all that survives of the original), a group of solo voices must have been placed at some distance from the main choir, to produce a polychoral effect. The sections "in medio chori" are, in the main, scored for high voices, and the total choral range in the full sections is more than three octaves—considerably above the normal, that is.

A reconstruction of the seven-part Service is now possible, owing to the recent discovery of several lost sources, although a tenor part is still lacking. When measured against the great six- and seven-part full anthems, it is something of a disappointment, although the seven-part texture is in itself impressive enough. The structure is consistently imitative and almost uninterruptedly in five or more parts. The key scheme is particularly unimaginative: the tonality rarely escapes from A "minor", whilst the melodic lines cover a very limited span and tend to hang around a pivot note, as the following extract from the Nunc dimittis will show:

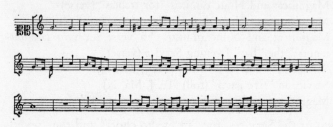

An impressive reconstruction of the five-part Service was published by Dr. Fellowes in 1937. It is based on the one surviving source, the "Batten" organ-book, which contains a very full keyboard reduction of the work. It is a pity, however, that Dr. Fellowes did not also print the organ part in its original form, since the extent of his own work would then have been more readily apparent.

The Amen to the Magnificat of this Service, as Dr. Fellowes has pointed out, is identical to the Amen of "O how amiable", which is also in five parts. There are links of a similar kind, too, between the seven-part Service and "O Lord arise", and between the Service "for trebles" and "Alleluia".

The Service "for trebles" poses an interesting problem since, as it stands in the Durham and Peterhouse books, it is incomplete. As has been pointed out in an earlier chapter, the term "treble" always implied at that time a boy's voice of unusually high range—a fourth or so above the normal or meane. Parts for treble voice were invariably notated in the treble clef (the G clef), and those for meane in either of the two highest C clefs. The Service "for trebles" is in verse form, and it might be expected that the high treble parts would be found in the solo verses. This, however, is not the case. The solo sections, as they stand in the existing sources, are reasonably complete and are for two ordinary boys (meanes) with subsidiary solo parts for tenor and bass voices. The full sections, however, are manifestly incomplete, and a comparison of the Nunc dimittis "Gloria" with the parallel section of "Alleluia" (see page 302) reveals that it is the treble part that is missing. Luckily, the reconstruction of this part causes no difficulty since it is supplied, though without words, in the organ part (organ and voices invariably double each other in the full sections of verse services and anthems). The term "for trebles" applies, therefore, to the choruses and not to the solo verses, which are for two meanes. Dr. Fellowes' misreading of the title has tended to confuse the issue since in none of the sources is the work described as the Service for *two* trebles.

Since Dr. Fellowes originally published his reconstruction of the work several of the missing parts have been found, showing that the original was by no means on the grand scale that had been envisaged. It is still, nevertheless, one of the most remarkable of all pre-Restoration settings, not least for the exceptional brilliance of the choral sections. The top Gs and As sound especially exciting in a resonant building.

ORLANDO GIBBONS

Several members of the Gibbons family had exceptional musical talent.[16] William—Orlando's father—and Ferdinando —one of his four brothers—were both professional waits, or town musicians; Ellis, the eldest but one of Orlando's brothers, was a composer of some stature (Thomas Morley included two of his madrigals in the *Triumphs of Oriana*, whereas no other composer in the collection, apart from Morley himself, is represented by more than one). Edward, the eldest of the four brothers, was successively Master of the Choristers at King's College, Cambridge, and Succentor of Exeter Cathedral. And one of Orlando's three sons—Christopher—was to take a leading part in London's musical life during the Commonwealth, becoming after the Restoration an Organist of the Chapel Royal, Private Organist to Charles II, and Organist of Westminster Abbey.

Orlando was born at Oxford in 1583. Shortly afterwards, the family moved to Cambridge, and from February 1596 until the spring of 1599 Orlando sang in the choir of King's College, his brother Edward then being Master of the Choristers. In the Easter term of 1598 he matriculated as a student of the college. Seven years later, in 1605, he won for himself a place in the Chapel Royal choir, and by 1615 he was sharing the duties of organist there with an elder colleague, Edmund Hooper.

In 1619 he was further rewarded with an appointment in the secular musical establishment "for the virginals to attend in his Highness' privy chamber"—an unusual honour for a Gentleman of the Chapel—and in 1623 he accepted yet another appointment, that of Organist of Westminster Abbey in succession to John Parsons. Two years later, whilst the Chapel choir was at Canterbury awaiting the arrival of Henrietta Maria, Orlando died of an apoplectic fit. He was then only forty-two years old.

All that now remains of his work is a set of madrigals, published in 1612; a great deal of unpublished music for keyboard instruments and consorts;[17] some forty anthems; a full Service; a verse Service; three sets of festal psalms; two sets of Preces and some seventeen hymn tunes—sixteen of which were published by George Wither in his *Hymnes and Songs of the Church* (1623).

Gibbons' "Short" Service in F fa ut—Venite, Te Deum, Benedictus, Kyrie, Credo, Magnificat, Nunc dimittis—is an unusually tuneful work, and for this reason, perhaps, it was quite the most popular setting of its day. Unlike the Tallis and Byrd Services, it is through-composed with none of the phrase repetitions and developments that characterise the earlier settings. The underlay of the outer voices is, on the whole, well managed; but the two inner parts are less satisfactory. In some places it is well nigh impossible to fit words and notes together comfortably. The countless underlay variants in the early sources bear ample witness to this. In the matter of word painting, Gibbons was strangely inconsistent. There are some very obvious examples of this:

and as-cended in - - to heaven

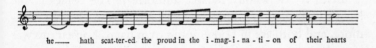

he___ hath scat-ter-ed the proud in the i-mag-i-na-ti-on of their hearts

but, on the other hand, the composer completely ignored the expressive potential of harmony and tonality—as indeed his predecessors had done—with the result that phrases such as "And was crucified also for us" and "He suffered and was buried" still have a curiously flat and almost pre-Reformation quality about them.

The verse Service consists of Te Deum, Jubilate, Magnificat and Nunc dimittis. There are two versions of the morning canticles, one being substantially shorter than the other. The scoring throughout is colourful and dramatic. The sterner verses of the Magnificat, for instance, are scored for the lower voices, whilst the fourth verse of the Nunc dimittis is arranged for meanes. In broad outline and particular detail, this work would seem to owe much to Morley's Service for verses.

Since the first collected edition of Gibbons' church music was published in 1925[18], seven of the thirty-nine anthems in the volume have proved to be the work of other composers. Four are to be found in the appendix of incomplete anthems —"Arise, O Lord" (Woodson), "Have pity" and "Sing we merrily" (Christopher Gibbons) and "Out of the deep" (attribution uncertain, but possibly by Byrd). Of the other three, "Have mercy" has long been known to be the work of Byrd and is to be found in the composer's *Psalmes, songs and sonnets* of 1611. Two other misattributions, however, have only recently come to light with the discovery of an organ-book, c. 1630, largely in the hand of Henry Loosemore, Organist of King's College, Cambridge.[19] The anthems in question are two very popular ones—"O Lord, increase my faith" and "Why art Thou so heavy". Before the discovery of the King's College organ-book, only one source of the two anthems was known—an early eighteenth-century copy in the hand of Thomas Tudway, Professor of Music at Cambridge (a useful if not wholly reliable authority). The copies in the King's College organ-book are both ascribed to Henry Loosemore, and both are in Loosemore's own hand. Loosemore was himself a composer of above-average ability, and there is no reason on stylistic grounds to doubt his word.

Two of the ten authentic full anthems are incomplete, and one—"Deliver us, O Lord our God"—may possibly lack an alto part. Certainly it is in places remarkably bare. Of the others, the small four-part "Almighty and everlasting God" and the four great full anthems—"Hosanna", "O clap your hands", "Lift up your heads" and "O Lord, in thy wrath"— are the most impressive. Gibbons experimented occasionally with various methods of musical repetition and development, as also did Weelkes. In the splendid "Hosanna to the Son of

David", he recapitulated much of the opening section ("Hosanna to the Son of David") towards the end of the anthem ("Hosanna in the highest heavens"). The text is a composite one, put together perhaps with such a possibility in mind. Both "Hosanna" and the six-part "Lift up your heads" would seem to have been very popular, to judge from the number of sources in which they are to be found, although the equally impressive eight-part setting of "O clap your hands" and the penitential anthem "O Lord, in thy wrath" were hardly known at all.

In years past there has been a tendency to look upon the verse music as experimental, to think of it in post-Restoration terms and to criticise it accordingly. The preface to the collected Services and anthems (1925 edn.) indeed, condemned most of Gibbons' verse anthems as "overloaded" and "mechanical":

> [Gibbons'] achievement in the traditional manner is magnificent . . . . When, however, we turn to his work in the new style we trace in all directions the groping and hesitation of the pioneer . . . . Only the shallow student will complain if in the pioneer work he finds the prentice hand. It would be easy to take a few works, such as "O God, the King of glory", "Lord, grant grace", and "If ye be risen" ["See, see, the Word is incarnate" and "Behold, thou hast made my days" are other verse anthems to be censured] and enlarge on their crudities. In the verse anthems his conception of the function of the solo voice is elementary, and the accompanying viol and organ parts are frequently so stuffed with imitations that they detract from the voice by their mechanical confirmations of its statements . . . .[20]

But to look backwards at the early seventeenth-century verse anthem from the Restoration is to miss the point entirely. For the early verse anthem is essentially polyphonic. The interplay of imitative ideas between instruments and voices is an indispensable feature of the style and one of its chief attractions.

Eight of the twenty-five extant verse anthems are incomplete. Of the others, "The secret sins" may well be the work of

William Mundy. The words of this anthem are in both the Chapel Royal anthem book (c. 1630) and in the second edition of James Clifford's *Divine Services and Anthems,* and in both cases Mundy is named as the composer. Mundy's setting seems to be lost, but all the extant sources of the Gibbons setting of these words are anonymous, save one or two of the Durham MSS. in which Gibbons' name is to be found. In the same books, however, Byrd's "Have mercy" is also ascribed to Gibbons, even though it had been published by Byrd himself in 1611! Clearly, the Durham attributions cannot wholly be relied upon. The anthem is strophic in form, and in this and many other respects it has much in common with William Mundy's "Ah, helpless wretch".

Practically all the verse anthems were composed for special occasions, and many have accompaniments for viols or other consort instruments (as usual, the instrumentation is not specified in the originals). The most popular anthem of all was undoubtedly "This is the record of John". Gibbons' mastery of the medium is apparent in every bar: in the shaping of phrases, in the declamatory quality of the melodic lines, and especially in the distribution of the cadences—for Gibbons took great care to match the verbal punctuation with its appropriate musical equivalents.

In common with his contemporaries, Gibbons used no one set structural plan for his verse anthems. As Table 31 on p. 316

shows, many of the full sections repeat and develop material from the preceding verses. One of the finest anthems— "See, see the Word is incarnate"—does not conform at all to this pattern, however. The text is in itself a very unusual one, covering in an almost impressionistic manner the story of Christ's birth, Ministry, Crucifixion and Resurrection:

See, see, the Word is incarnate; God is made man in the womb of a Virgin. Shepherds rejoice, wise men adore, and angels sing,/ Glory be to God on high: peace on earth, goodwill towards men./The law is cancelled, Jews and Gentiles all converted by the preaching of glad tidings of salvation. The blind have sight and cripples have their motion; diseases cured, the dead are raised, and miracles are wrought./Let us welcome such a guest with Hosanna./The Paschal Lamb is offered, Christ Jesus made a sacrifice for sin. The earth quakes, the sun is darkened, the powers of hell are shaken, and lo, he is risen up in victory./Sing Alleluia./ See, O see the fresh wounds, the gored blood, the pricks of thorns, the print of nails, and in the sight of multitudes/a glorious ascension./Now he sits on God's right hand, where all the choir of heaven all jointly sing,/Glory be to the Lamb that sitteth upon the throne. Let us continue our wonted note with Hosanna: Blessed be he that cometh in the name of the Lord; with Alleluia: We triumph in victory: the serpent's head bruised, Christ's kingdom exalted, and heaven laid open to sinners.

Gibbons' superb setting does much to enhance the forward drive of this unusual text. There are, indeed, only three emphatic cadences in the entire anthem and word repetition is kept to a minimum. The anthem, too, is through-composed in the sense that none of the verses are extended and developed either verbally or musically, in the following choruses. But there are one or two very effective and unusual recapitulations and developments. A rising quaver figure in the instrumental accompaniment of the first verse becomes the imitative point at the beginning of the first chorus; the second verse takes the form of a free canon between the two solo voices; the second, third and fourth choruses are largely sequential in structure,

TABLE 31

Verse Anthems of Orlando Gibbons

	Total length	Length and scoring of full sections	Scoring of verses
Almighty God, which hast given us	*90	40	incomplete
Almighty God, who by thy son	60	30 (MAATB)	A+MATB/MAATB
Awake up my glory		(festal psalm; mainly full, but first and last verses for solo voices and organ)	
Behold, I bring you glad tidings	100	60 (MAATB)	MA/MMAATB+A/AA/MMAA
Behold, Thou hast made my days	85	60 (MAATB)	A/A/A
Blessed are all they	95	60 (MAATB)	A/A+MMAATB+A/MMT+MAATB
Glorious and powerful God	105	60 (MAATB)	B+A/AB/AB
Grant, O Holy Trinity	75	45 (MAATB)	M/M/M
Great King of Gods	95	45 (MAATB)	A/A/AA/AB
If ye be risen again	100	60 (MMATB)	MM/MMA/MM
Lord, grant grace	55	60 (MMAATBB)	MM/MMAATTBB
Lord, we beseech Thee to pour	55	25 (MAATB)	A/MA/MM+AATB
O all true faithful hearts	70	incomplete	
O glorious God	100	40 (MAATB)	text only
O God, the king of glory	90	45 (MAATB)	MAAT/AA/MAT/MAT
Praise the Lord	120	85 for "trebles": incomplete	
See, see, the Word is incarnate	130	60 (M[M]AATB)	A/MA/ATB/AATT/A
Sing unto the Lord, O ye saints	120	35 (MAATB)	BB/AA/AB
So God loved the world	95	35	incomplete
The secret sins	70	50 (MAATB)	A/A/: probably by William Mundy
This is the day	95	text only	text only
This is the record of John	120	40 (MAATB)	A/A/A
Thou God of wisdom	175	35	incomplete
Unto Thee, O Lord		60 for "trebles": incomplete	
We praise Thee, O father	130	50 (MAATB)	MAB/TT/AA+MM/MMAATT

and fragments of the second and third choruses are repeated
in the fourth and last chorus. The whole work forms a
dramatic *tour-de-force* of the first order. Indeed, few of Gibbons'
European contemporaries could have matched the originality
of this design or the vitality of the music.

In a very different way, "Behold, Thou hast made my days"
is equally outstanding. Gibbons wrote the anthem for the
Dean of Windsor, Dr. Maxie, in 1618. Maxie seems to have
known at the time that he was dying, for the words that he
asked Gibbons to set come from Psalm 39, one of the two
psalms that are said or sung at the funeral service. The work
is very simply scored for solo counter-tenor and five-part
choir—the accompaniment being for strings or other consort
instruments—and there are reflective links between the three
verses and their succeeding choruses. The main idea in the
last chorus, and in the second half of its preceding verse, is
very like the rocking motive in one of the keyboard Pavans.[21]
It provides a most moving conclusion to the anthem:

It would be idle to claim that all the verse anthems are of
equal merit. Neither of the two royal anthems is of great
musical interest (Orlando wrote "Great King of Gods"

"for the king's being in Scotland"—the ambiguity may have been deliberate!—and "Grant, Holy Trinity" for the King's Day). Nor, perhaps, are "Almighty and Everlasting God" and "If ye be risen again" especially remarkable.

Two of the incomplete verse anthems are in a class of their own and call for some comment. Both are scored for solo voices and a chorus including high trebles, and both are in a very free rondo form. In "Praise the Lord" the first chorus is repeated note for note after the second and third verses. It is then extended to form a coda to the fourth and final verse. In "Unto Thee" the first chorus is repeated after the second verse, and the third chorus—completely new—reappears after verse four. To judge from the extant parts, the high trebles only sang the choruses, as in the Weelkes Service "for trebles".

Only two of the verse anthems are to be found in secular sources of the period, a fact that is probably explained by the very occasional nature of nearly all the anthems. No fewer than ten of the seventeen have accompaniments for consort instruments, and it is reasonably certain that at least two of the other seven were also consort anthems. Fragments of a wordless treble line are to be found in the Pembroke College version of "Behold, I bring you glad tidings", for instance, and there is an extra and wordless part in the Lambeth Palace version of "Almighty God, who by thy son".[22] No curious slips of this kind have yet been discovered in other music of the period, suggesting that Orlando may well have been especially attracted to the consort anthem medium.

OTHER CONTEMPORARIES OF THOMAS TOMKINS

Well over forty of Thomas Tomkins' younger contemporaries were writing Services, anthems and devotional songs during the early years of the seventeenth century. Many of these composers are very minor indeed, the quantity of their extant work being small and its quality for the most part indifferent: John Barnard and William Cranford of St. Paul's; Benjamin

Cosyn, music master at Dulwich College and Charterhouse; John Geeres of Durham Cathedral; John Gibbs, Master of the Westminster Abbey choristers; Richard Gibbs, Organist of Norwich Cathedral; John Heath, lay-clerk of Rochester Cathedral; Richard Hinde (probably of Lichfield); Thomas Holmes, Organist of Winchester Cathedral and Gentleman of the Chapel Royal; John Hutchinson, Organist of York Minster; Richard Hutchinson, Organist of Durham Cathedral; Randolph Jewett, Organist of the two cathedrals in Dublin; Robert Johnson, musician for the lutes and voices to Charles I; John Lugge, Organist of Exeter Cathedral; the author Thomas Mace, lay-clerk of Trinity College, Cambridge; George Marson, Organist of Canterbury Cathedral; Henry Molle, public orator to Cambridge University; Richard Nicholson, Organist of Magdalen College, Oxford, and first Heather Professor of Music; Henry Palmer of Durham Cathedral; Robert Parsons, vicar choral of Exeter Cathedral; Richard Portman, Organist of Westminster Abbey; William Stonard, Organist of Christ Church, Oxford; Daniel Taylor, singing-man of Westminster Abbey; Giles Tomkins, musician for the virginals to Charles I, Organist of the Chapel Royal and Organist of Salisbury Cathedral; John Tomkins, Organist of the Chapel Royal and of St. Paul's Cathedral; Edmund Tucker (possibly the Edward Tucker of Salisbury Cathedral); Thomas Warwick, Bull's assistant at Hereford and later Organist of the Chapel Royal; Thomas Wilson of Peterhouse, Cambridge; and Leonard Woodeson of St. George's Chapel, Windsor.

There were others, too, of greater distinction whose music deserves serious consideration, notably John Amner, Organist of Ely Cathedral; Adrian Batten and Martin Peerson, both of St. Paul's; Michael East, Organist of Lichfield; Thomas Ravenscroft, music master of Christ's Hospital; William Smith, minor-canon of Durham Cathedral; and John Ward, musician to the Fanshawe family.

Still others have left at least one or two devotional songs and anthems, though most of their work is of other kinds:

Thomas Bateson, Organist of Chester Cathedral and Holy Trinity, Dublin; George Kirby, the Suffolk madrigalist; the Thomas Lupos, musicians to Charles I; Francis Pilkington, lutenist and "chauntor" of Chester Cathedral; John Wilbye, musician to the Kytson family at Hengrave Hall, near Bury St. Edmunds; and the two recusant exiles Richard Dering and Peter Philips, who spent most of their time abroad in the service of the Catholic church.

Of the very minor composers, the more significant are perhaps Lugge, Nicholson and Stonard. Lugge's full setting of "It is a good thing to give thanks" reveals a competent technique and a lively rhythmic sense:

Nicholson's work is consistently well wrought. There are, in all, three solo songs (by "R. N.") and two five-part full anthems. The song "Come, Holy Ghost" is an ingenious combination of the "In nomine" cantus firmus (2nd viol) and the Sternhold "church" tune, an academic nicety that would doubtless have appealed to Nicholson's university colleagues:[23]

The full anthem "O pray for the peace of Jerusalem" shows the composer to belong to the William Mundy school, the texture being highly imitative and somewhat square:

whilst Stonard's consort anthem "Hearken all ye people" combines melody and polyphony in a pleasingly mellifluous way.

At least five of Stonard's ten extant anthems would seem to be restorable.

Batten, a "scholar" of the Winchester organist John Holmes, was, like his master, a prolific composer. His extant music is wholly liturgical in character, and not a note of it is to be found in contemporary secular sources. The divisions between the sacred and secular were already hardening in the 1620s and 1630s, a process that may not have been wholly unconnected with the Laudian movement. Of Batten's compositions there now remain more than fifty anthems, two sets of preces, six groups of festal psalms, a Litany, a morning, communion and evening Service for men, a "Short" Service, a "Great" or "Long" Service (both in full style), and four verse Services (the third and fourth being no more than evening Services). None of these would seem to have been especially popular. As can be seen from the following list, quite a few of the anthems have been lost:

TABLE 32

Adrian Batten's Anthems

Almighty God, which in thy wrath	v
Almighty God, which madest thy blessed son (text only)	
Almighty God, whose praise this day (text only)	
Behold, I bring you glad tidings	v
Behold, now praise the Lord (text only)	
Blessed are those that are undefiled	v
Bow down thine ear, O Lord (text only)	
But let all those (Pt. II of Haste thee, O God)	
Christ is risen (Pt. II of Christ rising)	
Christ our paschal Lamb	f4
Christ rising again (Pt. II: Christ is risen)	
Deliver us, O Lord	f4
God be merciful unto us (festal Ps. 67)	
Godliness is great riches	f5
Haste Thee, O God [I] (Pt. II: But let all those)	f4
Haste Thee, O God [II]	f4
Have mercy upon me, O God [I]	f5
Have mercy upon me, O God [II]	v
Hear my prayer, O God, and hide not [I]	f4
Hear my prayer, O God, and hide not [II]	f5
Hear my prayer, O Lord, and with thine ears	v
Hear the prayers, O our God	f5
Hide not Thou thy face	f4
Holy, holy, holy, Lord God almighty	v
I am the resurrection (text only)	
If ye love me (text only)	
I heard a voice	v
In Bethlehem town (text only)	
I will always give thanks	v

TABLE 32 (*continued*)

I will magnify Thee (festal Ps. 145)	
Jesus said unto his disciples	v
Let my complaint	f4
Lord, I am not high-minded	f5
Lord, we beseech Thee give ear	f4
Lord, who shall dwell	f6
My heart is inditing (festal Ps. 45)	
My soul truly waiteth	f4
Not unto us, O Lord (text only)	
O clap your hands	f8
O God, my heart is ready	v
O God, Thou art my righteousness	v
O God, the king of glory	v
O how happy a thing	v
O Lord, our governor	v
O Lord, Thou hast searched	v
O praise God in his holiness	v
O praise the Lord, all ye heathen [I]	f4
O praise the Lord, all ye heathen [II]	f4
O praise the Lord, all ye heathen [III]	f4
O sing joyfully	f4
O sing unto the Lord (text only)	
Out of the deep [I]	v
Out of the deep [II]	v
Out of the deep [III]	f
Ponder my words, O Lord	v
Praise the Lord, O Jerusalem (Pt. II of Praise the Lord, O my soul)	
Praise the Lord, O my soul, and all (Pt. II: Praise the Lord, O Jerusalem)	v
Praise the Lord, O my soul, while I live	f6
Save us, good Lord, waking (text only)	
Sing we merrily	f7
So God loved the world (text only)	
The king shall rejoice (festal Ps. 21)	
The Lord hear thee (festal Ps. 20)	
The Lord is my shepherd (text only)	
Turn Thou us, O good Lord	v
We beseech Thee, almighty God	f5
When the Lord turned again	f4

Batten's most popular anthems were the simple four-part settings, many of which have been republished in the octavo edition of the Tudor Church Music series. The composer is undoubtedly at his best in this vein, which stems directly from the much earlier style of Richard Farrant and John Hilton the elder:

Batten did attempt music of a more ambitious kind in the full style. His setting of "Hear the prayers, O our God" for MAATB is one of his best; and in the eight-part "O clap your hands" there are some interesting antiphonal effects and varied textures:

Three of the most popular verse anthems were "Holy, Holy, Holy, Lord God Almighty", "O Lord, Thou hast searched" and "Praise the Lord, O my soul" (Ps. 103). The following verse may serve as a typical example of Batten's writing for solo voices:

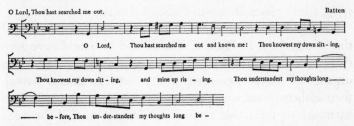

The word painting here, though obvious, is acceptable enough. It does get out of hand, however, in various places, as in the work of many minor composers of the period:

The larger Services and anthems reveal most clearly Batten's chief weakness—a lack of harmonic and tonal invention. All too often there are over-frequent cadences—cadences, moreover, that are centred on a single tonic and its relative major or minor. It is this, rather than any conservatism of style, which places Batten in the second rank.

Michael East was for much of his life Organist and Master of the Choristers at Lichfield Cathedral and he would have been there when Hammond and his friends visited the city: "The organs and voices were deep and sweet [Hammond wrote], their anthems were we much delighted with . . . the melodious harmony of the music invited our longer stay."[24] Between

TABLE 33

East's Anthems

As they departed	1624	v
Awake and stand up	1624	f6
Blow out the trumpet	1624	v
Haste Thee, O God	1618	v
How shall a young man	1624	v
I am the resurrection		f
I have roared	1624	v
I know that my redeemer liveth		f
O clap your hands I (text only)		f
O clap your hands II	1618	v
O Lord, of whom I do depend	1618	v
Sing we merrily	1624	v
Turn thy face	1610	v
When David heard	1610	f
When Israel came out of Egypt	1610	v

(All the verse anthems are scored for voices and viols)

1604 and 1638, East published no fewer than seven collections of his own compositions, two of which are entirely devoted to madrigals, two to instrumental pieces, two—the third and fourth sets of books, 1610 and 1618—to an assortment of madrigals, instrumental pieces and anthems, and one—the sixth set of books, 1624—to anthems alone. Several of the

published anthems are to be found in contemporary manuscripts, especially "As they departed", "O clap your hands",
"Sing we merrily" and, above all, "When Israel came out of
Egypt". The only unpublished compositions are two short
settings of sentences from the Funeral Service and a Magnificat
and Nunc dimittis "for verses", both in the Barnard books at
Lichfield.

All the anthems are on a very large scale, the funeral anthems
only excepted and most are subdivided into two or more
sections. They show East's fondness for rich sonorities and
polyphony in five and six parts. Like Thomas Tomkins, East
thought in terms of the development of melodic fragments
by imitation and sequence—a method that makes the frequent
repetition of text unavoidable. This is least satisfactory when
the composer is attempting some obvious illustration of a
word or phrase:

Several of the anthems contain particularly long instrumental
interludes and introductions and there are many effective
contrasts between instruments and voices in the solo verses.
East's music suffers none the less, as does Batten's, from static
tonalities and cadences that are at once too frequent and too
emphatic:

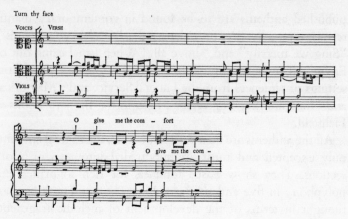

East's most remarkable composition is undoubtedly the sacred madrigal "When David heard", which is quite unlike any other early seventeenth-century setting of this popular text, in that it is wholly diatonic. Whether or not East deliberately intended this, or whether he lacked the technique and imagination to do otherwise, is a nice question. The setting none the less proves in performance to be extraordinarily moving in its stark simplicity:

Both Ward and Ravenscroft have much in common with East. Many of their extant compositions are for voices and viols and are sonorously scored in five and six parts. Much of this music must have been designed in the first instance for devotional use—for the children of Christ's Hospital and for the members of the Fanshawe household.

There now remain eleven anthems by Ravenscroft, of which nine are consort anthems. Only two of the eleven are to be found in choir part-books:

TABLE 34

Ravenscroft's Anthems

Ah, helpless wretch	v
All laud and praise (possibly by Peerson)	v
Behold, now praise the Lord	f5
In Thee, O Lord	v
O clap your hands	v
O Jesu meek	v
O let me hear thy loving kindness	v
O Lord, in Thee is all my trust	v
O woeful ruins	f5
This is the day	v
Wrapt up in mine abomination	v

Ward's extant music comprises two settings of Magnificat and Nunc dimittis, a Te Deum, Kyrie and Creed—all in the verse style—and some twenty devotional songs and anthems. "Let God arise" is to be found in an extraordinarily large number of pre-Restoration sources, both liturgical and secular. The other anthems, however, seem to have been virtually unknown.

TABLE 35

Ward's Anthems

Behold, I was shapen in wickedness	v
Bow down thine ear	v
Deliver me from blood-guiltiness	v
Down caitiff wretch	v
For look how high	v
Have mercy upon me	v
How long wilt Thou forget	f5
I heard a voice	v
I will praise the Lord	v
Let God arise	v
O let me tread	f4
O Lord, consider my great moans	f5
Praise the Lord, O my soul, and call	v
The days of man	v
The Lord executeth righteousness	v
The Lord hath prepared	v
This is a joyful day	v
Turn thy face	v
Unto Thee, O Lord	v

William Smith is now remembered solely for his superb set of Preces and Responses. The composer William Smith was not the late sixteenth-century minor canon of Durham Cathedral, but one who was sworn in as a minor canon of the cathedral on July 20th, 1627.[25] Smith is not known to have composed any Services, nor indeed any music other than the Preces, five sets of festal psalms and seven verse anthems:

TABLE 36

The Anthems and Psalms of William Smith

Anthems

Almighty and everlasting God (for the Purification)
Grant we beseech Thee (for Ascensiontide)
I will preach the law
I will wash mine hands
My heart is set
O God, which for our sakes (for the first Sunday in Lent)
O God, which hast taught (for St. Paul's Day)

Festal psalms

Be merciful unto me, O God	v
God be merciful unto us	v
I will give thanks unto the Lord	f
Lord, Thou art become gracious	f
O give thanks unto the Lord	v
The Lord said unto my Lord	v
The Lord shall send	v

Smith would seem to have been an admirer of Orlando Gibbons' music, and especially the consort anthems, for in his own work he uses similarly fragmented melodic lines and dramatic contrasts of texture:[26]

Smith does not differentiate at all between the style of the anthem and the festal psalm:

The Lord said unto my Lord (Festal Psalm for Evensong on Christmas Day)

Music of this kind would surely have been an anathema to Prebendary Smart! (see Chapter 2, page 47).

Of the composers so far mentioned in this group, Martin Peerson is certainly the least orthodox.[27] Of his twenty extant "anthems", no more than three appear in choir part-books—and of these only one, "Blow out the trumpet", was at all well known. This is a curious work, containing naïvely vigorous contrasts of rhythm and texture. The fragmented lines to the words "in his holy mountain" and the drumming rhythms of "sound an alarum" may be amusing enough to sing, but they would certainly sound somewhat oddly in a cathedral setting (see Chapter 5, page 151). Peerson is at his best in the more reflective moods, where the text gives little obvious scope for word-painting. His full and verse styles are well represented in the two following extracts; the strange words are not likely to appeal greatly to the modern reader (see page 333).

Although he may have been one of the first English composers to make use of the term "basso continuo", Peerson cannot by any means be considered an *avant garde* composer. There is, indeed, nothing in his music that is not to be found in the early seventeenth-century English madrigal, nor even is the basso continuo anything more than a normal English organ score, in which the outer parts (top and bottom) are

First setting of Man dream no more. Part II.

supplied, the inner parts only being improvised by the performer (see Table 37, page 334).

John Amner is in many ways the most interesting of the minor composers of the late sixteenth and early seventeenth

TABLE 37

Peerson's Anthems

Blow out the trumpet	v
Bow down thine ear	v
By Euphrates flowery side	f5
Fly ravished soul	f5
I am brought into so great trouble	f5
I am small	v
I called upon the Lord	v
I will magnify Thee, O Lord	v
Lord, ever bridle my desires	f5
Man, dream no more I	f5
Man, dream no more II	v
O God, that no time dost despise	f4
O God, when Thou wentest before the people	v
O go not from me	v
O let me at thy footstool fall (also attr. Palmer)	f5
O Lord, in Thee is all my trust	v
O Lord, Thou hast searched me out	v
O that my ways	v
Plead Thou my cause	v
Praise the Lord	v
Who will rise up with me	f5

(The italicised anthems are to be found in choir part-books.)

centuries. His extant works include two sets of Preces, a festal psalm for Christmas Day, three complete Services (two in verse form, the other an attractive "Short" Service for MATB), an evening Service "for verses" and some forty anthems and part-songs:

TABLE 38

Amner's Anthems

A stranger here	f6	1615
Away with weak complainings	f3	1615
Blessed be the Lord God	f4	
Christ rising again	f4	
Come, let's rejoice	f4	1615
Consider, all ye passers by	v	
Distressed soul	f3	1615

TABLE 38 (*continued*)

Glory be to God on high (also appears as a "Gloria in excelsis" to		
the "third" Service	v	
Hear, O Lord, and have mercy	v	
He that descended, man to be	f5	1615
How doth the city remain solitary	f5	1615
I am for peace	v	
I will sing unto the Lord as long as I live	v	
I will sing unto the Lord, for he	f5	1615
Let false surmises perish	f3	1615
Lift up your heads	f4	
Like as the hart	v	
Lo, how from heaven	v	1615
Lord, I am not highminded	f5	
Lord, in thy wrath	v	
Love we in one consenting	f3	1615
My Lord is hence removed and laid	v	1615
My shepherd is the living Lord	v	
O come hither	f5	
O come, thou spirit divinest	f3	1615
O God, my king	f4	
O Lord, of whom I do depend	f4	
O love, beseeming well	f3	1615
O magnify the Lord our God	v	
O sing unto the Lord a new song, let	f7	
Out of the deep	f3	
O worship the Lord	v	
O ye little flock	v	1615
. . . Rejoice, rejoice	v	
Remember not, Lord, our offences	f5	1615
St. Mary now	f4	1615
Sing, O heavens	f7	
Sweet are the thoughts	f4	1615
The King shall rejoice (text only)	v	
Thus sings the heavenly choir	f5	1615
. . . which hath not cast out my prayer	v	
Woe is me	f4	1615

1615 = published by John Amner in his *Sacred Hymnes* (italicised anthems are to be found in choir part-books.)

Roughly half of Amner's work is to be found in the *Sacred Hymnes*, which takes the form of an essay in contrasting moods, each piece being labelled either a "motect" or an "alleluia". Each "alleluia" includes a jubilant and usually melismatic setting of the word:

Thus sings the heavenly choir

final Alleluia, from Lo, how from heaven

Some of the smaller three-part "alleluias" are, in effect, devotional "fa-las" with the same binary structures and textures (see "Love we in one consenting", page 337).

The most brilliant "alleluia" of all, however, is the Christmas anthem "O ye little flock" for six viols, solo voices and six-part chorus. The work is of great length and is divided into three sections, each ending with a massive chorus. The "alleluia" comes at the end of section two (see CHORUS "Alleluia, alleluia", page 337).

Love we in one consenting

The exuberance of the instrumental writing in this anthem is well illustrated in this extract from the beginning of the second section:

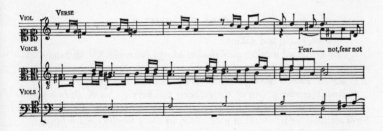

Among the "motects", the setting of the Litany prayer "Remember not, Lord, our offences" is especially memorable. The Amen is certainly one of the loveliest of its kind:

The little four-part motet, "Woe is me", is in its way equally fine:

A collected edition of the composer's music would seem to be long overdue.

NOTES TO CHAPTER 9

1. Stevens, D. (i); and Atkins.

2. The keyboard music is published in *Musica Britannica* XV, and some consort music in *Musica Britannica*, IX.

3. See the *English Madrigalists*, XVIII (Stainer and Bell, 1960).

4. Rough transcriptions of the anthems and Services by A. Ramsbotham, are deposited in the Music Library, University of London. The *Musica Deo Sacra* anthems are in course of publication by *Early English Church Music*.

5. Stevens, D. (i), p. 30.

6. Mr. P. James very kindly placed his reconstruction of the Sixth Service at the author's disposal.

7. Denis Stevens has published a version of "Above the stars," giving both organ and string parts; Concordia Publishing House, St. Louis, Mo.

8. Collins, W. (i) and (ii), p. 123.

9. Information very kindly supplied by Mr. J. H. Harvey, Hon. Archivist to Winchester College.

10. Chitty; and Cook.

11. Peckham (i and ii); Welch; and Dart (ii).

12. Welch, p. 4.

13. Brown, D.

14. *Musica Britannica*, XV, No. 41, for anonymous setting.

15. Dr. Fellowes failed to notice that Services No. 1 and 6 (his numbering, Fellowes (i), pp. 94–5) are one and the same.

16. Fellowes (iii).

17. See *Musica Britannica*, IX, for the consort music, and *Musica Britannica* XX for the keyboard music.

18. *Tudor Church Music*, IV.

19. Dart (i).

20. *Tudor Church Music*, IV, p. xxi.

21. *Musica Britannica*, XX, No. 17.

22. Information very kindly supplied by Mr. David Wulstan: see Wulstan (i), the "Introduction."

23. Mr. John Morehen very kindly placed his transcriptions of music by Nicholson and Stonard at the author's disposal.

24. Hammond (i).

25. Information very kindly supplied by Mr. H. W. Shaw.

26. Transcription very kindly supplied by Mr. J. Buttrey.

27. Jones, A.

10

William Child, his Contemporaries and the Stile Nuovo in England

Excellent though modern music may be, there is still nothing to suggest that it will ever be able to accomplish what ancient music accomplished ....

Vincenzo Galilei, *Diologo della musica antica e della moderna* (1581)[1]

It was this dissatisfaction with existing techniques of vocal composition that led the members of Count Bardi's famous

TABLE 39

The Contemporaries of William Child (1606–97)

Christopher Gibbons*	1615–1676
George Jeffries	*1610–1685*
Henry Lawes	1596–1662
William Lawes	1602–1645
Henry Loosemore	fl. 1630, d. 1670
Walter Porter	*1595–1659*
Robert Ramsey	fl. 1630
Benjamin Rogers	1614–1696

also

Beck, Bryne, Bullis (snr), John Cobb, Hugh Davies, Ellis, Foster, Hilton (the younger), Ive, *Jenkins*, Lowe, Thomas Mudd, Okeover, Pickaver, Pysinge, Rogers, Silver, John Wilson.

No information has yet come to light about any of the following: Bearsley, Belmagne, Blackwell, Blanks, Bolde, Broad, Richard Browne, Bucknam, *Bulman*, Butler, Carr, Cheyney, Corkine, Coste, Cutts, Richard Davies, Deane, Derricke, Fisher, Frost, Galle, Greggs, Hanford, Horsley, Hughes, Thomas Hunt, Kindersley, Laud, John Mace, Mallory, Mason, Nichols, Oxford, Partyne, Price, Read, Rutter, Simmes, Standish, Nicholas Strogers, Stubbes, Tozar and Wilkinson.

* Italicised dates are only approximate. Italicised names indicate that no liturgical anthems or Services are known by the composers in question.

340

"Camerata" in Florence to develop a new kind of vocal idiom, one that can best be described as a form of heightened oratory or, as Caccini put it in the preface to his *Le nuove musiche* (1602),[2] a kind of talking in harmony.

English interest in the *stile nuovo*, as it was generally called, first manifested itself in secular music and especially in the dramatic masque, which reached new heights of popularity under the patronage of the generous and improvident James I. The principal exponents of the new style in England were for the most part in royal service—Signor Angelo Notari (fl. c. 1610–66) and Nicholas Lanier II (1588–1666), musicians to Prince Henry, and subsequently to Prince (later King) Charles; Walter Porter (c. 1595–1659), self-styled pupil of Monteverdi and Gentleman of the Chapel Royal; Henry (1596–1662) and William (1602–45) Lawes, musicians to King Charles I; John Wilson (1595–1674), a "kinsman" of Porter's, musician to Charles I and subsequently Professor of Music at Oxford; and George Jeffries (c. 1610–85), organist to Charles I at Oxford during the Civil War. To these should be added the names of several other conservative yet influential composers, notably John Dowland (1563–1626); Alphonso Ferrabosco II (c. 1575–1628); Robert Ramsey (fl. 1610–45); and William Child (1606–97), Organist and Master of the Choristers at Windsor both before and after the Commonwealth.

To judge from the existing sources of manuscript and printed music, the *stile nuovo* began to make an impact in England shortly after 1600. There are Italian monodies in Robert Dowland's *Musicall Banquet* (1610), one of which is Caccini's famous "Amarilli", the international "hit" amongst art-songs of the early seventeenth century[3] (see "Amarilli", page 342).

There are many monodic songs, too, in Angelo Notari's *Prime musiche nuove*—published in London in 1613 (the composer had been musician to Prince Henry until the time of the young prince's tragic death in 1612) (see "Anima eletta", page 342).

Le nuove Musiche (1601)

Barring and note values original

Notari may not have been a very inspiring model for his English colleagues but this did not deter them from trying their hand at the new declamatory style, in some cases with remarkable success.

It was nevertheless some time before the new style was considered to be familiar enough for devotional and liturgical use. In his little treatise *Rules how to compose*[4] (c. 1610), John Cooper—alias Coperario—may have expressed an impatience with traditional techniques of composition, but his two devotional part-songs are both firmly rooted in the sixteenth century. The little four-part composition contains no unusual features. The more ambitious five-part setting of "O Lord, how do my woes increase" is certainly more dramatic, and yet there is nothing in it that cannot be found in the late-renaissance madrigal:

Alphonso Ferrabosco's "In death no man remembereth Thee", too, may contain some harmonic surprises, but the texture is none the less thoroughly contrapuntal:

The younger composers were more fully prepared to commit themselves—though never unreservedly—to the cause of the *stile nuovo*. Nicholas Lanier was by repute the first Englishman to attempt the "stilo recitativo"—the occasion being a masque, "Lovers made men", produced at Lord Hayes' house in 1617, for which he created both music and scenery. He appears to have written nothing for the Anglican rites, but there are Italianate part-songs and a motet of his in manuscripts at the Bodleian Library and Christ Church, Oxford, some of

M

which must surely have been familiar to the composer's Chapel Royal colleagues.

Understandably enough, the first church musicians to show a serious interest in the *stile nuovo* were both members of the Chapel Royal: Walter Porter and Henry Lawes. Unfortunately, all but one of Porter's anthems are now lost, but on the strength of the one extant composition Porter certainly emerges as a composer of considerable historical importance. No fewer than ten of his anthems are listed in the 1630 Chapel Royal anthem book—more than twice as many, that is, as are credited to Henry Lawes, his most Italianate colleague.

Little is known of Henry Lawes before he joined the Chapel Royal in 1625. He would then have been about thirty.[5] He soon made his mark at Court, and in 1631 he was honoured with an additional appointment as musician for the lutes and voices. At the time of his death, in 1662, he was both a Gentleman of the Chapel and composer in the private music for lutes and voices. He wrote some music for the stage, but the bulk of his work is liturgical and devotional in character. Besides the thirty three-part psalms in the *Choice Psalmes* (1648) and the simple hymn tunes in the Sandy's Psalter of 1638 (see Chapter 11, page 396) there are some twenty liturgical anthems, of which only six are at all complete:

TABLE 40
Anthems by Henry Lawes

Blessed is everyone		6346/1664
Happy sons of Israel	text only	1664
Hark, shepherd swains		
Haste Thee, O God	text only	1630
Hearken, O daughter	text only	1664
Hearken unto my voice	text only	1630/6346
Let God arise		
Lord, aloft thy triumphs raising	text only	1664
Make the great God thy fort	text only	1630
My song shall be of mercy		6346/1664
My soul, the great God's praises sing		1664
O sing unto the Lord	text only	
Rejoice in the Lord		
Sitting by streams		1663

TABLE 40 (*continued*)

Thee, and thy wondrous deeds		
The Lord in thy adversity	text only	1664
The Lord is king	text only	1630
The Lord liveth	text only	1664
They that put their trust	text only	6346/1664
Zadok the priest		6346/1664

1630 = Chapel Royal Anthem Book.
6346 = Chapel Royal Anthem Book.
1663 = James Clifford, *Divine Services & Anthems*/1664 = Clifford (2nd edition).

Not a note has yet come to light of the four anthems listed in the 1630 Chapel Royal anthem book, and of those in the Chapel Royal book of c. 1665 only "Zadok" now remains. "Zadok" was composed for the coronation of Charles II and, as might be expected under the circumstances, it is a very modest work. It does, nevertheless, achieve a certain dignity of expression. Sung boldly, with the enthusiastic support of wind, strings and brass, this opening would certainly have been quite impressive:

Apart from "Zadok", "My song shall be of mercy and judgement" was the only anthem to achieve any wide circulation. Its verses are in the somewhat disjointed arioso style currently favoured in England at that time—though by Italian standards, of course, it was then already many years out of date:

All but one of the other completable anthems are in a single source—possibly autograph. One is described as a "full song", though it is prefaced by an instrumental symphony of a dozen bars or so. The texture of the work is homophonic, the effect being of a harmonised recitativo arioso for treble and four accompanying voices:

The full sections of the verse anthems are similarly chordal, though enlivened here and there by small points of imitation:

Hark, shepherd swains

(original note values)

William Lawes[6] did not become a member of the King's
Music until 1635, when he joined his elder brother as a
musician for the lutes and voices. He was a prolific composer
with a particular interest in consort music, as became a pupil
of John Coperario. His liturgical anthems are few in number
(he was never a Gentleman of the Chapel Royal) and only
one of these—"The Lord is my light"—was at all well known.
He none the less wrote at least three others: "Before the
mountains were brought forth", "Who is this that cometh"
and "Let God arise", the last of which is to be found in a
number of early Restoration sources, including Durham, York
and St. Paul's. The loss of "When the mountains were brought
forth" is especially to be regretted since it is described in the
Chapel Royal anthem book of 1630 as a verse anthem "with
verses for cornetts and sackbutts". The composer was evidently
experimenting with a new kind of accompaniment in which
the solo singers were actually accompanied by wind instruments (as far as can be judged, wind instruments only played
in the full sections as a normal rule). Of the two completable
anthems, "The Lord is my light" is the less Italianate and, perhaps
for this reason, more widely sung. The work divides into two
substantial verses and two shortish choruses. The vocal lines
are smoothly imitative, and there is a good deal of chromaticism
of a simple but effective kind:

"Let God arise" is too naively dramatic to have any great appeal. Passages of the following kind could hardly be sung today with any degree of success, exciting though they may have sounded to Lawes' contemporaries:

William Lawes composed a good deal of devotional music besides, including twenty-six psalm settings in a trio sonata idiom (published posthumously in *Choice Psalmes* of 1648). Of especial interest are the "Psalmes, for 1, 2 and 3 partes, to the comon tunes", copies of which are in the library at Christ Church, Oxford, MSS. 768–70. They are notable not so much for their intrinsic musical worth, which is slight, but for their unusual style and form. Although they are described in the Oxford source as "Psalmes", they are quite unlike the earlier metrical psalms "with reports" of John Mundy and John Cosyn; for the psalm tunes are here used as chorus refrains, freely composed verses for solo voices and continuo being inserted in various ways between the refrains. The setting of the sixth psalm, for instance, runs as follows (the verse numberings are those of the Sternhold and Hopkins text):

vs. 1: Lord in thy wrath—verse for alto and bass

vs. 1: "Cho:" to the common tune, verse one being repeated (the tune is supplied in the MS above a simple unfigured bass)

vs. 2 and vs. 3 (first half): Verse for bass

vs. 4: "Cho:" to the common tune

vs. 5–6: Verse for solo bass

vs. 7: "Cho:" to the common tune

vs. 8–9: Verse for alto and tenor

vs. 10: "Cho:" to the common tune

Chorus 1 [the common tune]

There are, in all, nine such verse-psalms in the Christ Church books:

> All people that on earth do dwell
> Have mercy on us, Lord.
> Lord, in thy wrath reprove me not
> O God, my God, wherefore dost Thou forsake me
> O God, my strength and fortitude
> O Lord consider my distress
> O Lord, in Thee is all my trust
> O Lord, of whom I do depend
> O Lord, turn not away thy face

Among Lawes' younger contemporaries was the unusual and eccentric composer George Jeffries. To judge from the quantity of early seventeenth-century Italian music that he copied out,[7] and from the character of his own compositions, he was certainly more fully committed to the *stile nuovo* than any of his English contemporaries. The earliest datable compositions of his are the four songs "made for some Comedies by Sir Robert Hatton" in 1631, and a dialogue, solo and choruses for Dr. Halstead's Comedy called "The Rival Friends", acted before the King and Queen at Cambridge in 1632. Besides music for the stage, Jeffries wrote instrumental compositions of all kinds, Latin motets (well over sixty of which have survived) devotional part songs, and "songs for the church", as well as a morning and an evening Service, and several settings of various parts of the ordinary of Holy Communion. Whether any of the motets, anthems or devotional songs were written before the Civil War is an open question. Dates are attached to only a handful of pieces, and of these the anthem "Turn Thee again" (1648) is the earliest, whilst the latest is the anthem for Whitsunday (1669).

Just which of these pieces Jeffries intended for liturgical use is uncertain. The autograph score-book is divided into sections,[8] one of which is headed "Songs of 4 parts for the

TABLE 41

Anthems by George Jeffries

	Number of parts
Almighty God who madest thy blessed Son	5
A music strange (for Whitsunday) 1669	5
*Awake my soul**	4
Brightest of days (for the Epiphany)	5
Brightest sun, how was thy light (for the Epiphany)	3
Busy time (for the Blessed Innocents Day)	5
Glory to God on High (1652)	4
Great and marvellous are thy works	4
Hark shepherd swains (for the Nativity of our blessed Saviour)	5
Hear my prayer, O Lord, and with thine ears	3
He beheld the city and wept	4
How wretched is the state	4
In the midst of life (from the Funeral Service)	4
Look up, all eyes (for the Ascension)	5
Lord, who for our sins (made in the time of my sickness, October, 1657)	4
Praise the Lord, O my soul (Ps. 104)	2
Praise, the Lord, O my soul (Ps. 104)	3
Rise, heart, thy Lord is risen	5
See, the Word is incarnate (Pt. II The Paschal Lamb, Pt. III: Glory be to the Lamb (1662)	3
Show me thy ways, O Lord	3
Sing unto the Lord, O ye saints	3
The Lord in thy adversity	5
Turn Thee again, O Lord (1648)	4
Turn Thou thus, O good Lord (1655)	4
Unto Thee, O Lord, will I lift up	3
What praise can reach thy clemency (1665)	4
Whisper it easily	5
With notes that are both loud and sweet	2

(Italicised anthems are to be found in liturgical sources.)

church". And yet the only item in this section that could possibly have been sung as an anthem is the first, the Combination anthem "Turn Thou us". Certainly few of Jeffries' compositions would now be considered suitable for the church on either musical or textual grounds. The opening of the anthem for Holy Innocents Day—"Busy time"—is wholly typical in this respect. The lack of any regularly recurring pattern of harmonic change leads to unsatisfactory diffuseness of structure:

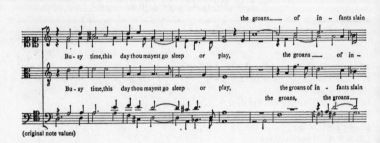

(original note values)

whilst the text is somewhat odd, to say the least:

> ... slain do count thy moments for thee, and their pain procures thy ease and gain. But blessed babes, all your laments and woes are but as ciphering Os. Herod did miss the figure, and 'till he comes to groan too, you cannot signify. When his precious death shall bide first by your side, you then shall come into eternity....

The anthem, like the others in five parts, is in a kind of verse form, but the sections run into one another in quite an unorthodox way. Almost every anthem and motet has some point of interest—an inventive declamatory line:

(original note values)

an unusual texture:

or a striking modulation:

The ability to sustain interest for any great length of time is lacking, however—a criticism which equally applies to so much of the early seventeenth-century Italian music that Jeffries admired.

By comparison, Robert Ramsey's church music is very conservative in style, though the biblical dialogue—"In guilty night", for three voices and continuo—and the two monodies

—"Go perjured man" and "What tears, dear prince"—
show the composer to have been fully conversant with
Italian *stile nuovo* techniques:

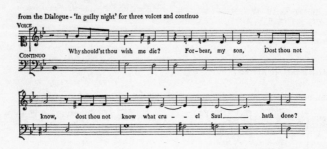

The anthems, motets and sacred madrigals are in a more
recognisably English idiom, though the madrigals and motets
contain some remarkably bold and effective progressions.
The following passage from Ramsey's "Commencement
Song", "Inclina domine", comes shortly after a firm cadence
in F "major":

whilst the following highly imaginative sequence of seventh-
chords, false relations and interrupted cadences is to be found
at the beginning of the third part of "How are the mighty
fallen":

The liturgical music is less experimental, though by no means unoriginal, as these two short extracts will show:

Almighty and Everlasting God

Ramsey's liturgical music comprises two Latin settings of Te Deum and Jubilate, a Latin and an English Litany, a fragment of an English Te Deum, a Short Service (Te, J, K, Cra, Ma, N) and the following anthems:

TABLE 42

Robert Ramsey's Anthems

Almighty and everlasting God, we humbly beseech	f5
Almighty and everlasting God, which hast given	f5
Almighty God, which hast given us	f5
Almighty God, which hast knit	f5
Almighty God, which through thine only begotten son	f5
God, which as upon this day	f5
Grant we beseech Thee, almighty God, that like	f5
Hear my prayer, O Lord, and consider	v
How are the mighty fallen	f6
How doth the city	f6
I heard a voice	v
My song shall be always	v
O come, let us sing	f5
O Lord, let me know mine end	text only
We beseech Thee, O Lord	f5
When David heard	f6

Although William Child was also an admirer of "the Italian way", he differed from the majority of his Italianate contemporaries in that he was primarily—and, indeed, almost wholly—a church musician. He started life as a chorister at Bristol Cathedral under the eminent contrapuntist, Elway Bevin. He became at the age of twenty-four a lay-clerk at St. George's, Windsor, and at twenty-seven, Organist and Master of the Choristers there. After the Restoration he resumed his Windsor appointment, accepting at the same time additional duties at Court as Organist of the Chapel Royal and composer in ordinary for his Majesty's wind instruments. After some initial bother, he managed to reconcile these various interests to the satisfaction of his colleagues at Windsor; and when he died in 1697, at the venerable age of 91, he was still nominally if not effectively in harness.

Nearly all of Child's extant work is for the Anglican rites, though the composer did publish a set of Italianate psalms in 1639 "for private chapels and other private meetings" (see Chapter 11, page 396). As a composer of Services, Child was very definitely the Stanford of his day—in quantity, if not in quality. There are, in all, some eighteen Services of various kinds. None of these settings, whether full or verse, are on anything like the scale of the early seventeenth-century "Great" and "Verse" Services of Byrd, Morley, Tomkins and Weelkes. Most, indeed, could properly be described as "Short". Child's modest music is not altogether without charm, especially in its gentle use of Italianate mannerisms, but its flow is constantly broken by heavy cadences and pauses. The opening of the E minor Magnificat—the Magnificat in "E la mi sharp", that is—may serve to illustrate the general style:

The most unusual Service is the setting of Magnificat and Nunc dimittis in D minor (D sol re flat) with verses throughout for four meanes, and full sections for five-part MAATB chorus. This work would certainly merit an occasional hearing:

At least two of the Services—the "Sharp" Service in "D sol re" and the Service in "Gamut" (G major)—date from before the Civil War, and they were among Child's most popular works. In music of the following kind, Child was most obviously the pupil of Elway Bevin:

TABLE 43
William Child's Services

Te, J "made for the right worshipful Dr. Cosin" (in Latin)
Two settings of Sa and G (one c. 1635)
G

Evening Service in A re	v	Ma, N
Short Service in A [minor]	f	Te, Bs, J, K, Cr, Sa, Ma, N
Last Service in A re	v	Ma, N
Service in B♭	v	Te, J, K, Cr, Sa, Ma, N
Evening Service in B mi ♭	v	Ma, N
Flat Service in C fa ut	v	Ma, N
Whole Service in C fa ut	f	Te, J, K, Cr, Ma, N
Sharp Service in D sol re	f	V, Te, J, K, Cr, Sa, Ma, N
Evening service in D sol re ♭, for four meanes	v	Ma, N
Evening Service in D [minor]	v	Ma, N
Short Service in D sol re ♭	v	Te, Bs, K, Cr, Sa, Ma, N
Service in E la mi ♭	v	Te, J, K, Cr, Sa, Ma, N
Sharp Service in E la mi	v	Te, J, K, Cr, Sa, Ma, N
Second Service in E la mi		Ma, N
Whole Service in F fa ut	f	Te, J, K, Cr, Sa, Ca, De
Whole Service in Gamut	f	V, Te, Bs, Be, J, K, Cr, Sa, G, Ma, N, Ca, De
Flat Service in G [minor]	v	Ma, N

(Italicised Services are contained in pre-Restoration manuscripts.)

Though by no means in the van of progress, Child was none the less one of the first to make any extensive use of unusual key signatures requiring accidentals other than the customary B and E flat. The "D sol re sharp" Service has, even in its pre-Restoration sources, a signature of F and C sharp, and it is effectively in D major, with modulations to nearby tonalities. The "Gamut" Service is very clearly in G major.

The Latin "Te Deum and Jubilate", "made for the right worshipful Dr. Cosin", and the "Sanctus" and "Gloria"—all in the Caroline part-books at Peterhouse—serve as a reminder that Child was himself involved in the Laudian or High Church movement of the 1630s. As far as is known, no composer had set either "Sanctus" or "Gloria in Excelsis" since the early years of the Edwardian reformation. In each of the nine Communion Services, Child provided a setting of "Sanctus", a practice that was to be followed by most of his younger contemporaries.

Well over fifty of Child's anthems are extant, no more than a handful of which have ever been published.

TABLE 44
William Child's Anthems

Alleluia. Awake my soul	v
Alleluia. O Holy Ghost	v
Alleluia. Therefore with angels	v
Alleluia. Thou who when all	v
* Almighty God, which hast knit	v
Behold, God is my helper	v
Behold, how good and joyful	v
Blessed be the Lord God, even the God	f4
Blessed be the Lord my strength	v
* Bow down thine ear, O Lord	f4
Charge them that are rich	f
* Give the King thy judgements	v
*Glory be to God on high	f8
* Hear me, O God	v
Hear me when I call	v
* Hear, O my people	v
* Holy, holy, holy, Lord God of hosts	f8
If the Lord himself (I)	f4
If the Lord himself (II)	v

(*Table 44 continued overleaf*)

TABLE 44 (continued)

I heard a voice	f
I was glad when they said	v
I will be glad	v
I will give thanks	v
Let God arise	v
Lord, who shall dwell	v
My heart is fixed	v
My soul truly waiteth (text only)	v
O clap your hands (I)	f4
O clap your hands (II)	v
* O God, wherefore art Thou absent	f4
O how amiable	v
* O let my mouth be filled	v
* O Lord God, the heathen (Pt. II: Lord how long)	f5
O Lord, grant the king a long life (I)	f4
* O Lord, grant the king a long life (II)	v
O Lord, rebuke me not in thine indignation (I)	f3
O Lord, rebuke me not in thine indignation (II)	v
O praise the Lord, all ye heathen	f4
O praise the Lord, laud ye	f5
* O praise the Lord of heaven	v
O pray for the peace of Jerusalem	f4
O sing unto the Lord a new song, for he	v
O that the salvation	f5
O worship the Lord (text only)	v
Praised be the Lord	f
Praise the Lord, O my soul, and all (I)	f4
Praise the Lord, O my soul, and all (II)	v
Praise ye the strength (text only)	f
Save me, O God, for thy name's sake	v
Sing unto God (text only)	v
*Sing we merrily	f8
The earth is the Lord's	v
The king shall rejoice (I)	f
The king shall rejoice (II)	v
The Lord only is my support (text only)	v
The spirit of grace (text only)	v
Thou art my king	v
Thy word is a lantern	v
* Turn Thou us, O Lord	v
* What shall I render unto the Lord	v
Why doth the heathen	f3
Woe is me that I am constrained	f4

* Indicates a date of composition not later than 1644.

The general level of interest is disappointingly low, though one or two of the pieces are exceptionally good. Three of the short full anthems are especially memorable for their very

Italianate chromaticism—"Bow down thine ear", "O God, wherefore art thou absent" and "Woe is me":

There is also the remarkable motet "O bone Jesu", which for no very clear reason Dr. Fellowes attributed to a later musician —Simon Child, Organist of New College from 1702–31. This is one of William Child's most successful essays in the *stile nuovo*. There are some memorable passages, too, in the verse anthem "Turn thou us", arguably his finest composition:

Child also had a firm grasp of the traditional techniques of polyphonic composition, and two of his anthems in the old manner are well worth hearing: "Sing we merrily", his B.Mus. exercise nominally in eight parts but effectively in seven, and the five-part "O Lord God, the heathen", composed "in the year 1644 on the occasion of the abolishing the

Common Prayer and overthrowing the constitution both in church and state."

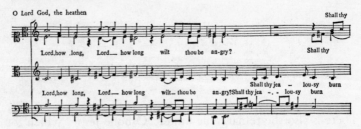

O Lord God, the heathen

Such was Child's mastery of the polyphonic style, and such was his ear for harmony, that it is hard to account for the dullness and even incompetence of so much of his extant work. For of the anthems that have not been mentioned, few are of more than historical interest. We see, as in some of Tomkins' anthems, a widening of the rhythmic range and the adoption of the crotchet as the standard metrical unit in place of the minim. We also see a move towards declamatory solo and choral writing, a *stile concitato* of the kind that Monteverdi had used so effectively in his "Madrigali guerrieri et amorosi" of 1683:

Te Deum and Jubilate for Dr. Cosin

Let God arise

(original note values)

let them al - so be mer - ry and joy - - ful.

let them al - so be mer - ry and joy - - ful.

let them al - so be mer - ry and joy - - ful.

We see, too, the final breakdown of the modal system and the use of clearly defined modulations to distant major and minor keys. We see, moreover, a new kind of melodic line that owes much of its character to the recitativo techniques of Nicholas Lanier and the Lawes brothers:

A Hymn for Christmas Day (verse anthem for A.T.B. and Continuo)

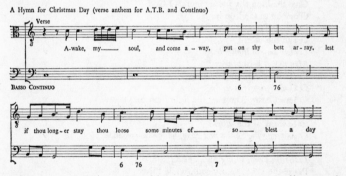

Verse

A-wake, my soul, and come a - way, put on thy best ar - ray, lest

BASSO CONTINUO   6   76

if thou long - er stay thou loose some minutes of so blest a day

6   76   7

That more than a handful of the anthems will ever be considered worthy of revival is unlikely, however. For though his finest compositions show him to have been a musician of surprising vision and ability, his minor ones suggest that he can only too often have been satisfied with less than the best.

In general, provincial musicians were less adventurous in the use of new ideas than their contemporaries at Court, though perhaps as much from lack of experience as from deliberate choice. Of Child's many immediate contemporaries, two comparatively conservative composers made a useful contribution to the repertory of liturgical music: Henry

Loosemore, Organist of King's College, Cambridge, from 1627 until his death in 1670, and Benjamin Rogers (1614–96), who started his career as Child's assistant at Windsor.

Of Loosemore's compositions there now remain some thirty anthems, two Services, a Latin Litany, a "Gloria in excelsis" and some instrumental pieces, including one for three viols and organ, and another—"A verse"—for sackbutt, cornett, violin and organ.

TABLE 45

Henry Loosemore's Anthems

Almighty and everlasting God . . . and that we may	f
Behold it is Christ	v
Behold now praise the Lord	f 8
Fear not, shepherd	v
Fret not thyself	v
Give the king thy judgements, O God	v
Glory be to God on high	v
I will give thanks unto Thee, O Lord	v
Let all the world	v
Lord, I am not high minded	v
Man that is born of woman	v
O eternal God, king of kings	v
O God my heart is ready	f 5
O Jesu Christ, Thou art the light (text only)	v
O Lord, increase our faith	f 4
O Saviour of the world	f
O sing unto the Lord a new song, let the congregation	v
O that mine eyes	v
Praise the Lord, O my soul, and all	v
Praise the Lord, O my soul, while I live	f 4
Put me not to rebuke, O Lord	f 4
Tell the daughter of Zion	f 5
The Lord hath done great things	v
Thou art worthy, O Lord	v
To Jesus Christ, the faithful witness	v
To Jesus Christ, the faithful witness	f
Truly, God is loving unto Israel	v
Turn Thee again, O Lord	v
Unto Thee lift I up mine eyes	f 5
Why art thou so heavy	f 4

(Italicised anthems are to be found in pre-Restoration sources.)

Both Services and the Litany date from the 1630s and are among his least interesting compositions, being in a very ordinary "Short" Service idiom. Such is the quality of his better work, however, that two of the anthems—"O Lord, increase my (our) faith" and "Why art thou so heavy"— have long been attributed unquestioningly to Orlando Gibbons. Both anthems are markedly unmodal in tonality, however, and in this respect are certainly untypical of Gibbons: "O Lord increase my faith" modulates through D minor, C minor/major, E major, A major and D major before coming to a final close in the tonic key of G minor; "Why art thou so heavy" passes through a similar range of keys. A third anthem "Put me not to rebuke", is little inferior to "O Lord, increase my faith", and it certainly merits some attention. The use of interrupted cadences is especially effective:

Loosemore's music did not have any wide circulation, and much of it is now sadly incomplete. Ironically enough, the two Cambridge sources of his music—the Caroline part-books at Peterhouse and the King's College organ-book— do not complement each other at all. Most of the Peterhouse anthems lack organ accompaniments, and the organ accompaniments in the King's Book lack voice-parts. To judge from the remaining fragments, the loss is much to be regretted.

Rogers was already thirty years old when choral services were interrupted by the Civil War, and yet not a note of his music is to be found in pre-Restoration manuscripts. There are some twenty anthems and at least six Services, none of which show any great originality. The composer's indebtedness to early Jacobean models is obvious enough though he used chordal textures, interrupted cadences, and major and minor tonalities in a distinctly mid-century fashion:

TABLE 46

Composers listed in the first and second editions of Clifford's
The Divine Services and Anthems (1663 and 1664)

	Numbers of anthems in the 1663 edition*	Numbers of anthems in the 1664 edition*		Numbers of anthems in the 1663 edition*	Numbers of anthems in the 1664 edition*
Anon	7	50	Leighton	—	1
Amner	1	4	Locke	—	4
Batten	33	—	Lowe	—	8
Bennett	1	—	Loosemore	1	6
Blow	—	3	Mason	—	1
Brown	—	1	Molle	2	1
Bryne	2	—	Morley	3	—
Bull	2	—	Mudd	—	1
Byrd	13	8	Mundy	7	3
Carre	—	2	Parsons	2	1
Child	1	5	Peerson	—	2
Cobb	1	—	Pelham Humphrey	—	5
Cooke	—	20	Phillips	1	—
Coste	1	—	Portman	—	2
Cranford	1	—	Price	2	—
Day	—	1	Ramsey	—	1
East	—	2	Rogers	—	2
R Farrant	2	—	Shepherd	3	—
A Ferrabosco	—	1	Ed. Smith	—	3
Fischer	1	—	H Smith	—	1
Ford	1	—	R Smith	—	6
C Gibbons	—	2	Stonard	1	3
O Gibbons	10	4	Stringer	—	5
Gibbs	3	—	Tallis	10	2
Giles	5	4	G Tomkins	—	1
Heath	—	1	J Tomkins	—	1
Hilton	1	—	T Tomkins	11	30
Hingston	—	2	Tucker	—	1
Holmes	—	3	Tye	6	—
Hooper	9	1	Ward	3	—
Hutchinson	—	4	Warner	—	1
Ives	1	—	Weelkes	9	4
Jeffries	3	—	White	2	1
Jewett	2	2	Wigthorpe	—	1
Johnson	2	—	Wilkinson	1	3
R Jones	—	2	J Wilson	1	—
H Lawes	2	9	Woodson	—	1
W Lawes	2	1			

* All the anthems in the first edition were reprinted in the second; the figures in the 1664 column represent additional items.

There were, besides Loosemore and Rogers, a host of very minor figures: Beck of Norwich; Bryne of St. Paul's Cathedral; the elder Bullis of Ely; Cobb of the Chapel Royal; Hugh Davies of Hereford; Ellis of Oxford; Foster of Durham; Simon Ive of St. Paul's; Edward Lowe of Christ Church, Oxford; Thomas Mudd of Peterborough; John Okeover of Gloucester; John Silver of Wimborne Minster; Thomas Wilson of Peterhouse, Cambridge; and others, too, such as Mallory and Mason, about whom nothing at all is known. All these men were encouraged by the lack of a published collection of Services and anthems to try their hand at composition. Little of their music passed into general circulation, and little of it is now in more than fragmentary condition.

With the resumption of choral services after the long silence of the Commonwealth, church musicians must have been pleasurably surprised to find that a remarkably large repertory of Services and anthems had somehow escaped destruction. St. Paul's Cathedral anthem book, edited by the Reverend James Clifford and published in 1663, includes the names of all the great Elizabethan and Jacobean composers and the texts of some hundred and seventy anthems. This was followed a year later by a greatly enlarged edition in which, Clifford claimed, had been included the texts of all the anthems that were in general use at the time. More than four hundred anthems are listed in this second edition, and well over two hundred and fifty of these are by late sixteenth- and early seventeenth-century musicians. It is almost as if the clock had been put back, and not merely twenty but forty years—for the Caroline composers are very poorly represented either in Clifford's lists or in Restoration scores and part-books (see Table 46). One may well wonder whether the repertory of the 1660s would have been quite such a reactionary one, had there been no long break in the Anglican tradition.

NOTES TO CHAPTER 10

1. Strunk, p. 302.
2. Strunk, p. 377.

3. Fortune, p. 464.
4. Coperario.
5. Evans, for a romanticised biography.
6. Lefkowitz.
7. British Museum MS. 31479.
8. British Museum MS. 10338.
9. See Thomson; see also Duckles; and Smallman, for discussions of the
English Dialogue. Smallman draws interesting parallels between the work of
Hilton, Ramsey, Portman and Francesco Aniero; Aniero published a number
of biblical dialogues at Rome in 1619 under the title *Teatro armonico spirituale.*

11

Published "... for the recreation of all such as delight in Musicke..."

In October 1530 an unknown printer launched into what was then in England a completely new field—to produce an anthology of music for a secular, domestic market. As a recent writer has observed,[1] this date marks the opening of the great era of Tudor and Stuart domestic music: one which was to reach, within the space of fifty years, the very highest levels of achievement. This first anthology—the *XX Songes*—like many later works of the kind, contains both secular and devotional music. The first piece is a setting of "Pater noster" by Cornysch, and there are Marian carols and prayers by Ashwell, Gwynneth and Cowper as well as much secular vocal and instrumental music. Between 1530 and 1588— the year in which Byrd published the first of his three English collections—more than a dozen sets of books were printed for the recreation of all such as delighted in music (see table of printed books in Appendix I).

The *Goostly psalmes and spirituall songes drawen out of the holy Scripture, for the conforte and consolacyon of soch as love to rejoyse in God and his worde*, which appeared some eight or nine years after the *XX Songes*, has an unmistakably Lutheran flavour about it. Its editor, Myles Coverdale, had been an Augustinian monk, as Luther himself had been. It was published at the time that Henry was known to be considering the possibility of an alliance with the Lutheran states, and it drew heavily upon Lutheran originals for words, music, prefatory material and title. There are in the *Goostly psalmes* some thirteen metrical psalms, as well as metrical versions of Magnificat, Nunc dimittis, the Lord's Prayer, Creed, Commandments and a dozen or so German and Latin hymns:

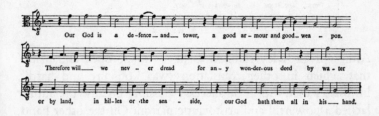

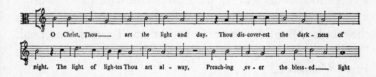

All the settings in Coverdale's book are unharmonised, unlike those of many early Lutheran books of *geistliche Lieder*— a reflection, perhaps, on the comparatively backward state of musical education in England at that time; a reflection too, no doubt, of the editor's desire to reach as wide a musical public as possible.

Soon after the demise of the Vicar General, Thomas Cromwell (Coverdale's patron), the *Goostly psalmes* was officially blacklisted, according to the martyrologist, John Foxe[2] and since no more than a single copy of the book has yet come to light it does seem that the work can have had only a limited circulation. Nothing further of any kind was published until 1549, when there appeared Robert Crowley's *Psalter of David newely translated into Englysh metre*. This is at once the first complete English metrical psalter and the first to contain harmonised music, even though the music in question consists of no more than a single chant-like tune:

Although Crowley claimed to have "made open and plain" that which in other translations was "obscure and hard", his psalter met with little success—possibly because the author lacked a powerful and aristocratic patron. On the other hand, a very modest collection of metrical psalms which also made an appearance in 1549 became within the space of twelve years the standard English psalter. Its author was Thomas Sternhold, "groom of the King's Majesty's robes" and Gentleman of the Privy Chamber.[3]

It is clear, from Sternhold's preface to the first edition of his psalter, that metrical psalms had for some time been in vogue at Court. In a dedicatory preface to the King, Sternhold wrote of the encouragement that the King had given him "to travail further in the said book of Psalms, trusting that as your grace taketh pleasure to hear them sung sometimes of me, so you will also delight not only to see and read them yourself, but also to command them to be sung to you of others". The first edition contained no more than nineteen psalms—seventeen in common metre, two in short metre. A second and posthumous edition appeared in December 1549 containing, in all, thirty-seven Sternhold translations and a further seven by Hopkins. Several reprints of this enlarged psalter appeared between 1550 and 1553.

The first "Sternhold and Hopkins" with music was published in Geneva in 1556. It was issued concurrently with "The forme of prayers . . . used in the English congregation at Geneva, and approved, by the famous and godly learned man,

John Calvyn" (no editions of the psalter, of course, were published in England during the Marian reaction). The 1556 Genevan Psalter contained new material by William Whittingham, then a member of the English community there and later Dean of Durham Cathedral (see Chapter 2, page 39). The preface to "The forme of prayers..." contains an unequivocal denunciation of the more elaborate kinds of church music:

> ... But as there is no gift of God so precious or excellent that Satan hath not after a sort drawn to himself and corrupt[ed]: so hath he most impudently abused this notable gift of singing, chiefly by the papists, his ministers, in disfiguring it, partly by strange language that cannot edify: and partly by a curious wanton sort, hiring men to tickle the ears and flatter the fantasies, not esteeming it as a gift approved by the word of God, profitable for the church, and confirmed by all antiquity ....

After this, it is hardly surprising to find that the tunes, as printed, are unharmonised and that the underlay is strictly syllabic. The tunes are wholly anonymous, but it does seem that they must have been the work of English musicians imitating, perhaps, French and German models.[4] The "Old Hundredth" (a French tune), for example, was obviously the starting point for the English tune to Psalm 3:

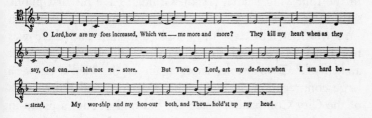

In subsequent editions, Whittingham and Keith broke away from the standard common and double metres to experiment with others that would permit the use of the original French and German tunes:

the Genevan edition of 1569

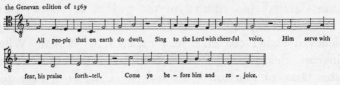

All peo-ple that on earth do dwell, Sing to the Lord with cheer-ful voice, Him serve with

fear, his praise forth-tell, Come ye be - fore him and re - joice.

With the accession of Elizabeth to the throne in September 1558 the Genevan psalter quickly found its way to England, and with it the Genevan practice of congregational psalm singing. Although John Day's 1560 edition of "Sternhold and Hopkins" was apparently the first to be published in England since 1553, psalms, canticles and prayers were already being sung "Geneva-ways" in London during the spring of 1559, if not earlier. At a funeral that took place in London in April 1559—so Machyn noted in his diary—the service was conducted by "the new preachers in their gowns, like laymen". Contrary to custom, there was "neither singing, nor saying till they came [to the grave], and before the body was placed in the grave there was a collect in English". After the burial, the whole company sang *Pater noster* in English, "both preachers and other and of a new fashion, and after, one of them went into the pulpit and made a sermon".[5]

Towards the end of September "began the new morning prayer at St. Antholyn's in Bage-row" after Geneva fashion, and everyone joined in the singing—men, women and boys. In the following March (1560), Grindall gave his first public sermon at St. Paul's Cross as Bishop of London, after which —so Machyn tells us—"the people did sing; and there was my Lord Mayor and the Aldermen, and there was great audience".[6] Two weeks later, again at St. Paul's Cross, a large congregation, including the Aldermen and the Masters of the City Companies, "sang all, old and young, a psalm in metre, the tune of Geneva ways", whilst on March 19th (two days later), at the induction service of the Vicar of St. Martin's, Ludgate, "all the bells of the church did ring a great peal, and after done, all the people did sing the tune of Geneva, and with the bass of the organs".

From then onwards, the metrical psalms of "Sternhold and Hopkins" rapidly established for themselves a firm place in public worship, both in London and the provinces. John Jewel, Bishop of Salisbury, described the process in a letter to Peter Martyr from London, dated March 5th, 1560:

... Religion is now somewhat more established than it was. The people are everywhere exceedingly inclined to the better part. The practice of joining in church music [i.e. the psalms] has very much helped this. For as soon as they had once begun singing in public, in only one little church in London, immediately not only the churches in the neighbourhood, but even the towns far distant began to vie with each other in the same practice. You may now sometimes see at St. Paul's Cross, after the service, six thousand persons, old and young, of both sexes, all singing together and praising God. This sadly annoys the Mass priests and the devil. For they perceive that by these means the sacred discourses sink more deeply into the minds of men, and that their kingdom is weakened and shakened at almost every note. . . .[7]

Naturally enough, there were those who disapproved. In spite of injunctions to the contrary, the Dean and Chapter of Exeter Cathedral did all they could to stop congregational singing at the cathedral services, and their attempts aroused a great deal of ill feeling:

December 16, 1559: *a letter from Lord Montjoye and others to the Dean and Chapter of Exeter*

After our hearty commendations. Whereas in the queen's majesty's late visitation in Exon, order was taken, that the vicars of your church should weekly, and by course say the morning prayer in the choir of your cathedral church, whereunto the people might at time convenient meet together to serve God; and they so resorting reverently, and in great numbers for their greater comfort and better stirring up of their hearts to devotion, appointed amongst themselves at every such meeting to sing a

N

psalm, and altogether with one voice to give praise unto God, according to the use and manner of the primitive church; which order, taken by the visitors, you promised by your corporal oath to see observed. We have now of late heard say, that contrary to the said order, and your own oath, certain of your vicars have scoffed and jested openly at the godly doings of the people on this behalf, and by divers and sundry ways have molested and troubled them; and that you the canons there, which of all others should most have rejoiced thereat, and should have encouraged the people to go forward, have very uncourteously forbidden them the use of your choir. . . .[8]

The Chapter replied that the congregation had been behaving outrageously, taking over the stalls in the choir and showing no respect at all for the cathedral clergy. In spite of this, however, Archbishop Parker wrote back to insist that the Chapter "quietly permit and suffer such congregation of people as shall be at any time hereafter congregated together in the said church, to sing or say the godly prayers in the morning, and at other times set forth, used and permitted in this Church of England . . . ."[9] We may be sure that the troubles at Exeter were not unique.

Several editions of "Sternhold and Hopkins" appeared between 1560 and 1562, the year in which the first complete edition was produced. From then onwards, every year saw the publication of at least one reprint or revised edition. Between 1560 and 1579 at least twenty different editions came out. Between 1580 and 1640 the numbers steadily rose—to over forty-five between 1580 and 1599, sixty-five between 1600 and 1620, and to more than a hundred between 1620 and 1640.[10]

The first harmonised "Sternhold and Hopkins" was Day's elegant print of c. 1563, entitled, *the whole psalmes in foure partes, which may be song to al musicall instrumentes, set forth for the encrease of vertue: and abolishyng of other vayne and triflyng ballades.* The four voice parts are printed separately in partbooks labelled "medius", "contratenor", "tenor" and "bassus", the music being liberally sprinkled with typographical errors in the publisher's best manner. Besides the hundred or so "church" tunes to be found in the earlier monodic psalters, there are thirty or so new tunes making a total of more than a hundred and forty in all. Rather more than half the harmonisations are by a William Parsons—perhaps the Parson who had been Organist of Wells Cathedral between 1550 and 1560. There are also a good number by Thomas Caustun, Gentleman of the Chapel Royal, and others by R. Brimley (probably the Durham musician), John Hake, N. Southerton and Richard Edwardes, Master of the Chapel Royal choristers. Many of the church tunes are harmonised in more than one way, and by different composers. The most popular are the "Quicunque vult", the 52nd psalm, the Magnificat, the Lord's Prayer and the Commandments, each with three different harmonisations; Psalms 51, 103 and 137, each with four; and Psalm 44 with no fewer than five. Could it be that the words of Psalm 44 had a particularly strong appeal during that time of rapid change?

> Our ears have heard our fathers tell, and reverently record
> The wondrous works that Thou has done in olden time, O Lord.
> How Thou didst cast the Gentiles out, and 'stroydst them with
> strong hand,
> Planting our fathers in their place, and gavest to them their land.

Most of the tunes are given to the tenor voice, as in the two settings of "Vater unser im Himmelreich" below, though a few harmonisations place the tune in the bass or treble:

Richard Edwardes

Our Fa-ther, which in hea-ven art, and makest us all one broth-er — hood

But with the heart deep sigh, and groan

Most of the harmonisations, like the one above, are in a simple chordal style, though a few are rather more elaborate in texture—notably the third setting of Psalm 137 by William Parsons, which has very much the texture of a setting of Psalm 44 by Brimley, which ends like this:

Day also included at the end of the books several prayers—two by Tallis, and one each by Shepherd, Caustun and William Parsons.[11]

No other harmonised version of the church tunes appeared until 1579, when one John Bull, citizen and goldsmith of London, published settings by William Damon, a Gentleman of the Chapel Royal. As it later transpired, Bull had not asked Damon's permission before going into print, and Damon seems to have been rather embarrassed by the appearance of his homespun music which he had only intended for private consumption. The harmonisations are of the simplest kind, with the exception of the first—a four-part polyphonic composition to the opening words of the prayer book Venite.

Six years later, John Cosyn produced a smaller but rather more ambitious collection of psalm settings dedicated to Queen Elizabeth's Principal Secretary and Privy Councillor, Sir Francis Walsingham. Cosyn intended these psalms, as he explained in the preface, "for the private use and comfort of the godly, in place of many other songs neither tending to the praise of God, nor containing anything fit for Christian ears". In all, his *Musike of six, and five partes* contains some forty-four block-chordal harmonisations, all for six voices, and some fourteen contrapuntal five-part consort songs which owe a good deal in style to the Scottish psalm "with reports".[12] A comparison may serve to illustrate the point:

But Cosyn's settings take the form rather more of contrapuntal chorale preludes, each line of melody being punctuated by imitative developments in the lower voices. None of Cosyn's music is to be found in pre-Restoration sets of choir part-books, but a setting of "Give laud unto the Lord", by John Mundy, in a very similar style, was certainly used as a liturgical anthem, with words fitted to parts that were obviously instrumental in their original form. As such, it is unique:

Six years later, there appeared two posthumous collections of harmonised "church tunes" by William Damon, to the words of Sternhold and Hopkins, entitled *The former Booke of the Musicke of M. William Damon* and *The second Booke of the Musicke*, both dedicated to Secretary Sir William Cecil, Knight of the Garter, Lord High Treasurer of England.

Shortly after the unauthorised publication of 1579, Damon had settled down to rework the tunes in that collection to suit the "learned ears" of the time. He had set each one twice, once in the tenor voice (*The former Booke*), once in the treble (*The second Booke*). In style, these psalms are not unlike the five-part versions of Cosyn—contrapuntal settings but with words set to all parts.

The "Sternhold and Hopkins" psalter formed the basis of four other collections—by Este, Alison, Barley and Ravenscroft—all basically reharmonisations of the established repertory of "church tunes". The first of these was Este's *The Whole Booke of Psalmes* (1592), "compiled by sundry authors, who have so laboured that the unskilful with small practice may attain to sing that part which is fittest for their voice". The dedicatee was Sir John Puckering, Lord Keeper of the Great Seal. Music is printed with every psalm, canticle and prayer, but many of the tunes are repeated and two by Hooper and Blanks each appear more than thirty times. Among the composers represented are Richard Alison, John Dowland, John Farmer and Michael Cavendish, none of whom were professional church musicians. The tunes are for the most part in the tenor voice, as they are in Day's *the whole psalmes* of 1563.

William Barley's *The Whole Booke of Psalms* appeared in 1599, cheaply printed as a pocket-sized edition. It is a curious work, for many of the settings—again in simple four-part harmony—are incomplete. Amongst the complete tunes however are four by Morley and five by John Bennet that had not before been published.

In the very same year, Richard Alison, "Gentleman Practitioner in the Art of Musicke", brought out his own simple hymn-like settings of the church tunes under the title *The Psalmes of David in Metre*, dedicating them to the Lady Ann, Countess of Warwick, the wife of his former patron. As with the earlier harmonised psalters, the tunes come mainly from the unharmonised Day psalter of 1579. Indeed, Alison obviously intended his work as a supplement to the current

Sternhold and Hopkins psalter, for he left out all the psalms that were without tunes in the 1579 edition and supplied only the first verses to the remaining ones. The four voice-parts are included in one book. Each setting occupies one complete opening, and optional parts for lute and cittern are supplied in the following manner:

The Lamentation

O Lord,— turn not a - way thy face from him that lies pros - trate.

The last harmonised "Sternhold and Hopkins" was Thomas Ravenscroft's *The Whole Booke of Psalmes* of 1621. It contains much music from earlier psalters, including settings by William Parsons and Tallis from Day's 1563 psalter, settings by Alison, Bennet, Blanks, Cavendish, Dowland, Farmer, Farnaby, Hooper, Kirby and Morley from the Este and Barley psalters, and new ones by John and Thomas Tomkins, Martin Peerson, Richard Palmer, John Milton (father of the poet), Ward, Stubbes, Cranford, Harrison and Ravenscroft himself. Most of the new contributors were professional church musicians, unlike those of the earlier collections. In an unusually interesting preface Ravenscroft addressed himself "to all that have skill or will unto sacred music". He stressed that he had taken especial care to select tunes "proper to the nature of each psalm", and he urged that singers should bear the following points in mind:

1. "That psalms of tribulation be sung with a low voice and long measure"—these included Psalms 6 (misprinted in the first edition as 9!), 32, 38, 51, 102, 130 and 143.

2. "That psalms of thanksgiving be sung with a voice indifferent, neither too loud, nor too soft, and with a measure neither too swift nor too slow."

3. "That psalms of rejoicing be sung with a loud voice [and] a swift and jocund measure" (these included Psalms 33-4, 47, 84, 95-6, 98-9, 108, 113, 117, 135-6, 145, 147-8 and 150).

Ravenscroft's own version of Psalm 130 will serve as an example of the later work. In its use of minor melodic and harmonic intervals it happens to conform to current harmonic theories of expression as expounded by Zarlino and Morley. Most of the settings in the collection do not, however.

Lord, to Thee I make my moan, When danger me op - press. I call I sigh, plain and groan, Trusting to find re - lease.

Only those publications that were based on both the words and music of the "Sternhold and Hopkins" psalter have so far been mentioned. But much else was published, too, including free polyphonic settings of verse by Sternhold and Hopkins, and settings of other contemporary texts, both verse and prose. The simplest kinds of composition were those in which only a single musical line was supplied, usually in the alto or tenor clef. The music in some half-dozen books is of this kind (see Appendix I, asterisked titles), including William Slatyer's very curious *Psalmes or songs of Sion, turned into the language, and set to the tunes of a strange land*, which makes use of popular tunes of the day, such as "Goe from my window" (Psalms 8 and 11), "Barow Faustus dreame" (Psalm 19),

"Susan", "Sweet Robin", "The New Sa Ho" and "The Queen of love".

The two earliest collections containing harmonised settings of contemporary verse (other than that of "Sternhold and Hopkins") were Francys Segar's *Certayne psalmes* (dedicated to the Lord High Steward, John, first Earl of Bedford) and Christopher Tye's *Actes of the Apostles* (dedicated to Edward VI), both published in 1553. In Segar's work there are nineteen metrical psalms and two "tunes", one of a fairly elaborate kind, the other being no more than a simple hymn tune:

Tye's work comprises the first fourteen chapters of the Acts of the Apostles—turned into verse by the composer himself and supplied with music—a monody, and two imitative pieces for MATB. The music was rescued by the Victorians and provided with alternative texts, the most popular being "Come, Holy Ghost, eternal God" and "O Lord, thy word endureth", but it is of no great distinction. The word accentuation is stiff and the imitative points are rather mechanically contrived.

The next important work to appear in print was Archbishop Parker's psalter, issued privately it would seem, in about 1567.

As Parker explained in the course of a twenty-seven-page preface, he had originally turned the psalter into metrical verse for his own private use. He had, however, been persuaded by friends to go into print and to publish both the psalter and the nine tunes that Thomas Tallis had composed to go with it. Parker's interesting comments on Tallis' music show that he had very clear ideas of his own as to the moods that the Tallis tunes evoked:

> First [he wrote in the preface to the psalter] you ought to conjoin a sad tune or song with a sad Psalm, and a joyful tune and song with a joyful psalm, and an indifferent tune and song with a psalm which goeth indifferently.

He then went on to describe his own reactions to Tallis' tunes:

> The first is meek, devout to see,
> The second, sad, in majesty,
> The third doth rage, and roughly brayeth,
> The fourth doth fawn, and flattery playeth,
> The fifth delighteth, and laugheth the more,
> The sixth bewaileth, it weepeth full sore,
> The seventh treadeth stout, in forward race,
> The eighth goeth mild, in modest pace.

> ... not yet, by this, meaning to prescribe a rule to prejudice any man's peculiar spirit or ear, for as there are diversities of tastes in men's palettes ... so also in their ears ...

During the last three or four years of his life, Parker employed the composer Thomas Whythorne to direct the music in his private chapel. A year or so before entering the Archbishop's service, Whythorne had published a collection of his own secular and devotional part-songs under the title *Songs for three, fouer, and five Voyces*. Most of the three- and five-part pieces are settings of secular texts, but the bulk of the four-part works are devotional in character, some having Prayer Book texts but the majority metrical verses of Whythorne's own devising. The *Songs* sold badly (neither verse nor music is of much merit) and Whythorne was inclined to blame his publisher, John Day, for his failure to advertise the work adequately. He also wondered whether the public might not have been wary of buying music from Day, knowing that Day "had heretofore printed music which was very false printed!"[13] Whythorne published one other work, a collection of fifty-two two-part pieces for voices and/or instruments, appropriately entitled *Duos* and dated 1591. There are altogether fifteen canons, some twenty-five untexted and presumably instrumental pieces, and a dozen or so settings of biblical texts.

Three years before the publication of this second book, William Byrd had produced the first of his three great English collections, the *Psalmes, Sonets, and songs of sadness and pietie*. The title is misleading, for it implies a concentration upon subjects of a grave and sober kind. There are, however, some sixteen very secular compositions, both sad and gay, besides ten metrical psalms and seven devotional songs, one of which is the extraordinary "Susanna fair"—perhaps the oddest of all the Elizabethan "moral" songs.[14] Most of the 1588 pieces had been written some time before they were published, and all but one of the psalms and songs of sadness and piety had originally been scored for solo voice and an instrumental accompaniment, probably of viols. The exception, "O God, give ear", is a fine anthem for MAATB. It is to be found in several sets of choir part-books, whereas the consort-song adaptations are with one exception exclusive to the secular sources. Disparaging remarks are usually made about Byrd's English "anthems", and especially about those in the 1588 collection. As consort-songs, however, these "anthems" have great charm. The unhappy underlay that mars the adapted songs is, of course, entirely absent from the originals, and the contrast between instruments and solo voice adds a new dimension to the music.

The Psalmes, Sonets, and songs met with such success that Byrd was encouraged to publish a second work of a similar kind only a year later, the *Songs of sundrie natures*, containing music "lately made and composed" "for the delight of all such as take pleasure in the exercise of that Art". Byrd dedicated it to Sir Henry Carye, who, as "Lord Chamberlain to the Queen's most excellent Majesty", had the charge of the musicians of the Queen's household. Most of the 1589 *Songs* are secular, but there are some three-part settings of the penitential psalms, and eight "anthems"—three in verse form—and five full settings in four and six parts. Within the limits imposed by a three-part texture, Byrd's music is of considerable interest. The seven penitential psalms are set in minor modes, and the underlay is unexpectedly—and appropriately—melismatic. By comparison, the four- and six-part anthems are something of a disappointment. The underlay is persistently syllabic, and there is little of the imaginative freedom that characterises the best of the music in the 1611 volume.[15]

Byrd published his third and last collection of English compositions—the *Psalmes, songs, and sonnets*—in 1611, when he was little short of seventy years old. The charming preface speaks of the composer's "best endevour" to give content and of his confidence that the music will "deserve liking" if it is "well expressed". This collection does indeed contain some of Byrd's very finest English anthems. There are two splendid verse anthems—"O God, that guides" (written surely for the Twelfth Night celebrations at Court) and the penitential prayer "Have mercy upon me"—together with no fewer than seven large-scale full anthems, rather in the style of the madrigalian motets in the 1589 and 1591 *Cantiones Sacrae*. Surprisingly, only one of the 1611 anthems is to be found in any contemporary manuscript source (can they already have seemed old-fashioned by then?) Even in the small three-part pieces there is a much greater freedom of line, a bolder use of rhythm, and a much richer harmonic vocabulary, qualities that are even more apparent in the larger anthems.[16]

At least five sets of early Jacobean part-songs are entirely devotional in character. These include an English version of Giovanni Croce's *Musica Sacra* (1608), Sir William Leighton's *The Teares or Lamentacions of a Sorrowfull Soule* (1614), two sets of *Sacred Hymns* by Robert Tailour and John Amner (both published in 1615), and Michael East's *The Sixt Set of Bookes*, which appeared in 1624 together with a sixth and much simpler work, George Withers' *The Hymnes and Songs of the Church*.

Croce was very highly esteemed in England during the late sixteenth and early seventeenth centuries. His compositions are to be found in many English manuscripts and in two "Englished" collections of Italian madrigals that were published in 1597. *Musica Sacra* first came out in 1599 at Nuremberg, and only nine years later it was issued by the English printer Thomas Este in a crude English adaptation. The work comprises six-part settings of the penitential psalms. The beginning of "Shew mercy, Lord, on me" may serve as a fair example of Croce's contrapuntal, colourful, yet conservative style:

Sir William Leighton's *Teares*, which came out eight years later, is a curious work. Leighton, a Gentleman Pensioner to James I, had been imprisoned in 1609 for debt—unjustly, as he claimed. During his confinement, he had whiled away the hours by writing metrical psalms and devotional verse, and on his release from prison he had published the fruits of his labours. Being keenly interested in music, and himself an amateur composer, he had somehow managed to persuade most of the leading composers of the day to set his verses to music

—only Tomkins' name, indeed, is missing. The anthology falls into three main divisions: "consort songs" for Morley's "broken consort" of lute, pandora, cittern, treble viol, bass viol and recorder (but with, of course, the addition of voices),

(original note values)

"songs of four parts", and "songs of five parts", both un-accompanied. There are fifty-three pieces in all. Leighton himself contributed eight of the seventeen consort songs, the other composers being John Bull,[17] Coperario, John Dowland, Ford, Giles, Hooper, Robert Johnson, Kindersley and John Milton. In spite of Leighton's poor verse, many of the contributors managed to produce music of remarkably high quality. Byrd wrote no fewer than four settings, two in four and two in five parts.[18] These are Byrd's last published vocal compositions, and they are not far removed in style from the more dramatic *Gradualia* motets. Gibbons wrote two splendidly sonorous pieces for Leighton, and Weelkes produced a short but beautiful consort song—his only essay in this medium. The other composers who accepted Leighton's invitation to contribute were Alphonso Ferrabosco, Robert Jones, Thomas Lupo, Peerson, Pilkington, Ward and Wilbye.

Two further collections of devotional music and verse came out in the following year—one by Robert Tailour, musician to Prince Charles, and the other by the Organist of Ely Cathedral, John Amner. Tailour's work is the less substantial of the two. It consists of "*Fifti Select Psalms of David and others . . . set to be sung in Five parts, as also to the Viole, and Lute or Orpharion . . .*". Sir Edwin Sandys' verse reaches no great heights and Tailour's music is unremarkable. Only the treble part is underlaid, suggesting that the composer primarily intended the pieces to be consort songs and not, despite the preface, "a-capella" anthems. As this extract will show, the music is in the English consort-song tradition:

John Amner's *Sacred Hymnes* is altogether more interesting. It contains in all some twenty[19] compositions in from three to six parts, some of considerable length and subdivided into separate sections. Many are to be found in contemporary manuscripts (unlike the Tailour *Sacred Hymns*) and it is clear that Amner's music achieved a certain justifiable popularity at the time. The quality of both music and verse is uneven. There are some embarrassing literary naiveties of which this short extract is typical:

> St. Mary now, but erst the worst of many, when with dishevelled hairs, she wiped the feet that she with tears had washed before, with knees full lowly bent, and many a grievous groan to heaven sent. . . .

On the other hand, strange though the verse may be, the best of it has a lightness of touch that accords well with

Amner's madrigalian music (see p. 337). The two most ambitious *Hymnes* are the Christmas verse anthems for voices and viols. Of the two, "O ye little flock" is the more substantial and it seems to have been the more widely known. There are copies of it in several sets of pre-Restoration part-books. The other, "Lo, how from heaven", suffers somewhat from its text, but it too has some very impressive moments (see p. 336). All but three of the Amner *Hymnes* are settings of contemporary verse. The exceptions—"Woe is me", "How doth the city" and "Remember not, Lord"—are all of considerable merit.

George Wither's *The Hymnes and Songs of the Church* (1623) is, by comparison, a very modest production, though its history is not without interest. Wither tells in *The Schollers Purgatory* how he was "by some of the clergy ... invited to collect and translate into lyric verse the hymns dispersed throughout canonical scriptures". This he did, "adding unto them such parcels of Holy Writ, Creeds, and Songs" as he considered "proper and necessary to be sung", and suitable "for the ordinary public occasions" of the Church. But the Stationers Company discouraged sales of the book—or so Wither claimed—on the grounds that it was "popish and tending to the maintenance of supersitition", though we may suspect that the quality of Wither's verse was the major deterrent!

The Song of Solomon: First Canticle, Song 13

> Oh, my love, how comely now,
> And how beautiful art thou!
> Thou of dove-like eyes a pair
> Shining hast within thy hair,
> And thy looks like kidlings be,
> Which from Gilead hill we see.

Popish or not, the hymns were certainly far removed from the familiar metrical psalmody of Sternhold and Hopkins, and it is easy to understand why they met with some opposition. Even so, the book passed through several reprints in the course of the first two years. As is well known, Gibbons supplied music for the hymnal—eight tunes in all[20] consisting of a melody and a bass, the middle parts being supplied, presumably, by the organist. This is, in fact, the first hymnal proper of the Church of England, designed from the outset for congregational use.

Many other sets of late sixteenth- and early seventeenth-century music books, while not wholly devoted to sacred music, contain much that is devotional in character. John Mundy's collection of *Songs and Psalmes*, published in 1594, is very similar in scope to the Byrd anthologies mentioned above, but it does not seem to have been anything like as popular—to judge, at least, from the contents of contemporary manuscripts. This is difficult to understand, for Mundy writes well for voices; and his use of suspended and passing dissonance, in particular, is original and highly effective.

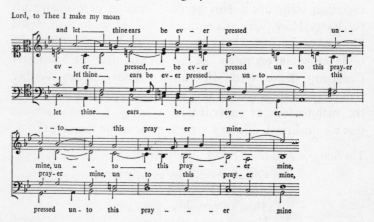

Other collections of the kind to note are Thomas Greaves' *Songes of Sundrie Kindes* (1604), Michael East's third, fourth and sixth sets of books (1610, 1618 and 1624), Thomas Tomkins' *Songs* of 1622, Francis Pilkington's *Second Set of Madrigals* (1624), and Walter Porter's *Madrigales and Ayres* of 1632.

Little is known of Greaves, beyond the fact that he was lutenist to Sir Henry Pierrepoint of Holm in Nottinghamshire.

The music in his *Songes* is of three kinds: airs to be sung to the lute and bass viol, songs of sadness for the viols and voice, and madrigals for five voices. By design or accident, all the songs of sadness are in minor keys. The accompaniments, though scored for viols, show very clearly the influence of the lute. Alison framed his *Howres Recreation* "for the delight of gentlemen and others which are well affected to that quality". Most of the pieces have a total range of three octaves or more, and most call for two high trebles—a feature, so Alison claimed, that would appeal especially to "private families". The tone of the collection is set by the first song:

> The man upright of life
> Whose guiltless heart is free
> From all dishonest deeds
> Or thoughts of vanity.
>
> That man needs neither towers
> Nor armour for defence,
> Nor secret vaults to fly
> From thunder's violence.

And although there are one or two charming pastorals, including a setting of Campian's delightful "There is a garden in her face", most of the items are designed to improve the mind rather than to titillate. The set ends with three substantial anthems (with parts for the normal meane, and not for the treble), "Behold, now praise the Lord", a full five-part anthem for general occasions, and two for November 5th: "O Lord, bow down thine ear" (MAATB) and "The sacred choir of angels", a verse anthem for solo meane, four viols and five-part choir in a suitably festive triple metre.

Michael East—an industrious composer—produced, in all, seven sets of books; the first in 1604, the last in 1638. In three of these sets he published full-scale liturgical anthems, many of which are to be found in contemporary choir part-books. There are two large verse anthems for voices and viols in the 1610 set (the third), which possibly date from the year or so previously when East had been a lay-clerk at Ely. In the fourth set (1618), there are four more verse anthems for voices and viols—three in five parts, the other in six—and an austere but immensely effective setting of "When David heard". East was by then Organist and Master of the Lichfield choristers. The sixth set is entirely devoted to anthems and is dedicated to John Williams, Bishop of Lincoln—a former Dean of Westminster Abbey and a noted patron of the Arts.[21] Williams had apparently bestowed an annuity upon the composer, after hearing performances of some motets of his, though the two had never met. The music of these three collections has been discussed in greater detail above.

The four sacred madrigals or anthems in Tomkins' *Songs of 3. 4. 5. and 6 parts* (1622) are all of considerable interest. The five-part setting of "When David heard" ranks as one of the outstanding sacred madrigals of the time. Its tonic is effectively C minor though the key signature contains only two flats, a most unusual tonality at that time. There is much modulation into the sharper keys, both major and minor, and a great deal of suspension and passing dissonance:

The other three songs are distinguished by similar qualities, and the opening of "Woe is me" is especially fine.

Sacred songs are also to be found in one or two of the thirty or so lutenist song-books, all of which were published between 1597 and 1622, notably John Bartlett's *A Booke of Ayres* (1606), Thomas Campion's *Two Bookes of Ayres. The First contayning Divine and Morall Songs* (1610), John Dowland's *A Pilgrimes Solace* (1612) and John Attey's *The First Booke of Ayres* (1622).

Of these, the most substantial is Dowland's *A Pilgrimes Solace*. As they are printed, they may be sung as full anthems with or without the support of lute and viols or as solo songs with obbligato accompaniment. Dowland clearly scored the songs for solo voice and instruments in the first place, however, since the underlay of the subsidiary parts is repetitious and contrived. Much use is made of sharp tonalities (the very nature of lute tablature must have encouraged an experimental approach to tonality) and the settings are full of unexpected modulations and augmented intervals:[22]

Attey's *The First Booke of Ayres* and Tomkins' *Songs* of 1622 mark the end, to all intents and purposes, of the polyphonic madrigal and the consort song in England. There followed a period of transition in which the vertical or harmonic elements became increasingly important, and during which the continuo bass principle was firmly established. Changes in this direction are already much in evidence in the music of Peter Philips and Richard Dering, and they may well have been hastened in England by the return of Dering in 1625 from Brussels as a member, and possibly as director, of Queen Henrietta Maria's private chapel—though Dering's work was mostly to Latin texts, it would seem, and none was published in England until the Restoration.[23]

Martin Peerson was the first composer to publish English devotional music with figured basses. He published two sets of compositions, one entirely secular in content, the other a mixture of secular and devotional songs, entitled *Mottects or Grave Chamber Musique*, "Containing Songs of five parts of severall sorts, some ful, and some Verse and Chorus. But all fit for Voyces and Viols, with an Organ Part; which for want of Organs, may be performed on Virginals, Base-Lute, Bandora, or Irish Harpe." Both the full and the verse compositions are very much in the Dowland *"Pilgrimes Solace"* tradition, with great emphasis on expressive effects involving the use of chromaticism and madrigalian harmonic rhythms.

Two years later Walter Porter, a Gentleman of the Chapel Royal, produced a volume of *Madrigales and Ayres* "of two, three, foure and five voyces, with the continued bass" in which he included a large-scale verse anthem for virtuoso treble and tenor soloists, and a five-part choir—music far beyond the reach, one would imagine, of all but the most skilled performers.

In 1636 George Sandys, Gentleman of the Privy Chamber to Charles I, brought out his metrical psalter, and two years later there appeared *A Paraphrase upon the Psalmes of David, by G.S. Set to new Tunes for private Devotion: And a thorow Base, for Voice, or Instrument, by Henry Lawes, Gentleman of His Majesties Chappell Royall* .... It was dedicated to the king, "the best of men and most excellent of princes". The tunes, twenty four in all, are simple hymn-like settings, the outer parts only being given, with words against the lower part. The best of them have a pleasing strength and a tonal shape that is foreign to the earlier "church tunes" of Sternhold and Hopkins. Many are still in use today:

In 1639 William Child, Organist of St. George's Chapel, Windsor, brought out his *First set of Psalmes of III Voyces*

"fitt for private chappells, or other private meetings with a Continuall Base, either for the Organ or Theorbo, newly composed after the Italian way", and reprints followed in 1650 and 1656 under the title *Choise Musick*. The music is neatly engraved in a flowing Italic hand, and the music itself bears ample proof of Italian influence, being in the trio-sonata idiom for two upper voices and a bass (see Plate 8). There is much parallel movement in thirds and sixths, as well as a good deal of sequential development. The line of succession stems from Viadana, through Viadana's younger contemporaries, and especially Alessandro Grandi, to Philips, Dering and Nicholas Lanier, Master of Music to Charles I.

The strength of Child's collection lies in the fact that the composer has, in the main, used the biblical and Prayer Book versions of the psalms as his texts. The music, unfortunately, nowhere measures up to the best of his purely liturgical work.[24]

Nine years later, Henry Lawes published a similar collection of three-part psalms, *Choice Psalmes put into musick*, but to the verse of George Sandys. The work is prefaced by laudatory poems from many of Lawes' distinguished contemporaries, including the composers John Wilson, John Hilton, John Jenkins and Simon Ive, and the poet John Milton himself. It is, indeed, in this very volume that Milton's well-known tribute to Henry Lawes is to be found:

> Harry, whose tuneful and well measured song
> First taught our English music how to span
> Words with just note and accent. . . .

The volume contains well over sixty compositions, roughly thirty each by the two brothers, Henry and William. After such high praise, the music itself comes as something of an anti-climax. Both composers use a trio-sonata idiom, much as Child had done, and their work suffers, as Child's does, from overmuch movement in thirds and sixths and from an overall lack of continuity. The idiom was fairly new to English ears at the time, however, and it is easy on this account to understand its early popularity:

Quite the most extraordinary publication of the entire period was the *Psalterium Carolinum*, "The devotions of his Sacred Majestie in his Solitudes and Sufferings, Rendered in Verse. Set to Musick for 3 Voices and an Organ or Theorbo, by John Wilson, Dr. and Musick Professor of Oxford" (1652). That Wilson dared to publish such a work at that time is a tribute to his royalist loyalties if not to his common sense. He seems, nevertheless, to have escaped serious trouble with the authorities, though there is some evidence that he was quickly forced to withdraw the book from circulation. According to Antony à Wood, Wilson was a "kinsman" of Walter Porter and on terms of close friendship with the Lawes brothers. If Henry Lawes' fulsome verse is to be depended upon, Wilson was indeed one of the foremost exponents of the Italian style, cutting a path "where there was none before":

> For this I know, and must say't to thy praise,
> That thou hast gone, in music, unknown ways,
> Hast cut a path where there was none before
> Like Magellan traced an unknown shore.
> Thou taught our language first to speak in tone,
> Gavest the right accents and proportion.
> And above all (to show thy excellence)
> Thou understandest good words, and dost set sense. . . .

Wilson's settings are again for trio sonata ensemble—two trebles (the G clef is used, but not with the earlier implication of a high tessitura) and a bass, with a simply figured bass for keyboard continuo. All are fairly short—between forty and fifty measures long—and key signatures of up to three flats and sharps are used. Wilson's style is more homogeneous than that of Child and the Lawes brothers, but it does not escape tonal monotony, for each piece tends to remain closely rooted to its primary key. These few bars from "Lord, thou whose beauty" may serve to illustrate Wilson's technique:

The last publication to fall within the period is Walter Porter's *Mottets of Two Voyces* (1657) "for Treble or Tenor and Bass. With the Continued Bass or Score: To be performed to an Organ, Harpspycon [*sic!*], Lute or Bass-Viol". In the book there are some seventeen settings of metrical psalms, all but two being the George Sandys versions of 1636. In a short preface, Porter laments the "scarcity of voices, it being difficult and troublesome to get two voices, much more three or four together, to sing sure and masterlike". His aim, he says, has been to provide "good air, variety, and to marry the words and notes well together" (similar aims were expressed by Lawes and Child in their earlier volumes). In comparison with the large anthem discussed above from the 1632 *Madrigales and Ayres*, these short "motets" are very straightforward in style and remarkably similar to the psalms of the Lawes brothers.

Some are "full" throughout, others are arranged as simple verse anthems—there being one or more "verses" for solo voices and a short concluding "chorus" in two parts for treble (or tenor) and bass:[25]

Mofet No. 5   Porter (1657)

I will lift up mine eyes to heaven, I will lift up mine eyes to heaven from whence is my salvation given

NOTES TO CHAPTER 11

1. Harrison, F. Ll. (ii), p. 348.

2. Foxe.

3. The courtly origins of the English and French Psalters are discussed in Terry.

4. Pratt, ch. 10, for discussion of the diffusion of French tunes outside France.

5. Nichols (i), p. 193.

6. Nichols (i), pp. 226–8.

7. Robinson (iii), p. 71.

8. Wilkins, p. 201.

9. Bruce, p. 107.

10. Figures taken from Schnapper.

11. A somewhat inaccurate score is to be found in the British Museum Add. MS. 31,855: a single part-book, British Museum Add. MS. 15166, contains a number of comparatively elaborate psalm-settings by John Shepherd.

12. See *Musica Britannica*, XV.

13. Whythorne, xlvi.

14. See the *English Madrigal School*, XIV, for the original text.

15. Compare, too, the motet "Ecce quam bonum", and "Behold how good and joyful a thing"; Byrd, *Collected Works*, V and XIII.

16. See, for instance, "Turn our captivity", Byrd *Collected Works*, XIV, for bold suspensions and melismatic underlay, and "This day Christ was born", for madrigalian rhythms.

17. See "In the departure of the Lord", in *The Treasury of English Church Music*, II, for the original scoring. On his arrival in England in 1602 the Duke of Stettin-Pomerania was welcomed by musicians playing 'viols and pandoras"; his secretary recorded in the Duke's diary, "throughout England it is the custom, even in small villages, for musicians to wait upon the traveller for a small fee; in the morning, when it is time to get up, they stand outside the room playing sacred songs (geistliche lieder)".

18. *Collected Works*, XI: note however that the clefs of "Look down" are "C" 5, "C" 5, "C" 3, and "F" 3, and of "I laid me down", "C" 5, "C", 5 "C" 3, "C" 2, and "F" 2.

19. Twenty-six, if each part is counted separately.

20. Bridges and Wooldridge, nos. 23–5, 28, 35, 38, 56, and 94.

21. Hacket; and Phillips.

22. For the four-part version see *Musica Britannica*, VI.

23. See ch. 3 for discussion of Dering and Henrietta Maria's private chapel.

24. A score of the Child *Psalmes* is in the British Museum, Add. MS. 34,289.

25. There are unpublished psalm-settings for two and three voices by Thomas Ford, and John Jenkins, Christ Church, Oxford, MSS. 736-8.

Appendix I

Published "... for the recreation of all such as delight in Musicke..."

A list of printed books containing devotional music

Anon	1530	*XX Songs*
*Coverdale, Myles	c. 1539	*Goostly psalmes and spirituall songes*
Crowley, Robert	1549	*The Psalter of David newely translated into Englysh metre*
Sternhold, Thomas	1549	*Certayne Psalmes*
S[egar], F[rancys]	1553	*Certayne psalmes*
Tye, Christopher	1553	*The Actes of the Apostles*
Beard, Richard	1553	*A godly psalme of Marye Queene*
*Sternhold, Hopkins and others	1556	*One and fiftie psalmes of David (Geneva)*
Day, John	1563	*... the whole psalmes in foure partes*
*Hall, John	1563	*The Courte of Vertu*
Parker, Matthew	c. 1567	*The whole psalter translated into English metre*
Whythorne, Thomas	1571	*Songs for three, fouer and five Voyces*
Damon, William	1579	*The psalmes of David in English metre*
*Hunnis, William	1583	*Seven Sobs of a sorrowfull soule for sinne*

* Monodic, unharmonised music only.

Cosyn, John	1585	*Musike of six, and five partes*
*Fetherstone, Christopher	1588	*The Lamentation of Jeremie*
Byrd, William	1588	*Psalmes, Sonets and songs*
	1589	*Songs of sundrie natures*
Whythorne, Thomas	1590	*. . . duos, or songs for two voices*
Damon, William	1591	*The former Booke of the Musicke of M. William Damon*
	1591	*The second Booke of the Musicke*
[Drayton, Michael	1591	*The harmonie of the church,* Not extant]
Este, Thomas	1592	*The Whole Booke of Psalmes*
Mundy, John	1594	*Songs and Psalmes*
Lasso, Orlando di	1598	*[Duos]Novae Aliquot (London)*
Farnaby, Giles	1598	*Canzonets to Fowre Voyces*
Alison, Richard	1599	*The Psalmes of David in Metre*
Barley, William	1599	*The Whole Booke of Psalms*
Greaves, Thomas	1604	*Songes of Sundrie Kindes*
Alison, Richard	1606	*An Howres Recreation in Musicke*
Bartlett, John	1606	*A Booke of Ayres*
Croce, Giovanni	1608	*Musica Sacra . . . Newly Englished (London)*
Campion, Thomas	1610	*Two Bookes of Ayres. The First contayning Divine and Morall Songs*
East, Michael	1610	*The Third Set of Bookes*
Byrd, William	1611	*Psalmes, songs and sonnets*
Dowland, John	1612	*A Pilgrimes Solace*
[Barlow, William	1613	*Psalmes and hymnes of praier and thanksgiving.* Not extant]
Campion, Thomas	1613	*Songs of mourning*
Leighton, William	1614	*The Teares or Lamentacions of a Sorrowfull Soule*
Amner, John	1615	*Sacred Hymnes*
Tailour, Robert	1615	*Sacred Hymns*
East, Michael	1618	*The Fourth Set of Bookes*
Ravenscroft, Thomas	1621	*The Whole Booke of Psalmes*

* Monodic, unharmonised music only.

Attey, John	1622	*The First Booke of Ayres of Foure Parts*
Tomkins, Thomas	1622	*Songs*
Wither, George and Gibbons, Orlando	c. 1623	*The Hymnes and Songs of the Church*
Pilkington, Francis	1624	*The Second Set of Madrigals*
East, Michael	1624	*The Sixt Set of Bookes*
Peerson, Martin	1630	*Mottects or Grave Chamber Musique*
Porter, Walter	1632	*Madrigales and Ayres*
*Anon	1632	*All the French Psalm tunes with English Words* [also 1650]
Slatyer, William	1635	*Psalmes, or songs of Sion*
*Braithewaite, William	1638	*Siren Coelestis*
Lawes, Henry	1638	*A Paraphrase upon the Psalmes of David*
Child, William	1639	*The First set of Psalmes of III Voyces* [Second edition 1650]
Barton, William	1644	*The Book of Psalms in Metre* [subsequent editions in 1645, 1646 and 1654]
Lawes, Henry and William	1648	*Choice Psalmes*
Wilson, John	1652	*Psalterium Carolinum*
Porter, Walter	1657	*Mottets of Two Voyces*

* Monodic, unharmonised music only.

Appendix II

Organ Music available in Modern Editions

1. "The Mulliner Book", ed. D. Stevens, *Musica Britannica*, I (1951); see nos. 3–10, 11–22, (24?), 26–34, 36–41, 46–69, 72–75, 77, 86, 91–109, 119, (120?). Much of this music is of pre-Reformation origin; the composers are Allwood, Blitheman, Carleton, Farrant, Heath, Newman, Redford, Shelbye, Shepherd and Tallis

2. "John Bull, Keyboard Music: I", ed. John Steele and Francis Cameron, *Musica Britannica*, XIV (1960); see nos. 1–4, 6–16, 18–31, 33–51, 53–61

3. "Keyboard Works, I", *The Collected Works of William Byrd*, XVIII (1950); possibly some of the Preludes and Fancies, though Preludes 1–2, are more probably virginals music, and the first, sixth and seventh Fancies are transcriptions of string music. The second Voluntarie may originally have been written for liturgical use

4. "Keyboard Works, III", *The Collected Works of William Byrd*, XX (1950); possibly the plainsong fantasias (two settings of "Gloria tibi trinitas", two of "Miserere" and two of "Veni Creator Spiritus", and the three "Ut, re mi" Variations; there are also two settings of "Clarifica me pater" in the *Fitzwilliam Virginal Book*, ed. J. A. F. Maitland and W. B. Squire, (1899), Dover Reprint (New York, 1963).

5. *Three Voluntaries for organ*, by Benjamin Cosyn, ed. J. Steele, Novello (1959)

6. "Orlando Gibbons: Keyboard Music", ed. G. Hendrie, *Musica Britannica*, XX (1962); see nos. 1–14

7. *Three Voluntaries for double organ* by John Lugge, ed. S. Jeans and J. Steele, Novello (1956)
8. *Thomas Tallis: Complete Keyboard Works*, ed. D. Stevens, Hinrichsen-Peters (1953)
9. "Thomas Tomkins: Keyboard Music", ed. S. D. Tuttle, *Musica Britannica*, V (1955); see nos. 21 and 27–33. Many of the other plainsongs and "Ut, re mi's" may have been written for the organ, if not for liturgical use
10. Weelkes, *Pieces for keyed Instruments*, ed. M. Glyn, Stainer and Bell (1924)

There are unpublished compositions by Amner, Elway Bevin, Brown, Burton, Carleton (II), B. Cosyn, Coxsun, Ellis, Facey, Edward Gibbons, Thomas Holmes, Kyrton, John Lugge, Thomas Mudd, Portman, Preston, ap Rhys, Nicholas Strogers, Thorne, Robert White, Woodson and Wynslade.

Appendix III

Modern Editions

COLLECTED EDITIONS

TUDOR CHURCH MUSIC, Volumes I–X (Oxford University Press, 1923–9)

- I   John Taverner (Part 1)
- II   William Byrd (Part 1)
- III   John Taverner (Part 2)
- IV   Orlando Gibbons
- V   Robert White
- VI   Thomas Tallis
- VII   William Byrd (Gradualia)
- VIII   Thomas Tomkins (Part 1; Services)
- IX   William Byrd (Masses, *Cantiones Sacrae* and Motets)
- X   Hugh Aston, John Marbeck and Osbert Parsley

EARLY ENGLISH CHURCH MUSIC, Volumes I– (Stainer & Bell, 1962–)

- I   Early Tudor Masses (Part 1)
- II   William Mundy (Latin Antiphons and Psalms)
- III   Orlando Gibbons (Verse Anthems 1)
- IV   Early Tudor Magnificats (Part 1)
- V   Thomas Tomkins (*Musica Deo Sacra* 1)
- VI   Early Tudor Organ Music (Part 1)
- VII   Robert Ramsey
- VIII   Early Tudor Masses (Part 2)

MUSICA BRITANNICA (Stainer & Bell, 1951–)

- V   Thomas Tomkins (Keyboard Music)
- VI   John Dowland (Ayres for Four Voices)
- XIV   John Bull (Keyboard Music, Part 1)

XV   Music of Scotland, 1500–1700
XX   Orlando Gibbons (Keyboard Music)
XXIII   Thomas Weelkes (Collected Anthems)

THE COLLECTED WORKS OF WILLIAM BYRD, 20 Volumes
(Stainer & Bell, 1937–50)

THOMAS MORLEY. Collected Motets (Stainer & Bell, 1959)
ANTHEMS FOR MEN'S VOICES, 2 Volumes (OUP. 1965)

SEPARATE PUBLICATIONS

Items printed in **bold type** are included in le Huray (ii)

(1) MUSIC TO ENGLISH TEXTS

ALISON, RICHARD (fl. 1600)
    Behold, now praise the Lord   SB.
    O Lord, bow down thine ear   SB.
    The sacred choir of angels   SB.

AMNER, JOHN (c. 1585–1641)
    A stranger here   SB.
    Away with weak complainings   SB.
    Come, let's rejoice   SB.
    He that descended, man to be   Y.
    Lift up your heads   OUP.
    Love we in one consenting   OUP.
    O come, O come, thou Spirit divinest   Y.
    O ye little flock   C.M.S.(OUP.)
    Remember not, Lord our offences   BP.

ANON.
    O Lord, the maker (Wanley MSS.)   OUP.
    This is the day   OUP.

BATESON, THOMAS (c. 1570–1630)
    Holy, Lord God almighty   N.

BATTEN, ADRIAN (before 1590–c. 1637)
    Communion; The Short Service   CMS.(OUP.)
    Service for Men (Magnificat and Nunc   CMS.(OUP.)
        dimittis)
    Fourth Service (Magnificat and Nunc   OUP.
        dimittis)

Deliver us, O Lord our God	OUP.
Haste thee, O God	OUP.
Hear my prayer, O God	OUP.
Hear my prayer, O Lord	S.
Hear the prayers, O our God	S.
Let my complaint	N. OUP.
Lord, we beseech thee	OUP.
Lord, who shall dwell	O.
My soul truly waiteth	O.
O clap your hands together	S.
O Lord, thou hast searched me out	S.
O praise the Lord, all ye heathen	OUP.
O praise the Lord, all ye heathen	BP.
O sing joyfully	OUP.
Out of the deep	S.
Sing we merrily	N.
We beseech thee, almighty God	S.
When the Lord turned again	OUP.

BEVIN, ELWAY (fl. 1575–after 1634)

Morning and Evening Service (Te Deum, Benedictus, Kyrie, Creed Magnificat, Nunc dimittis)	BCM.

BRYNE, ALBERTUS (?–1668?)

Morning and Evening Service (Te Deum, Jubilate, Sanctus, Kyrie, Creed, Magnificat, Nunc dimittis)	N.

BULL, JOHN (c. 1563–1628)

Almighty God, who by the leading of a star	OUP.
Attend unto my tears	SB.
In the departure of the Lord	BP. SB.
O Lord my God	C.
O Lord, turn not away thy face	SB.

BYRD, WILLIAM (1543–1623)

The Great Service (Venite, Te Deum,	OUP. SB.(X)*

*Roman numerals refer to the Volume in the *Collected Works*: items in square brackets have been transposed for modern performance.

Benedictus, Kyrie, Creed, Magnificat, **Nunc dimittis**)	BP.
The Short Service (Te Deum, Benedictus, Kyrie, Creed, Sanctus, Magnificat, Nunc dimittis)	OUP. SB.(X)*
The Third Service (Magnificat, Nunc dimittis)	OUP. SB.(X)
Preces, Responses and Litany	CMS. OUP. SB. (X)
Alack, when I look back	SB.(XI)
An earthly tree	SB.(XI)
Arise, Lord, into thy rest	SB.[XI](XIV)
Arise, O Lord, why sleepest thou	OUP. SB. (III)[XI]
Attend mine humble prayer	SB.(XIII)
Be unto me [O Lord] a tower	N. SB.(XI)
Behold, O God	SB.(XI)
Blessed is he that fears	SB.(XII)
Bow thine ear	CMS.(OUP.) SB.(II)[XI]
Christ rising again	L. SB.(XIII)
Come help, O God	CMS.(OUP.) N. SB.(II)[XI]
Come let us rejoice	OUP. SB.[XI] (XIV)
From depth of sin	SB.(XIII)
From Virgin's womb	SB.[XI](XIII)
Have mercy upon me	SB.[XI](XIV)
Help, Lord, for wasted are those men	SB.(XII)
How long shall mine enemies	SB.(XI)
If that a sinner's sighs	SB.(XII)
I have been young	SB.(XIV)
I laid me down to rest	N. SB.(XI)
Lift up your heads	SB.(I)
Look down, O Lord	N. SB.(XI)
Lord, hear my prayer	SB.(XIII)
Lord, in thy rage	SB.(XIII)
Lord, in thy wrath correct me not	SB.(XIII)
Lord, in thy wrath reprove me not	SB.(XII)
Make ye joy to God	SB.[XI](XIV)

* Roman numerals refer to the Volume in the *Collected Works*: items in square brackets have been transposed for modern performance.

Mine eyes with fervency   SB.(XII)*
My soul oppressed with care   SB.(XII)
O God, give ear   C. SB.(XII)
O God that guides the cheerful sun   SB.(XIV)
O God, the proud are risen   SB.(XI)
O God, which art most merciful   SB.(XIII)
O God, whom our offences   OUP. SB.(XI)
O Lord, make thy servant Elizabeth   SB.(XI)
O Lord, my God   SB.(XIII)
O Lord, turn thy wrath (Ne   OUP.
    irascaris)   BP. (another version)
O Lord, who in thy sacred tent   SB.(XII)
O praise our Lord, ye saints   SB.(XI)
Praise our Lord, all ye Gentiles   SB.(XIV)
Prevent us, O Lord   CMS. OUP. SB.(XI)
Rejoice, rejoice   SB.(XIII)
Right blest are they   SB.(XIII)
Sing joyfully   BP. N. SB.(XI)
Sing we merrily   SB.[XI](XIV)
Sing ye to our Lord   SB.[XI](XIV)
Teach me, O Lord   BP. CMS.(OUP.)
This day Christ was born   SB.[XI](XIV)
Turn our captivity, O Lord   SB.[XI](XIV)
Unto the hills   SB.(XIII)
What unacquainted cheerful voice   SB.(XV)
When Israel came out of Egypt   SB.(X)

CAUSTUN, THOMAS (before 1535–69)
Service "For Children" (Te Deum,   N. OUP.
    Benedictus, Kyrie, Creed, Magnifi-
    cat, Nunc dimittis)
Service "for men" (Nunc dimittis)   BP.
Rejoice in the Lord   Y

CHILD, WILLIAM (1606–97)
Service in D ["sharp"] (Te Deum,   BCM.
    Jubilate, Kyrie, Creed, Magnificat,
    Nunc dimittis)

* Roman numerals refer to the Volume in the *Collected Works*: items in square brackets have been transposed for modern performance.

Service in E [minor] ("with the lesser   BCM.
  third") (Te Deum, Jubilate, Kyrie,
  Creed, Magnificat, Nunc dimittis)
If the Lord himself   N.
O God, wherefore art thou absent   BP.
  from us?
O Lord God, the heathen   BP.
O Lord, grant the King a long life   N.
O pray for the peace of Jerusalem   N.
Praise the Lord   N.
Sing we merrily   N.
Turn thou us   OUP.

COPERARIO, JOHN (c. 1575–1626)
  I'll lay [lie] me down to sleep   N.

DOWLAND, JOHN (1562–1626)
  An heart that's broken   N.
  "Seven Hymn Tunes"   OUP.
  See also *Musica Britannica*, Volume VI

EAST, MICHAEL (c. 1580–1648)
  As they departed   MAS.
  Blow out the trumpet   MAS.
  Haste thee, O God   SB.
  How shall a young man   MAS.
  I have roared   MAS.
  O clap your hands   SB.
  Sing we merrily   MAS.
  Turn thy face   MAS.
  When David heard   S. SB.
  When Israel came out of Egypt   OUP. SB.

FARMER, JOHN (before 1575–?)
  The Lord's Prayer   BP.
  O Lord, of whom I do depend   SB.

FARRANT, JOHN (1575–1618)
  Morning and Evening Service (Te   OUP.
  Deum, Jubilate, Magnificat, Nunc
  dimittis)

FARRANT, RICHARD (before 1535–1581)
    Morning and Evening Service
    (Te Deum, Benedictus, Magnificat,   OUP.
      Nunc dimittis)
      (Kyrie, Creed)   BCM.
    Call to remembrance   OUP.
    Hide not thou thy face   BP. OUP.
    Lord, for thy tender mercy's sake BP. N. OUP.
      (also attributed to John Hilton the
      Elder)

FERRABOSCO, ALPHONSO (ii) (1575–1628)
    In death no man remembreth thee   N.
    In thee, O Lord   SB.

FORD, THOMAS (c. 1580–1648)
    Almighty God, who hast me brought N.
    Let God arise   MAS.
    Not unto us   N.

GIBBONS, ORLANDO (1583–1625)
    The Short Service (Te Deum, Bene- BP. OUP.
      dictus, Magnificat, **Nunc dimittis**)
    The Short Service (Kyrie, Creed)   BCM.
    The Verse Service (Magnificat, Nunc OUP.
      dimittis)
    Almighty and everlasting God   OUP.
    Almighty God, who by thy Son   OUP.
    Behold, thou hast made my days   OUP.
    Blessed be the Lord God   N.
    Deliver us, O Lord   N.
    Glorious and powerful God   N.
    God is gone up (part II of "O clap
      your hands")
    Great King of Gods (see "Great Lord
      of Lords")
    Great Lord of Lords   SB.
    Hosanna to the Son of David   N. OUP.
    If ye be risen   N.
    Lift up your heads   N. OUP.

O all true faithful hearts — N.
O clap your hands — N. OUP.
O God, the King of glory — OUP.
O Lord, how do my woes increase — N.
O Lord, I lift my heart — N.
O Lord, increase my faith (see Loose-more)
O Lord, in thy wrath rebuke me not — BP. OUP.
See, see, the Word is incarnate — BP. SB.
The eyes of all wait — N.
This is the record of John — N. OUP.
See also *Tudor Church Music*, Volume IV and *Early English Church Music*, Volume III.

GILES, NATHANIEL (c. 1558–1633)
God which as at this time — OUP.
Out of the deep — OUP.

HILTON, JOHN (The Elder) (before 1565–after 1612)
Call to remembrance — OUP.
Lord, for thy tender mercy's sake—
see RICHARD FARRANT

HOOPER, EDMUND (c. 1553–1621)
The Full Service (Magnificat, Nunc dimittis) — OUP.
The Verse Service (Magnificat, Nunc dimittis) — OUP.
Behold, it is Christ — S.
Teach me thy way, O Lord — CMS.(OUP.)
The collected anthems are published in the *Early English Church Music* series

HUNT, THOMAS (?. 1600)
Morning and Evening Service (Venite, Te Deum, Benedictus, Magnificat, Nunc dimittis) — OUP.

JONES, ROBERT (fl. 1600)
Lament my soul .... AMP.

LAWES, HENRY (1596–1662)
Lord, to my prayers .... BP.
Now the Lord his reign begins .... BP.
Who trusts in Thee .... BP.
With sighs and cries .... BP.

LAWES, WILLIAM (1602-45)
The Lord is my light .... BCM.

LOOSEMORE, HENRY (?–1670)
Litany .... N.
O Lord, increase my faith (attr. O.   L. N. OUP.
Gibbons)

LUPO, THOMAS (?–1628)
Out of the deep .... OUP.

MERBECKE, JOHN (c. 1510–85)
The booke of Common praier noted   BP.
**(Nunc dimittis, Communion
Anthem and Agnus Dei only)**
See also *Tudor Church Music*, Volume
X

MILTON, JOHN (1563–1647)
I am the resurrection .... WP.
If that a sinner's sighs .... WP.
O had I wings like to a dove .... WP.
O Lord, behold my miseries .... WP.
Thou God of might .... WP.
When David heard .... WP.

MORLEY, THOMAS (1557–1603)
The First Service (Magnificat, Nunc   OUP.
dimittis)
The Short Service (Magnificat, Nunc   OUP.
dimittis)
The Burial Service (I am the Resur-   BCM.
rection; I know that my Redeemer
liveth; We brought nothing into
this world; Man that is born of

woman; In the midst of life; Thou
knowest, Lord; I heard a voice
from heaven)

Preces and Responses   CMS.(OUP.)
Nolo mortem peccatoris   BP. OUP. SB.
Out of the deep (Full Anthem: adapted SB.
 from "De profundis")
Out of the deep (Verse Anthem) BP. N. OUP.
See also Morley's *Collected Motets* (SB.)

MUDD, JOHN (?–1631?)
 Let thy merciful ears   OUP
 O God, who hast prepared   N. OUP.

MUNDY, JOHN (?–1630)
 Hear my prayer, O Lord   OUP.
 In deep distress   OUP.
 Sing joyfully   OUP.
 Sing ye unto the Lord   OUP.
 See also: *English Madrigalists*, Volume SB.
 XXXV B

MUNDY, WILLIAM (c. 1530–91)
 The First Service (Magnificat, Nunc N.
 dimittis)
 Ah, helpless wretch   BP.
 O Lord, the maker of all things BP. OUP.
 See also *Early English Church Music*,
 Volume II

NICHOLSON, RICHARD (?–1639)
 O pray for the peace of Jerusalem OUP.
 When Jesus sat at meat   OUP.

PARSLEY, OSBERT (1511–85)
 Morning and Evening Service (Te OUP.
 Deum, Benedictus, Magnificat,
 Nunc dimittis)
 See also *Tudor Church Music*, Volume
 X

PARSONS, ROBERT (?–1570)
| The First Service (**Nunc dimittis**) | BP. |
| Deliver me from mine enemies | N. |

PARSONS, WILLIAM (c. 1515–after 1561)
| **In trouble and in thrall** | BP. |

PATRICK, NATHANIEL (?–1595)
| Morning and Evening Service (Te Deum, Benedictus, Magnificat, Nunc dimittis) | CMS.(OUP.) |

PEERSON, MARTIN (c. 1580–1650)
Blow out the trumpet	S.
Lord, ever bridle my desires	S.
Man, dream no more	S.
O God, that no time dost despise	S.
O God, when thou wentest forth	S.
O let me at thy footstool fall	S.

PILKINGTON, FRANCIS (?–1638)
Care for thy soul	SB.
Hidden, O Lord	AMP.
High, mighty God	N.
O gracious God of heaven	SB.
O praise the Lord, all ye heathen	SB.

PORTER, WALTER (c. 1595–1659)
| **Praise the Lord** | BP. |

RAMSEY, ROBERT (fl. 1630)
Almighty and everlasting God	S.
God, who as upon this day	S.
My song shall be alway	S.
O come let us sing	S.
When David heard	S.

See also *Early English Church Music*, Volume VII

RAVENSCROFT, THOMAS (c. 1590–c. 1633)
Ah, helpless soul	CMS.(OUP.)
O Jesu meek	CMS.(OUP.)
Remember God's goodness	N.

[REDFORD, JOHN (?–1547)]

    Rejoice in the Lord alway (attribution   OUP.
    uncertain)

ROGERS, BENJAMIN (1614–98)

    Morning and Evening Service in D   BCM.
    ("with the greater third") (Te
    Deum, Jubilate, Kyrie, Creed,
    Magnificat, Nunc dimittis)

    Evening Service in A minor (Magni-   N.
    ficat, Nunc dimittis)

    Evening Service in F (Magnificat,   BA.
    Nunc dimittis)

    Behold, how good and joyful   O.

    Behold, now praise the Lord   O.

    Lord, who shall dwell   N.

    O give thanks   O.

    O pray for the peace of Jerusalem   N.

    Teach me, O Lord   O.

SHEPHERD, JOHN (c. 1520–63?)

    Haste thee, O God   N. OUP.

    I give you a new commandment   OUP.
    (attributed to Tallis)

    O Lord of hosts   CMS.(OUP.)

    Steven first after Christ (see Hawkins,
    Sir John, *History of Music*, Vol. II)

SMITH, WILLIAM (fl. 1630)

    Preces and Responses   CMS.(OUP.)

STONE, ROBERT (1516–1613)

    The Lord's Prayer   BP. N.

TALLIS, THOMAS (c. 1505–85)

    The Short Service (Te Deum, Bene-   BCM.
    dictus, Kyrie, Creed, Magnificat,
    Nunc dimittis)

    The Short Service (Magnificat, Nunc   OUP.
    dimittis)

    Te Deum for Five Voices   OUP.

    Preces and Responses   CMS.(OUP.)

    Litany   N.

Blessed be thy name | OUP.
Hear my prayer | OUP.
Hear the voice and prayer | N.
I call and cry (O sacrum convivium) | OUP.
I give you a new commandment | OUP.
If ye love me | BP. OUP.
O God, be merciful | OUP.
O Lord, give thy Holy Spirit | OUP.
O Lord, in thee is all my trust | OUP.
Purge me, O Lord | OUP.
This is my commandment | OUP.
Wherewithal shall a young man cleanse his way? Festal Psalm | BP.
With all our hearts and mouths (Salvator mundi) | BP.
 | CH. (another version)
See also *Tudor Church Music*, Volume VI.

TOMKINS, THOMAS (1572–1656)

Evening Service in C (Magnificat, Nunc dimittis) | N.
The Second Service (Te Deum, Jubilate, Magnificat, Nunc dimittis) | OUP.
The Third Service (Magnificat, Nunc dimittis) | OUP.
The Fourth Service (**Nunc dimittis**) | BP.
The Fifth Service (Magnificat, Nunc dimittis) | OUP.
Preces and Responses | CMS.(OUP.)
Almighty and everlasting God | H.
Almighty God, the fountain | S.
Arise, O Lord, into thy resting place | BP.
Behold, the hour cometh | S.
God, who as at this time | H.
Great and marvellous | OUP.
Hear my prayer | S.
He that hath pity | N.
I am the Resurrection | N. OUP.

I heard a voice	N.
My beloved spake	S.
My shepherd is the living Lord	SB.
O give thanks	OUP.
O God, wonderful art thou	OUP.
O how amiable are thy dwellings	CMS.(OUP.)
O Lord, I have loved	H.
O praise the Lord, all ye heathen	OUP.
O pray for the peace of Jerusalem	OUP.
O sing unto the Lord a new song	S.
Praise the Lord, O my soul	OUP.
Then David mourned	H. S.
Thou art my King, O God	AMP. SB.
When David heard	SB.
Woe is me	SB.

See also *Tudor Church Music*, Volume VIII, and *Early English Church Music*, Volume V.

TYE, CHRISTOPHER (c. 1505–72)

Magnificat and Nunc dimittis (also attributed to Parsley)	OUP.
Nunc dimittis	BP.
Give alms of thy goods	OUP.
I will exalt [extol] thee	OUP.
O come, ye servants of the Lord	SB.
O God, be merciful	OUP.
Praise [ye] the Lord, ye children	OUP.
Sing unto the Lord	OUP.

WARD, JOHN (fl. 1620)

The First Service (Magnificat, Nunc dimittis)	N.
O let me tread	CMS.(OUP.)
O Lord, consider my complaint	N.

WEELKES, THOMAS (c. 1575–1623)

The Short Service (Te Deum, Benedictus, Magnificat, Nunc dimittis)	SB.
Magnificat and Nunc dimittis (in Five Parts)	OUP.

Magnificat and Nunc dimittis (in   OUP.
    Seven Parts)
Magnificat and Nunc dimittis ("for   SB.
    Trebles")
Alleluia, I heard a voice   SB.
All people, clap your hands   MAS.
Give ear, O Lord   BP. SB.
Gloria in excelsis Deo   BP. OUP. SB.
Hosanna to the Son of David   OUP.
Let thy merciful ears (See MUDD)
O how amiable   OUP.
O Jonathan, woe is me   AMP. S.
O Lord, arise into thy resting place   OUP.
O Lord, grant the King a long life   OUP.
O mortal man   C.
When David heard   AMP. N.
See also *Musica Britannica*, Volume
    XXIII (Collected Anthems).

WHITE, ROBERT (c. 1535–74)
O how glorious   WI.
O praise God in his holiness   OUP.
The Lord bless us   WI.
See also *Tudor Church Music*, Volume
    V.

WILBYE, JOHN (1574–1638)
I am quite tired   SB.
O God the rock   N. SB.
O Lord, turn not thy face   N.

(2) MUSIC TO LATIN TEXTS

BYRD, WILLIAM (1543–1623)
Mass for Three Voices (Kyrie, Gloria,   CH. SB.(I)*
    Creed, Sanctus, Agnus Dei)
Mass for Four Voices (**Kyrie**, Gloria, CH. SB.(I) BP.
    Creed, Sanctus, Agnus Dei)
Mass for Five Voices (Kyrie, Gloria,   CH. SB.(I)
    Creed, Sanctus, Agnus Dei)

* The Roman numerals refer to the Volume in the *Collected Works*.

Alleluia, ascendit Deus	SB.(VIII)*
Alleluia, cognoverunt discipuli	N. SB. (VI)
Aspice, Domine	SB.(I)
Assumpta est Maria	C. SB.(IV)
Attolite portas	SB.(I)
Ava Maria, gratia plena	BP. CH. SB.(IV)
Ave Regina	CH. SB.(V)
Ave verum corpus	BP. OUP. SB.(V)
Beata es, Virgo Maria	CH. SB.(IV)
Beata viscera Mariae Virginis	CH. SB.(IV)
Cantate Domino	OUP. SB.(III)
Christe, qui lux es	OUP. SB. (VIII)
Christus resurgens	CN. SB.(V)
Civabit eos	CH.
Civitas sancti tui	CH.
Confirma hoc, Deus	CH. N. SB.(VII)
De lamentatione	SB.(VIII)
Dies sanctificatus	N. SB.(VI)
Ego sum panis vivus	CH. SB.(VI)
Emendemus in melius	SB.(I)
Exsurge, quare obdormis	OUP.
Felix es, sacra Virgo	SB.(IV)
Haec dies	N. OUP. SB.(III) (VI)
Justorum animae	SB.(IV)
Laetentur coeli	N. OUP.
Laudibus in sanctis	SB.(III)
Libera me	SB.(I)
Lumen ad revelationem	N.
Miserere mei	OUP. SB.(III) (VIII)
Ne irascaris (O Lord, turn thy wrath)	BP.
Non vos relinquam	CH. SB.(VII)
O Lux beata Trinitas	SB.(I)
O magnum mysterium	CH. SB.(VI)
O quam gloriosum	OUP. SB.(II)
O quam suavis	CH. N. SB.(VI)
O rex gloriae	CH. SB.(VII)
O sacrum convivium	CH. N. SB.(V)

* The Roman numerals refer to the Volume in the *Collected Works*.

Oculi omnium | SB.(V)*
Peccantem me quotidie | SB.(I)
Psallite Domino | SB.(VII)
Rorate coeli | OUP. SB.(IV)
Sacerdotes Domini | OUP. SB.(V)
Salve Regina | CH. SB. (III)
Salve, sancta parens | CH. SB. (IV)
Senex puerum portabat | CH. N. SB.(IV)
Siderum rector | SB.(I)
Surge illuminare | N. SB.(VI)
Te deprecor | SB.(I)
Terra tremuit | N. SB.(VI)
Tu es pastor ovium | CH. SB.(VII)
Tu es Petrus | SB.(VII)
Tui sunt coeli | N. SB.(VI)
Veni, Sancte Spiritus | SB.(VII)
Victimae paschali | OUP. SB.(VI)

DERING, RICHARD (c. 1580–1630)
Factum est silentium | BP.
Jesu, summa benignitas | CH.
Quem vidistis, pastores | CH. N.

JOHNSON, ROBERT (c. 1490–c. 1560)
Dum transisset Sabbatum | CH.

KIRBYE, GEORGE (?–1634)
Vox in Rama | SB.

LUPO, THOMAS (?–1628)
O vos omnes | CH.

MORLEY, THOMAS (1557–1603)
Agnus Dei | SB.
De profundis clamavi | OUP. SB.
Domine, dominus noster | SB.
Domine, fac mecum | N. SB.
Domine, non est exaltatum | SB.
Ehu, sustulerunt Dominum | N. SB.
Laboravi in gemitu meo | OUP. SB.
See also Morley's *Collected Motets* (SB.).

* The Roman numerals refer to the Volume in the *Collected Works*.

OKELAND, ROBERT (fl. 1560)
  Kyrie · · · CH. SB.

PHILIPS, PETER (c. 1565–c. 1635)
  Alma redemptoris mater · · · CH.
  Ascendit Deus · · · BP. OUP.
  Ave Regina · · · CH.
  Cantantibus organis · · · N.
  Elegi abjectus esse · · · CH.
  Gaudent in coelis · · · N.
  Ne reminiscaris, Domine · · · N.
  O virum mirabilem · · · CH.
  Regina coeli · · · CH.
  Surgens Jesus · · · N.
  Viae Sion lugent · · · N.

SHEPHERD, JOHN (?–1563?)
  Playnsong Mass for a Meane · · · CH.
  The French Mass · · · CH.
  Alleluia, confitemini Domino · · · N.
  Haec dies · · · CH.

TALLIS, THOMAS (c. 1505–85)
  Audivi vocem · · · OUP.
  Dum transisset Sabbatum · · · CH.
  Gloria Patri · · · N.
  In jejunio et fletu · · · CH.
  In manus tuas · · · SB.
  Lamentationes · · · OUP.
  Laudate Dominum · · · CH.
  O nata lux · · · OUP.
  O sacrum convivium · · · SB.
  O salutaris hostia · · · CH.
  Salvator mundi (With all our hearts) · · · BP. (another version)
  Rubum quem viderat · · · CH.
  Salve, intemerata Virgo · · · OUP.
  Spem in alium (40 parts) · · · OUP.
  Te lucis ante terminum · · · N.
  See also *Tudor Church Music*, Volume VI.

TYE, CHRISTOPHER (c. 1505–72)

Euge Bone Mass	WI.
Omnes gentes, plaudite	CH.
Rubum quem viderat	CH.

WHITE, ROBERT (c. 1535–74)

Christe, qui lux es et dies	BP. CH. OUP.
Lamentations	SB.
Libera me, Domine	OUP.
Precamur, sancte Domine. See Christe, qui lux es et dies.	

KEY

AMP.	Associated Music Publishers, New York
BA.	Banks & Son, York
BCM.	Boyce's Cathedral Music
BP.	Blandford Press
BUA.	Burns & Allen, New York
C.	Curwen
CH.	Chester
CMS.	Church Music Society Reprints (OUP.)
H.	Hinrichsen
L.	Lawson Gould, New York
MAS.	Musical Antiquarian Society (Chappell)
N.	Novello
O.	Ollivier
OUP.	Oxford University Press
S.	Schott
SB.	Stainer & Bell
WI.	Joseph Williams (Galliard)
WP.	Williams & Parker (Old English Edition)
Y.	Year Book Press (Ascherberg, Hopwood & Crew)

The list of Music to English texts has been compiled from "The Sources of English Sacred Music" by R. T. Daniel and P. G. le Huray; (published in the *Early English Church Music series:* Stainer & Bell).

The list of Music to Latin texts is taken from Denis Stevens' *Tudor Church Music* (Faber & Faber, 1961).

Appendix IV

Bibliography

ANDREWS, H. K. (i) *The Technique of Byrd's Vocal Polyphony* (1966)
(ii) "Transposition of Byrd's Vocal Polyphony", *Music and Letters*, XLIII:1 (1962)

ANON. "English Cathedral Music", *British and Foreign Review*, XVII, No. 33 (1844)

ARBER, E. *A Transcript of the Registers of the Company of Stationers 1554–1640* (1875–94)

ARKWRIGHT, G. E. P. (i) "The Chapel Royal Anthem Book of 1635", *Musical Antiquary*, II (1910–11)
(ii) *Catalogue of the Music in the Library of Christ Church, Oxford*, I–II (1915)

ARNOLD, D. " 'Seconda pratica', A background to Monteverdi's Madrigals", *Music and Letters*, XXXVIII:4 (1957)

ARNOLD, F. T. *The Art of Accompaniment from a Thorough Bass* (1931)

ASCHAM, R. (i) *Toxophilus* (1545), ed. E. Arber (1868)
(ii) *The Scholemaster* (1570)

ASHMOLE, E. *The Institution, Laws and Ceremonies . . . of the Garter* (1672)

ATKINS, SIR I. "Early Occupants of the Office of Organist . . . ", *Worcester Historical Records* (1918)

ATKINS, W. M. and MATTHEWS, W. R. *A History of St. Paul's Cathedral* (1957)

AUSTEN, G. "The Statutes of the Church", *York Minster Historical Tracts*, No. 18. (1928)

AYRE, J. (ed.) "The Catechism of Thomas Becon, with other pieces written by him in the reign of King Edward the Sixth", *Parker Society* (1844)

BACON, F. *Certain Considerations touching . . . the Church of England* (1604)

BAILLIE, H. *London Churches, their Music and Musicians* (1485–1560), unpublished dissertation for the degree of Ph.D., Cambridge, 1958: see also, "Some Biographical Notes on English church musicians, chiefly working in London, 1485–1569, *Royal Musical Association Research Chronicle*, II, 1962

BAKER, T. *History of St. John's College, Cambridge* (1869)

BANNISTER, A. T. *The Cathedral Church of Hereford* (1924)

BARLEY, W. *The pathway to Musicke* (1596)

BARLOW, W. *Summe of the Conference before the King's Majestie* (1604)

BASTWICK, J. *The Answer of John Bastwick . . . to the exceptions made against his Litany* (1637)

BATES, E. S. *Touring in 1600* (1911)

BEAUMONT, R. M. *The Chapter of Southwell Minster* (1956)

BECON, *see* AYRE, J.

BEVERLEY BOROUGH RECORDS, *Yorkshire Archaeological Society Record Series*, LXXIV (1933)

BINDOFF, S. T. *Tudor England* (1950)

BIRCH, T. *The Court and Times of Charles I* (1848)

BISHOP, E. and GASQUET, F. A. *Edward VI and the Book of Common Prayer* (1890)

BLACKSTONE, B. *The Ferrar Papers* (1938)

BOSTON, N. "The Musical History of the Cathedral Church of Norwich", *Friends of Norwich Cathedral*, 10th Report (1939)

BOTSTIBER, H. "Musicalia in der New York Library", *Sammelbände der Internationalen Musikgesellschaft* (1902–03)

BRADLEY, E. T. *Annals of Westminster Abbey* (1904)

BRADSHAW, H. and WORDSWORTH, C. *Lincoln Cathedral Statutes* (1897)

BRENNECKE, E. *John Milton the Elder and his Music* (New York, 1938)

BRETT, P. (i) "The English Consort Song", *Proceedings of the Royal Musical Association*, LXXXVIII (1961–62)

(ii) "The Songs of William Byrd", unpublished dissertation for the degree of Ph.D., Cambridge, 1965

BRETT, P. and DART, R. T. "Songs by William Byrd in manuscripts at Harvard", *Harvard Library Bulletin*, XIV:3 (1960)

BRIDGE, J. C. "The Organists of Chester Cathedral", *The Journal of the Chester and North Wales Architectural . . . Society*, XIX:2 (1913)

BRIDGEMAN, G. T. P. "The History of the Church and Manor of Wigan", *Chetham Society* (1889)

BRIDGES, R. and WOOLDRIDGE, H. E. (ed.) *Yattendon Hymnal* (1920)

BRIGHTMAN, F. E. *The English Rite*, I–II (1915)

BROOK, V. J. K. *A Life of Archbishop Parker* (1962)

BROOKBANK, J. *The Well-Tuned Organ* (1660)

BROWN, C. *Annals of Newark on Trent* (1879)

BROWN, D. "The Anthems of Thomas Weelkes", *Proceedings of the Royal Musical Association*, XCI (1964–65)

BROWN, G. F. *History of St. Catharine's College* (1902)

BROWN, R. (ed.) *Calendar of State Papers Venetian*, V (1534–54) (1873)

BROWN, R. and BENTINCK, G. C. *Calendar of State Papers Venetian*, VII (1558–80) (1890)

BRUCE, J. (ed.) "Correspondence of Matthew Parker D.D.", *Parker Society* (1853)

BULOW, G. VON, "The Diary of Philip Julius, Duke of Stettin-Pomerania", *Transactions of the Royal Historical Society*, VI (1892)

BUMPUS, J. S. *English Cathedral Music*, I (1908)

BURNE, THE VEN, R. H. V. "The History of Chester Cathedral", *The Journal of the Chester and North Wales Architectural . . . Society*, XXXIX (1952)

BURNEY, C. *A General History of Music*, III (1789)

BURTON, E. (ed.) *Three Primers put forth in the reign of Henry VIII* (1834)

BUTLER, C. *The Principles of Musik* (1636)

BUXTON, J. *Elizabethan Taste* (1963)

CAMPIAN, T. *A New Way of making Fowre parts in Counterpoint* (1613)

CANTERBURY CATHEDRAL, *The Statutes of the Cathedral . . . Church of Christ, Canterbury* (privately printed 1925)

CARPENTER, N. C. *Music in the Medieval and Renaissance Universities* (Oklahoma, 1958)

CASE, J. (?) *The Praise of Musick* (1586)

CHAMBERS, E. K. *The Elizabethan Stage* (1923)

CHANCELLOR, E. BERESFORD, *Historical Richmond* (1885)

CHITTY, H. C. "The Organist and the Quiristers' Master", *The Wykehamist* (1917)

CLAPHAM, SIR J. *A Concise Economic History of Britain* (1949)

CLAY, THE REV. W. K. (ed.) "Private Prayers put forth by authority during the reign of Queen Elizabeth", *Parker Society* (1851)

CLIFFORD, J. *The Divine Services and Anthems* (1st edn. 1663; 2nd edn. 1664)

CLOGY, A. *Memoire of the Life and Episcopate of Dr. William Bedell*, ed. W. W. Wilkins (1862)

CLUTTON, C. and NILAND, A. *The British Organ* (1963)

COCKSHOOT, G. *The Sacred Music of Alphonso Ferrabosco* (Father) (1543–1588). Unpublished dissertation for the degree of Ph.D., Oxford, 1964

COCLICO, ADRIAN PETIT, *Compendium Musices* (1552), ed. M. Bukofzer (Kassel, 1954)

COLE, E. "In search of Francis Tregian", *Music and Letters*, XXXIII:1 (1952)

COLE, R. E. G. "Chapter Acts of the Cathedral Chapter of St. Mary of Lincoln, 1547–1559", *Lincoln Record Society*, XV (1917)

COLLINS, A. *Letters and Memorials . . .* (1746)

COLLINS, W. S. (i) *The Anthems of Thomas Weelkes*, unpublished dissertation for the degree of Ph.D., Michigan (1960)

(ii) "Recent discoveries concerning the biography of Thomas Weelkes", *Music and Letters*, XLIV:2 (1963)

COOK, A. K. "About Winchester College", *The Wykehamist* (1917)

COPERARIO, J. *Rules how to compose* (c. 1610) ed. M. Bukofzer (Los Angeles, 1952)

COX, J. C. "Churchwardens Accounts", *The Antiquaries Books* (1913)

COZENS-HARDY, B. and WILLIAMS, J. F. "Extracts from the two earliest Minute Books of the Dean and Chapter of Norwich", *Norfolk Record Society*, XXIV (1953)

CRUM, M. C. "A Seventeenth-century Collection of Music belonging to Thomas Hamond", *Bodleian Library Record*, VI:1 (1957)

CULMER, R. "Cathedral News from Canterbury", *Archaeologia Cantiania* X, (1876)

DANIEL, R. T. and LE HURAY, P. G. "The Sources of English

Sacred Music, 1549–1644", *Early English Church Music* (1967)

DART, R. T. (i) "Henry Loosemore's Organ Book", *Cambridge Bibliographical Society* III:2 (1960)

(ii) "Music and Musicians in Chichester Cathedral, 1545–1642", *Music and Letters*, XLII:3 (1961)

DART, R. T. and SCHOFIELD, B. "Tregian's Anthology", *Music and Letters*, XXXII:3 (1951)

DAVEY, H. *History of English Music* (1895)

DAWLEY, P. M. *John Whitgift and the Reformation* (1955)

DICKENS, A. G. *The English Reformation* (1964)

DICKINSON, E. *Music in the History of the Western Church* (1902)

DICKSON, W. E. *A Catalogue of Ancient Choral Services* (1861)

DOUGLAS, C. E. and FRERE, W. L. (eds.) *Puritan Manifestoes* (1954)

DUCKLES, V. "John Jenkins, settings of lyrics by George Herbert", *Musical Quarterly*, XLVIII:4 (1962)

DUGDALE, SIR W. *Monasticon Anglicanum*, ed. J. Coley, H. Ellis and B. Bondinal. I–VI (1815)

DUNLOP, I. *Palaces and Progresses of Elizabeth I* (1962)

EARLE, J. *Microcosmographie* (1629)

EASSON, D. E. *Medieval Religious Houses in Scotland* (1957)

ECCLES, S. *A Music Lector* (1667)

EINSTEIN, A. "The Elizabethan Madrigal and Musica Transalpina", *Music and Letters*, XXV:2 (1944)

ELTON, G. R. *The Tudor Constitution* (1960)

ELY CATHEDRAL (i) The Statutes of the Collegiate Church of Ely (1817)

(ii) Statuta ecclesiae Cathedralis Eliensis (1867)

EPPS, D. "John Gerarde", unpublished dissertation, being part of the examination for the degree of D.Mus., Edinburgh, 1964

EVANS, W. M. *Henry Lawes, Musician and Friend of Poets* (1941)

FALKNER, J. M. and THOMPSON, A. H. "The Statutes of the Cathedral Church of Durham", *Surtees Society*, CXLIII (1929)

FARMER, H. G. *A History of Music in Scotland* (1947)

FELLOWES, E. H. (i) *English Cathedral Music* (4th edn. 1948)

(ii) *William Byrd* (2nd edn. 1948)

(iii) *Orlando Gibbons* (1951)

(iv) "The Organists . . . of St. George's Chapel", *Windsor Historical Monographs* (1939)

(v) "The Vicars and Minor Canons . . . of St. George's Chapel", *Windsor Historical Monographs* (1945)

(vi) *A Catalogue of the Manuscripts in the Library of St. Michael's College, Tenbury* (Paris, 1934)

FLOOD, W. H. GRATTON, "Master Sebastian of Paul's", *Musical Antiquary*, III (1911–12)

FORD, W. K. "An English Liturgical Partbook of the Seventeenth Century", *Journal of the American Musicological Society* XII:2–3 (1959)

FORTUNE, N. (i) *Italian Secular Song from 1600–1635*, unpublished dissertation for the degree of Ph.D., Cambridge (1954)

(ii) "Italian 17th Century Singing", *Music and Letters*, XXXV (1954)

FOSTER, C. W. "The State of the Church", *Lincoln Record Society*, XXIII (1926)

FOSTER, M. B. *Anthems and Anthem Composers* (1901)

FOXE, J. *Actes and Monuments* (1563)

FREEMAN, A. (i) "The Organ of All Hallows, Barking", *The Organ*, VIII:30 (1928)

(ii) "The Organs of Eton College", *The Organ*, IV:15 (1924–25)

FREEMAN, E. A. *see* HOWSON, J. S.

FRERE, W. H. "Edwardine Vernacular Services before the First Prayer Book", *Alcuin Club Collections*, XXXV (1940)

FRERE, W. H. and DOUGLAS, C. E. *see* DOUGLAS.

FRERE, W. H. and KENNEDY, W. P. M. "Visitation Articles and Injunctions of the Period of the Reformation", *Alcuin Club Collections*, XIV–XVI (1910–   )

FROST, M. *English and Scottish Psalm and Hymn Tunes, c. 1543–1677* (1953)

FROUDE, J. A. *Life and Letters of Erasmus* (1894)

FULLER, T. (i) *Church History of Britain to 1648* (1655)

(ii) *History of the University of Cambridge* (1655) ed. M. Prickett and T. Wright (1840)

FULLER-MAITLAND, J. A. and MANN, A. H. *Catalogue of the Music in the Fitzwilliam Museum, Cambridge* (1893)

GALPIN, F. W. "The Sackbut", *Proceedings of the Royal Musical Association*, 1906–07

GASQUET, J. A. *see* BISHOP, E.

GEE, H. *The Elizabethan Prayer Book and Ornaments* (1902)

GIBBONS, A. *Episcopal Records of Ely Cathedral* (1891)

GIUSTINIANI, V. *Discorso sopra la Musica*, tr. C. MacClintock, in *Musica Disciplina*, XV, 1961

GLOUCESTER CATHEDRAL *The Statutes of Gloucester Cathedral* (1918)

GOOCH, G. P. *Political Thought in England, Bacon to Halifax* (1955)

GRAY, A. (i) *A College Chronicle 1557–1643* (c. 1893)

(ii) *A History of Jesus College, Cambridge* (1902)

GREEN, M. A. E. (ed.) (i) "Life of Mr. William Whittingham", *Camden Miscellany*, XVI (1870)

(ii) *Calendar of State Papers Domestic* (Addenda), *1566–79* (1871)

(iii) *Calendar of State Papers Domestic, 1598–1601*

GRINDAL, E. *see* NICHOLSON, W.

GROVE, *Dictionary of Music*, E. Blom, ed., 5th edn. (1954)

HACKET, J. *Scrinia Reserata* (1692)

HAMILTON, W. D. (ed.) "Wriothesley's Chronicle", *Camden Society*, I–II (1875 and 1877)

HAMMOND (i) *A Relation of a Short Survey of Twenty-Six Counties*, (1634) ed. L. G. W. Legg (1904)

(ii) "A Relation of a Short Survey of the Western Counties", (1635) ed. L. G. W. Legg, *Camden Society*, XVI (1936)

HARDIE, J. *A Report of a Discourse concerning Supreme Power* (1606)

HARRISON, F. (i) *York Minster* (1931)

(ii) "The Sub-Chanter and the Vicars Choral", *York Minster Historical Tracts*, XXII (1928)

HARRISON, F. Ll. (i) *Music in Medieval Britain* (1958)

(ii) *New Oxford History*, III (1960)

HARRISON, G. B. (i) *The Elizabethan Journals* (New York, 1939)

(ii) *A Jacobean Journal* (New York, 1941)

(iii) *A Second Jacobean Journal* (Michigan, 1957)

HARRISON, W. *A Description of England*, II (1577), ed. F. J. Furnivell (1877)

HAWKINS, SIR J. *A General History . . . of Music* (1776) (Dover Reprint, 1963)

HENTZNER, P. *Travels in England*, ed. J. Jeffrey (1797)

HEYLYN, P. *Ciprianus Anglicanus* (1668)

HEYWOOD, J. and WRIGHT, T. *The Ancient Laws . . . for King's College and Eton College* (1850)

HILLEBRAND, H. M. (i) "The Early History of the Chapel Royal", *Modern Philology*, XVIII (1920)

(ii) "The Child Actors, A Chapter in Elizabethan Stage History", *University of Illinois Studies in Language and Literature*, XI, 1926.

Historical Manuscripts Commission "Calendar of the Manuscripts of the Dean and Chapter of Wells", II (1914)

Historical Manuscripts Commission, "Fourth Report and Appendix", I (1874) [Visitation Articles and Replies, 1634/5 for the cathedrals of Canterbury, Exeter, Salisbury, Wells, Bristol, Rochester, Gloucester, St. Paul's and the colleges of Eton and Winchester.]

HOOKER, R. *Laws of Ecclesiastical Polity*, V (1597)

HOPE, SIR W. ST. JOHN, "Inventories of the College of Stoke by Clare", *Proceedings of the Suffolk Institute of Archaeology*, XVII (1921)

HORSLEY, I. "Improvised Embellishment in the Performance of Renaissance Polyphonic Music", *Journal of the American Musicological Society*, I (1951)

HOTSON, L. *The First Night of Twelfth Night* (1954)

HOWSON, J. S. (ed.) *Essays on Cathedrals* (1872)

HUGHES, DOM A. *Catalogue of the Musical Manuscripts at Peterhouse, Cambridge* (1953)

HUGHES, P. *The Reformation in England* I–III, 5th edn. (1963)

HUGHES-HUGHES, A. *Catalogue of Manuscript Music in the British Museum*, I (1906)

HUME, M. A. S. (ed.) *Calendar of Letters and State Papers Spanish, 1558–1567* (1892)

HUNNIS, W. *A Handful of Honisuckles*, [and other writings] (1589)

HUNT, J. E. *Cranmer's First Litany, 1544, and Merbecke's booke of Common praier noted, 1550*: facsimile edn. (1939)

HUTTON, W. H. *St. John the Baptist College* (1898)

IZON, J. "Italian Musicians at the Tudor Court", *Musical Quarterly*, XLIV:3 (1958)

JACKMAN, J. "Liturgical Aspects of Byrd's *Gradulia*", *Musical Quarterly*, XLIX:1 (1963)

JACKSON, N. G. *Newark Magnus* (1965)

JAMES, W. A. *An Account of the Grammar and Song Schools at Newark* (1927)

JEANS, LADY S. "The Musical Life of Exeter Cathedral, 1600–1650", *The Quarterly Record*, XLIII:172 (1951)

JEBB, J. "Catalogue of Ancient Choir Books", *The Ecclesiologist*, XX (1859)

JENKINSON, W. *London Churches before the Great Fire* (1917)

JOHNSON, F. R. "Notes of English Retail Book Prices 1550–1645", *The Library*, Fifth Series, I:2 (1950)

JONES, A. *The Life and Works of Martin Peerson*, unpublished dissertation for the degree of M.Litt., Cambridge (1957)

JONES, W. B. and FREEMAN, E. A. *The History and Antiquities of St. David's* (1856)

JULIAN, J. *A Dictionary of Hymnology* (1925)

KENNEDY, W. P. M. *see* FRERE, W. H.

KENNEDY, W. P. M. "Elizabethan Episcopal Administration", *Alcuin Club Collections*, XXVI–XXVII (1924)

KERMAN, J. (i) *The Elizabethan Madrigal* (1962)
(ii) "The Elizabethan Motet", *Studies in the Renaissance*, X (1962)
(iii) "Byrd's Motets: Chronology and Canon", *Journal of the American Musicological Society*, XIV:3 (1961)

KIRBY, F. E. "Hermann Finck on Methods of Performance", *Music and Letters* XLII:3 (1961)

KITCHEN, G. W. and MADGE, F. T. *Documents of Winchester Cathedral 1541–1547* (1889)

KLARWILL, V. VON, *Queen Elizabeth and some foreigners* (1928)

KNIGHT, C. B. *A History of the City of York* (1944)

KNOWLES, D. *The Religious Orders in England*, I–III (1959)

KNOWLES, D. *see* HADCOCK, R. N.

KÖKERITZ, H. *Shakespeare's Pronunciation* (Yale, 1953)

LAFONTAINE, H. C. DE, *The King's Musick* (1909)

LATIMER, J. *Annals of Bristol in the Seventeenth century* (1900)

LAUD, W. *Collected Works*, ed. W. Scott (1847–60)

LAW, E. *The History of Hampton Court*, I–III (1885–91)

LEACH, A. F. "Visitations and Memorials of Southwell Minster", *Camden Society*, XLVIII (1891)

LEFKOWITZ, M. *William Lawes* (1960)

LEGG, J. W. (i) "English Orders for Consecrating Churches", *Bradshaw Society*, IV (1911)
(ii) *The Coronation Order of King James I* (1902)

LEGG, J. W. and HOPE, W. ST. J. *Inventories of Canterbury Cathedral* (1902)

LE HURAY, P. G. *see* DANIEL, R. T.

LE HURAY, P. G. (i) "Towards a Definitive Study of Pre-Restoration Anglican Service Music", *Musica Disciplina*, XIV (1960)

(ii) *The Treasury of English Church Music, 1540–1650* (1965)

(iii) "The English Anthem, 1580–1640", *Proceedings of the Royal Musical Association*, LXXXVI (1959)

LEIGH, A. *King's College* (1899)

LEMON, R. (ed.) *Calendar of State Papers Domestic 1547–1580* (1856)

LONDON, W. *A Catalogue of the Most Vendible Books* (1657–58)

LOWINSKY, E. (i) "The Concept of Physical and Musical Space in the Renaissance", *Papers of the American Musicological Society* (1941)

   (ii) "Music in the Culture of the Renaissance", *Journal of the History of Ideas*, XV (1954)

   (iii) "Early Scores in Manuscript", *Journal of the American Musicological Society*, XIII, 1–3 (1960)

   (iv) "On the Use of Scores by sixteenth-century Musicians", *Journal of the American Musicological Society*, I (1948)

MACE, T. *Musick's Monument* (1676)

MADGE, F. T. *see* KITCHEN, G.W. and STEPHENS, W. R. W.

MAGDALEN COLLEGE, OXFORD. *The Oxford University Archaeological Society* (by M. D. N.) (1950)

MANN, A. H. *see* FULLER-MAITLAND, J. A.

MASON, W. M. *The History and Antiquities of St. Patrick's* (Dublin, 1820)

MATHEW, D. (i) *The Age of Charles I* (1938)

   (ii) *The Jacobean Age* (1938)

MATTHEWS, W. R. *see* ATKINS, W. M.

MELLOWS, W. T. "The Foundation of Peterborough Cathedral, A.D. 1541", *Northants Record Society*, XIII (1941)

MENDEL, A. "Pitch in the sixteenth and early seventeenth centuries", *Musical Quarterly*, XXXIV:1–4 (1948)

MERBECKE, *see* HUNT, E. J.

MERSENNE, M. *Harmonie Universelle* (1636) trans. R. E. Chapman (Hague, 1957)

MEYER, E. *English Chamber Music* (1946)

MORE, P. E. and CROSS, F. L. *Anglicanism in the seventeenth Century* (1935)

MORISON, S. *English Prayer Books* (1949)

MORRIS, C. *Political Thought in England: Tyndale to Hooker* (1953)

MORLEY, T. *A Plaine and Easie Introduction to Practicall Musicke* (1597), ed. R. A. Harman 1952

MORYSON, F. *Itinerary*, Pt. 3. (Glasgow, 1897)

MULCASTER, R. *Positions* (1581)

MUSIK IN GESCHICHTE UND GEGENWART (1949–)

NEALE, J. E. *Queen Elizabeth* (1934)

NEEDHAM, R. and WEBSTER, A. *Somerset House* (1905)

NICHOLS, J. G. (ed.) (i) "The Diary of Henry Machyn", *Camden Society*, XLII (1848)

  (ii) "Chronicle of the Grey Friars of London", *Camden Society*, LIII (1852)

NICHOLSON, W. (ed.) "The Remains of Edmund Grindal", *Parker Society* (1843)

NORRIS, J. P. *Statutes of Bristol Cathedral* (1870)

NORTH, R. *see* WILSON, J.

OGILBY, J. *The Entertainment of his most Excellent Majestie, Charles II* (1662)

OLLARD, S. L. "Fasti Wyndesoriensis", *Historical Monographs* (1950)

ORNITHOPARCUS, *Micrologus*, trans. J. Dowland (1609)

ORNSBY, G. (ed.) "The Correspondence of John Cosin, D.D.", *Surtees Society*, LII and LV (1868 and 1870)

OVERTON, J. H. *The Church in England* I–II (1897)

PAGET, G. "The Organs of Norwich Cathedral", *The Organ*, XIV: 54 (1934)

PALMER, G. H. "The Elements of Plainsong", *Plainsong and Medieval Music Society* (1904)

PARKS, E. *The Hymns and Tunes found in the English Metrical Psalters* (New York, 1966)

PATTISON, B. *Music and Poetry of the English Renaissance* (1948)

PEACHAM, H. *The Compleat Gentleman* (1634)

PEARCE, E. H. *Annals of Christ's Hospital* (2nd edn. 1908)

PECKHAM, W. D. (i) "The Vicars Choral of Chichester Cathedral", *Sussex Archaeological Collections*, XXXVII (1937)

  (ii) "The Acts of the Dean and Chapter of the Cathedral Church of Chichester, 1545–1692", *Sussex Record Society* (1959)

PEEL, A. (ed.) *The Seconde Parte of a Register* (1915)

PHILLIPS, A. *Life of Williams* (1700)

PINE, E. *The Westminster Abbey Singers* (1953)

PLATT, P. *Richard Dering*, unpublished dissertation for the degree of B.Litt., Oxford (1953)

PLAYFORD, J. *A Brief Introduction to the Skill of Musick* (1654)

PRATT, W. S. *The Music of the French Psalter of 1562* (New York, 1939)

PRESCOTT, J. E. *The Statutes of the Cathedral Church of Carlisle* (1879)

PROCTOR, W. *A History of the Book of Common Prayer* (1902)

PROCTOR, W. and WORDSWORTH, C. W. *Statutes and Customs of the Cathedral Church of Salisbury* (1915)

PRYNNE, W. (i) *Histrio-Mastyx* (1633)
  (ii) *A Breviate of the Life of William Laud* (1644)
  (iii) *Canterburies Doome* (1644)

RAVENSCROFT, T. *A Brief Discourse* (1614)

REESE, G. *Music in the Renaissance* (1954)

REYNOLDS, T. *Wells Cathedral* (1881)

RIDLEY, J. *Thomas Cranmer* (1926)

RIMBAULT, E. F. "The Cheque Book of the Chapel Royal", *Camden Society*, III (1872)

ROBERTSON, D. H. *Sarum Close* (1938)

ROBINSON, H. (ed.) (i) "Original Letters Relative to the English Reformation", I. *Parker Society*, (1846)
  (ii) "Original Letters Relative to the English Reformation", II, *Parker Society*, (1847)
  (iii) "Zurich Letters", I, *Parker Society* (1842)
  (iv) "Zurich Letters", II, *Parker Society* (1845)

ROCHESTER CATHEDRAL, *The History and Antiquities of the Cathedral Church of Rochester* (1717)

ROGERS, C. C. *The History of the Chapel Royal of Scotland* (Edinburgh, 1882)

ROPER, H. T. "King James and his Bishops", *History Today* (1955)

ROSS-WILLIAMSON, H. *Four Stuart Portraits* (1949)

ROUTLEY, E. *The Music of Christian Hymnody* (1957)

RYE, W. B. *England as seen by Foreigners* (1865)

SCHNAPPER, E. B. *The British Union Catalogue of Early Music printed before 1801* (1957)

SCHOLES, P. A. *The Puritans and Music* (1934)

SCHRADE, L. *Monteverdi* (1951)

SCOTT, H. S. (ed.) *Camden Miscellany*, X (1902)

SHAW, H. W. (i) "A Contemporary source of English music of the Purcellian Period", *Acta Musicologica*, XXXI:1 (1959)
  (ii) "Thomas Morley of Norwich", *Musical Times* (1965)

SIMPKINSON, E. H. *Life and Times of Archbishop Laud* (1894)

SIMPSON, W. S. *Registrum Statuorum et Consuetudinem Ecclesiae Cathedralis Sancti Pauli Londinensis* (1873)

SMALLMAN, B. "Endor revisited: English Biblical Dialogues of the Seventeenth Century", *Music and Letters*, XLVI:2 (1965)

SMART, P. *The Vanity and Downfall of Superstitious . . . Ceremonies* (Edinburgh, 1628)

SMITH, A. (i) "Elizabethan Music at Ludlow: a new source", *Music and Letters*, 1967.

(ii) "Parish Church Musicians in the reign of Elizabeth I: an annotated register", *Royal Musical Association Research Chronicle*, IV, 1967.

SMITH, E. T. *Annals of Westminster Abbey* (1904)

SQUIRE, W. B. "Musik-Katalog der Bibliothek der Westminster Abtei", *Monats-heften für Musikgeschichte* (35th year, Leipzig, 1903)

STEELE, J. *English organs and organ music*, unpublished dissertation for the degree of Ph.D., Cambridge (1958)

STEELE, R. "The Earliest English Music Printing", *Bibliographical Society* (1903)

STEPHENS, W. R. W. and MADGE, F. T. "Winchester Cathedral Documents", *Hampshire Record Society*, I (1897)

STEVENS, D. (i) *Thomas Tomkins* (1957)

(ii) *Tudor Church Music* (1961)

(iii) "The Mulliner Book", *Musica Britannica*, I (1951), *The Mulliner Book, a Commentary* (1952)

STEVENS, J. *Music and Poetry in the early Tudor Court* (1961)

STOPES, C. C. "William Hunnis and the Revels of the Chapel Royal", *Materialen zur Kunde des älteren Englischen Dramas* (Louvain, 1910)

STOW, J. (i) *Chronicles of England* (with additions to 1631 by E. Howes) (1631)

(ii) *The Survey of London* (enlarged by A. M.) (1633)

STRUNK, O. *Source Readings in Musical History* (1950)

STRYPE, J. *Annals of the Reformation* (1709)

SUMNER, L. W. *The Organ* (1953)

SWAINSON, L. A. *The History and Constitution of Chichester Cathedral* (1880)

TANNER, T. *Notitia Monastica*, ed. J. Nasmith (1787)

TAYLOR, J. *An Apology for Authorised and Set Forms of Liturgy* (1649)

TAYLOR, W. F. *Charterhouse of London* (1912)

TERRY, SIR R. R. *Calvin's First Psalter* (1932)

THOMSON, E. "Robert Ramsey", *Musical Quarterly*, XLIX:2 (1963)

TREVELYAN, G. M. *England under the Stuarts* (1947)

TRINITY COLLEGE, CAMBRIDGE, *Statuta Collegii Sanctae et Individuae Trinitatis* (1846)

USHER, R. W. G. *Reconstruction of the English Church* (New York, 1910)

VICARS, J. *Gods arke overtopping the worlds waves* (1646)

VICTORIA COUNTY HISTORIES

WAILES, M. "Martin Peerson", *Proceedings of the Royal Musical Association*, LXXX (1954)

WALCOTT, M. E. *The Early Statutes of the Cathedral Church . . . of Chichester* (1877)

WALKER, J. *A History of Music in England* (3rd edn. 1952)

WALKER, T. A. *Peterhouse* (1935)

WALLACE, C. W. (i) "The Children of the Chapel at Blackfriars, 1597–1603", *The University Studies of the University of Nebraska*, VIII (1908)

 (ii) *The Evolution of the English Drama up to Shakespeare* (Berlin, 1912)

WALLER, A. R. and WARD, A. W. *Cambridge History of English Literature*, VI (1908–16)

WALTERS, H. B. *London Churches at the Reformation* (1939)

WALTON, I. *Walton's Lives* [J. Donne, Sir H. Wotton, R. Hooker, R. Sanderson and G. Herbert], ed. S. B. Carter (1951)

WARNER, G. F. *A Catalogue of the Manuscripts and Monuments of Dulwich College* (1881)

WARTON, T. *The History of English Poetry*, IV, ed. W. C. Hazlitt (1871)

WEBSTER, A. *see* NEEDHAM, R.

WEDGEWOOD, C. V. *The King's Peace 1637–1641* (1955)

WELCH, C. E. "Two Cathedral Organists", *Chichester Papers*, VIII (1957)

WEST, J. E. *Cathedral Organists* (1899)

WESTON, W. *William Weston, The Autobiography of An Elizabethan*, trans. P. Caraman (1951)

WESTRUP, J. A. (i) "Domestic Music under the Stuarts", *Proceedings of the Royal Musical Association*, LXVIII (1942)

(ii) "Foreign Musicians in Stuart England", *Musical Quarterly*, XXVII:2 (1941)

WHITELOCKE, SIR J. "Liber Famelicus", ed. J. Bruce, *Camden Society* (1858)

WHITTINGHAM, W. *see* GREEN, M. A. E. (ed.)

WHYTHORNE, T. *The Autobiography of Thomas Whythorne*, ed. J. M. Osborn (1961)

WILKINS, D. *Concilia Magnae Britanniae*, IV (1737)

WILLETTS, P. J. ' Music from the Circle of Anthony Wood at Oxford", *British Museum Quarterly*, XXIV:3-4

WILLEY, B. *The Seventeenth Century Background* (1934)

WILLSON, D. H. *King James VI and I* (1956)

WILSON, H. A. *Magdalen College* (1899)

WILSON, J. *Roger North on Music* (1959)

WILSON, T. "The State of England in 1600", *Camden Miscellany* (1936)

WOODFILL, W. *Musicians in English Society* (Princetown, 1953)

WOODRUF, C. E. and DANKS, W. *Memorials of Canterbury Cathedral* (1912)

WOOLDRIDGE, *see* BRIDGES, R.

WOOLDRIDGE, H. E. "The Polyphonic Period, II", *Oxford History of Music*, II (1932)

WORDSWORTH, C. W. *see* PROCTOR, W.

WOTTON, A. *Answere to a Popish Pamphlet* (1605)

WULSTAN, D. (ed.) (i) "Orlando Gibbons, Verse Anthems", *Early English Church Music*, III (1963)

(ii) "The Problem of Pitch in sixteenth-century English vocal music", *Proceedings of the Royal Musical Association*, XCIII (1966–67)

Index of Musical Examples

General Index

446